Supercharging Productivity with Trello

Harness Trello's powerful features to boost productivity and team collaboration

Brittany Joiner

‹packt›

BIRMINGHAM—MUMBAI

Supercharging Productivity with Trello

Copyright © 2023 Packt Publishing

All rights reserved. No part of this book may be reproduced, stored in a retrieval system, or transmitted in any form or by any means, without the prior written permission of the publisher, except in the case of brief quotations embedded in critical articles or reviews.

Every effort has been made in the preparation of this book to ensure the accuracy of the information presented. However, the information contained in this book is sold without warranty, either express or implied. Neither the author, nor Packt Publishing or its dealers and distributors, will be held liable for any damages caused or alleged to have been caused directly or indirectly by this book.

Packt Publishing has endeavored to provide trademark information about all of the companies and products mentioned in this book by the appropriate use of capitals. However, Packt Publishing cannot guarantee the accuracy of this information.

Group Product Manager: Alok Dhuri
Publishing Product Manager: Uzma Sheerin
Book Project Manager: Manisha Singh
Senior Editor: Kinnari Chohan
Technical Editor: Maran Fernandes
Copy Editor: Safis Editing
Proofreader: Safis Editing
Indexer: Sejal Dsilva
Production Designer: Aparna Bhagat
DevRel Marketing Coordinators: Deepak Kumar and Mayank Singh

First published: August 2023

Production reference: 1210723

Published by Packt Publishing Ltd.
Grosvenor House
11 St Paul's Square
Birmingham
B3 1RB, UK.

ISBN 978-1-80181-387-7

www.packtpub.com

To my partner, Vy Tran – thank you for making life not just possible but enjoyable when I add more side projects to our plate. I couldn't have written this without you cheering me on and being my 90 on days when I could only be 10. And thank you to all the adorable critters in my life (Levi, Lucas, Artie, Melman, Blackjack, and Finn) that snuggled with me and kept me smiling while I wrote more about Trello than any human thought possible.

– Brittany Joiner

Contributors

About the author

Brittany Joiner is a Trello expert with over a decade of experience. An active member of the Atlassian Community, Brittany has answered user questions and helped countless people learn how to use Trello to streamline their workflow and boost their productivity. She's also a contributor to the Trello blog, writing about how to use Trello to increase personal and team productivity.

After working in marketing for several years, Brittany became a developer. She regularly speaks about Trello, automation, and how to help individuals move into technical careers. Brittany lives with her partner and her pets. You'll find her nerding out about technology, traveling the world, and making Trello-related puns.

I want to thank my technical reviewers, Lauren Moon, Andy Gladstone, and Robin Warren, for spending almost as much time on this book as I did! And special thanks to the Atlassian CommuniTEAM (Stephanie Grice, Erica Finley, Moonie, Monique van den Berg, and Cassie Mayes, to name a few) that have encouraged and supported me in every way possible on my journey to becoming a Trello super-fan. Also, thanks to Lane Simon, for handling the house while I got away on much-needed airplane rides that forced me to sit down and write!

About the reviewers

Andy Gladstone is currently the **chief operating officer** (**COO**) at Fidelity Payment Services, a FinTech company that specializes in the payments space. He is passionate about tools and strategies that increase collaboration, break down information silos, and create efficiencies for groups and organizations. Andy has been a community leader in the Atlassian Online Community for the past two years and is an avid user and ambassador for Atlassian's global mission and products, especially Confluence, Jira, and Trello. As COO, Andy still wears the hat of Atlassian Admin in his organization due to the deep love and satisfaction he gains from creating a group of users whose sum is greater than its parts.

Robin Warren lives in beautiful Teignmouth on the UK's southwest coast.

He runs a small software company that builds add-ons (power-ups) for Trello and has previously worked as a software developer and development team lead.

When he's not doing that, he's either hanging out with his wife and kids or out doing something on, in, or under the water. ☺

Table of Contents

Preface — xv

Part 1 – Trello Foundation

1

The Structure of Trello — 3

What is Trello?	3	**Boards**	**9**
But why Trello?	5	Creating a board	9
Where can you use Trello?	5	Finding your boards	10
Via the web	5	Top toolbar options for a board	10
Trello desktop app	5	**Lists**	**23**
Trello mobile app	5	Add a card	24
What kinds of things do people use Trello for?	6	Copy	25
		Move	25
Work-related use cases	6	Watch	25
Non-work-related use cases	6	Sort by	26
		Actions for cards within a list	26
Getting started	7	Archive list	27
Creating an account	7	**Cards**	**27**
Workspaces (previously called Teams)	8	**Summary**	**28**

2

Trello Card Starter Pack — 29

Card views	30	**Labels**	**31**
Name and description	31	Creating and editing labels	32
Editing descriptions	31		

Dates	**34**	**Comments and activity details**	**39**
Start and due dates	34	Commenting on a card	39
Adding start and due dates to a card	34	Activity details	40
Members	**37**	**Card actions**	**41**
Adding members to a card	37	**Quick actions from the card front**	**42**
Watching	**38**	**Summary**	**44**
Configuring watching on a card	38		

3

Leveling Up Your Cards   45

Attachments	**45**	Viewing all your checklist items	59
Attaching items to a card	45	Viewing the progress of checklists	59
Inline attachments	51	**Locations**	**60**
Custom fields	**52**	Setting a location on a card	60
Creating a custom field	53	**Covers**	**61**
Setting a custom field value	56	Adding a card cover	62
Checklists	**57**	**Link cards**	**64**
Adding a checklist	57	Disabling link cards	65
Advanced checklists	58	**Summary**	**65**

4

Viewing Cards Your Way   67

Filters	**67**	**Calendar**	**75**
Dimensions to filter by	69	Changing the cadence	76
Activity	71	Editing dates on a card	77
Filter logic	71	Adding a card	77
Removing a filter	72	Syncing with your calendar	78
Accessing alternative board views	**72**	Using the Calendar Power-Up	78
Dashboard	**73**	**Timeline**	**79**
Adding a new tile	74	Adding another dimension	79
Editing an existing tile	75	Adding a card	80

Table	80	Adding a new card	83
Editing cards	80	**Workspace views**	**83**
Adding a card or list	81	Workspace calendar views	84
Maps	**81**	Workspace Table view	85
Setting a location on a card	83	**Summary**	**86**

5

Real World Trello Boards — 87

Understanding Trello templates	**87**	**Meeting planner**	**97**
Viewing template information	88	Board structure	97
Copying a template	89	Cards are agenda items	98
Using Trello for Kanban and Agile workflow management	**91**	**Product roadmap**	**99**
		Board structure	100
Board structure	92	Cards represent features or bugs in your product	100
Cards represent tasks	93		
Cross-team project management	**94**	**Creating your own Trello template**	**102**
Board structure	95	**Summary**	**104**
Cards represent objectives	95		

Part 2 – Automation in Trello

6

Initiating Trello Automations — 107

Getting ready to automate	**107**	When a card is archived/unarchived	113
When are you ready to automate?	107	When a list is created/renamed/archived/unarchived	113
Triggers	108		
Actions	108	Automation variables	114
Accessing triggers	**109**	When a list has a specific number or range of cards	114
Pro tip – advanced mode	110		
Card move	**111**	**Card changes**	**115**
When a card is added to the board	112	When a specific (or any) label is added to a card	115
When a card is added to a specific list	112	When an attachment is added/removed	116

When you or someone else is added to/removed from a card	116	When an item is added to/removed from a checklist	122
When a specific user is added to/removed from a card	117	**Card content**	**122**
When a vote is added to/removed from a card	117	Advanced pro-tip	123
		When the name/description of a card contains specific text	124
Dates	**117**	When a comment is posted to a card	124
When a start/due date is set on a card	118	When a person is mentioned in a card	124
When the due date is marked complete/incomplete	118	**Fields**	**125**
When you or someone else enters a card name containing a date, set the due date	119	When all custom fields are completed	126
		When custom fields are completed	126
Checklists	**119**	When a custom field is set	126
When a specific checklist is added to/removed from a card	120	When a custom field is set to a specific value	126
When a checklist is completed/made incomplete in a card	120	When a checkbox custom field is checked/unchecked	127
When an item is checked/unchecked	121	When a number custom field is set to a specific number/range of numbers	127
When a due date is set on/removed from an item	121	When a date custom field is set	127
		Summary	**128**

7

Common Automation Actions — 129

Accessing automation actions	**129**	**Dates**	**136**
Move	**131**	Mark a due date as complete/incomplete	136
Move/copy the card to the top/bottom of the list	131	Set the due/start date to ___	137
		Move the due/start date to _	138
Move the card to the top/bottom of the current list	132	Move the due/start date by the same amount of time	138
Archive/unarchive the card	132	**Checklist actions**	**138**
Add/Remove	**132**	Add/remove checklists to a card	140
Create a new/unique card	133	Add an empty checklist	140
Add/remove a label to a card	134	Add/remove items to a checklist	140
Add/remove a sticker to a card	134	Assigning the item to someone	141
Add/remove a link	134	Set the item due date	141
Remove (just about anything) from the card	135	Move the item due date	141
		Remove the due dates from the checklist	142

Remove the due date from the item	142	Add a member at random/in turn to a card	146
Check/uncheck an item	142	Remove all the members from a card	147
Check/uncheck all the times in a/all checklist(s)	142	**Content actions**	**147**
Reset all the checklists on a card	143	Rename the card to ___	148
Remove items from checklists	143	Set the card's description to ___	148
		Post a comment	148
Member actions	**144**	Send an email notification to ___	149
Join/leave a card	145	Get/post/put to URL	149
Subscribe/unsubscribe to a card	145		
Add/remove a specific user to a card	145	**Summary**	**150**

8

Advanced Actions — 151

Field actions	**151**	Find/lookup a card titled/with link	159
Clear custom field ___	152	For each card linked in the attachments	160
Set custom field ___ to ___	153	For each card linked from an item in checklist	160
Check/uncheck custom field	153	For each checklist item	160
Increase/decrease the number in custom field ___ by ___	153	Link/unlink the cards together	161
		Link the card with the item	161
Set date custom field ___ to ___	154	Convert the item to a linked card	161
Move the date in custom field ___ to ___	154	Convert items in a checklist to cards/linked cards	162
Sort actions	**154**	Collect all the cards into linked items/links/items in checklist	162
Sort list by ___	155		
Sort by custom field ___	156	**Other tool actions**	**163**
Sort by label ___	156	Jira	164
Cascade actions	**157**	Bitbucket	165
Find/lookup the first/last card linked in the attachments	158	Slack	166
		Summary	**168**

9

Building Automation with Triggers — 169

Accessing Automation	**170**	Creating a rule	172
Rules	**171**	Testing your rule	175

xii   Table of Contents

Editing existing automations	176	Card buttons	178
Other automation settings	177	Board buttons	184
Button automation	**178**	**Summary**	**190**

10

Date-Based Automation   191

Scheduled automation	**191**	New triggers for Due date automation	197
New triggers for schedule automation	192	Creating a due date automation	200
Creating a scheduled automation	194	Testing a due date automation	201
Testing your scheduled automation	195	**Summary**	**202**
Due date automation	**196**		

Part 3 – Power Up Your Boards

11

Power-Ups Built by Trello   205

What are Power-Ups?	**206**	**Read Me**	**218**
Accessing Power-Ups	**206**	Adding the Read Me Power-Up	218
Power-Ups for Integrations	**210**	Previewing the Read Me	220
Tools Trello integrates with easily	211	Editing the Read Me	220
Adding the Slack Power-Up	212	**Voting**	**221**
Viewing notifications in Slack	214	Adding the Voting Power-Up	222
List Limits	**214**	Voting on a card	223
Adding the List Limits Power-Up	215	Sorting a list by votes	225
Configuring List Limits	215	**Other Trello-made Power-Ups**	**226**
Using List Limits	217	**Summary**	**227**

12

General-Use Power-Ups   229

| **Approvals for Trello** | **229** | Adding Approvals for Trello to your board | 230 |

Creating an approval	231	Updating a field	242
Approving or rejecting an approval	233	Additional features	243
Viewing cards by approval status	234	**Bulk Actions**	**244**
Advanced features	235	Adding Bulk Actions	245
Amazing Fields	**236**	Selecting multiple cards to edit	247
Adding Amazing Fields	236	Making changes to multiple cards	248
Creating a field	238	**Summary**	**250**

13

Syncing Info Between Boards and Tools — 253

Forms by Blue Cat	**253**	**Unito**	**265**
Adding Forms by Blue Cat	254	Creating a flow	266
Creating a form	255	Testing a flow	272
Sharing a form	261	**Summary**	**272**
Testing a form	263		

14

Reporting in Trello — 273

Blue Cat Reports	**273**	Default attributes for reporting	293
Adding reports to your board	274	Adding widgets and reports	294
Quick lists	275	**Screenful**	**298**
Reports	**279**	Getting started	299
Placker	**286**	Insights	299
Getting started	287	CHARTS	304
Mapping a board	287	REPORTS	306
Viewing multiple boards together	290	**Summary**	**309**

Index — 311

Other Books You May Enjoy — 318

Preface

Why, Tr-hello there! (If you know me, of course you knew I'd be starting this book with a Trello pun.) This book is designed to be your comprehensive guide to understanding and utilizing the true power of Trello.

Trello is a collaboration and project management tool that helps individuals and teams stay organized, productive, and focused. It utilizes a visual interface consisting of boards, lists, and cards, allowing users to create and manage tasks, projects, and workflows in a flexible and structured manner. It's easy to get started with, and powerful enough to handle your most complicated workflows.

Whether you're an individual seeking an organized approach to your personal tasks or a team looking for a collaborative project management solution, Trello has got you covered, and I'm going to show you how.

In this book, we'll explore Trello from its fundamental components to advanced features, automation, and integrations! My goal is to equip you with the knowledge and tools needed to maximize your productivity and efficiency with this amazing tool.

Part One lays the foundation by diving into the core components of Trello. I'll walk you through the basics of boards, cards, and lists and illustrate how they can be utilized effectively. You will discover customizable templates and real-world use cases that provide inspiration to organize your personal and professional projects. Even if you are familiar with Trello, I'll bet you will still learn a thing or two in this section!

Part Two shines a spotlight on automation within Trello. I'll unravel the world of triggers and actions, enabling you to streamline repetitive tasks and supercharge your productivity. With practical examples and recipes, I'll be your Trello sherpa and guide you in automating various activities, such as adding members to cards, creating checklists, and moving cards between lists. You will gain a deeper understanding of how automation can be tailored to your specific needs and be confident to build out your own automations.

Part Three explores Trello's integrations; we call them Power-Ups. I'll explain the concept and purpose of Power-Ups and show you how to discover and leverage the vast array of options available. With examples of my favorite Power-Ups developed by Trello, as well as other Power-Ups addressing common use cases, you will have the tools to customize Trello to suit your unique requirements. I'll even talk about special integrations and Power-Ups to help you navigate the reporting landscape, comparing the different options available. You will gain insights on how to measure progress, track performance, and extract meaningful data from your Trello boards.

Throughout this journey, I'll empower you to harness the full potential of Trello's capabilities, enabling you to become a professional of organization, collaboration, and automation. And I'll even show you how to dive deeper and find the answers to anything else that may come up as you go.

I hope that this book will be your companion, providing inspiration, guidance, and practical solutions to enhance your Trello experience. And I hope it even makes you laugh in a place or two.

So, without further ado, let's embark on this adventure together and unlock the true power of Trello! I need some more nerds to chat about this stuff with.

Happy Trello-ing!

Who this book is for

This book is meant for individuals and teams seeking a comprehensive guide to harnessing the full potential of Trello. Whether you are new to Trello and eager to learn its fundamental features, or already familiar with the platform and looking to explore its advanced functionalities, this book is your go-to resource. It caters to a wide range of readers, including professionals in various industries, project managers, entrepreneurs, students, and individuals aiming to enhance personal productivity. Regardless of your background or level of Trello knowledge, this book will equip you with the knowledge, tips, and strategies necessary to effectively utilize Trello and optimize your workflows, allowing you to stay organized, collaborate efficiently, and achieve your goals with ease.

What this book covers

Chapter 1, The Structure of Trello, helps you discover the fundamental structure of Trello – a digital whiteboard adorned with sticky notes and versatile LEGO-like components. Explore boards, lists, and cards as the building blocks of efficient organization and collaboration. Learn how to create an account, navigate boards and lists, and customize essential settings, forming a strong foundation to harness Trello's potential.

Chapter 2, Trello Card Starter Pack, explores the core elements of Trello cards, from names and descriptions to labels, dates, members, and comments. Discover essential actions such as copying, archiving, templating, sharing, and moving cards, enabling efficient organization and collaboration in Trello.

Chapter 3, Leveling Up Your Cards, dives into more useful card features, such as attachments, custom fields, checklists, and the location feature, showcasing how these elements enrich your Trello boards and cards with enhanced functionality and customization options.

Chapter 4, Viewing Cards Your Way, teaches you how to utilize filters to narrow down by attributes and explore Trello's various views, including calendar, map, table, and dashboard views, for better organization and productivity.

Chapter 5, *Real-World Trello Boards*, unlocks the versatility of Trello as we explore specific use cases and templates. From finding relevant templates in the gallery to employing Trello for Kanban, cross-team project management, meetings, and product roadmaps, this chapter provides practical guidance to maximize Trello's capabilities.

Chapter 6, *Initiating Trello Automations*, start the journey of automation in Trello, showing you what you need to know before automating in Trello. Learn how to find the automation section in Trello and understand the various sections. Then, you'll deep dive into triggers, which are activities that Trello can monitor to initiate automation. This chapter comprehensively covers every available trigger, offering practical guidance, instructions, and real-world examples to utilize them effectively.

Chapter 7, *Common Automation Actions*, shows you how to leverage Trello's automation capabilities to perform actions on your behalf. Learn how to move cards, modify fields, set dates, manage checklists, assign members, and so on. With comprehensive explanations, recommended triggers to pair with these actions, and real-world examples, this chapter equips you with valuable insights and practical knowledge to make the most of Trello's automation features, maximizing efficiency and productivity within your workflow.

Chapter 8, *Advanced Actions*, dives deep into more advanced Trello automation actions and how you might use them to unlock powerful possibilities to streamline workflows. Learn how to modify custom fields, sort cards or lists, and cascade actions to automate processes across multiple items. You'll even jump into actions with Slack and Jira. With detailed explanations and practical examples, this chapter equips you with the knowledge and tools to take your Trello automation skills to the next level, making you an expert and allowing you to build just about anything you can dream of.

Chapter 9, *Building Automation with Triggers*, explores the synergy of triggers and actions within Trello to build comprehensive automation rules. Learn how to bring together triggers and actions to automate actions behind the scenes. You'll also learn how to create board and card buttons to engage automation. With practical insights, examples, and step-by-step guidance, you'll bring everything together to build the automation you need.

Chapter 10, *Date-Based Automations*, examines date-based automation in Trello, including scheduled automations and actions tied to card due dates. Discover how to automate recurring tasks and leverage dynamic actions based on a task's due dates. This chapter provides practical examples and guidance to optimize your workflow and ensure timely task management.

Chapter 11, *Power-Ups Built by Trello*, starts the section of the book dedicated to add-ons for Trello. Explore a variety of Power-Ups built by Trello, including integrations with popular tools such as Twitter, Zendesk, Google, GitHub, and Slack. Additionally, we will delve into commonly used Power-Ups that facilitate tasks such as card counting, documentation creation, and feedback gathering through card voting.

Chapter 12, *General-Use Power-Ups*, explores Power-Ups that offer broad utility across various use cases, enhancing nearly every Trello workflow. Discover Power-Ups that facilitate seamless approval processes, enable the creation of custom and styled fields within your cards, and give you the ability to make bulk edits across multiple cards.

Chapter 13, *Syncing Info between Boards and Tools*, discusses Power-Ups specifically designed to help you get info in and out of your boards. These Power-Ups enable seamless integration of content from external sources, such as forms hosted in URLs. Additionally, learn how to use Unito to sync cards between Trello boards and other platforms such as GitHub, Jira, and Google Sheets! With practical examples and insights, this chapter equips you with the knowledge to streamline information flow, enhance collaboration and let each person do their work where they work best.

Chapter 14, *Reporting in Trello*, discovers the options for reporting in Trello and how to use them. This chapter guides you through the process of effectively managing and analyzing your data in Trello and how to choose from three common reporting tools. Gain insights into the features and capabilities of each tool, empowering you to make an informed decision based on your reporting needs. From generating progress reports to tracking performance, this chapter provides practical guidance to ensure accurate and insightful reporting within the Trello platform.

To get the most out of this book

It will help to have a basic understanding of Trello and to have used it to have more context for the examples and content provided, but even if you've never heard of Trello, I'll bring you up to speed in the first chapter!

Software/hardware covered in the book	Operating system requirements
Trello	Windows, macOS, or Linux

Conventions used

There are a number of text conventions used throughout this book.

Bold: Indicates a new term, an important word, or words that you see on screen. For instance, words in menus or dialog boxes appear in **bold**. Here is an example: "Select **System info** from the **Administration** panel."

> **Tips or important notes**
> Appear like this.

Get in touch

Feedback from our readers is always welcome.

General feedback: If you have questions about any aspect of this book, email us at `customercare@packtpub.com` and mention the book title in the subject of your message.

Errata: Although we have taken every care to ensure the accuracy of our content, mistakes do happen. If you have found a mistake in this book, we would be grateful if you would report this to us. Please visit www.packtpub.com/support/errata and fill in the form.

Piracy: If you come across any illegal copies of our works in any form on the internet, we would be grateful if you would provide us with the location address or website name. Please contact us at `copyright@packt.com` with a link to the material.

If you are interested in becoming an author: If there is a topic that you have expertise in and you are interested in either writing or contributing to a book, please visit authors.packtpub.com.

Share Your Thoughts

Once you've read *Supercharging Productivity with Trello*, we'd love to hear your thoughts! Scan the QR code below to go straight to the Amazon review page for this book and share your feedback.

https://packt.link/r/1801813876

Your review is important to us and the tech community and will help us make sure we're delivering excellent quality content.

Download a free PDF copy of this book

Thanks for purchasing this book!

Do you like to read on the go but are unable to carry your print books everywhere? Is your eBook purchase not compatible with the device of your choice?

Don't worry, now with every Packt book you get a DRM-free PDF version of that book at no cost.

Read anywhere, any place, on any device. Search, copy, and paste code from your favorite technical books directly into your application.

The perks don't stop there, you can get exclusive access to discounts, newsletters, and great free content in your inbox daily

Follow these simple steps to get the benefits:

1. Scan the QR code or visit the link below

   https://packt.link/free-ebook/9781801813877

2. Submit your proof of purchase
3. That's it! We'll send your free PDF and other benefits to your email directly

Part 1 – Trello Foundation

We start our Trello journey by exploring what Trello is and its core components – boards, lists, and cards. We'll dive into all of the fields on cards and how to use them in productive (and even fun) ways so that every individual contact, task, or item has all the information you need. Zooming out, we'll learn how to see all your cards in useful views that highlight what you need when you need it and demonstrate some of the most common ways people use Trello.

This part has the following chapters:

- Chapter 1, The Structure of Trello
- Chapter 2, Trello Card Starter Pack
- Chapter 3, Leveling Up Your Cards
- Chapter 4, Viewing Cards Your Way
- Chapter 5, Real-World Trello Boards

1
The Structure of Trello

Before you can start using Trello, you'll need to understand what it is and how it works. In this chapter, we're going to walk through what you need to know to get started with Trello.

We'll talk about the following:

- Analogies to help you understand Trello
- Where you can use Trello
- Why it's preferred over other tools
- Creating a Trello account
- Making your first board and list

Ready? Let's get started!

What is Trello?

I've talked to many people about Trello – more than I can count. I always return to one metaphor to explain Trello and a second metaphor to explain how it works: **a digital whiteboard**.

I bet you've used a whiteboard to keep your projects organized. And you likely put sticky notes on that whiteboard to help you keep track of items for that project. You use squeaky dry-erase markers to create stages or lists under which your sticky notes fall.

When a sticky note changes, you move it to another whiteboard section. You jot down extra notes on it or add a sticker to it. You use specific colors of sticky notes to differentiate between them. You might use different colors based on who is working on those tasks or what team is responsible for them.

Because of this whiteboard process, you have the big picture of your project and can see what is completed, what's in progress, and what's still left to do. And any time you need to zoom in, you refer to a sticky note.

The whiteboard is fantastic and a classic approach. But there are a couple of problems with it.

One – it's not portable.

Whiteboards only work well when you and your team are all working in close physical proximity. After all, the whiteboard is only as effective as the people updating it. If no one can see it, check its status, or move items as they have changed, the whiteboard isn't functional.

If you use one at your home office, it's only useful when you're sitting at home, and you can't check it on the go. You can't reference and update it while you're traveling, and no one on your team can edit it.

And two, sticky notes are only so powerful!

You can change colors, add stickers, and sort sticky notes differently. But there's only so much you can do to help them stand out and keep information about their task. They won't hold any data, such as relevant files or images. They're small, so you can only add a little detail to them.

Enter Trello... the digital whiteboard.

Imagine a whiteboard, but better. That's what Trello is. It's a digital whiteboard with super-charged sticky notes.

It's a whiteboard but without the problems. It's more powerful for collaborating with your team and keeping track of everything.

A Trello board holds cards (sticky notes) organized by lists – no dry-erase marker is required. You move your cards around and between the lists, as you would your sticky notes. And it takes up less room than a massive physical board with sticky notes!

The cards are customizable too, but we'll discuss those in greater detail in *Chapter 2*.

Now that you understand what Trello is, let's talk about how it works.

It's like LEGO bricks!

While Trello has much in common with a whiteboard, it also has much in common with something else we've all used (although, maybe it's been a few years).

How does a project management tool have anything in common with a kid's toy?

It's because you can build just about anything you want with Trello. It's a highly customizable platform that is flexible and can be more than just a whiteboard. There are a million different things you can build with it – just like LEGO.

How many different LEGO kits exist in the world? Hundreds, thousands? Maybe more? You can build a Hogwarts Castle, a Death Star, racecars, dinosaurs, villages... you can even build the Titanic!

Because LEGO bricks are versatile, you can shape and mold them to be whatever you like. You only need a creative person to plan where they need to go. Lucky for you, I just happen to be that creative person!

But why Trello?

You're not sitting here reading this book because I'm an expert in Asana or Monday.com. There's a reason I chose Trello over those tools, but I won't get into bashing other tools in this book, probably. They all have their place, and in some cases, other tools do work better for some folks.

The magic of Trello is that it's extremely versatile yet powerful.

We're going to get technical in this book and explain all the ins and outs of how to use Trello, and as I'm writing this, I realize there's just so much to say because you can customize it and perfect it to work just the way you want it to.

It integrates with just about any software you can think of and is one of the most well-known tools on the market. It's owned by Atlassian, a massive company focused on producing quality tools for improving workflows.

How to tweak the experience to make it exactly what you need it to be might not be super clear from the moment you open a board, but everything you need is there. Just like a sculptor, you need to carve and work it to make it a beautiful work of art for you and your team.

Where can you use Trello?

You can use Trello in a few places. This makes it more powerful than other tools that can only be accessed in the browser.

Via the web

You can use Trello from any browser as a web-based application. Head to `trello.com` and log in, and you'll have access to all features, keyboard shortcuts, and more from Chrome.

Trello desktop app

If you prefer computer apps, you can access the Trello desktop app for Windows and Mac computers. The app provides notifications, access to Power-Ups, and more keyboard shortcuts.

Trello mobile app

Trello is perfect for use on the go, and this can be done via its Android and iOS apps. It's a great way to create and access cards while away from your computer.

What kinds of things do people use Trello for?

Many teams use Trello for more than just project management. Let's take a look.

Work-related use cases

Here are some examples of work-related use cases:

- Customer support teams use Trello to create an organized flow for responding to customer requests
- Sales teams use Trello to keep track of leads through a pipeline as they convert them into deals and revenue
- Marketers use Trello boards to plan content calendars and track the content creation process
- Event planners use Trello to ensure nothing falls through the cracks and to create a timeline of tasks
- Engineering teams use Trello to track bugs and features throughout the development cycle
- Product teams use Trello for roadmapping, and often publicly share what new features are coming out in apps via their boards
- Small businesses use Trello for managing operations and coordinating with stakeholders.
- Agencies use Trello for collaborating with clients and keeping track of deliverables.
- Law firms use Trello for managing pleadings for clients, while keeping track of billable hours
- Non-profit teams use Trello to organize internal operations and coordinate fundraising efforts
- Churches use Trello for organizing worker schedules and tasks to be completed for Sunday services

Now, let's look at non-work-related use cases.

Non-work-related use cases

People also use Trello outside of work for a myriad of personal uses, some of which are as follows:

- Organizing books to read
- Meal planning
- Household chores and products
- Trip planning
- Storing addresses and contact records
- Workout planning and tracking
- Saving articles
- Online shopping cart with links to products

And more!

The possibilities are endless. So, now you see why it's like LEGO!

It's exciting but also intimidating. When I only see a bunch of bricks and a picture of Hogwarts Castle, I have no idea how I will get there. How do these little bricks combine to make something so cool?

That's the purpose of this book. Imagine this as your instruction manual that comes with your LEGO. I'll help you make your Hogwarts Castle. But before we can start building, you need to understand what the bricks are.

So, let's examine the contents of this LEGO kit we've opened and see what we have to work with.

Getting started

Before you can dive into the elements of Trello, you'll need to create an account and create your first workspace.

Creating an account

Go to `trello.com` and click **Sign up**. You'll be directed to an Atlassian login page. You can use your existing Atlassian login if you use other Atlassian products (such as Jira, Confluence, or Bitbucket). This makes it extremely easy to get started and keeps everything under one login if you use multiple tools. Otherwise, you'll need to create a new account.

You can do that by typing an email address or choosing one of the social account options, such as Gmail:

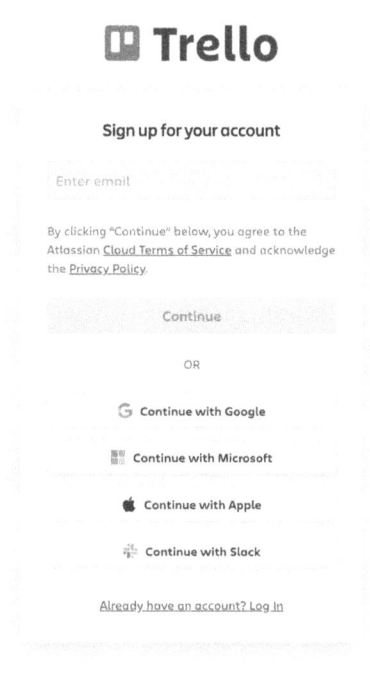

Figure 1.1 – Trello sign-up modal

Workspaces (previously called Teams)

The wizard will walk you through the sign-up flow and help you create your first workspace. Think of a workspace as your department or organization, or a type of project:

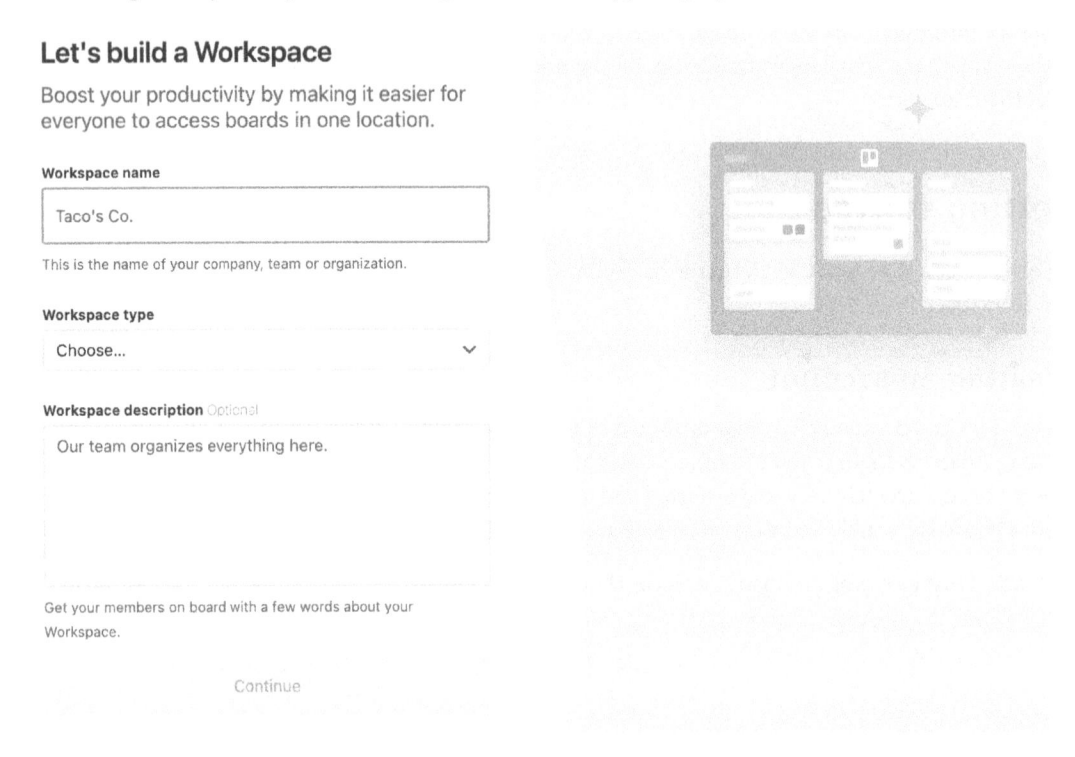

Figure 1.2 – Form to create a Trello workspace

Each workspace is charged by the number of members in that workspace. You can have free workspaces, and you can have as many workspaces as you wish. Select your team type you are to get specific template recommendations. Next, invite team members via email address, or skip this process for now and invite them later.

Now that you've got a Trello account squared away, you're ready to start playing around and getting your hands dirty. It's time for the rubber to meet the proverbial road because we're going to start creating boards and lists and understand what those things are, as well as how to use them.

Let's dive into what Trello is most known for... its boards!

Boards

The first principal component of Trello is the digital whiteboard – that is, "the board." You can have several boards in Trello (up to 10 per workspace in the free plan and unlimited boards in paid plans).

A board is a collection of cards, but we'll get to those later. Think of a board as a topic or a goal. It could be a specific project you're working on, or it could be a team.

Don't worry too much about what your board should be, as it will likely change over time, and you'll find yourself operating on multiple boards. It's easy to adjust as you go.

Are you ready to put your fingers on the keyboard? It's time to start digging in.

Creating a board

To help you explore boards, we will create one so that you have a visual as I explain what's going on inside the board.

From the top toolbar in Trello, click the **Create** button and choose the first option that appears – that is, **Create board**:

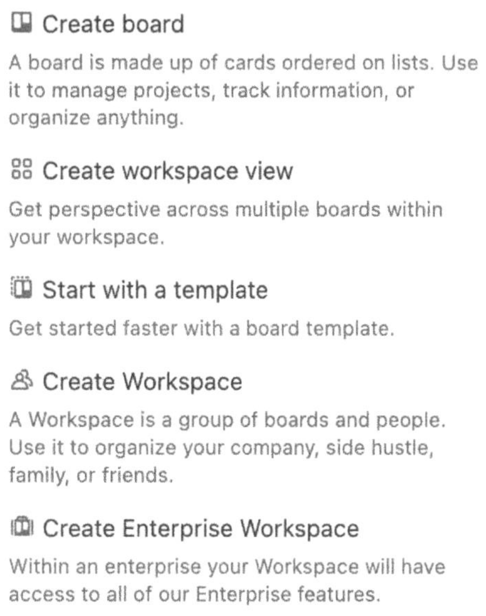

> **Create board**
> A board is made up of cards ordered on lists. Use it to manage projects, track information, or organize anything.
>
> **Create workspace view**
> Get perspective across multiple boards within your workspace.
>
> **Start with a template**
> Get started faster with a board template.
>
> **Create Workspace**
> A Workspace is a group of boards and people. Use it to organize your company, side hustle, family, or friends.
>
> **Create Enterprise Workspace**
> Within an enterprise your Workspace will have access to all of our Enterprise features.

Figure 1.3 – Create options in Trello

Name your board. You can call it `To Do` or `Team Tasks`.

Next, confirm the workspace you want the board to be in. You can leave the default option or click the name of the board to select another available workspace.

Lastly, you'll choose a level of visibility – that is, who has access to view your board. For now, stick with the default option, which is **Workspace visible**. If no one else is part of your workspace, this is effectively the same as private visibility. If you aren't sure and would prefer to hide this board, you can set the visibility to **Private**.

Once you click **Create**, you'll go straight to your new board.

Finding your boards

Go to `trello.com` to see the boards you have joined or created:

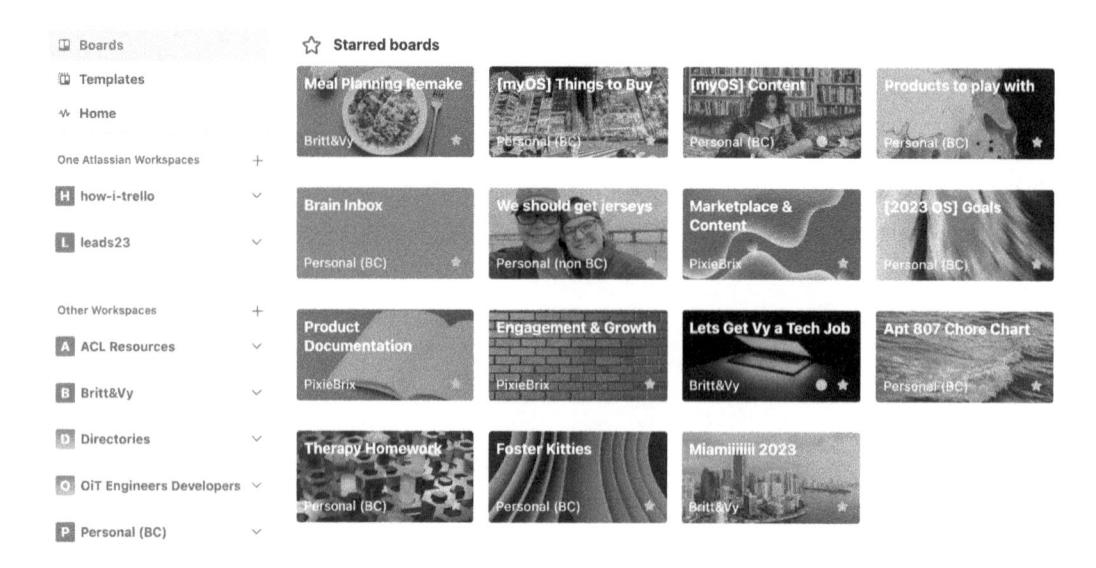

Figure 1.4 – Trello board home page

View all boards, starting with starred ones, then your recently viewed ones, and finally the remaining boards. You can view only boards from a specific workspace by selecting a workspace name on the left-hand side.

To go to a board, click on its tile.

Top toolbar options for a board

Though boards can look very different, navigating them is the same. They all have a top toolbar with items for personalizing your board.

Although other tools have the "board" concept, did you know Trello was the first to promote this type of organization? Trello also offers the best customization and set of features at a board level that I've seen across all other similar tools.

Starring a board

The first item you will see is the board's name; immediately next to it will be a star. If it's filled yellow, this means that the board is "starred" and will show up at the top of your **Trello Boards** page.

You can also access these boards from the **Starred** menu in the very top toolbar in Trello.

By default, the starred field will be unselected. Click it to star it, and click again to un-star it:

Figure 1.5 – Board title with star icon for favoriting

Setting board visibility

The next option you'll see is your board's visibility. When creating a board, by default, it will be set to **Workspace visible**. This means that anyone who is part of your workspace can view the board and join it.

To change this, select the current visibility option – a menu will appear with options to change it:

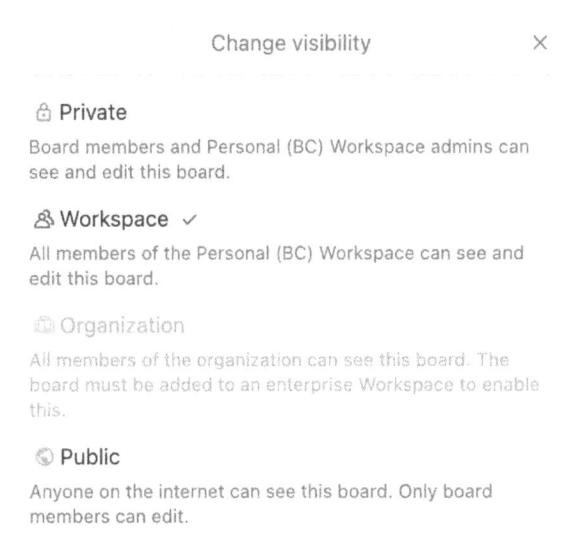

Figure 1.6 – Board visibility options

You have at least three visibility options, and a fourth one if you are on an Enterprise version of Trello.

Private means that only you and the people who you invite can see the board and its contents, with one exception – workspace admins are also able to see the contents of any board (so make sure not to say anything about your boss in your boards 😆).

You can find your workspace admins by opening the panel on the left-hand side of the board and selecting **Members**:

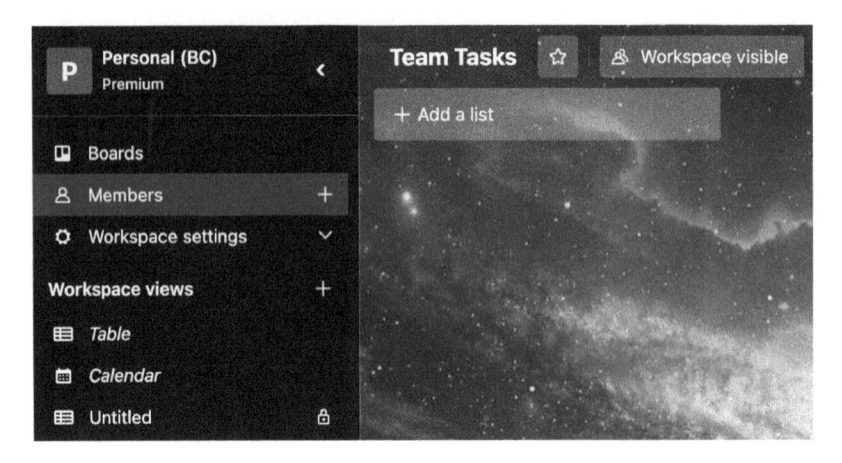

Figure 1.7 – Board member settings

If you want others to view your content and engage in a board, you can invite them to the board, even if its visibility is **Private**. Click the **Share** button in the top-right toolbar of your board to see a modal appear:

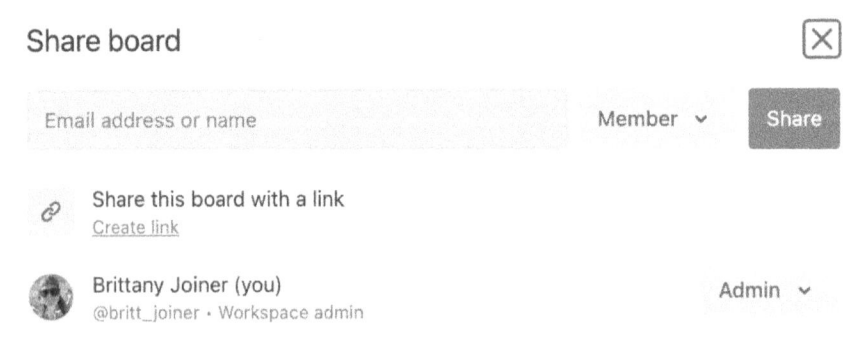

Figure 1.8 – Board sharing and invite options

Here, you can type a member's name or email address. If they're not on Trello, you can send an invite to their email address.

You can also click the **Create link** button below the text field to create a link that you can send to someone to join the board. This link is not public, but anyone you send it to will be able to join the board. You can revoke this link any time after you create it.

Workspace visible means that anyone who is part of your workspace can see the contents of your board. They'll also be able to join it and edit. This is great for any information that is relevant to your wider group of colleagues and doesn't contain sensitive information.

Public visibility means that anyone can see this board, even if they don't have a Trello account. Sometimes, this is actually kind of useful! For instance, perhaps you want to distribute information, such as a roadmap or resources. Although anyone can see this board, they can't edit it.

It's also important to note that as of 2022, Google does not index Trello boards, so they will not appear in Google search results. Bummer for folks who had Trello boards with links that were getting tons of traffic!

Organization visibility is only available to Trello Enterprise accounts. It means anyone using Trello with the same company email domain (for example, `mary@coolcompany.com` and `john@coolcompany.com`) can view this board.

Next to the visibility settings, you'll see options for board views. If you want to learn about them now, skip to *Chapter 4*.

There's another button called **Power-Ups**, but once again, we won't cover these until a later chapter because we've got a lot of ground to cover there. These add-ons super-charge your Trello board to do even more powerful things. It's best to start with Trello's native features before diving into the extras. We will discuss those in *Chapters 11, 12, 13*, and *14*.

You'll also see a button for **Automation**, which allows you to customize rules for managing items in Trello. You will learn more about this in *Chapter 6*.

Filtering a board

One more button you'll see in your top bar is the **Filter** button. If you don't have any cards on your board, it won't be very useful, but once you add cards, you can select which cards you want to see:

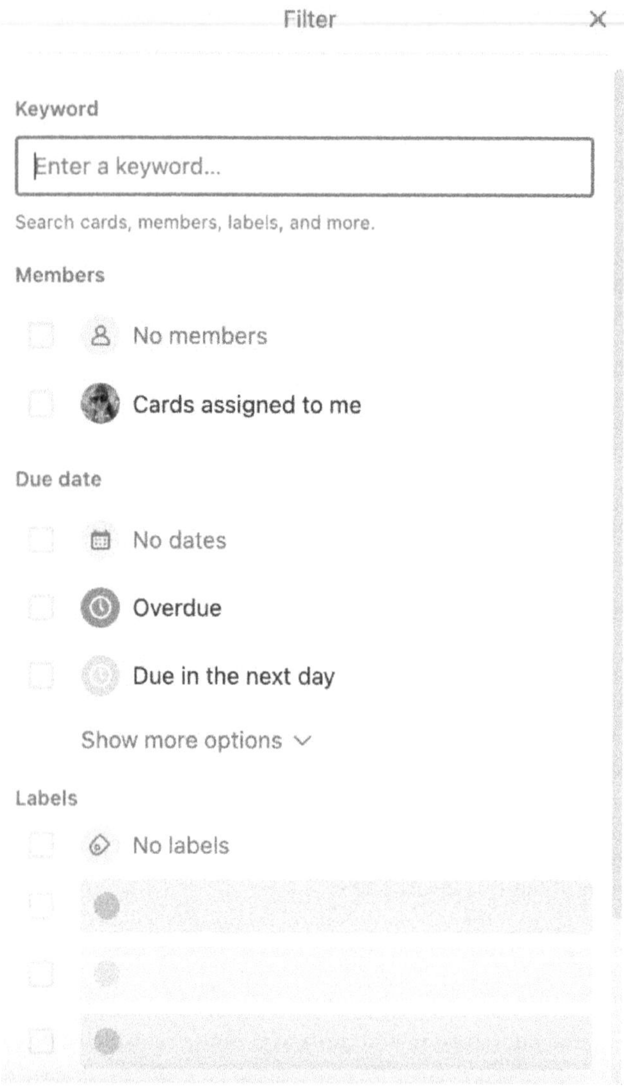

Figure 1.9 – Board filtering options

Here, you can filter to only show your cards (or another member's) or filter by due dates. You can even filter by keywords, labels, or recency of activity. It's a great tool for drilling down to exactly what matters, and helpful when you have a busy board.

Adding members and setting roles

You'll also notice avatars on the top right-hand side of your board, which indicate who has joined the board. Click on an avatar to view that member's information. If you need to change their role, click the **Share** button. You can also see a list of all the members and their roles here.

By default, everyone is a **member**, which means they can edit the content on a board, such as creating cards, lists, and more.

Admins have superpowers and can rename a board and close a board.

If you're on a Trello Premium or higher plan, you'll have access to another role type: **Observer**. These users can view content and comment on a card, but they aren't able to edit anything on the board. This is helpful if you don't want to make a board public, but need your team to see the content without having the power to break anything.

Accessing the board menu

The last stop on the board menu is an ellipsis on the right-hand side of the top toolbar. Click it to reveal extra settings for configuring your board:

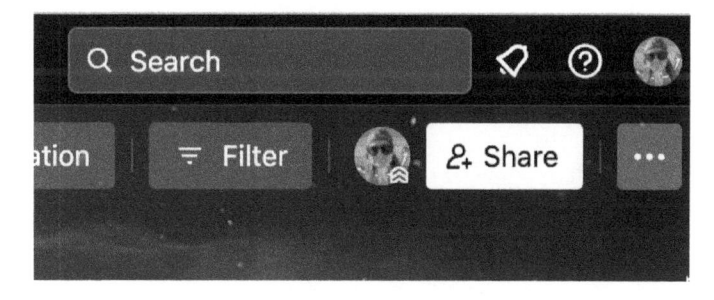

Figure 1.10 – Menu navigation on Trello boards

Description

A board description is a place where you can summarize the board. It's helpful for others to understand the context of the board and also a great place to save related links. Let's go ahead and set this:

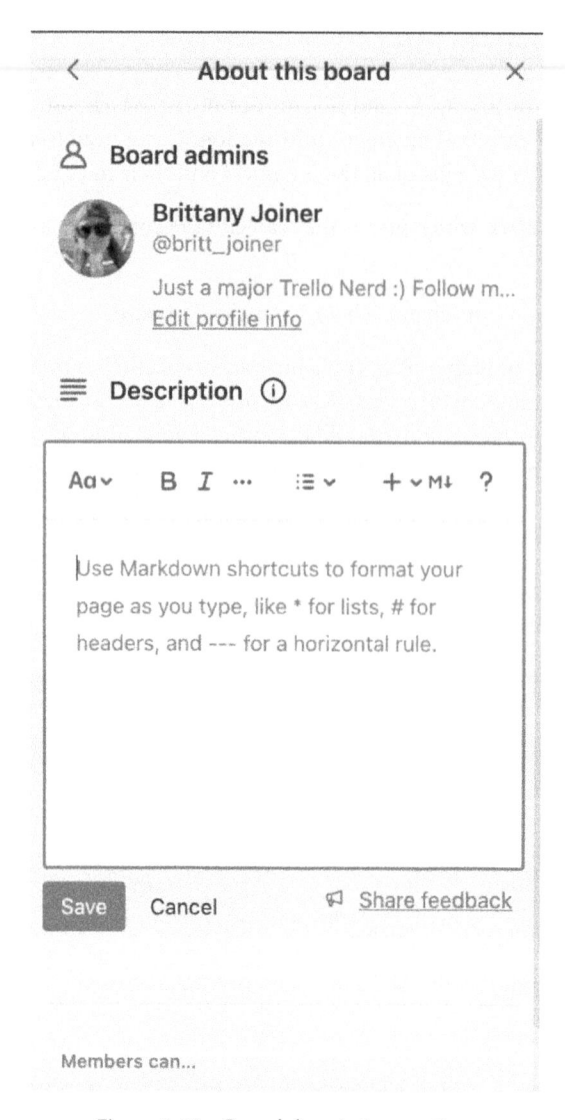

Figure 1.11 – Board description section

Use the rich text editor to style your text with headers, bullet points, and anything else you want. When you're done, click **Save**.

Background

The next setting allows you to change the background to another color, a stock photo, or a custom image.

Click **Custom** to upload a file, or search for keywords to find photos from Unsplash:

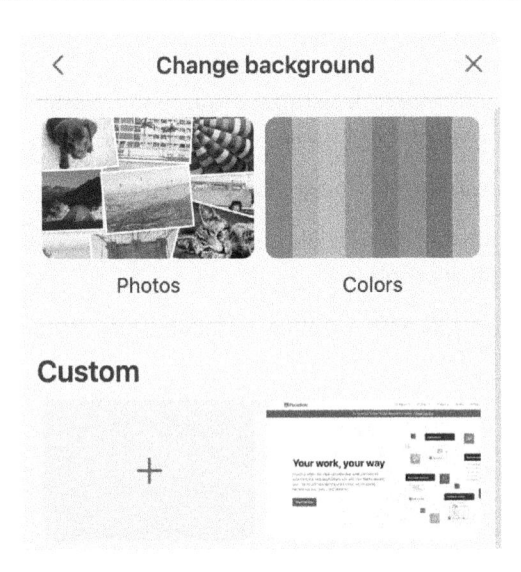

Figure 1.12 – Board background customization options

Not every tool lets you customize and style your workspace. Trello lets you make the board your own rather than being limited to using the default light or dark mode background.

Stickers

If you want to add flair to your board, you can add stickers to style cards. Open the stickers menu, search for a keyword, select the sticker, and then drag it over to a card. You can remove a sticker by hovering over it and clicking the **x** button:

Figure 1.13 – Trello board stickers

Additional settings

Click **More** to view another hidden layer of settings. If you choose the first option, called **Settings**, you'll see options to change the board's workspace.

You can also enable or disable card covers (images that prepend to the top of a card).

Lastly, you can change the permissions of who is allowed to perform various actions on a board, such as commenting on cards or adding people.

You can even edit the ability for workspace members to join the board without an invite:

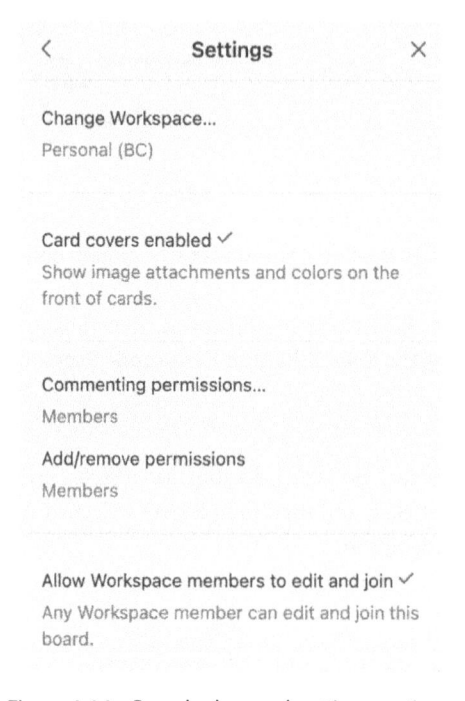

Figure 1.14 – Board advanced settings options

Collections

Collections are kind of like folders for your Trello boards. If you'd like to organize multiple boards together, you can add them to a collection. This feature is only available for Premium and higher plans.

Archived items

Trello makes it very hard to accidentally delete something. If you seem to be missing something, there's a good chance it was just archived! You can find your archived items here. Click this option to see anything archived in this board, sorted by card or list:

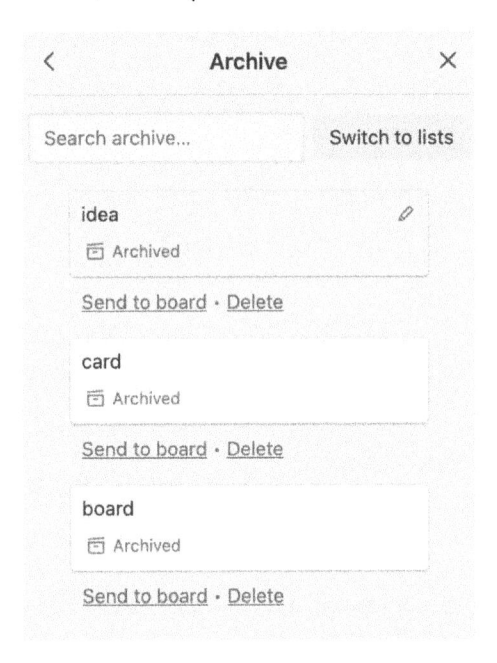

Figure 1.15 – Archived items in Trello

To bring something back, click the **Send to board** button.

This is one of the reasons I prefer to use Trello – because it's hard to lose something. In other tools, you might delete something as the default action. This makes it difficult to restore if it was an accident. But when using Trello, if you find that something's missing, it's easy to recover it.

Email address

Did you know that you can email something to a Trello board? Every board has a unique email address. You can use the **Email-to-board settings** area to view the board's address, generate a new one, and configure which list to add new items to:

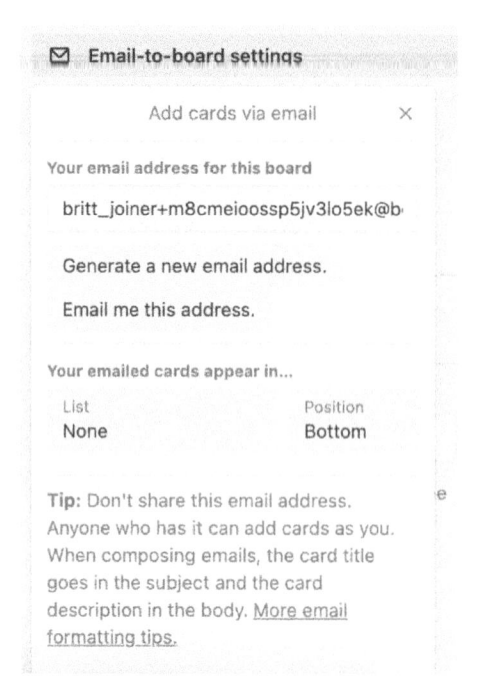

Figure 1.16 – Board email options

Go ahead and try it! Copy the email address and head to your email. Send an email with the subject Hi and something in the body. Then, head back to Trello and watch it appear on your board within seconds!

Watching

If you want notifications about everything that happens to anything on this Trello board, click the **Watch** button. But fair warning – that's a lot of notifications! You'll get a notification whenever something happens to any card on this board:

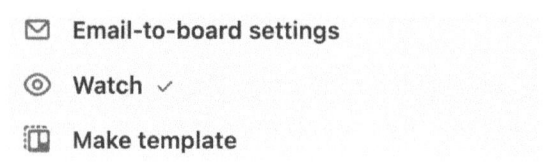

Figure 1.17 – The board's Watch button checked

You can confirm whether you're watching a board or not in this section, as it will show a checkmark if you are. Or, in the toolbar, you'll see a watch button. You can toggle it off if you're getting too many notifications.

Template

Once you have your board set up the way you like, you might want to share it as a template that you or others can use in the future. This is a great way to customize and reuse boards so that you don't have to set them up from scratch each time:

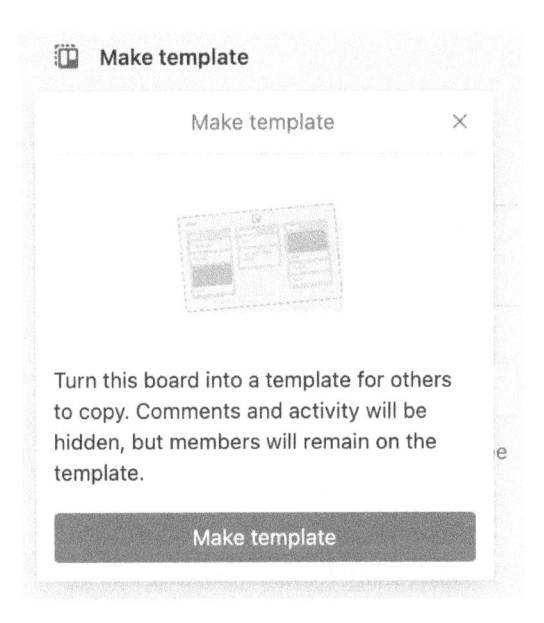

Figure 1.18 – The Make template button

You can even publicize a template to help more people discover more uses for Trello! To view templates others have contributed to, head to `trello.com/templates`.

Copy

You don't have to make a board a template to be able to copy it. Click the **Copy** button to duplicate the board and choose which parts you want to copy over, such as members and cards:

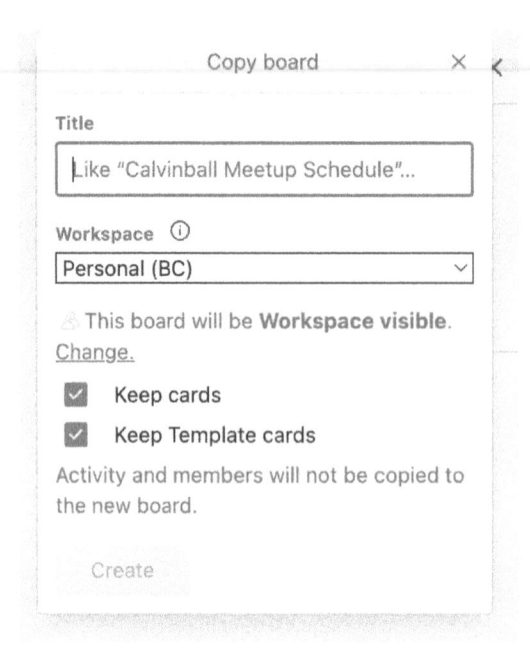

Figure 1.19 – Settings to copy a board

Try it out and make a copy of your current board. Make a duplicate board named `House Projects`.

Exporting

As much as you'll enjoy working in Trello, you might find that you need to get your information out of Trello. There are multiple ways to do that – you can print your boards, export them as a CSV, or export them as a JSON object (pro tip – you can also view your board as a JSON object in your browser by appending `.json` to the URL):

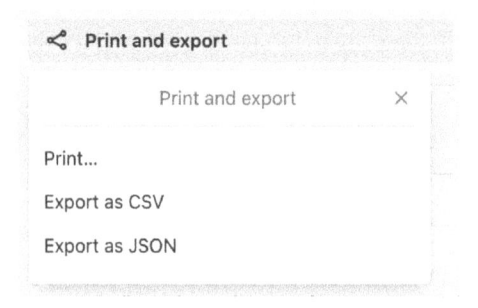

Figure 1.20 – Board export options

At the moment, our board is pretty empty, but if you want to test it out, add a few cards and try it out!

Close board

If you ever want to delete a board, you can close it. Even after you close it, you can undo it if you change your mind! Simply click **Reopen board**. You can also find your closed boards from your **Boards** page (to get there, click the Trello logo in the top-left corner from anywhere in Trello). From there, scroll to the bottom of the page, then click the **View all closed boards** button.

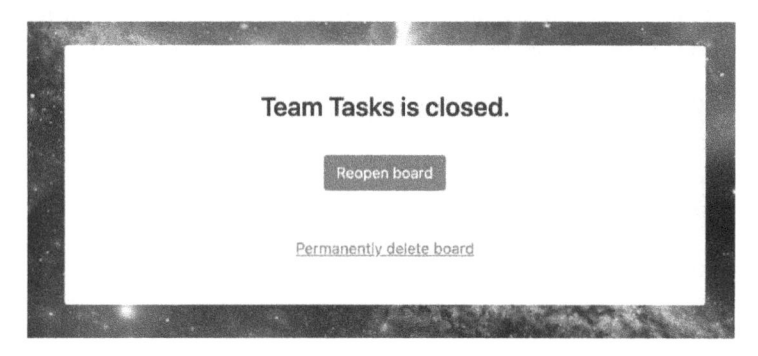

Figure 1.21 – Reopening a closed board

Go ahead and try it out! Close your board, and then bring it back.

Lists

The second major component of your Trello board is your **lists**. Lists are how you organize sticky notes inside the board. While there are a million strategies for how you can use lists, they're often used as stages of your workflow.

In many cases, it's as simple as **To Do**, **Doing**, and **Done**.

It's easy to change the names of lists and drag them around, so don't worry too much about what you call them and whether the name will change.

To create your first list, click **Add a list** in the box under your board's name. Type anything you want, but if you need inspiration, call this one `Ideas`. Press *Enter* to create your first list:

Figure 1.22 – Empty board before adding a list

Go ahead and create a few more. You'll follow the same process – just type the name and press *Enter* in the box to the right of the list.

Add the **To Do**, **Doing**, and **Done** lists.

If you put them in the wrong order or want to move a list, drag a list to move it to a different spot.

Just like boards have actions, lists have actions for managing groups of cards. Click the three-dot menu at the top right of a list to access the list menu:

Figure 1.23 – The three-dot menu to access list actions

Add a card

The first option is to add a card to a list. This isn't the only way to add a card, but it's available if you like it. Click **Add a card** to name a card, after which it will be added to your list. Go ahead and try it!

Figure 1.24 – Adding a card to a list

Make a card that says `Add cards to my Trello board`. Press *Enter* to save it. And voilà! It will appear on your list!

Copy

The next action in the list menu is to copy a list. This does just what it sounds like – it duplicates the list and adds it right next to the current list, including any cards in that list. Go ahead and try it out! Click **Copy** to see another list appear with the card you just created.

Move

Lists also have a **Move** option. You can drag a list to move it to another place within the board, or you can use this action to move it. You can even move the list to another board entirely! You might want to do this when you're figuring out how to organize your board, or after you've completed a project.

Watch

You can also watch a list, similar to watching a board.

This sends notifications about anything that happens to any card in this list. It's perfect if you're managing a particular stage of a workflow.

For instance, if you're in charge of reviewing content for your blog, you may want a notification about every card in the **Review** list:

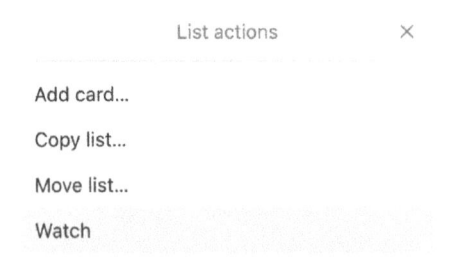

```
               List actions              ×

               Add card...
               Copy list...
               Move list...
               Watch
```

Figure 1.25 – Available actions in a list

Select the **Watch** option for this **To Do** list so that you can get notifications whenever a new card is added to this list.

Sort by

You can use the **Sort list** action to sort cards in a list by certain attributes. Here, you can order cards by their name, date created, or by the due date (if you have cards with due dates in that list):

```
       <        Sort list            ×

       Date created (newest first)
       Date created (oldest first)
       Card name (alphabetically)
```

Figure 1.26 – List sorting menu

Actions for cards within a list

The following two options apply to all the cards in a list, but not the list itself. You can move all the cards to another list while leaving the list column in its current place. You might do this at the end of the week by moving all the cards in your **Done This Week** list to another **Done** list:

```
       Move all cards in this list...
       Archive all cards in this list...
```

Figure 1.27 – Actions for cards within a list

The next action is to archive all the cards in the list while keeping the actual list itself. This is useful if you're done with the cards in the list and want to clear them out but still plan to continue using that list.

Archive list

The last action in the **List** menu is to archive the list, which will archive the cards *and* the list itself. This is useful if you realize you no longer need the list. If you accidentally archive a list (or cards in a list), you can go to the board settings in the **Archived items** area and send the list back to the board.

Cards

The final element of a Trello board is the super-charged sticky note. Your board holds your lists, which contain your cards. You can easily move cards between lists (and boards), name them whatever you want, and do so much more.

That's why *Chapters 2* and *3* will dive deep into the core features of Trello that are nested inside these cards.

For now, just know that these are the sticky notes of your board and can be moved between lists. They have superpowers, allowing you to add more detail than you could ever imagine to each sticky note:

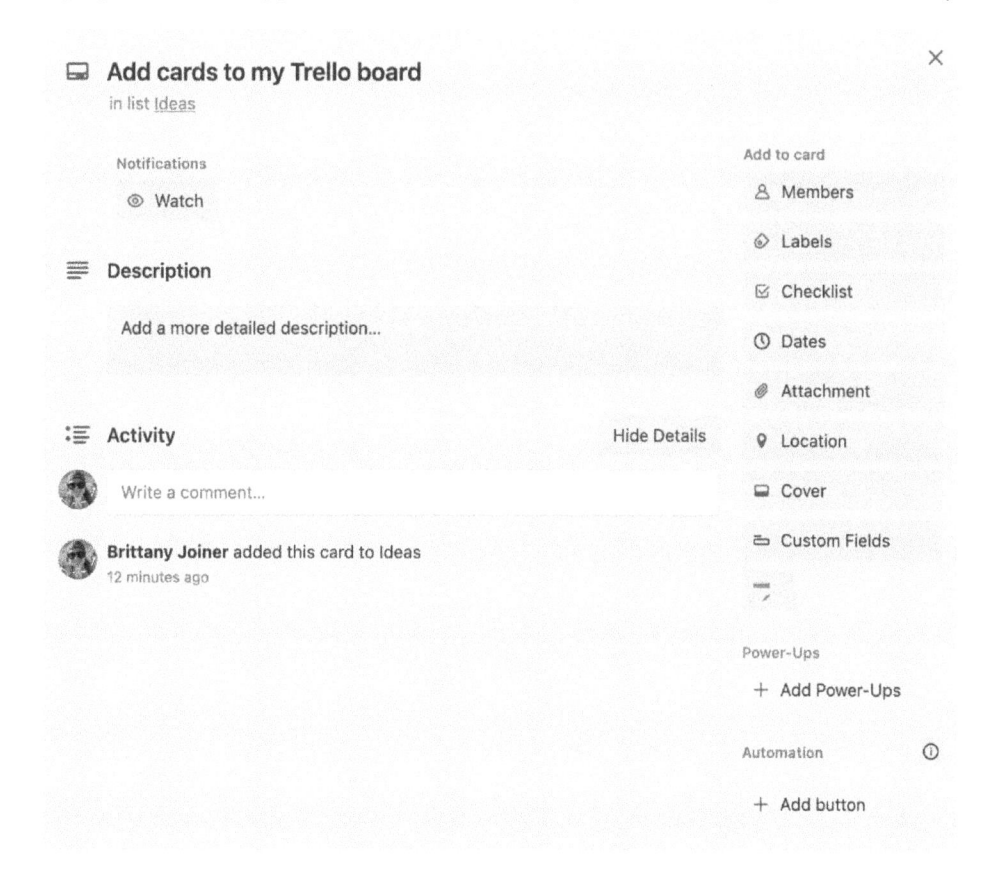

Figure 1.28 – Trello card

Summary

In this chapter, we learned how Trello is a digital whiteboard with sticky notes. You can build nearly anything you want with it because, like LEGO, it's so versatile. Many different types of teams and people find value in Trello!

When building, you'll use three components – boards, lists, and cards – to design your masterpiece. Boards are a collection of cards – super-charged sticky notes – and lists organize those cards across the board. There are many options for customizing your board to make it your own.

Alright you've made it through the tough set up content, now it's time to have some fun and dive into Trello cards.

2
Trello Card Starter Pack

Trello's key component is the super-charged sticky notes that we call **cards**. Everything in Trello centers around the cards – it's the core of Trello! To get the most out of Trello, you'll need to understand a card's different functions.

In this chapter, we're going to cover the most important things you need to know about cards, including the fields that are used most commonly. By the end of this chapter, you'll be able to create cards with clear descriptions and stylish labels, adding members and dates to them. You'll also be able to move things around with ease.

Although there's a lot to cards, here's what we'll focus on in this chapter:

- Card views
- Name and descriptions
- Labels
- Dates
- Members
- Watching cards
- Comments

We'll talk more about other features in cards, such as checklists, custom fields, and attachments, in *Chapter 3*.

Card views

Trello cards have two views – the **card front** and the **card back**.

The front view is what you see from the board, without clicking to open the card:

Figure 2.1 – The card front

The back view is what you see when you open a card. This shows the full details of a card and allows you to interact with it.

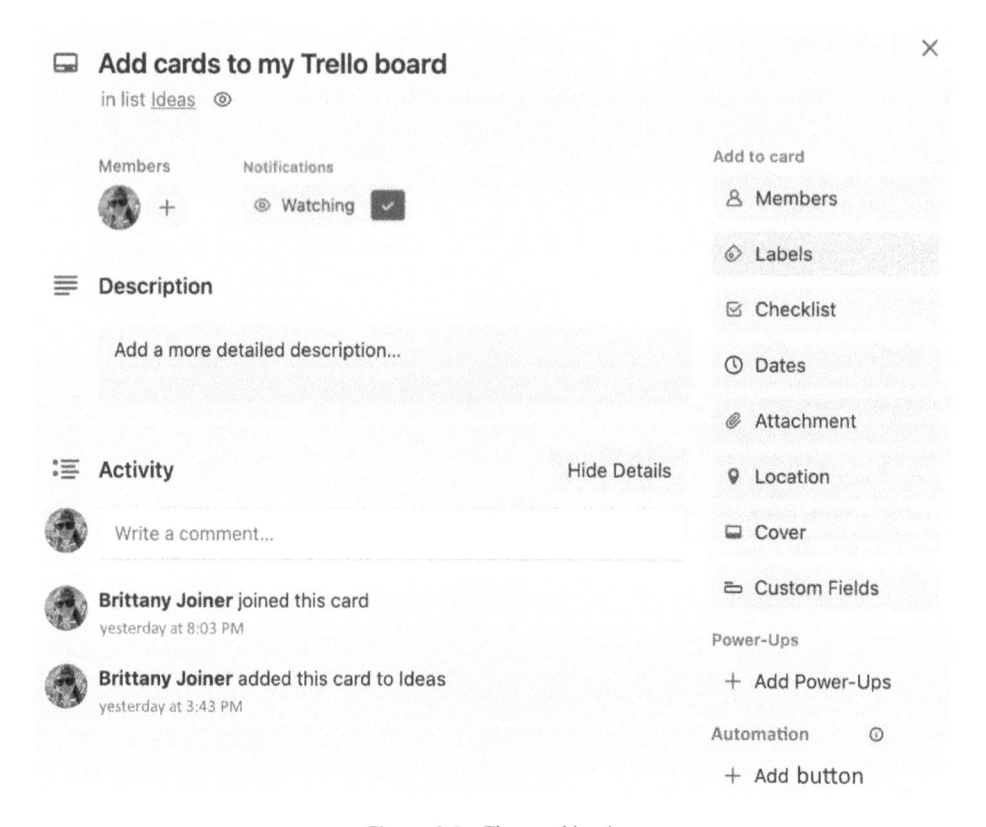

Figure 2.2 – The card back

Name and description

Every Trello card must have a title. This is visualized at the top of the card. Below that is the description field.

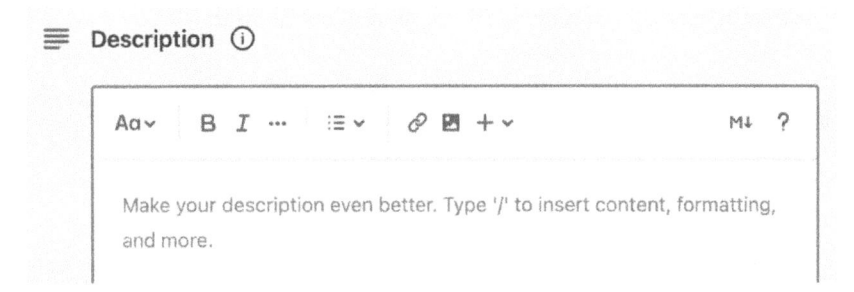

Figure 2.3 – The card description editor

The description field allows you to provide detailed information about a task or project. This is particularly useful to provide context or additional information that may not be immediately apparent from the title of the card.

> **Why use descriptions?**
> Descriptions are a great place to keep notes about a task or project and provide additional details. For instance, if you're a marketer using a card to represent a campaign, the description can hold the items you would include in a campaign brief. This eliminates the need to link to another document somewhere else. If you're a project manager, you can combine notes from all the stakeholders and list the objectives and goals of a project in the description. An engineer might use the description to describe a bug and include a screenshot of a broken feature. You can also include information in attachments, which we'll talk about in *Chapter 3*.

Editing descriptions

To add a description to a card, click on the name of the card from the board view to open the card. Then, select the box prompting you to make a description, and type anything that comes to mind.

The description field accepts Markdown, but if you prefer, you can use the rich text editor to style the text with headers, bold, italics, created links, added links, images, and more! If you need to export the card description to Markdown, select the **M↓** button, and then copy the text.

Labels

Labels are used to categorize cards. They are color-coded and can be customized to suit your needs. For example, you can use labels to indicate the priority of a task, the type of task, the status of a project, or anything else you can imagine!

> **Why use labels?**
>
> Labels add visual tags to your cards so that you can quickly get relevant details about them without having to open the card. They're also useful to filter your board, allowing you to view a subset of your cards at any given time. We'll talk more about filters in *Chapter 4*.

Creating and editing labels

There are two places to edit labels – the board menu or from directly within a card. Both processes are the same – the only difference is where you access it!

From within a card, click the **Labels** button on the **Add to card** menu located on the right side of the card:

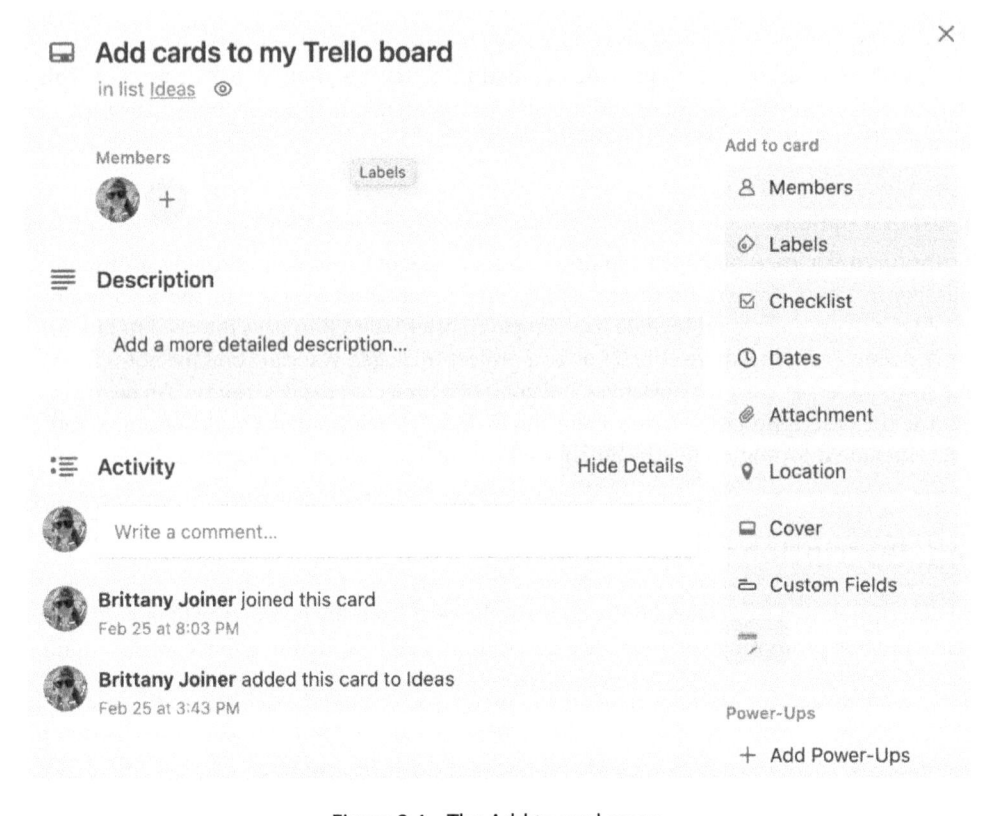

Figure 2.4 – The Add to card menu

This opens a modal, allowing you to select a current label or create a new one:

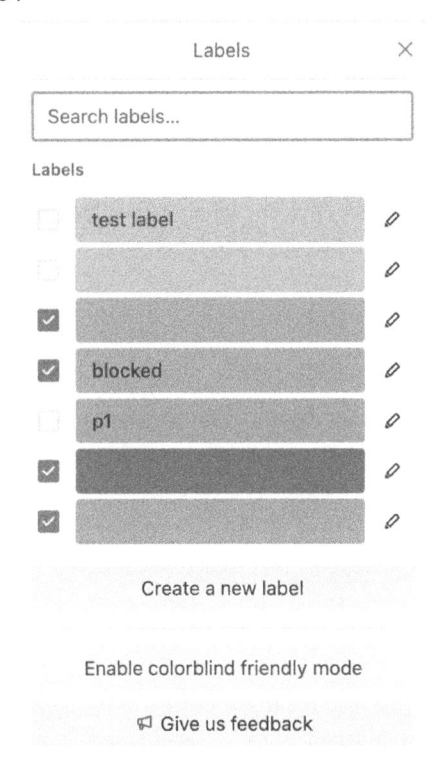

Figure 2.5 – The Labels modal

Search for existing labels in the search box by typing a name. To create a label, click the **Create a new label** button, or the pencil icon next to an existing label that you'd like to edit. A box will then appear, allowing you to add a title for the label, which is the text displayed on the label.

You can also change the color of a label to any of the 30 shades available in the palette chooser. If you'd prefer only text and no color, the label will be hidden from the front of the Trello card and will only appear when the card is open.

Figure 2.6 – An example of a colorless label

Once you've named a label and selected the color, click **Save**.

If you'd prefer more color blind-friendly options, click the button below the labels to turn on **Colorblind friendly mode**. This changes the labels to various patterns instead of just colors, which can be more accessible for anyone with difficulty discerning colors.

To remove a label, click the pencil to the right in the menu, and then select the red **Delete** button.

After you've created the labels you want, click the label or the checkbox next to a label to add it to the current card. Exit the card, and you can click the label from the card front to show or hide the text of the label.

Dates

The start and due date fields are used to set deadlines for a task or project. The due date is the date by which a task or project should be completed, while the start date is the date on which work should begin. Can't get enough and need more dates? We'll talk about how to add more dates in *Chapter 3* when we discuss custom fields.

To set a start or due date, simply click on a card and select the appropriate date from the calendar.

Start and due dates

A card can have both the start and due date fields set, neither of the fields set, or one of each set. Both fields offer a date value, but only the due date field accepts a time value as well.

> **Why use dates?**
>
> Dates are useful to visualize deadlines and prioritize your tasks. Cards with a due date can be plotted on a Timeline or Calendar view, which we'll discuss in more detail in *Chapter 4*.
>
> Sorting cards by the due date in a list is a useful way to prioritize your workload for the week. If you'd prefer to only see tasks that are due soon, you can use board filters to show only cards due today or in the next week, or cards that are overdue.

Adding start and due dates to a card

From the board, click a card to open up the back view. Click **Dates** from the **Add to card** menu on the right side of a card. This opens a modal with start and due date options.

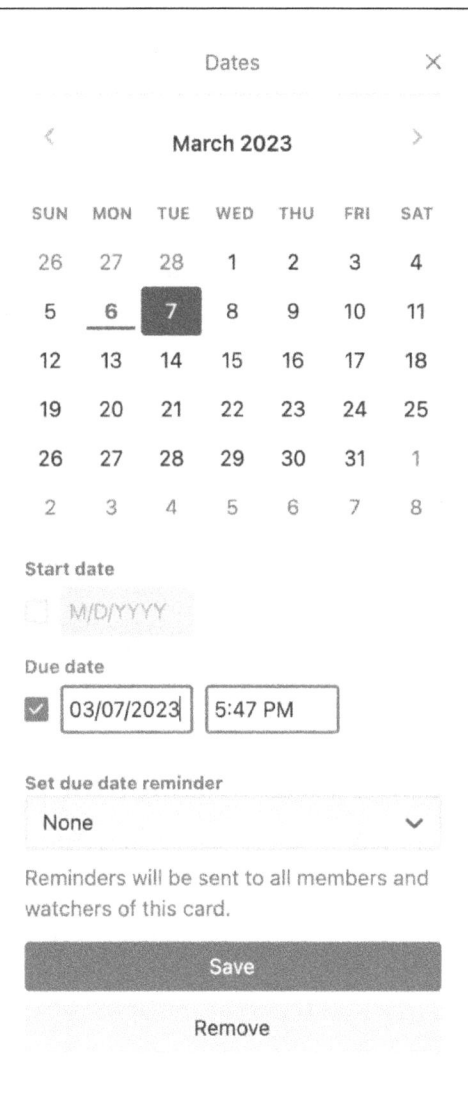

Figure 2.7 – The Dates modal

Use the arrows to the right and left of a month name to navigate to past or future dates.

By default, the start date is disabled, but clicking any date will automatically set the due date. If you want, you can adjust the time by selecting the time box just to the right of the date and typing another time.

To set the start date, select the checkbox in front of the grayed-out date below the **Start date** label. Immediately, the start date will be set to one day before the current due date. To change this, click another date on the calendar above, or type the desired date in the start date field.

If you'd like a notification before the card is due, use the dropdown option to set a reminder. The options are similar to reminders for an upcoming meeting in calendar tools.

Figure 2.8 – The due date reminder options

You can set a reminder for a card from the moment it's due up to two days before. If you need something further ahead, this is possible, but only with Trello automation. We'll cover due date automation more in *Part 2*.

The reminders will appear wherever you have Trello notifications configured. For instance, if you allow notifications in the mobile app, you'll receive a push notification about a card at the time you set it. You'll also receive an email or desktop notification if you have those types of notifications configured.

It's also important to note that anyone who is a member on the card or watching it will receive reminders about the due date – not just you!

If you'd prefer to not receive notifications about a card that is due, simply leave this field as is, since the default option is **None**.

When you're satisfied with your start date, due date, and reminder configurations, click the blue **Save** button at the bottom of the card.

Figure 2.9 – How the start and due dates appear on the front of a card

If you want to clear the dates from a card, click the gray **Remove** button.

The card dates will be visible in the card details above the description and below the card name when the card is open, and they are also visible from the Board view, so you can reference the dates without needing to open the card.

Members

The **Members** field allows you to assign team members to a task or project. This field is handy to track who is responsible for parts of a task and divide responsibilities across multiple teammates.

> **Why use members?**
>
> Adding members to cards is key to ensuring that task owners are notified about their projects and are aware of any changes happening to things they're working on. It's also useful to separate tasks on a board so that each person can filter it to only see their tasks, while project managers can still use the board to view everything in one place.
>
> Using the Timeline view, you can also view cards plotted by date and member, which is a helpful way to understand bandwidth and capacity for a given period. We'll talk more about views in *Chapter 4*. If you are using the free version of Trello, you can still view cards organized by members in lists with the Swimlanes Power-Up. We'll talk more about Power-Ups in *Part 3*.

Adding members to a card

Open a card by clicking it from the board. From the card back, select the **Member** button that appears at the top of the **Add to card** menu. This opens the **Members** modal.

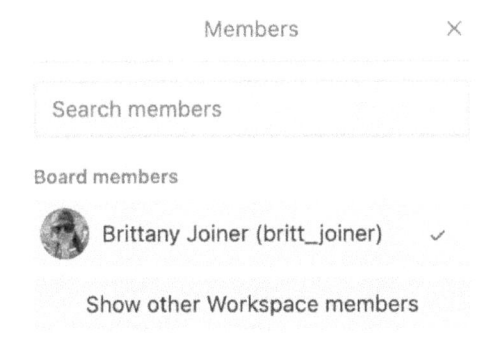

Figure 2.10 – The Members modal

Search for a member who is part of the board or select them from the names listed. If a user is already a member of a card, a checkmark appears next to their name. The member will receive a notification that you added them to the card.

To remove a user from a card, click their name to de-select them. They will also receive a notification about their removal.

You can add as many members to a card as you like. If you want to add someone but don't see them listed, you'll need to add them to the board first. Go back to *Chapter 1* if you need a refresher on adding a user to a board.

All members of a card appear with their avatar just below the card title. They're also visible from the front of a card so that you can see who is assigned without opening a card.

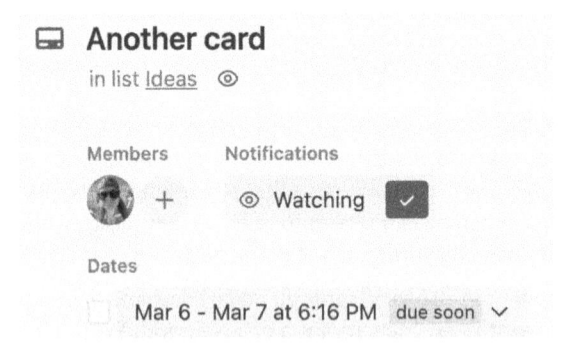

Figure 2.11 – The member section of a card

Watching

When someone is a card member, their avatar appears on the card, and they're assigned the item. However, sometimes you might want notifications about activities that happen on a card without it being assigned to you in Trello. You can do this in Trello, and it's called **watching**.

> **Why watch a card?**
> Watching a card is useful when you need notifications about a card but don't want it to appear as one of your designated tasks. It's also great for when the results of a task are relevant to you but there's no action you can take to make progress on the card.

Configuring watching on a card

Open a card and look just below the name to see a section called **Notifications**. Below that, there's a gray **Watch** button with an eye icon.

Figure 2.12 – The watch section of a card

By default, the box is unchecked. Click the button to begin watching the card. A checkbox appears next to **Watch**, and an eye icon appears near the top of the card next to the list name.

To stop watching a card, click the **Watch** button again to remove the check.

Comments and activity details

The bottom section of a Trello card offers a log of activities on the card as well as comments added from users. The comments are particularly useful to communicate with team members or provide updates on the status of a task or project.

> **Why use comments?**
> Comments are useful to discuss anything that relates to a card. Rather than needing to send emails or messages over Slack, it's easier to have a conversation within the card itself. Comments are always saved to cards, and even when a card is archived, you can still access the card and see the comments, showing a historical account of any decisions made relating to that task or item.

Commenting on a card

To add a comment to a card, open it by clicking it from the main board, and then scroll to the bottom of the card, below the description and any checklists or attachments. You'll see a section called **Activity**, and below that is an input field to type a comment.

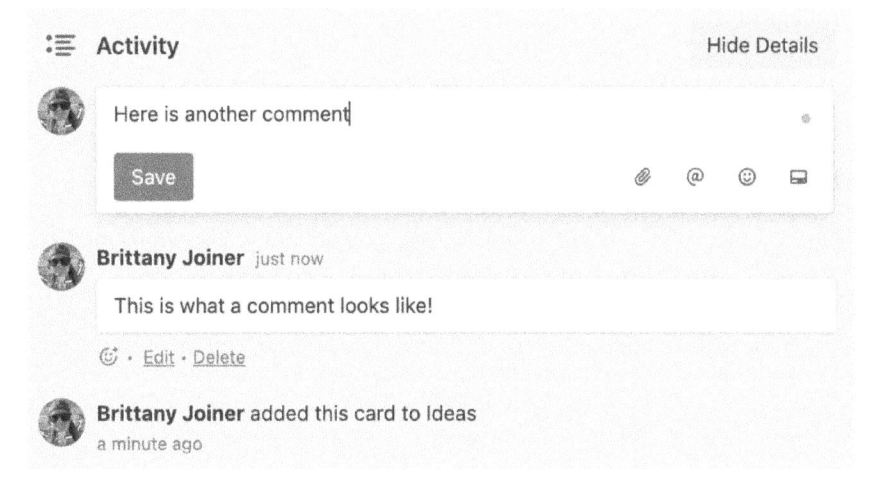

Figure 2.13 – The comment section of a card

Click the field and start typing some text. You can attach files, mention another user to send them a notification, add emojis for style, or even reference another card. When you're finished, click the blue **Save** button just below your text.

After you've posted, you can still edit or delete a comment with the actions below it. If someone else has posted a comment, you'll see options to **reply**, which automatically starts a new comment and mentions the user.

Finally, you can react to comments. Click the emoji button below a posted comment and select from one of the options, or search for the right one.

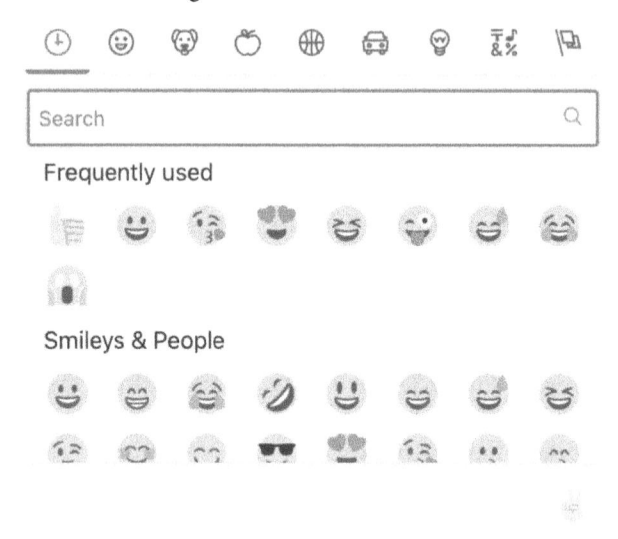

Figure 2.14 – The emoji picker to react to comments

Activity details

In between comments on a card, you will see other updates about things happening on a card, such as changes to members, dates, labels, custom fields, attachments, or even a description. While this is typically helpful when you want to see what happened to a card or aren't sure who changed a field on a card, if you find these updates unnecessary or cluttering up your card, you can turn them off. Click **Hide Details** to remove those updates and only show comments.

If you ever change your mind, you can bring them back by clicking **Show Details**.

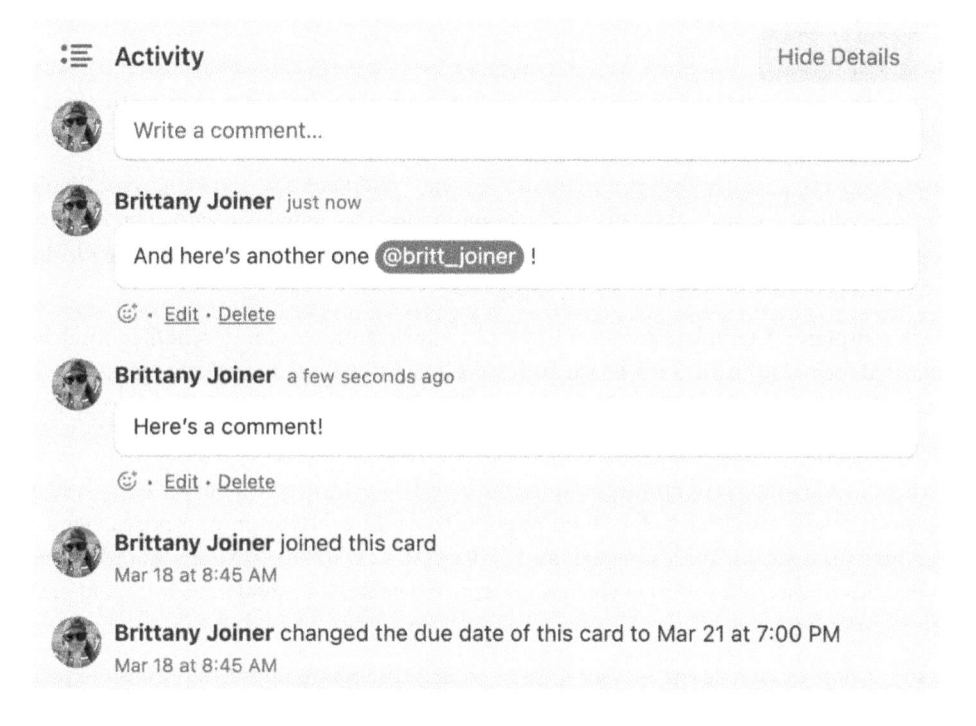

Figure 2.15 – Activity details listed at the bottom of a card

Card actions

We've already discussed a lot of things you can do to a card, but everything we've mentioned so far mostly refers to adding information. There are a few more important actions you can take with cards.

Figure 2.16 – The card action menu

The card action menu is found on the right side of a card at the very bottom of the card options, below any Power-Ups and automation buttons. These actions are useful to do something with the entire card:

- **Move**: Use this action to move a card to another list or board. You can specify the position, such as whether you want to add it to the top or bottom of the list. Keep in mind that you can also easily move a card around a board by simply clicking and dragging.
- **Copy**: Copying a card allows you to duplicate a card and keep the parts you want. You can copy everything, and a checklist gives you the option to avoid copying over certain items such as attachments, checklists, or comments. Just like the **Move** option, you can specify which list and board you want the copied card to appear on.
- **Make template**: A template card is a way to let your teammates know whether you have a preferred format for cards on a board and make it easy for them to copy that format. While you can copy any card on a board, template cards make it extremely clear how to copy a card and give new users an easy way to reference them.
- **Archive**: Archiving a card removes it from the board. Don't worry – it's never really lost! You can easily send a card back to the board by going to **Archived Items** in your board menu and searching for the card. There's no real need to delete it, as you don't have any storage limits in your archived data, but some people may prefer to delete it if it's confidential information they never want resurfacing.
- **Share**: In some cases, you may want to share a card. The **Share** option allows you to print a card or export it in the JSON format. You can also view and copy a card's short link, generate a QR code for the card, or grab the embed code to view it on a web page. (Note that this doesn't enable people who do not have access already to see the card.) You can also get the email address for the card. Anything sent to that email will appear as a comment on the card.

Card actions can be useful, so take your time to get to know these actions. You can also use a keyboard shortcut – typing the letter C while a card is selected to archive it. With these tips, you'll avoid scrolling to the **Card actions** menu to perform those actions.

Quick actions from the card front

Everything we've discussed so far was from the card back, when you have it open. However, you can make changes to cards without clicking them to open them. While hovering over a card, click the pencil icon to the right of the card name.

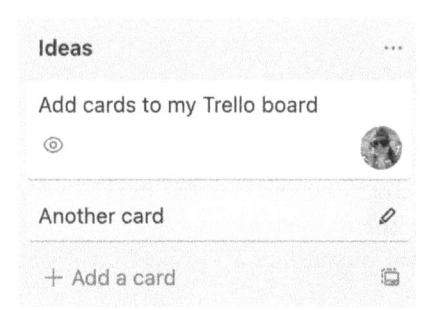

Figure 2.17 – Editing a card from the board view

This opens a menu that allows you to access the fields of a card and open those modals, without needing to go into the card itself.

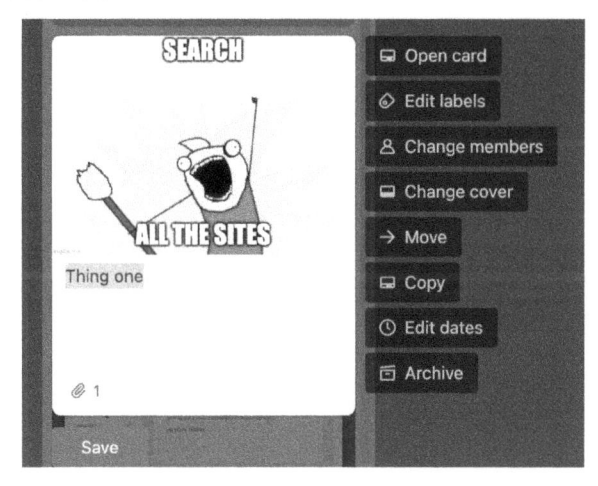

Figure 2.18 – A list of all card quick actions

Clicking any of the options that appear opens the same menu you would find inside the card, such as a menu to add members, select the due and start dates from a calendar, move a card, and add labels. There are also keyboard shortcut options to go straight to one of them – check out `trello.com/shortcuts`.

Summary

Whoa! We've gone through a lot in this chapter. If you're thinking, "*Wow, Trello does a lot!*", you're right. That's the beauty of it. Rather than get overwhelmed, give yourself a chance to see the possibilities!

Let's recap. We learned the elements of a card and the attributes you can assign to it, such as members, dates, and labels. You're also now comfortable navigating around a card and performing actions, showing details, and making edits as you please.

Now that you know about the most useful parts of a card, it's time to dive even deeper. We've only scratched the surface of everything you can do inside these super-charged sticky notes, so let's keep going!

3
Leveling Up Your Cards

If your head is still spinning from all the things you can do with a card, buckle up because we're just getting started. While adding members, dates, and labels is most common, there are many other things you can include in your Trello cards to make them more powerful.

In this chapter, we'll discuss how to add files, links, and any other attachments to your cards. We'll also talk about locations, checklists, and card covers and how to use all of those fields to give even more context to your cards. In case you think of an input we haven't already mentioned, you'll learn how to create custom fields to store any other info you can imagine.

Attachments

While you can add a lot of info to a Trello card description or through some of the other fields we've already talked about, sometimes you'll have data or files that live in other places. This is where attachments come in handy.

> **Why use attachments?**
> I'm not naïve enough to think that Trello is the only tool you'll ever use. Heck, even I still use other things such as spreadsheets to organize financial info or Canva to create images for blog posts, and even Google Docs or Confluence to collaborate with others through text. Attachments make it possible to keep everything in one place, without needing to sacrifice using the best tool for the job. You'll also be using multiple Trello cards and boards that relate to each other, so being able to quickly get to relevant items while you're working on a card is critical.

Attaching items to a card

The easiest way to attach items to a card is to drag and drop a file or paste a link over the card. You can do this while it's open (card front) or closed (card back).

Another way to attach cards is via the **Attachment** action from the **Add to card** menu. A modal appears prompting you to select the type of attachment.

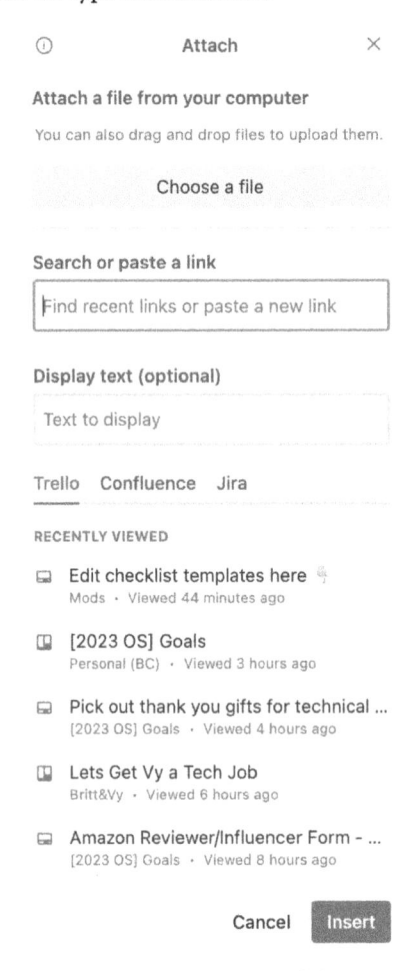

Figure 3.1 – Attachment modal options

There are multiple types of attachments you can add to a card, and the process for adding one varies slightly depending on what you'd like to attach.

Computer files

If you have files saved to your computer, such as PDFs, spreadsheets, images, presentations, videos, or audio files, you can add them to the card and others can preview or download the attachments.

Select the **Computer** option and a file picker modal appears asking you to select a file from a directory on your computer.

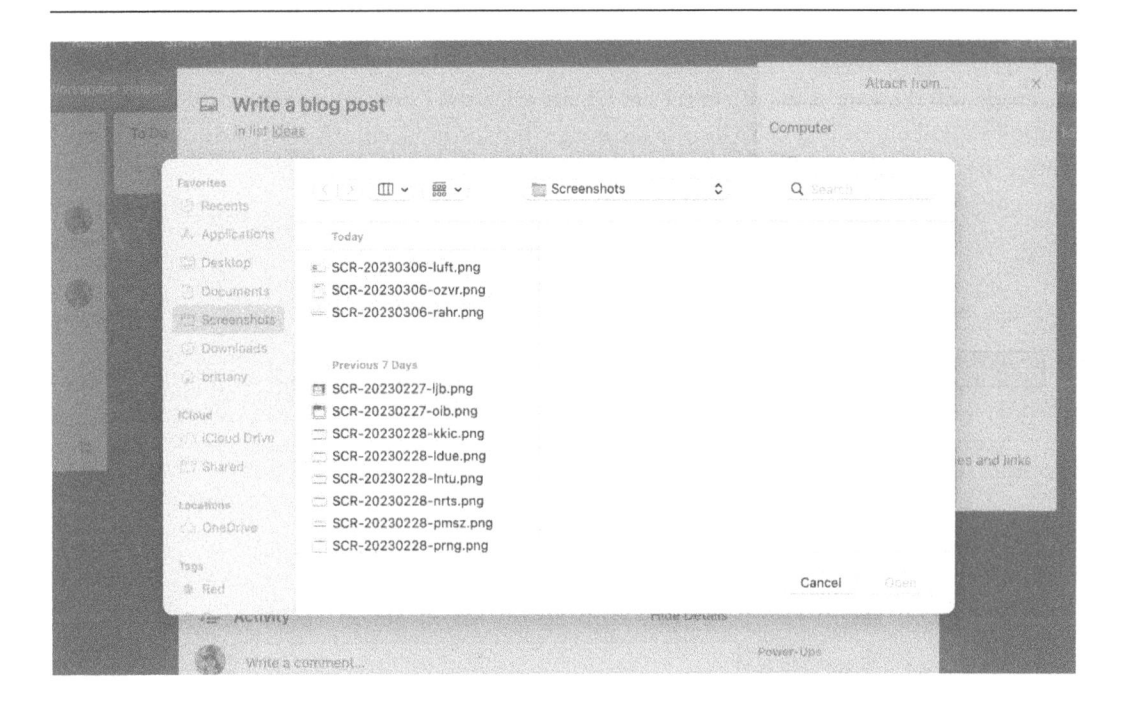

Figure 3.2 – File picker

Select the file and as it loads to the card, you'll see a loading notification. Once it's been added, the attachment appears below the card description and above any checklists on the card.

Figure 3.3 – Image attachment displayed in the Attachments section

If the file is an image or PDF, clicking the name or item will open a preview of the item. To download the resource, click the arrow icon after the filename.

If you'd like to rename the item, click **Edit** to change the name and make it clearer. This is useful if someone sends you a screenshot name "Screenshot-12345" and no one knows what that means.

Leveling Up Your Cards

If you add an image to a card, Trello automatically sets it as the card cover. This means that a thumbnail of the image will show up at the top of the card, both when the card is open and when the card is closed and viewed on the board. To disable the image from previewing, select **Remove cover** from the image in the **Attachments** section inside the card.

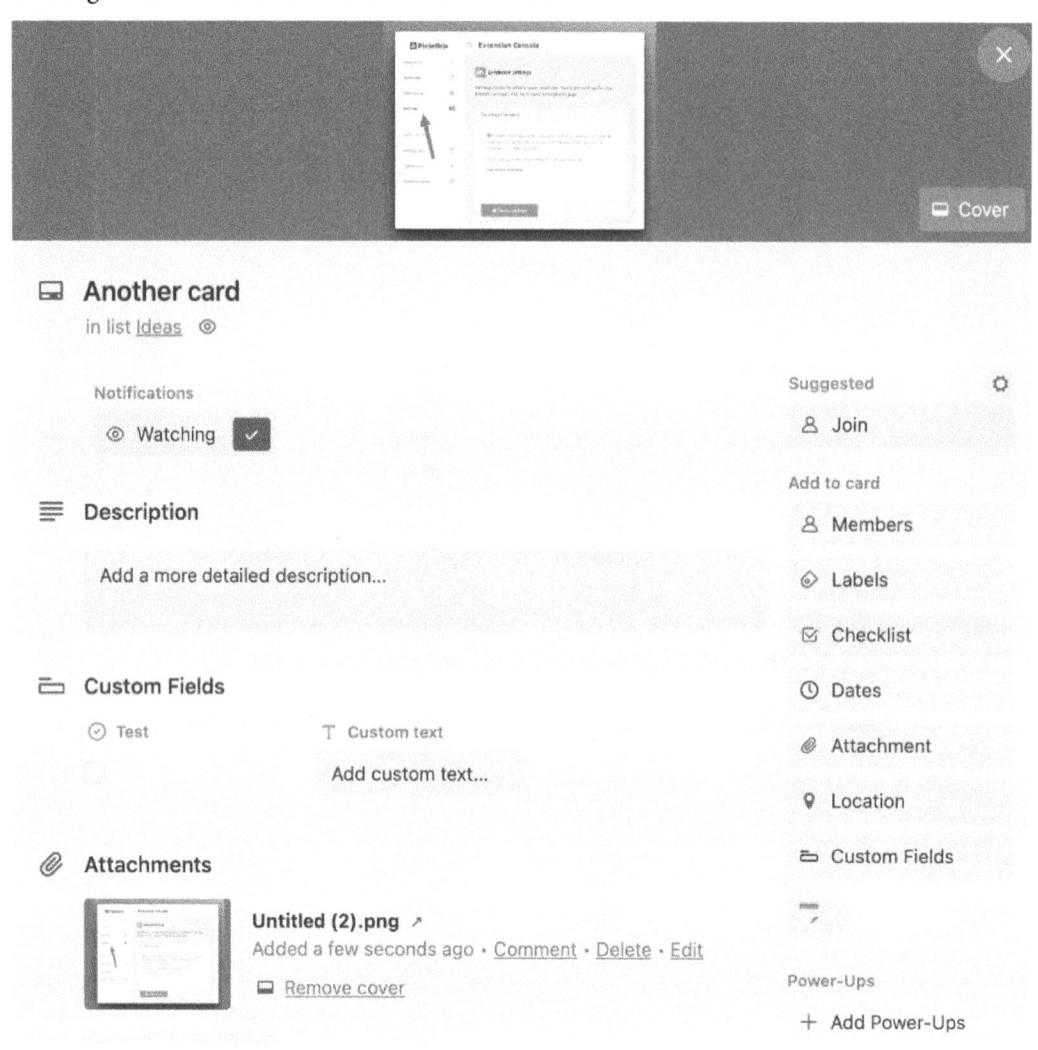

Figure 3.4 – Image added to the top of a card as a card cover

Trello cards and boards

You can also attach Trello items to a card, making it easy to quickly reference other boards or cards.

Click **Trello** from the attachment options and a new modal appears asking you to search for a card or board to add to the card. Search for a name, type a link, or select one of the cards or boards that appears automatically.

A new section of your card is created called **Trello attachments** and it shows the item you've selected. It's a great way to preview a card's key information without having to actually go to the card.

Figure 3.5 – Preview of attached card

If you attach a board, your attachment shows a preview of the board background with the board name, and you're just a click away from going straight to the board.

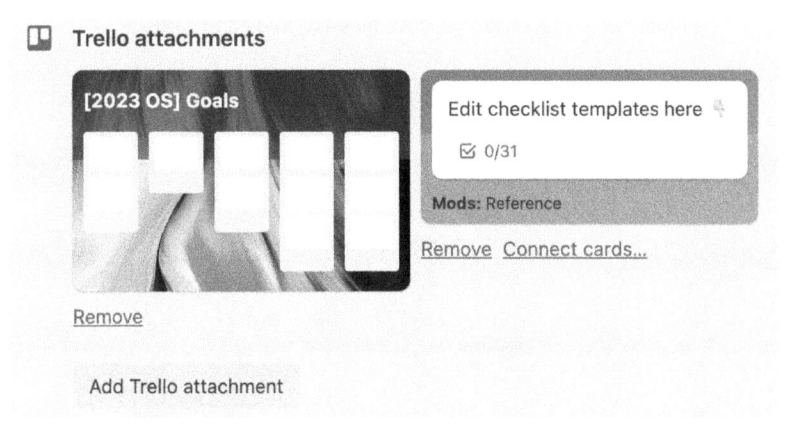

Figure 3.6 – Preview of attached board and card

Note that if a member of the card does not have access to the board for the attached Trello item, they will not be able to preview the attachment. This can be useful for you to quickly reference something from a private board as you view a card, while not permitting others to see that item.

You'll notice next to option to search for Trello items, you also see Confluence and Jira. Since Trello is owned by Atlassian, there's a tight integration with these other Atlassian tools, allowing you to search for and select Confluence pages and Jira tickets in the menu.

Cloud drives

Many of us use tools to share documents in the cloud, such as Google Drive, Box, Dropbox, and OneDrive. Attaching cloud files works very similarly, regardless of the platform.

Previously, Trello's attachments had sections for some of those, such as Box and Google Drive. But with recent updates to their Attachment menu, those have moved away. If you want to incorporate Cloud files in your board, you can search for a Power-Up (such as the Google Drive Power-Up), or you can attach those files via their link, which we'll talk about in a minute.

Figure 3.7 – Attach Google Drive files and folders to cards

You'll see a new section appear on the card with the cloud document provider and a preview of the image.

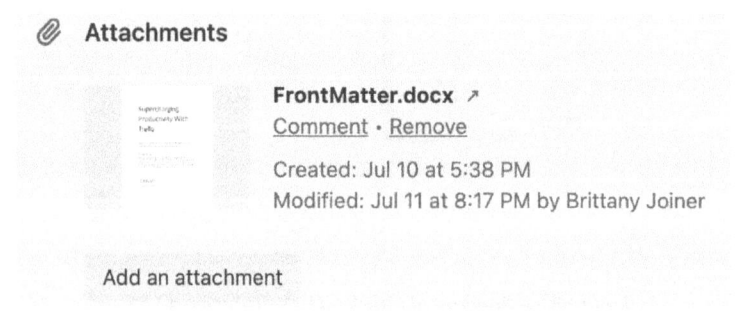

Figure 3.8 – Google sheet attached to a card

Click Comment to start a comment that links to the file. This is useful if you've added a file and you want to make sure folks on the card know the file is there and invite them to take any action needed with the file.

Links

In some cases, you might just want to attach a link to an article. Simply paste the link in the box at the top of the **Attachment** menu.

The Display text field below the link gives you the option to name your link. This is optional and gives you a quick way to clarify the name for that field if the default text that appears isn't clear enough. I find this particularly helpful with Notion links, which come across as a useless string of letters and numbers. I can rename them to for example, `Mod Promo Playbook`.

When you're happy with the link and name, click the blue **Insert** button.

Inline attachments

Rather than attaching links to a card via the **Attachments** section, you can incorporate them inside descriptions and comments. Try it out!

Paste a link into a comment. I used to hate recording myself, but now I actually prefer communicating thoughts over Loom rather than typing a long comment, so I'll paste in a link from Loom.

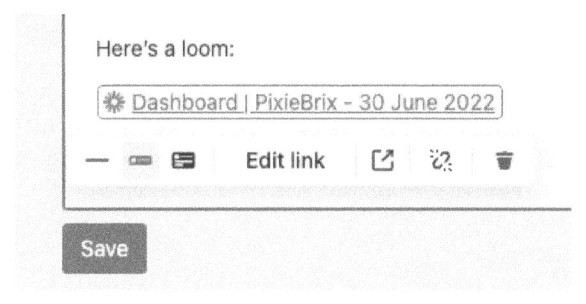

Figure 3.9 – Smart link options in card comment

Click the link to see a menu with options for changing how the link looks. You can keep it simple and include only the exact copy of the link, you can choose the middle option (which is the default) showing a logo and the title hyperlinked, or you can choose the third option, which is like an embeddable view of the content from the link.

Figure 3.10 – Full embed of smart link in card comment

To see which services this works for, check `support.atlassian.com/trello/docs/link-cards/#supported-services` for the most up-to-date information, as I'm sure they add more all the time. These work very similarly to link cards, which you'll read about later in this chapter.

Custom fields

We've already discussed a lot of specific fields for a card. You can define dates, assign members, update a description with any info you'd like, attach files, and more! But sometimes, you still just need something else.

This is where custom fields come in! Trello users on Standard, Premium, and Enterprise plans can create custom fields to track additional information about a task or project. This field is particularly useful for tracking information that is specific to your organization or workflow.

Custom fields are set at the board level and appear on every card on the board. You can't set fields to only show on certain cards, or make them appear on the front of the card unless they're filled in. You also have the option to remove them from the card front altogether if you prefer.

I use custom fields on just about every board that I create. While you can use labels to add information and details about a card, I find custom fields to be much easier to work with and more straightforward for defining relevant details about a card.

They're also fantastic for turning your Trello cards into a form. With custom fields, you can tell someone to create a Trello card and fill out the fields that appear, rather than describing all of the information they should be typing into the card description.

> **Why use custom fields?**
>
> Once you get in a groove with your workflows in Trello, you'll want to make them as smooth as possible. Custom fields help you do that and also provide guardrails to make sure others using the board are adding correct data to the cards and ensuring nothing is forgotten. It's also a way to completely customize Trello to be the tool you need it to be, rather than just your run-of-the-mill project management tool. This is really one of the building blocks that allow you to build Trello to be anything you need it to be.

Are you interested in custom fields but not sure what to create for your board? Here are some ideas based on how you use Trello:

Content Calendar	Ad title, Publish date, Content topic
Sales Pipeline	Lead email, Deal amount, Status
Support Tickets	Ticket ID, Customer email, Support level/tier
Engineering Sprint	Estimated story points, Actual story points, Priority
Product Roadmap	Votes for feature, Key stakeholder

Project Management	Milestone date(s), Impacted team
E-commerce Orders	Order ID, Estimated delivery date

Creating a custom field

You can create a custom field from within a card or the board menu. Select the **Custom Fields** button at the bottom of the **Add to card** menu on the right side of a card.

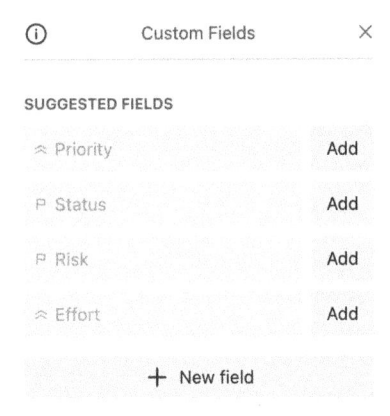

Figure 3.11 – Custom field creation modal

Trello suggests a few custom fields, such as **Priority** and **Status**. If you want to add one of those, simply select **Add**. These are commonly used custom fields and a great way to get started.

Click the gray **+ New field** button to create your own field. You'll be prompted to select a title for the field, which shows up on the card. Then you can choose from one of the five types of fields.

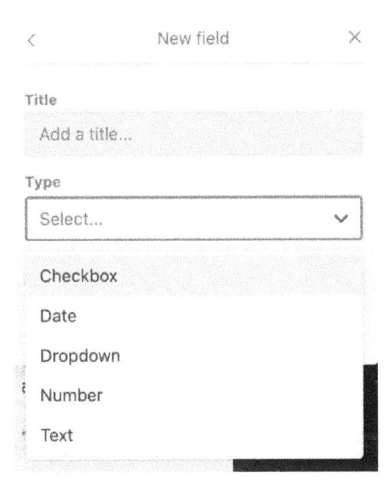

Figure 3.12 – Options for custom field types

You might use a **Checkbox** field if the value of something is yes or no. This is a great way to show whether something has been approved or to see whether a card has been through a specific stage of a workflow.

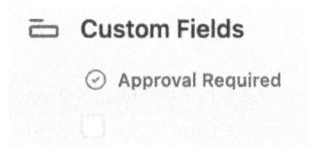

Figure 3.13 – Custom fields with a Checklist type

I love using this as a toggle on a card to help determine whether it meets some criteria (such as **Needs review from a senior manager**). This is helpful in automation because you can specify actions to occur on cards that have a field checked, such as moving a card to a list when the field is checked, or moving it to another list when it's un-checked.

A **Date** field is a timestamp field with date and time values. It's useful if you want to add another date to your card, besides just start and due dates.

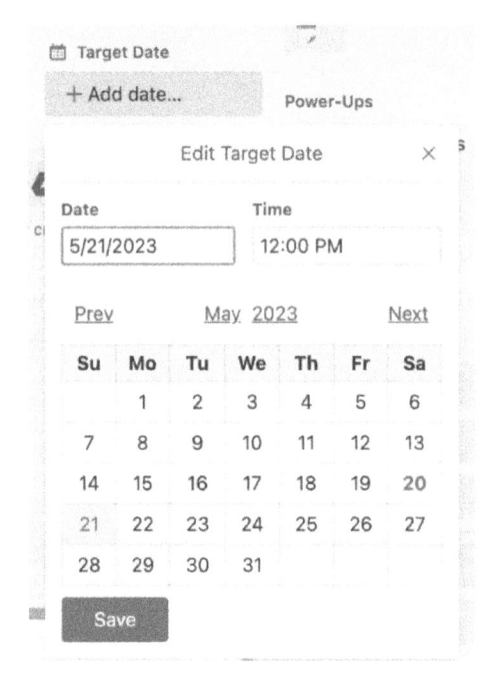

Figure 3.14 – Custom fields with the Date type

You might use this to track actual completion dates or a draft due date that is a week before the final due date. Some even prefer to use these as start and end dates instead of the native Trello date fields. It's easy to build automation that sets the date field of a card based on when you perform actions, so you could create a date field for tracking when it moves into its current list or when the card was created.

The **Dropdown** field allows you to preset options that people can select from a dropdown. This is perfect for data validation and to prevent having inconsistent text values as fields on a card.

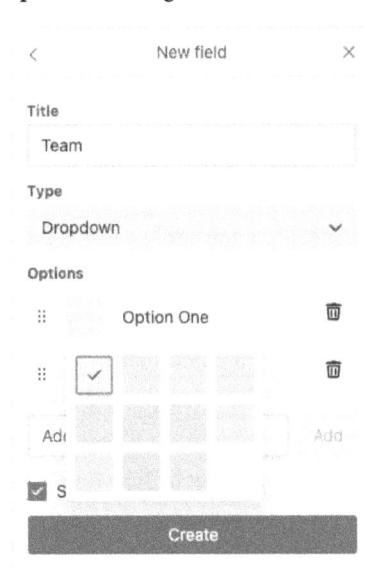

Figure 3.15 – Custom fields with the Dropdown type

You might use this to set a card's priority to high, medium, or low. Add colors to a **Dropdown** option to help the different answers stand out.

Number values are just that—numbers. You can perform calculations and report on aggregates of these values with third-party Power-Ups, which we'll discuss in *Part 3*.

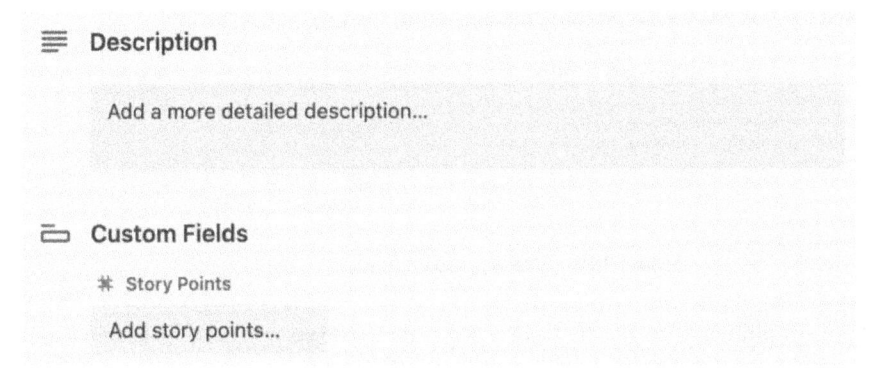

Figure 3.16 – Custom fields with the Number type

This type is useful for tracking hours or story points on a project or budget.

Text fields are useful for just about anything that doesn't fit into the other types.

⊟ **Custom Fields**

T Reason

Add reason...

Figure 3.17 – Custom fields with the Text type

You might use a text field to store a contact's email address, a note about the task, or other relevant information for the task.

Once you've selected the type and defined any preset options for a drop-down field, you can decide whether you want to show the field on the front of a card (when viewed from the board alongside other cards) or whether you only want to see it when you open a card. Finally, create the field by clicking the **Create** button below the options.

If you no longer need a custom field, you can delete it by selecting the option from the **Custom Field** menu on a card or from the **Board** menu. Click **Delete field** and then type the name of the field to enable the red **Delete field** button. This is meant to prevent any accidental deletion of data from your boards.

Setting a custom field value

You can find the **Custom Fields** section of a card just below the card description and above the attachments. Interact with the field just like you would any other field on the card. If it's a checkbox, click the box to show whether the task is complete or incomplete. Click a text or number field to input a value. Select a date field to open a calendar. Click a drop-down field to view the configured options.

There's no need to click **Save**—simply moving away from the field saves the input!

⊟ **Custom Fields**

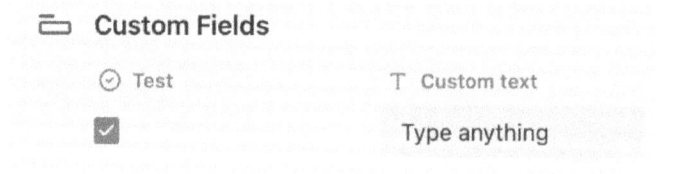

⊙ Test   T Custom text

☑   Type anything

Figure 3.18 – Setting custom fields on a card

If you need more inspiration with custom fields, head to the Trello section of the Atlassian Community to ask questions or see what other folks are doing with their boards—you'll find many cool uses of custom fields!

Checklists

The checklist feature lets you create a list of subtasks that need to be completed in relation to the task or project. This field is particularly useful for breaking down complex tasks into smaller, more manageable pieces.

> **Why use checklists?**
> Checklists are helpful for ensuring you follow a specific set of tasks for routine procedures or making sure you don't forget any essential parts of a task. They're also a great way to delegate responsibilities if you have multiple members assigned to a card.

Adding a checklist

To add a checklist to a card, open the card and select the **Checklist** button from the **Add to card** menu.

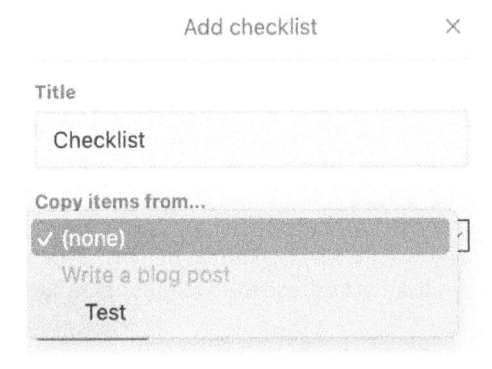

Figure 3.19 – Checklist creation modal

If you've already created a checklist in the current board, you can select it from the dropdown to create a duplicate version with the same items as in the current card. Otherwise, you can simply give it a title and click the blue **Add** button.

Figure 3.20 – Checklist on a card

Add specific items to the checklist by typing in the box that says **Add an item**. Press *Enter* or click the blue **Add** button to create the item. Pro tip — you can copy and paste a list of items from a document or spreadsheet and it will create a new item from each line break!

If you accidentally created an item, you can edit the name by selecting the text. But if you're really done with it, you can remove it by hovering over the card and clicking the ellipses at the end of the row, then click Delete.

Sometimes you might create an item as a subtask but realize it's actually a better fit as its own card. It's easy to change that! Click the ellipses at the end of the row of a task and click **Convert to card**. The checklist item becomes a new card in the same list as the original card. When you're done, just click out of the checklist.

Advanced checklists

Standard, Premium, and Enterprise Trello users can use advanced checklists, which allow you to add due dates and members to checklist items. This is especially useful if you have multiple people involved in completing a card. You can see what tasks still need to be done and who is up next.

To add a due date or member to an existing checklist item, hover over the item and you will notice a clock icon and user icon appear. Clicking the clock icon opens a modal similar to the due date picker, allowing you to set a due date for the item. Clicking the user icon allows you to add one member to the checklist item.

You can also add a member and due date while creating an item. Type the name of a task in the checklist. Before pressing *Enter* or clicking **Add**, use the **Assign** or **Due date** button on the right side.

Figure 3.21 – Modal for adding advanced checklist items

Don't have a paid Trello plan? You can still mention someone in a checklist item by clicking the @ icon. This doesn't assign them the item, but it does hyperlink their profile and send them a notification. Clicking the emoji button allows you to add style to your checklist items by selecting an emoji from the emoji picker. When you're done, click the blue **Add** button.

Viewing all your checklist items

If you've been assigned checklist items across multiple cards, you can view them all by going to your home view at `trello.com`. It shows the next upcoming items you've been assigned. Click **Show more** to see all of your checklist items.

Figure 3.22 – Home section in Trello showing assigned checklist items

You can check off items from this view or click an item to go to the card and view more information.

Viewing the progress of checklists

Check off items on a checklist by checking the box to the left of the checklist name.

Figure 3.23 – Semi-completed checklist

A bar appears underneath the checklist title showing you the percentage of items that have been completed. A line is crossed through any items that have been checked off. If you'd prefer to only see the remaining tasks that haven't been completed, click **Hide checked items** next to the checklist name.

You can also view the progress of a checklist from the front of a card. Close the card to view a fraction on the front of the card, displaying the number of completed items and total items in the card.

Figure 3.24 – Card checklist progress fraction on the card front

To remove a checklist, click **Delete** from inside the card, just to the right of the checklist name.

Locations

Many of the fields we've discussed are available on other productivity and project management tools, but this one is not something I've seen anywhere else!

This field type stores a location value from Google Maps as a field in your cards. While this may not be useful for every board, if you work with location data for jobs or are planning events or trips, this field will prove invaluable for helping you literally map out your workflow.

Note that this field is only available for Premium and Enterprise workspaces.

> **Why use location?**
> Although not every board will need to use location, it can be incredibly handy if you need to see multiple locations and how they relate to each other. With the Map view, you can view all of these cards plotted on a map and see how close they are in relation to others. It's perfect for planning an order delivery, creating itineraries for trips, or organizing an address book.

Setting a location on a card

To set a location on a card, click the **Location** button from the **Add to card** menu on the right side of a card. This opens a modal allowing you to search for a location in Google Maps.

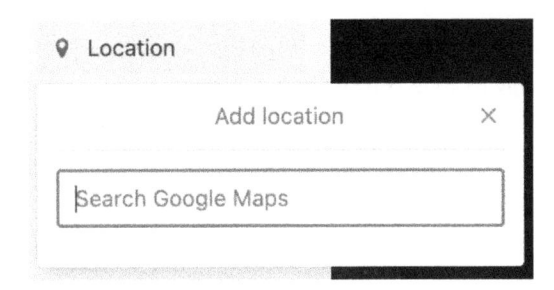

Figure 3.25 – Add location modal

Type an address or the name of a destination, such as Disney World. As you type, options appear below. Select one to see a new section of your card appear that adds a preview of a map. Clicking the arrow opens a new tab with the location in Google Maps.

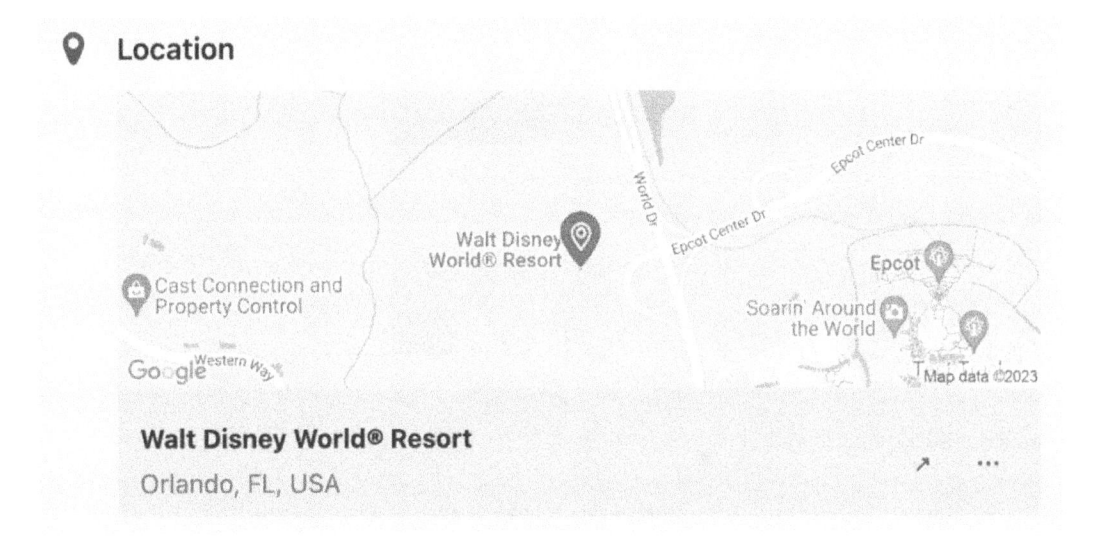

Figure 3.26 – Location preview on a card

You can change the location or remove it by selecting the ellipses at the end of the row.

Covers

Card covers are the perfect way to make your board more visual. These covers are displayed behind or above the card title. There are two types of covers you can add to your cards: colors and images.

62   Leveling Up Your Cards

> **Why use card covers?**
>
> Card covers are a great way to style your boards. Colors are useful for creating sections or headers in your lists. Images are useful for visualizing important aspects of a card. They also work well for organizing galleries of images for products, portfolios, or anything else that's visually dependent.

Adding a card cover

To add a cover to a card, click the **Cover** button on the **Add to card** menu on the right side of a card. If you've already added an image to the card, Trello might have automatically set that image as the cover. In that case, the **Cover** menu will be at the top of the card, in the bottom-right corner of the displayed image. Once you click **Cover**, it will open a menu.

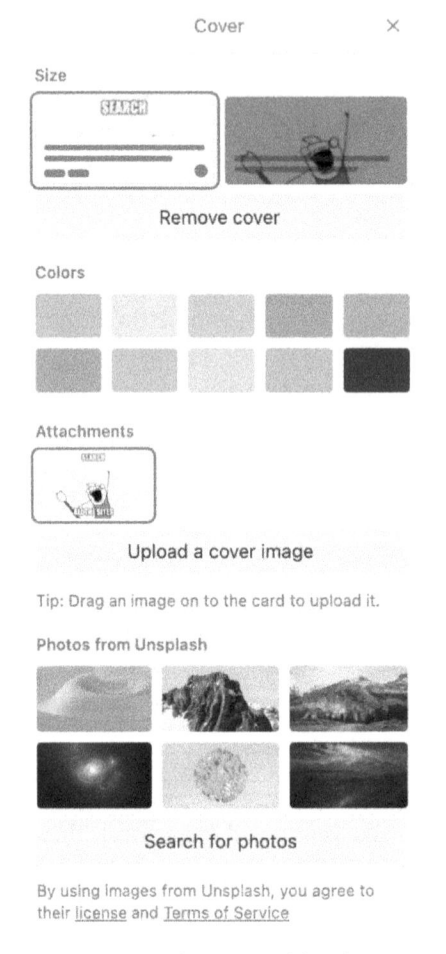

Figure 3.27 – Card cover modal with options

You can configure a few things about your card cover.

First of all, you can configure the size. By default, the image or color appears above the card name, but choosing the option to the right will place the image as the background of the card front and place the card name over the image. Choosing this option removes additional information from the front of the card, such as labels, members, number of attachments, checklist progress, and custom fields. But it can be a strategic design choice if your cards are graphic dependent, for instance, if you have a board that organizes images that you can use for ads or destinations for a trip. They also make nice list headers to give instructions on how to use a list.

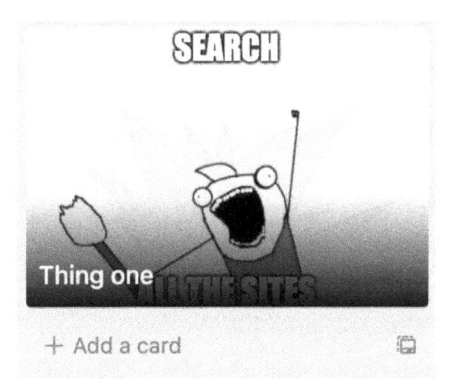

Figure 3.28 – Front of a card with image cover as background

When you select this style of card cover for images, you'll be able to select the color of the text (black or white) that will lay over the image.

If you haven't attached an image to the card, you can still add one to the cover. Search for photos from Unsplash at the bottom of the cover options.

Aside from images, you have another option you can use for card covers—colors! Colors are useful for styling your cards as dividers and creating sections for your lists.

Figure 3.29 – Front of a card with color cover

Link cards

If you create a Trello card with a link as the name, the card gets a bit fancy. Trello integrates with certain tools to embed links on your board, making it even easier to interact with other tools you use.

For example, if you paste a YouTube video link as a card name, the card shows an embedded YouTube video on your Trello board.

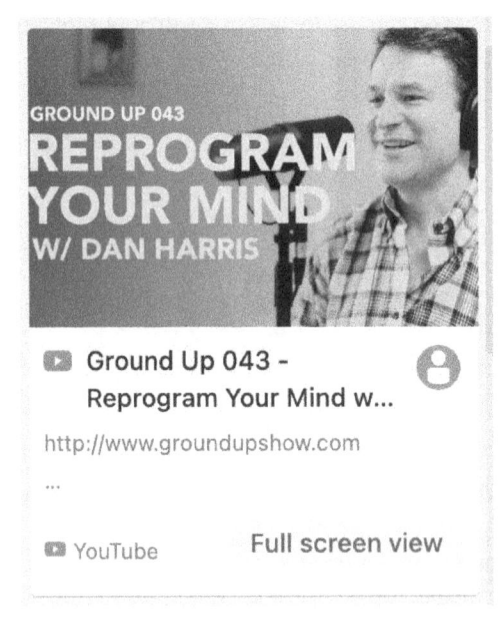

Figure 3.30 – YouTube video embedded Trello card

A thumbnail appears with the video and the title below, as well as a **Full screen view** button. Clicking the button opens a YouTube video player, allowing you to watch the video from YouTube without leaving your Trello screen.

Try this out with other links you use regularly! Creating a new card with a Google Sheets or Google Doc link as the name allows you to preview and edit the Google Doc without leaving Trello.

Learn more about service link cards support on this page: `support.atlassian.com/trello/docs/link-cards/`.

Disabling link cards

If you ever want to actually use a link as a normal card, click the pencil icon in the top-right corner while hovering over a card and select **Convert to regular card**.

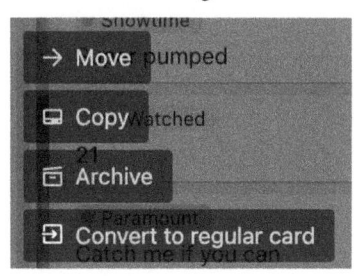

Figure 3.31 – Link card menu options

There are so many ways to add information to your card! Hopefully, it's clear now how you can really keep everything in Trello.

Summary

Now you can truly put anything you need in your Trello cards. You've learned how to attach items—whether digital files or links or other Trello cards! You can literally map out data in your boards by adding location fields to cards. Your worries about delegation and quality assurance are gone because you can add checklists to your cards.

You're well on your way to becoming a Trello expert since you can confidently navigate your cards! Now, it's time to talk about how we use all of these attributes of cards to analyze our cards in different views in Trello.

4
Viewing Cards Your Way

Now that you know everything you can add to a card, you might be bursting with ideas of what to put in your Trello boards. Since organizing a lot of information is easy in Trello, you'll find yourself adding many cards to a board. While seeing everything laid out in a board style is helpful, there are multiple ways to view your cards that unlock additional insights.

In this chapter, we'll discuss how to change the data in your board so that you can view the cards that are most relevant to you. You'll learn how to do the following:

- Set filters to show only the most relevant cards
- Create and view charts that visualize information about cards
- Plot your cards by date on a calendar and timeline
- Make your board look like a spreadsheet
- View your cards by location on a map

Filters

Filters can be used with every Trello view except **Dashboards**. They do exactly what they sound like – they filter all of the cards on the board(s) to only show a subset of cards based on criteria that you set.

Follow along and set up a filter with the cards you've already created. To access filters, click the gray **Filter** button at the top right of your board, just next to the **Automation** button:

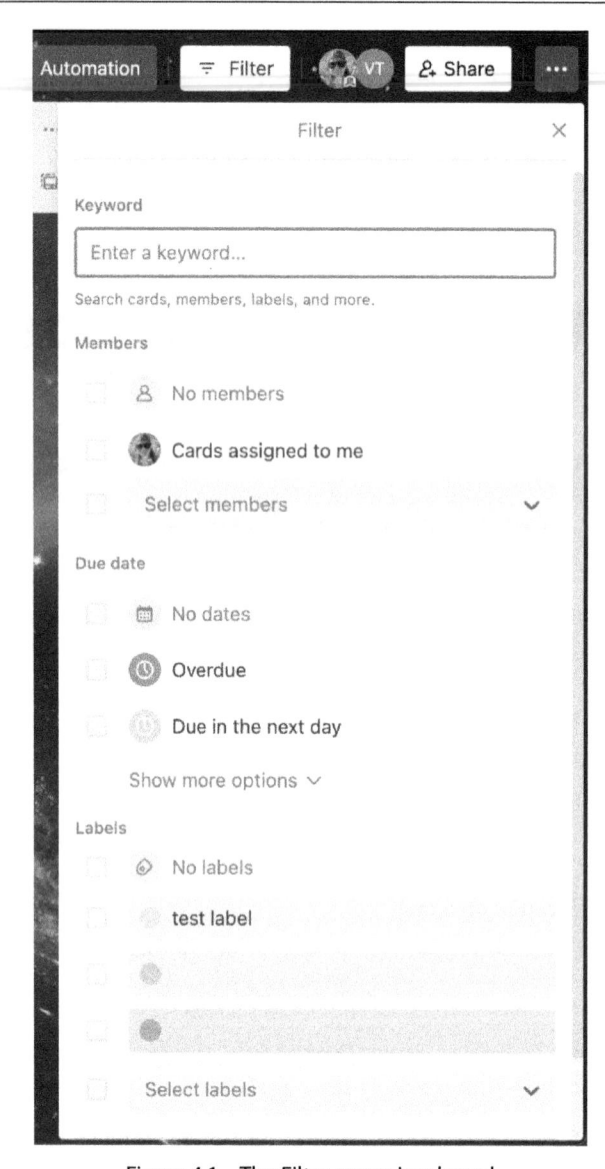

Figure 4.1 – The Filter menu in a board

Clicking the **Filter** button reveals a menu of options showing you the filtering capabilities.

Dimensions to filter by

Filters are powerful for querying multiple dimensions of a card. You can combine them to get a clear picture of exactly what you're looking for, such as your tasks for the week that are currently blocked, or what client tasks must be completed today.

Keywords

You can search for a word or phrase to only show cards that have that text in some aspect of the cards. This searches by name, labels, or members.

Start typing in the box to search for a term; the filter will be applied immediately and remove any cards from the board that don't match the text.

Members

Speaking of members, a popular filter shows cards that belong to a specific member. For example, you might share a board with your entire team, and while it's nice to see what everyone is working on when you are planning or coordinating your day-to-day work, sometimes you may just want to see your own tasks.

If you're a project manager, you might want to filter by cards that do not have a member assigned so you can decide which tasks need to be delegated and assigned an owner:

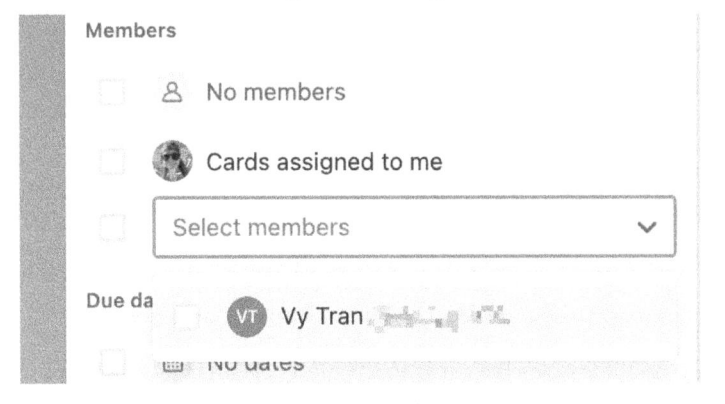

Figure 4.2 – Additional members filter in the Filter menu

To use the **Members** filter, check the box to the left of the filter you prefer or search for a specific member in the **Additional members** field. You can select one or multiple. Selecting multiple is great if you have many people on your board but want to see what a specific team of a few people is working on.

Since filtering by your own cards is a common practice, you can press Q on your keyboard when you're on a board to automatically apply the **Cards assigned to me** filter.

Due dates

Perhaps you've narrowed down the cards on the board so that you are viewing just your cards, but there might still be many! Using the dates filter helps you see which are upcoming so that you can be aware of urgent items.

These are most helpful for assessing your current workload and seeing whether you've planned too much or whether anything is falling behind.

You can filter for cards with no dates to see whether there are any tasks you need to plan or use the **Marked as complete** filter to view cards that have been completed. This is especially helpful if you aren't using a *Done* list to indicate a card's status:

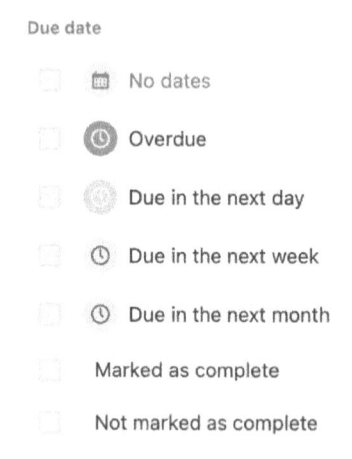

Due date

- No dates
- Overdue
- Due in the next day
- Due in the next week
- Due in the next month
- Marked as complete
- Not marked as complete

Figure 4.3 – Date filter options in the Filter menu

To set a date filter, check the box next to the option you'd prefer. Check another box if you change your mind.

Labels

The **Labels** filters are useful for viewing cards that have a certain status or are part of a category. Sometimes, I use labels for priority, so applying a filter for a red "p1" label would filter the board to show my highest priority cards or a "blocked" label would show any cards that I may need to raise to my manager:

Figure 4.4 – Labels filter options in the Filter menu

You can select a specific label by checking the box to the left of one. If you don't see a label, click the **Select labels** dropdown. You can also filter by cards that do not have a label, which is useful for tagging newly created cards on a board.

Activity

Trello recently added the option to filter cards by activity so you can see which cards have been most active over a certain period of time. That's helpful for seeing cards that people have been working in recently.

You can also filter by cards without activity in the last four weeks, which is a great way to see if any cards are being neglected.

Filter logic

By default, filters use OR logic. This means that if one of the criteria is true, a card will appear on the board:

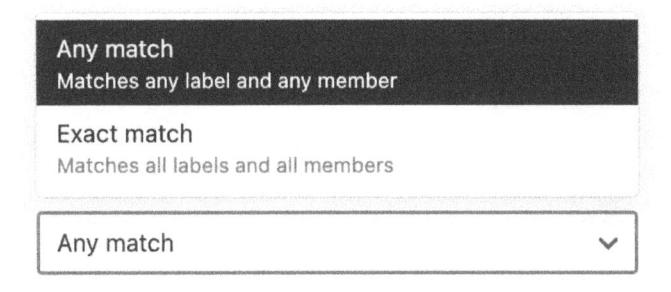

Figure 4.5 – Filter logic settings in the Filter menu

72 Viewing Cards Your Way

If you prefer to only see cards that meet ALL the criteria, such as cards assigned to me AND cards with a yellow label, apply the **Exact match** setting at the bottom of the Filter modal.

Removing a filter

Removing a filter is as simple as clicking the **X** button in the filter box in the board's toolbar. Many people open an empty board and wonder what's happened to their cards! They didn't disappear, there's just likely a filter that's hiding them! Always check for a filter when you're missing cards on your board.

I'll leave this section on filters with a pro filter tip for you: although there is no feature to save a filter view, it's still technically possible. Every filter changes the URL of a board. When you apply a filter, you'll see that the URL changes based on the selected filter. Bookmark a URL to save those filters and return to a specific view at any time.

Accessing alternative board views

While filters help control which cards appear on your board, Board views give you alternative ways to display the cards that are shown. To access the other views in your Trello board, click the arrow next to the **Board** button on the top toolbar of your Trello board, just to the right of the board's name:

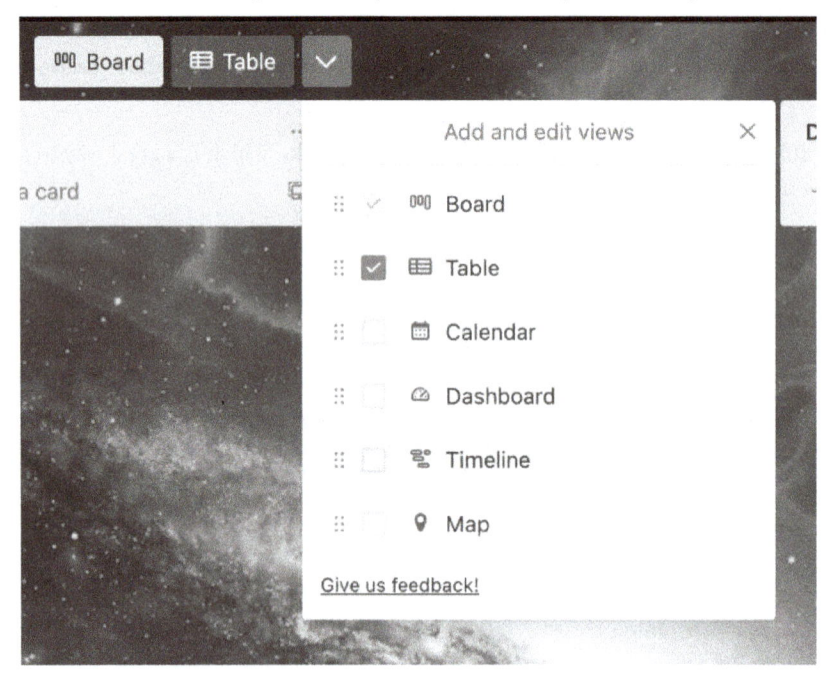

Figure 4.6 – Board views picker

In the dropdown that appears, check the box next to the views you'd like to see. For each one that is checked, a button will be added to your board toolbar to help you navigate to that view. If you don't have a **Trello Premium** account, you'll be prompted to start a trial of Trello Premium to access these views.

Go ahead and check all of the boxes – we'll be exploring each of these views in this chapter. To go to a view, click the button that specifies the view's name, such as **Calendar**.

The rest of this chapter will look at each of these views in detail, so to follow along, click the name of the button that matches the section.

Dashboard

The Dashboard view is a lightweight solution for visualizing statistics about your cards. Users get a quick overview of their boards and cards and see how they compare across various attributes:

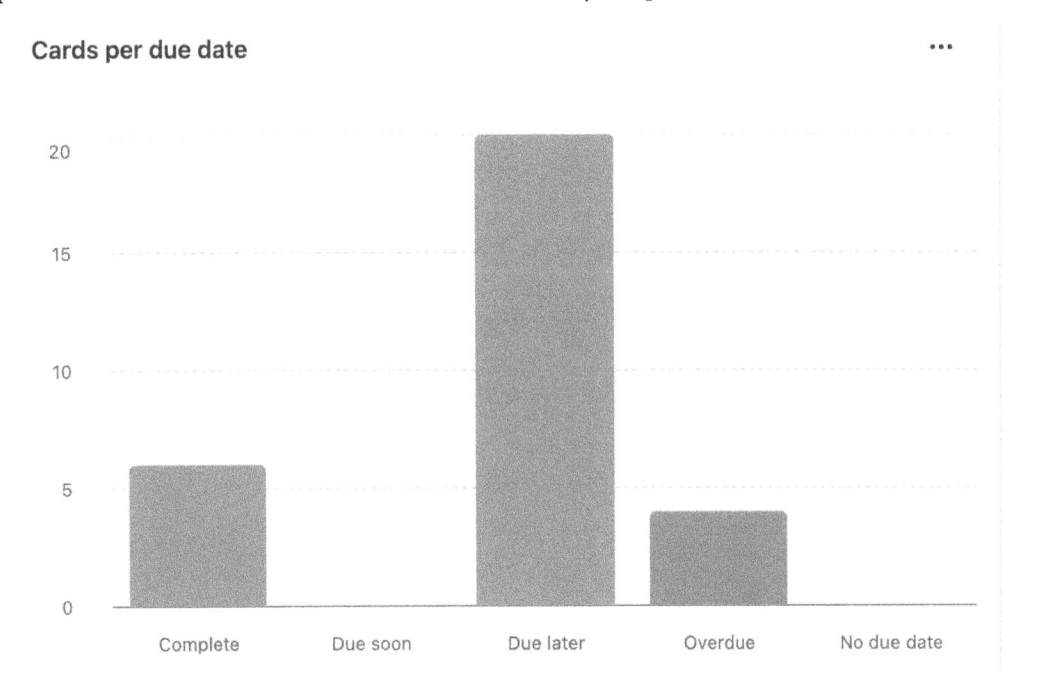

Figure 4.7 – Charts (tiles) on a Dashboard view

If you need robust reporting features, you'll likely need to add a third-party Power-Up to get more customized charts and insights. We'll talk more about those in *Chapter 14*, but if you're looking for some quick insights about your workflows, the Dashboard view can highlight workload balance, the feasibility of timelines, or blocks in your workflow stages.

Adding a new tile

To customize your dashboard, you can add new charts or remove existing ones. To add a new chart, click the + button in the gray box at the bottom of the existing charts (called **tiles**):

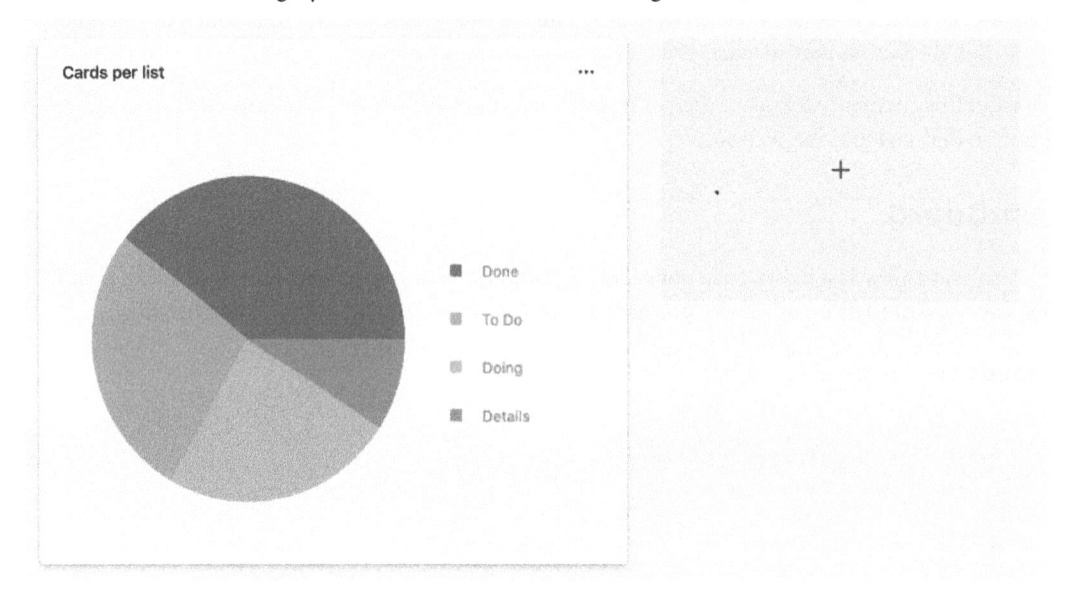

Figure 4.8 – Tile with an empty box for adding a new tile

A modal will appear, asking you to select the type of tile you want to add. Choose one of the three charts, as shown here:

Figure 4.9 – Types of tiles that can be created

Select the one that best represents how you'd like to visualize the information, but don't stress about picking the right one – you can easily change it in the next step, or even after you've created your tile. Click the blue **Next** button.

Next, choose one of four attributes to display your cards:

- **Cards by list**: This helps you visualize whether any cards are getting stuck in certain stages of your workflow
- **Cards per label**: This attribute shows you whether you're spending too much (or too little) time on a certain type of card over another
- **Cards per member**: This attribute is great for capacity planning and ensuring that team tasks are being assigned fairly
- **Cards per due date**: This type helps you visualize whether you have too many tasks coming up too quickly

By selecting the blue **Add tile** button in the bottom-right corner, your new chart will appear in your dashboard!

Editing an existing tile

To edit or remove an existing tile, click the ellipses that appear in the top-right corner of a tile when you're hovering over it. A menu will appear with two options: **Edit** and **Delete**.

The **Edit** menu gives you the option to change the type of chart and the attributes of data.

Calendar

While due dates are valuable for reminders, notifications, and filtering your boards, they're also useful for visualizing your cards in a calendar format. This is most helpful for anyone working with dates to check bandwidth and quickly redistribute or change deadlines as needed.

Although used by a variety of teams, the ones that will find this most valuable are those with content calendars, shift schedules, or event planners:

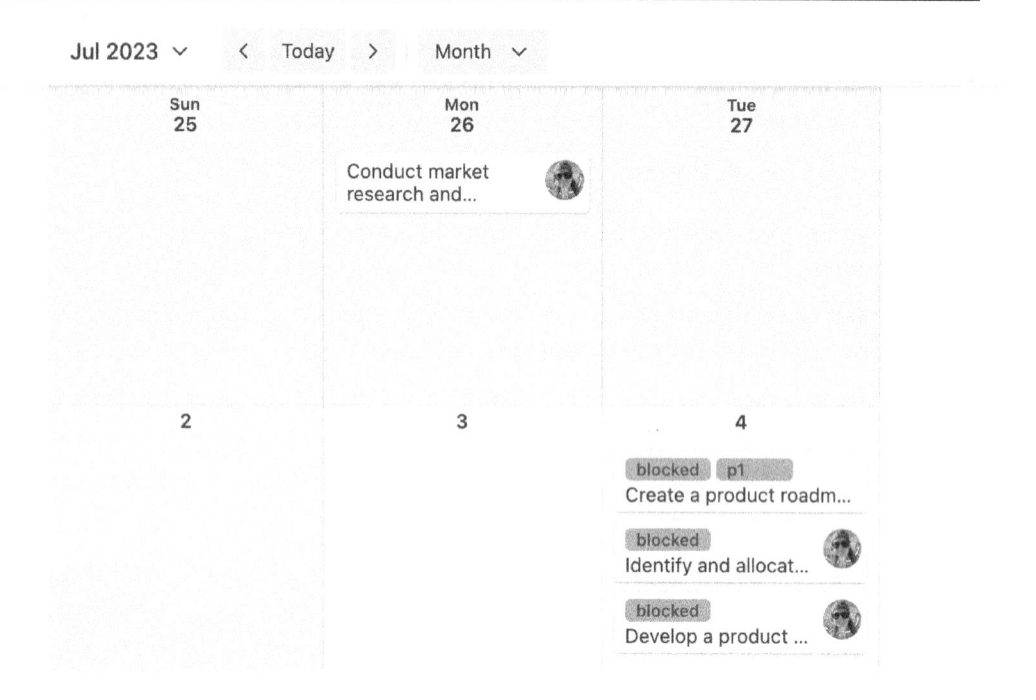

Figure 4.10 – Cards organized in the Calendar view

Cards and checklist items appear over the day(s) from their dates, including the start date if one is provided. This helps you analyze how long projects might take and create your own Gantt charts.

From this view, you can see the card names, labels, and members. To view other details about the card, simply click on it from the calendar – the back of the card will appear, just like from the Board view.

Changing the cadence

If you'd like a more granular or zoomed-out view of your cards, you can select another cadence from the settings in the top left, above the calendar:

Figure 4.11 – Calendar view options

Here, you'll be able to change the amount of time shown every **Day**, **Week**, or **Month** to view this week's task, or zoom out and plan out an entire month. You can also go to a specific date by selecting the month and year from the leftmost side of the Calendar toolbar. If you only need to go forward or backward by smaller increments, use the arrows to the right and left of **Today** to quickly advance or go back.

Editing dates on a card

Perhaps the best feature of the Calendar view is easily changing start and due dates. Instead of opening the card, selecting new dates from the date menu, and then saving those dates and closing the card, you can drag and drop the card to another spot on the calendar – by doing this, the dates will update.

You can drag the left-hand side of the card to an earlier date to set the start date and drag the right-hand side of the card to a future date to set the due date. Dragging an entire card from the middle keeps the duration but shifts the dates.

This is helpful when you see that you have too much work at the same time and need to quickly redistribute it.

Adding a card

You can add cards directly from this view without having to switch back to the Board view. Double-clicking on any date in the grid will make a modal appear where you can set card details:

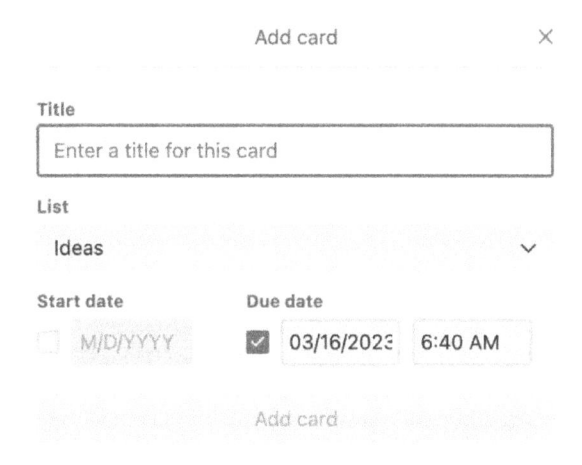

Figure 4.12 – Adding a card modal from the Calendar view

Name the card and choose the list. By default, the due date will be set to the date that you clicked, but you can click the date field to change it to another date. By checking the box next to **Start date**, the start date will be set to the day before the due date. You can type a new date in the date field if you'd like to change it.

Once you're done, click the **Add card** button at the bottom of the modal and view your newly created card on the calendar or your board.

Syncing with your calendar

If you'd like your Trello cards to appear on another calendar, such as a Google Calendar, you can get a URL for subscribing to a calendar. This will update your calendar with events from your Trello cards.

Select the **Sync to personal calendar** button at the top right, above the calendar. A modal will appear, saying that the URL is disabled. However, clicking the ellipses next to it gives you the option to enable it:

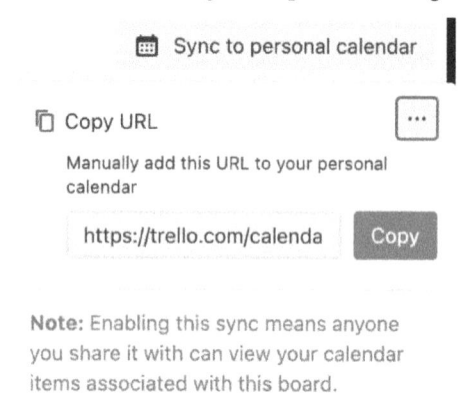

Figure 4.13 – Trello calendar URL for syncing to your calendar

Copy the link that appears and add it to your calendar of choice. If you ever need to turn this off, click those same ellipses in the menu and click **Disable**.

Using the Calendar Power-Up

While Trello Premium users have access to this view, even free Trello users can still get most of the same features from the **Calendar Power-Up**. You can find this by clicking the **Power-Ups** button at the top of the board's toolbar and selecting **Add Power-Ups**. You'll be taken to the Power-Up marketplace. We'll talk more about Power-Ups in *Part 3*, but this marketplace allows you to add more features to your board.

Search for `Calendar` in the search box on the left and select **Calendar Power-Up**. Although there are others, the one with over 10 million boards is the official Calendar Power-Up made by Trello:

Figure 4.14 – Calendar Power-Up in the Power-Up Marketplace

Upon clicking **Add**, a new button will appear in your top toolbar called **Calendar Power-Up**. Click that button to see a similar view to what we've already described.

The main difference between the Power-Up and the Premium view is that Power-Up is limited to showing only by week or month, and there is no date picker for adjusting the period. You'll need to manually click the arrows to get to the exact date you're looking for.

You can still sync to a personal calendar with Power-Up. Simply click the gear icon at the top right to get the link for subscribing.

Timeline

The Timeline view is similar to the Calendar view as it also plots your cards by date, but it allows you to add another attribute to help you get a clearer view of your cards.

This view is most helpful for managers or anyone coordinating a project that needs to be aware of time frames and priority, status, capacity planning, or anything else represented by lists or labels:

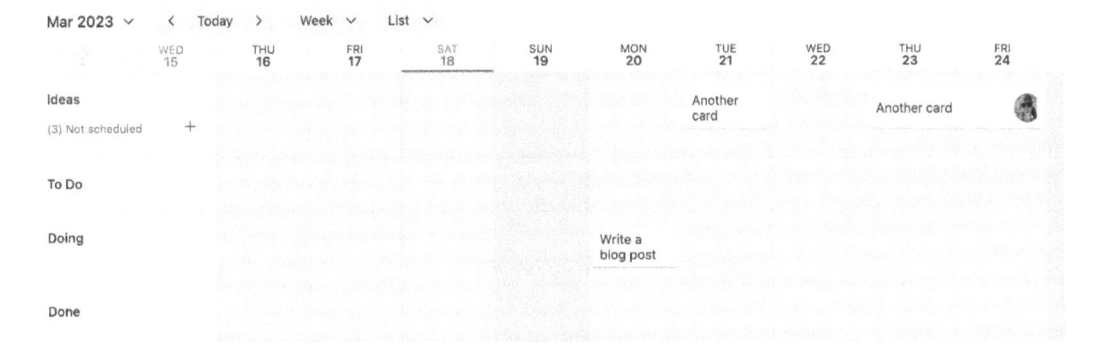

Figure 4.15 – Cards grouped by date and list

Just like the Calendar view, you can select the period and cadence that appears by using the calendar picker or select the **Week** button to get more cadence options, such as **Day**, **Week**, **Month**, **Quarter**, and **Year**.

From this view, the front of the card shows its name and members. To view more information, click the card to open it and view all the fields.

Adding another dimension

The beauty of the Timeline view comes from its last configuration, which is the vertical axis. By default, this view shows cards by list, allowing you to not only see the date a card has been assigned but also the list it's currently in. This is helpful as you're checking progress throughout the week to ensure a card that's due tomorrow is going through the pipeline and hasn't been ignored.

Aside from showing by list, you can sort by other attributes, such as **Members**, which helps you view your capacity and see whether a certain teammate has too much on their plate, or someone else has extra bandwidth.

Viewing by **Labels** can help you batch similar work together. For instance, if you prefer to work on content tasks at the same time, you can see all your cards with the content label that are due this week in grouped format, even if they're in separate lists.

Adding a card

Just like with the Calendar view, you can add another card by double-clicking in any space. This new card will default to the date and the member, list, or label from the section you double-clicked. As with the Calendar view, you can adjust these fields and click **Add card** when you're done.

Table

If you love Trello but miss your spreadsheets, you might just love the Table view. Instead of plotting your cards on a Kanban board, this view shows the fields of your cards as rows of a table:

Card	List	Labels	Members	Due date
Finalize product features and specifications	Backlog	·	👤	🕐 Jul 19
Create marketing collateral (e.g., brochures, videos)	Backlog	·	👤	🕐 Jul 19
Build a landing page or website for the product	Backlog	·	·	🕐 Jul 19

Figure 4.16 – Cards organized in rows

This view is particularly helpful for showing a group of tasks together that might be across multiple lists. For instance, if you want to share a screenshot of what your team is working on this week, you can gather it easily here. If you need to view more information about a card, click the card's name to view the back of the card. The Table view is also useful if you need to quickly update many cards.

Editing cards

While you can't add more columns to this view, you can see the most important properties, such as name, list, members, and due date. You can quickly edit these properties by clicking their sections of the row. This is much easier than opening a card and setting those values, then closing out the card and picking another:

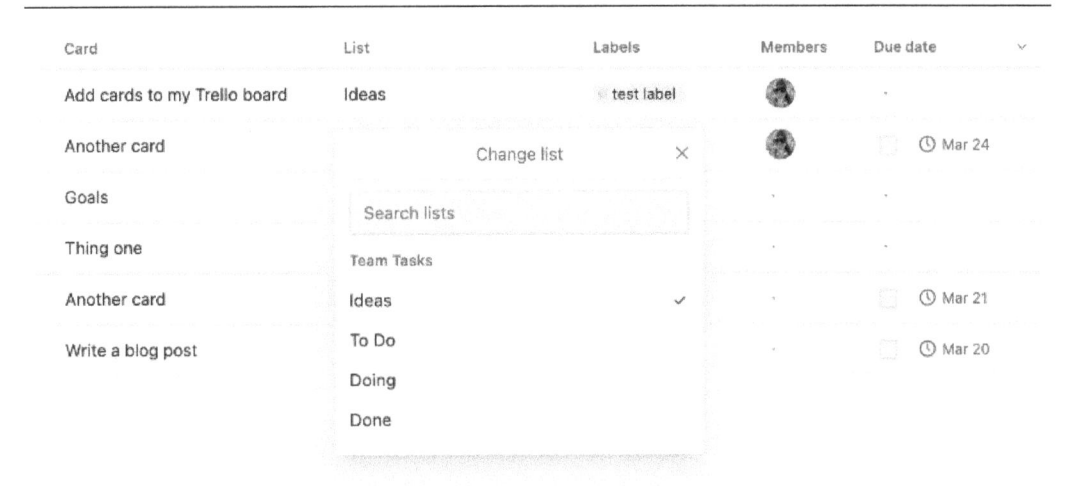

Figure 4.17 – Editing a card in the Table view

For this reason, I prefer to use this view when I'm doing my weekly reviews and planning. I can see what I've done for the week and quickly plan what's on deck for next week.

If you'd prefer to change the order of the cards listed, hover over a card's name until dots appear on the left-hand side, then click and drag to reorder it:

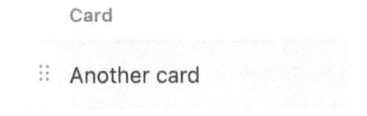

Figure 4.18 – Reordering a card in the Table view

Adding a card or list

The table view lets you not only create new cards on a board but also create a new list on the board! To add either, simply click the gray + **Add** button in the bottom-left corner of your table. Choose the **card** or **list** choice and set the related details.

Once you've set the list or card name and confirmed the other properties, click the blue **Add** button and you're all set.

Maps

This is perhaps the most unique view I've ever experienced in a project management tool. While other tools will typically offer calendar or table formats of their data, I've yet to see another one that provides a native feature that allows you to view your cards plotted on a map!

While the Map view is not useful for every board, whenever you're dealing with location data in your cards, this is a game-changer. It's helpful for anyone planning routes, such as a local repair company sorting out jobs for a day or a flower shop making deliveries. For personal use, it's perfect for planning trips and grouping nearby activities on the same day:

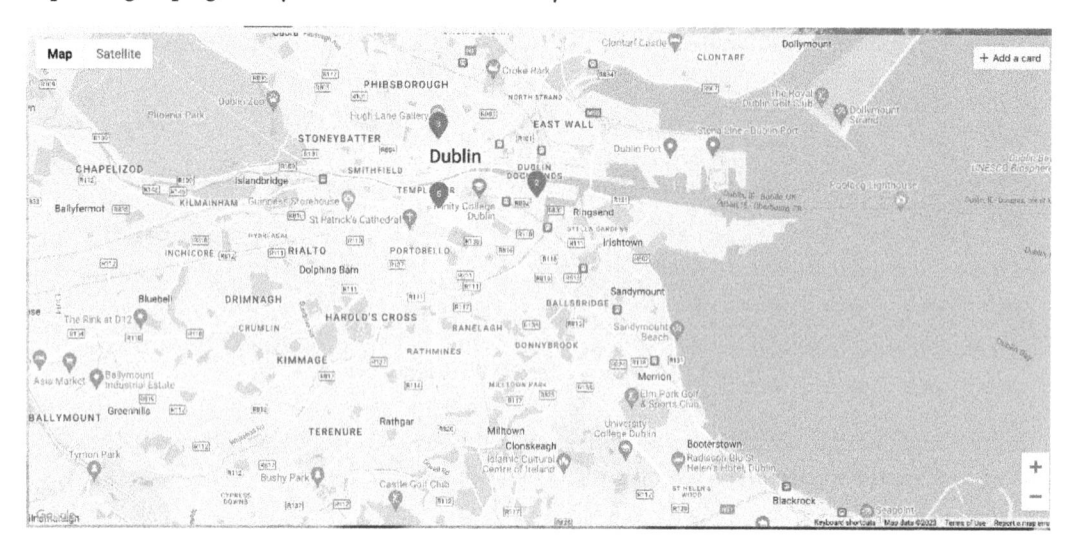

Figure 4.19 – Cards plotted over a map

The Map view plots your cards by their location, which is set on the card. A blue pin represents each card, and if they're close to each other, you can see groups of cards once you've zoomed out far enough. Click the number to zoom in to that area and view the cards associated there. You can also click a specific pin to view the front of the card, including its cover image, due dates, members, and the number of checklists or attachments on the card:

Figure 4.20 – Card front in the Map view

To view more details about the card, click it; this will show you the back of the card.

Setting a location on a card

To add a location to a card, open a card and click **Location** from the right side of the card underneath the **Add to card** section. In the search box that appears, start typing the name or address of a location. Google Maps shows results based on what you type. Upon selecting the most relevant one, a preview of your address will appear on the card.

Adding a new card

To add a new card from this view, click the **Add card...** button at the top right of the board:

Figure 4.21 – Modal to add a card from the Map view

Set a card name, and search for the name or address of a location in the box below. Confirm the list or click the field to select another list. Once you're happy with your card details, click the blue **Add** button at the bottom of the modal. This newly created card will now appear on your map!

Workspace views

So far, all the views we've discussed relate to cards on a specific board. If you'd like to create views that incorporate cards from multiple boards, you'll want to use Workspace views.

Workspace calendar views

We talked about viewing cards in a calendar from a single board, but what if you want one calendar that shows cards from all of your boards? This is possible with the **Workspace Calendar view**.

You can access this view from the left sidebar on any board. If this panel is not already showing, click the > arrow just before the board name or press [on your keyboard. Click the **Calendar** option near the top of the menu in the **Workspace views** section:

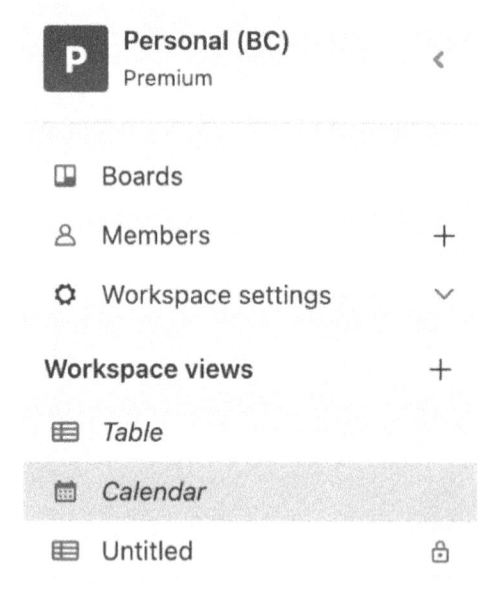

Figure 4.22 – The left-hand side panel of a Trello board showing workspace settings and views

This will open a Calendar view that looks just like the view we saw on our board, but this time, we will also see cards from recent boards in the workspace. This view functions the same as a single-board Calendar view, except you cannot create a new card by double-clicking on a date. There will also be a small display just before a card's name to help you visualize what board the card is from.

To adjust which boards and cards are displayed, click the **Filter** option at the top right of your view and select which boards and lists cards you want to include:

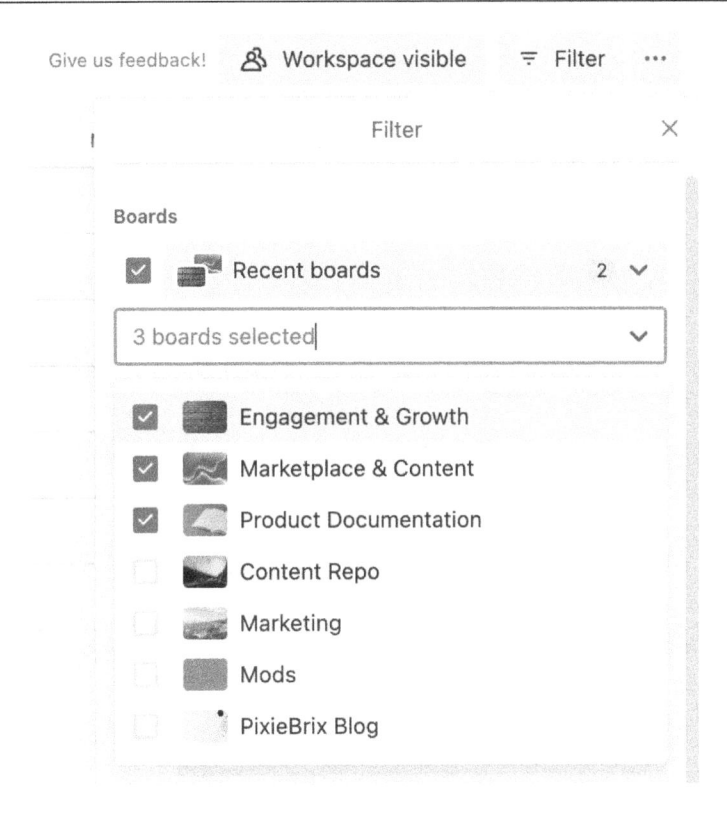

Figure 4.23 – Workspace view filter options for choosing boards

This is helpful if you want to track only cards that are in progress or at a certain stage of your workflow, or if you only want to see your own cards across multiple project boards.

Workspace Table view

Just like the Workspace Calendar view, you can access this view from the left-hand side panel of your board by clicking the > icon just before the board name or pressing [on your keyboard. Upon selecting **Table** under the **Workspace views** section, your table will transform and include data from other recent boards.

To customize the cards that appear, click the **Filter** button at the top right to select the boards, lists, members, labels, dates, and other criteria for the cards you wish to include in the view:

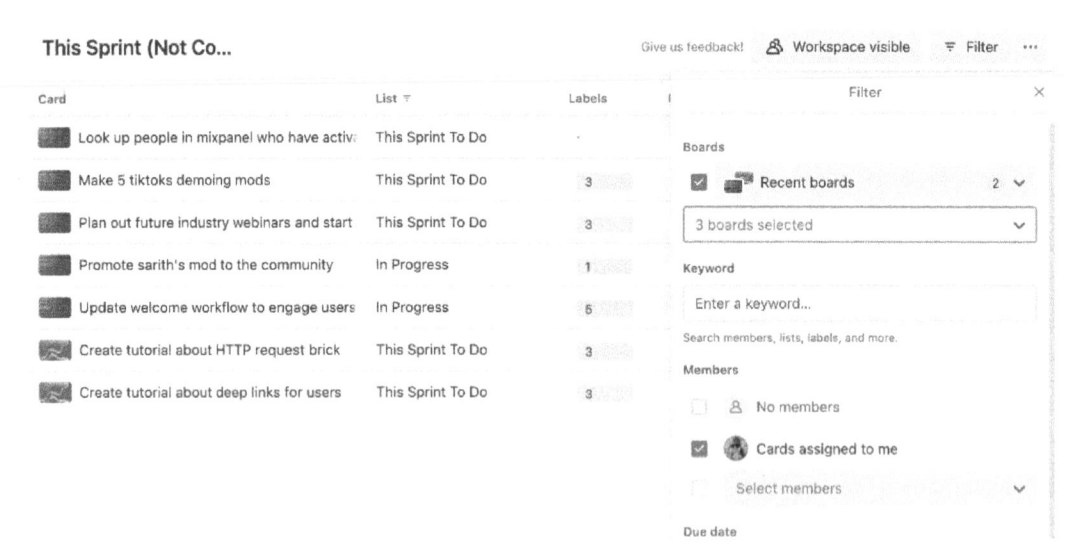

Figure 4.24 – Table view with filter options

The main differences between board vs workspace views are that you cannot reorder cards in the Workspace Table view. However, you do get another column in the Workspace Table view that shows you the board that the card is from.

Summary

In this chapter, we discussed the different ways you can view your cards in Trello. Although Trello is perhaps best known for its Kanban-style Board view, having these extra views gives you more information about your cards and helps you quickly figure out actions to take.

You can filter cards to zoom into the information you need at any moment, and you can visualize your cards in the ways that are most important for you and your team. In the next chapter, we'll talk about how to bring it all together with specific use cases and templates!

5
Real World Trello Boards

Now that you know how to view your cards, it's time to bring them all together with practical use cases. In this chapter, we'll go through Trello board templates that demonstrate common uses of Trello.

This chapter will explore boards that show common applications of Trello's features. By following these templates, you'll be able to visualize how you might use Trello and even get a head start on setting up your workflows.

This chapter will help you organize your tasks and track progress with ease. So, let's dive in and discover how you can make the most out of Trello for your projects.

After this chapter, you'll be able to do the following:

- Manage your team (or personal goals) in a sprint on Trello
- Coordinate all the moving parts for an upcoming project
- Improve your meetings with effective Trello boards
- Define the direction of your company with a product roadmap board

Let's get started!

Understanding Trello templates

To explore Trello templates, head to `trello.com/templates`. Once you're there, you can browse through a bunch of prebuilt Trello boards that you can copy and customize yourself. Here's a screenshot that gives you an idea of what the Trello template gallery looks like:

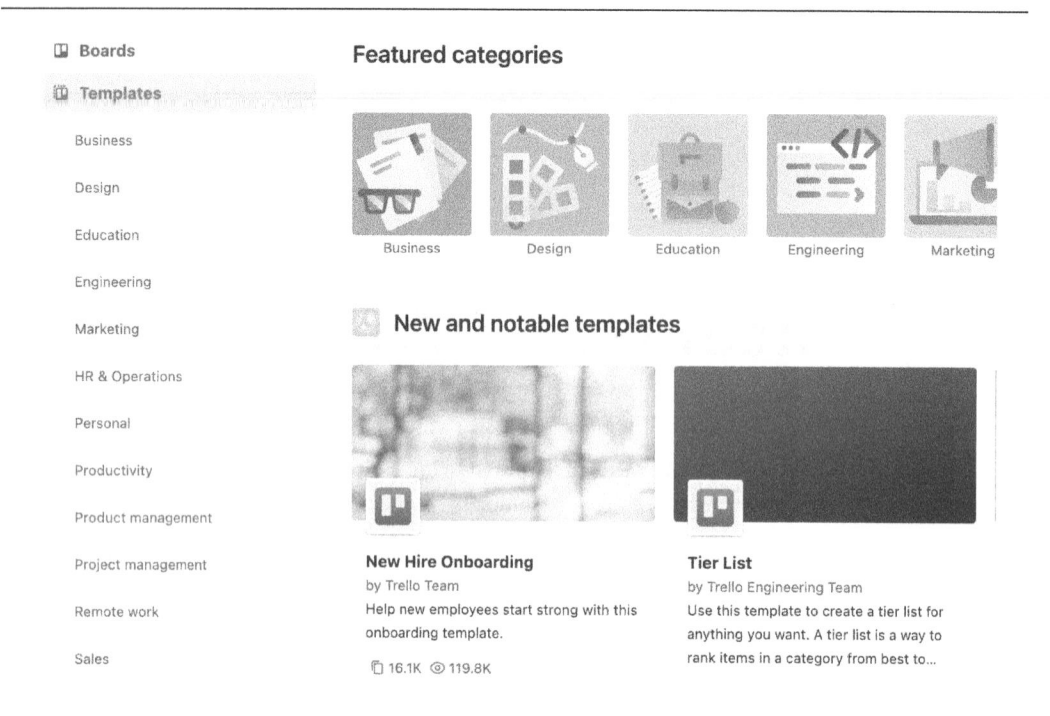

Figure 5.1 – Trello template gallery

To find the Trello board template you need, you can select a category from the options listed on the left-hand side of the template gallery. This will filter the templates and show only the ones that match your chosen category.

Alternatively, you can use the search box in the top-right corner of the page to look for a specific keyword or term. This will bring up all the templates that match your search term.

Once you've found a template you're interested in, click on it to view more details. You'll be able to preview the template, read a brief description, and see how many people have used it before. If it looks like a good fit for your needs, you can click the **Use template** button to make a copy and start customizing it.

Viewing template information

In the **Viewing template information** area, you can see more details about the template and an explanation of how it's meant to be used. You can also see how popular the template is by the number of times it's been copied and viewed.

Below the text description is an embedded version of the template that you can scroll through to get an idea of the structure of the board, as well as the types of cards that are used. It's great to scroll through but you might want to go to the template to take a closer look.

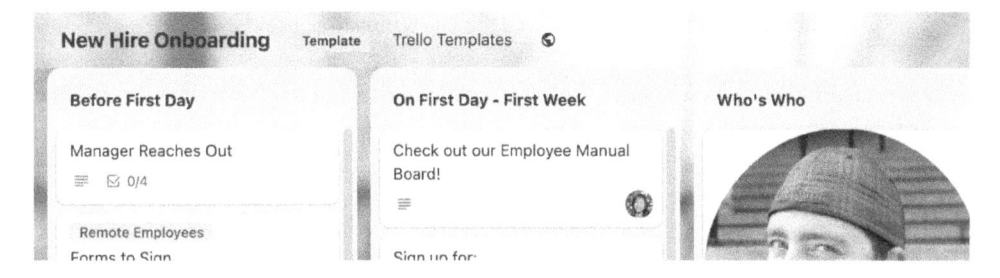

Figure 5.2 – Viewing template information

Go to the bottom right of the embed and look for the link that says **View template**. Upon clicking it, you'll go directly to the template! (You will not pass go and you will not collect $200.)

Once you're there, you can open cards and see examples of how the cards might be set up. You can see the order of the lists and get more comfortable with the settings. Click the ellipses in the top-right corner of the board to open the board menu and view the board's description. Once you're done previewing, you can click the back button in your browser to return to the template listing page. Alternatively, if it's a good fit, you can start using the template right away.

Copying a template

If you've found a template that strikes your fancy, you can easily copy it and try it out. If you're currently previewing the template and inside a Trello board, click the **Create board from template** button at the top of the page:

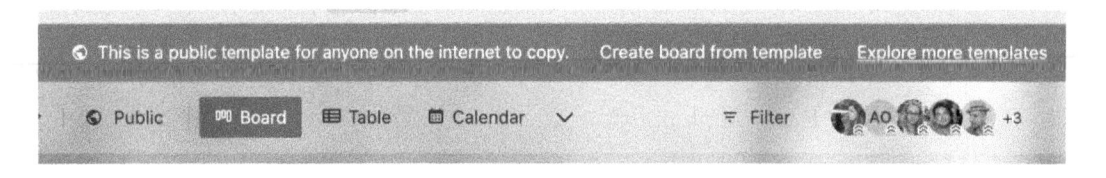

Figure 5.3 – Template description bar at the top of the page

If you're on the template description page, click the **Use template** button to the right of the template's name:

Figure 5.4 – Template headline and the Use template button

A modal will appear, asking you to select the workspace you'd like to add it to, as well as if you'd like to keep the cards from the template.

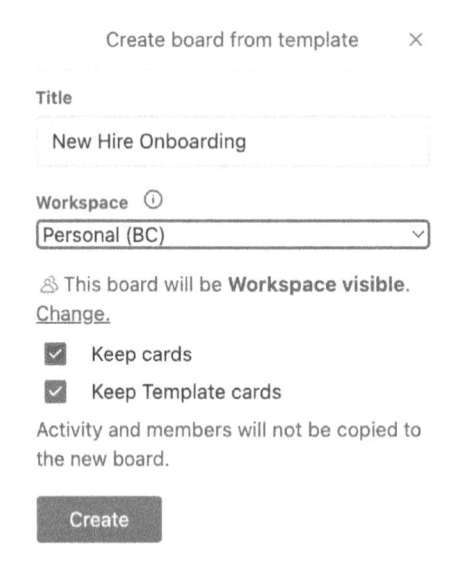

Figure 5.5 – Modal for creating a new board from a template

To make it your own, rename the board! You also have the choice of keeping cards (template cards or all cards) as part of the copy. You might leave those unchecked if you're only interested in the list structure, board description, and suggested Power-Ups. In some boards, I am interested in keeping the cards themselves as they might be critical to the template. Typically, I copy everything and use the **Archive all cards in this list** action to remove cards as they become unnecessary. Click **Create** when you're happy with the settings.

Once you've copied a board, it's yours to adjust and edit as you see fit. You are the owner and admin of the new board, so your changes will only reflect on your copied board. This is a great way to make the board your own!

You might decide to rename a list or move a list around. You also might add or remove some of the cards that were copied over. You can add your own style by adding stickers to cards or changing the board's description. Head back to *Chapter 1* if you need a refresher on all the things you can customize within your board menu.

Now that you know how to find and use Trello board templates, let's take a look at a specific template, one that shows how Trello can be used for specific project management methodologies, such as Kanban and Agile.

Using Trello for Kanban and Agile workflow management

Trello is best known for its Kanban-style board. Kanban is a visual workflow and scheduling system that's used as a lean management system and is often used in Agile software development. However, many teams across various industries have adopted this process as a way to increase productivity and streamline workflows. At its core, Kanban involves breaking down work into manageable tasks and visualizing the flow of work through a board, which can help teams identify bottlenecks, prioritize tasks, and make more informed decisions about how to allocate resources.

In this section, we'll explore how to implement a Kanban-style board in Trello to help streamline your team's workflow and improve productivity.

These types of boards are used to help teams visualize their workflow and identify opportunities for improvement. These boards categorize tasks into columns, allowing you to easily track your progress and efficiently handle tasks.

You can see how Trello might lend itself naturally to this process! Let's walk through the Amazing Kanban Project Management Template. You can find it in the Trello templates gallery at `trello.com/b/WHOzj88m/amazing-kanban-project-management-template/`.

This is what the template looks like. It's a board with six lists, each describing a stage in a workflow:

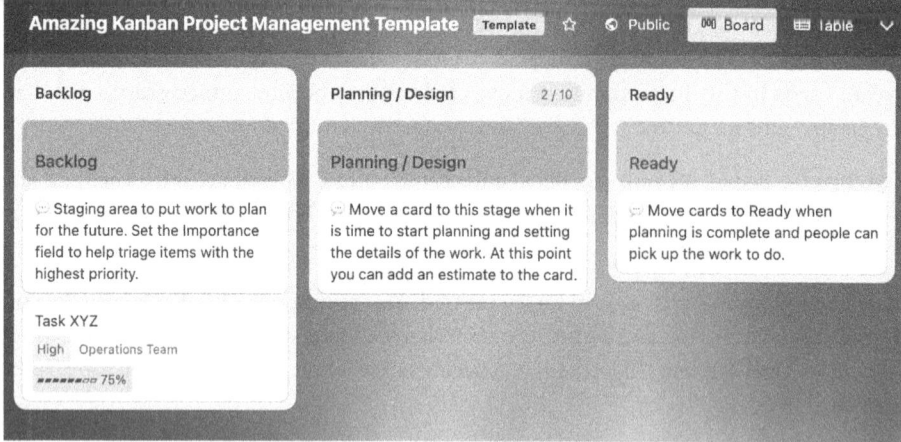

Figure 5.6 – Kanban template board structure

Let's dive into how this board is organized and learn about the best practices for using it.

Board structure

In this board, each list is a stage of your team's workflow. You can be as specific as you want by listing the exact stages. For example, if your team owns your company's blog, then your stages might be Ideation, Prioritized, Drafting, Reviewing, Publishing, and Promoting.

But in other cases, you might have a lot of different tasks that don't all go through the same stages in a workflow. In that case, you can still use a Kanban/Agile board, but you may just want to make the lists a bit more generic, such as lists named Backlog, To Do, Doing, and Done.

If you want something in the middle, use the lists provided in this template. Most tasks will go through these stages, although you might call it something else, depending on the task. Let's look at the default lists in this template and how you might use them:

- **Backlog**: Think of these as ideas. This is where you collect all your ideas and any requests from other teams.
- **Planning/Design**: Before you start to work on tasks, there might be some more prep work that you need to do, or you might need to flesh out the idea a bit more. Using this list, you can move something that you do want to work on but that might need more definition before someone can take action on it.
- **Ready**: A task in this list means it's ready to be worked on. If you have multiple people on your team, a card in this list means anyone can grab it and begin working on it. If you've already

assigned it, that member will know they can start working on this item. You can think of this list as your to-do list.

- **Review**: Cards in this list have been worked on and are awaiting review. This could be a manager needing to give approval, or going through a formal code review in your development team.
- **Done**: This one's probably obvious… it's the cards that you've completed! It's personally my favorite list to celebrate.
- **In Progress**: The tasks in this category are being worked on. They've at least been started, but they're not quite complete. This is useful for seeing what is in flight for your team. If cards spend too much time in this list, you might be assigning too many tasks that can't be completed.

You're free to rename the lists to anything you'd like! Now, let's dive into what's happening inside these lists. Time to talk about cards!

Cards represent tasks

In this type of board, cards represent specific tasks or items that relate to your team's primary job. If you manage a blog, each card will represent a blog post. If you're a software team, each card may represent a user story for implementing a new feature or fixing an existing bug:

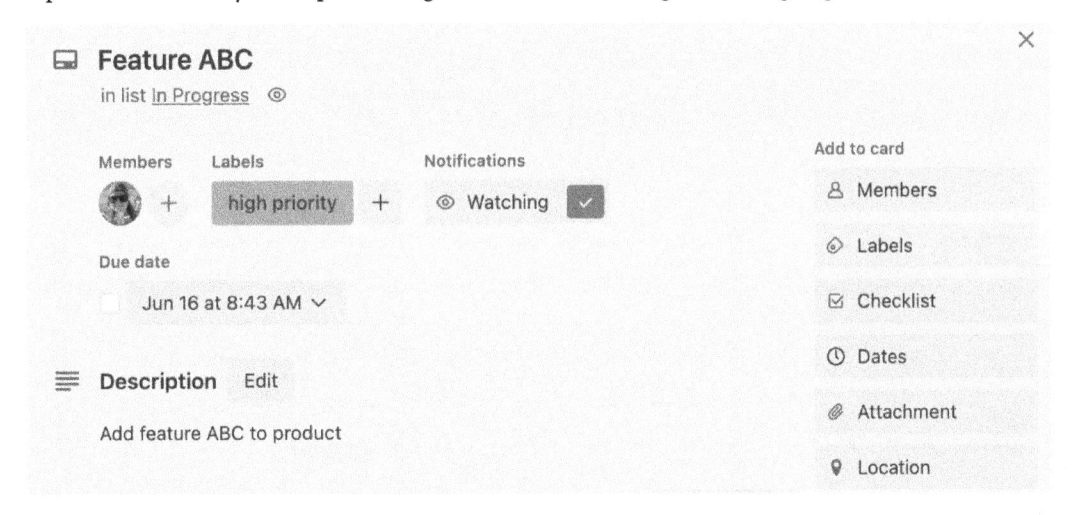

Figure 5.7 – Sample card with a task

Move the cards through the lists to indicate their status. If one person on your team manages a stage of the process (such as reviewing), they will be able to pick up the task there and carry it to the next step. You can also add comments or change owners to indicate who else is needed to carry a task to the next stage. Keep as much information inside the card as you can. Note that there are many fields and sections to document anything you might need to know about a task. With these, you can describe a task, explain its importance, assign members, show progress, and even request reviews if you'd like.

You can also use labels to provide more details about tasks or categorize them. If you're a software team, you might use labels to indicate whether a task is a bug or feature. If you're a marketing team, labels could differentiate between the types of content you're creating, such as blog posts, videos, or e-books.

It's worth noting that many of the principles and strategies we've discussed for Kanban and Agile workflow management in Trello can also be applied to cross-functional teams working on larger projects. We'll take a look at this next!

Cross-team project management

In some cases, you might find yourself needing to work with multiple teams to make a specific project happen. For example, let's say you're about to launch a new product in your company. There are multiple stakeholders, and your team will be dependent on other teams to complete everything. It's like you're choreographing a big dance!

In this case, it might not make sense to have lists for each stage. Instead, you could create a list for each of the departments or teams that are involved in the project. Check out this template: `trello.com/b/hyBcI9lX/pm72-single-project-board`.

Let's look at this template and learn how to effectively coordinate with other teams to move a project forward:

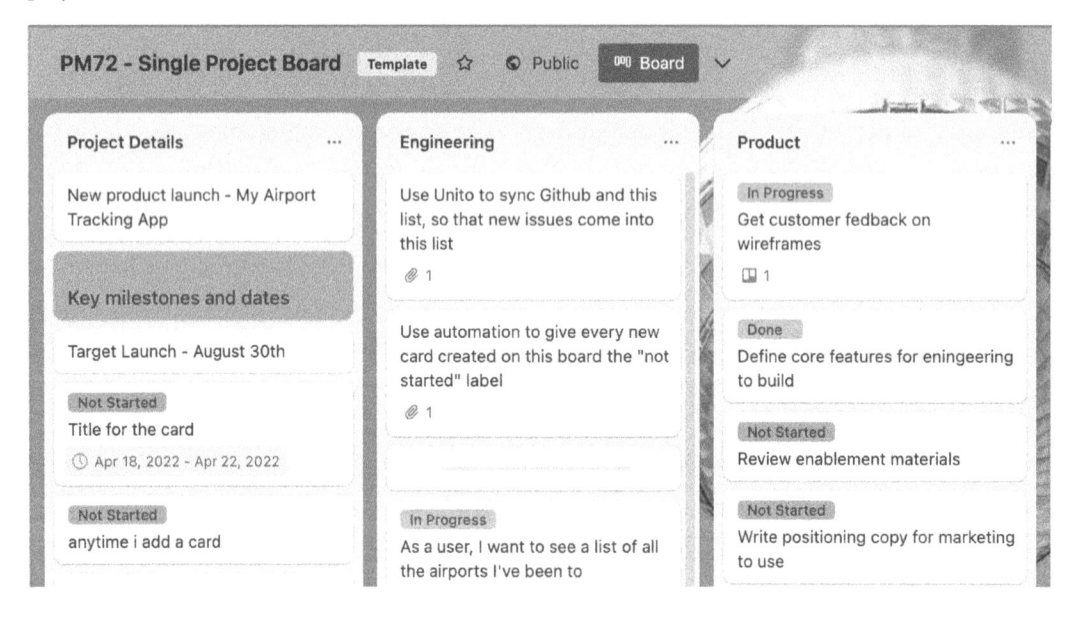

Figure 5.8 – Project management template board structure

Board structure

In this template, the first list is a resource or details list. This is used to collect all the links and related information about a specific project. Here, you can include any project briefs, reports, blueprints, designs, or anything else that is relevant to the project. You may also want to include a section for FAQs on this list.

I like to create sections of a list by creating a card that is just a horizontal line. To do that, simply create a new card and type - - - - - as the name. This will create a card that has a line in it, which is great for breaking up items inside a list:

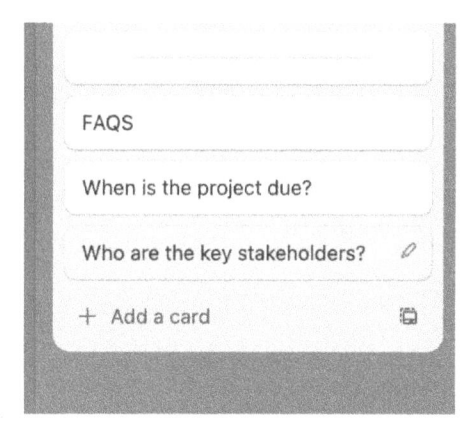

Figure 5.9 – Separator card in a Trello list

The other lists on the board can be for the different teams or types of activities involved in the project. In this template, I Engineering, Product, Marketing, Sales, and Support.

Cards represent objectives

On this board, cards *can* represent tasks, or they can be larger initiatives. Since this type of board is often used for larger products that require teams to collaborate, there are likely a *lot* of tasks that need to be done, and listing them all could clutter the board and make it difficult to read.

Another way to organize the cards is by objective. Consider a product launch, for instance. The marketing team might have several objectives, such as creating a landing page, writing a blog post, creating ads, and organizing influencers. It might make sense to list those cards and then let the marketing team sort out specific action items in the **Checklist** area of a card:

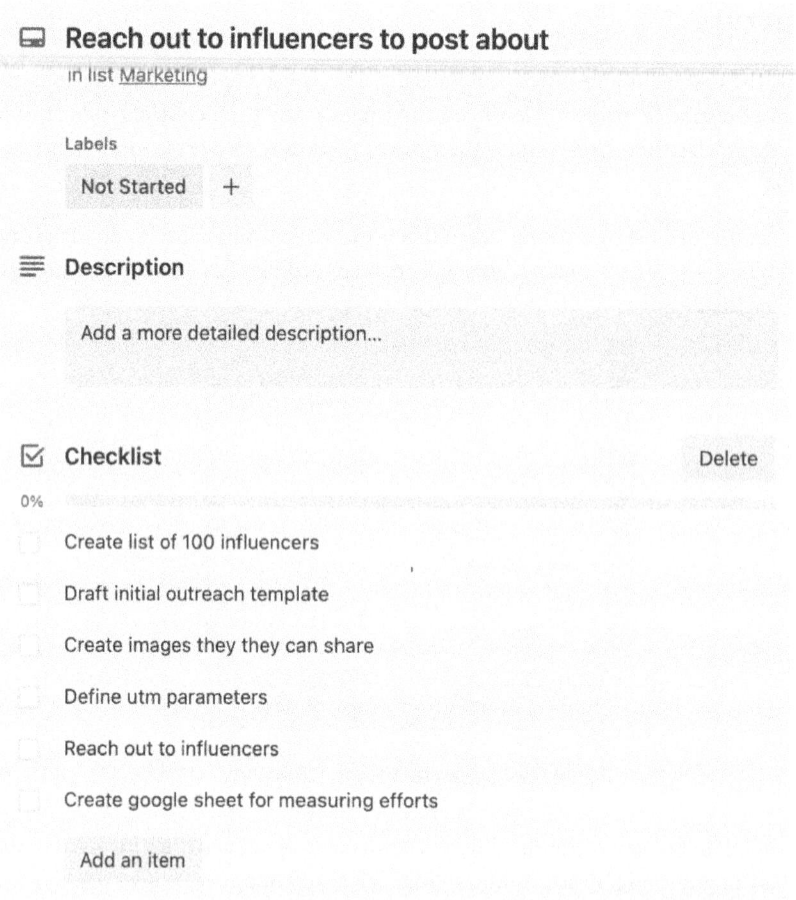

Reach out to influencers to post about

in list Marketing

Labels

Not Started +

Description

Add a more detailed description...

Checklist — Delete

0%

- Create list of 100 influencers
- Draft initial outreach template
- Create images they they can share
- Define utm parameters
- Reach out to influencers
- Create google sheet for measuring efforts

Add an item

Figure 5.10 – Trello card with checklist items

Labels can be used to indicate the status of an objective from a high-level view. This is helpful because lists are grouped by team, so it's harder to immediately see what's in flight and what's been completed. Adding labels that show the status solves this because you can visualize a card's status by the color and text on the card, and you can filter a board to show only cards with a certain label. You can use filters to see which tasks have not been started when you need to know what remains on your to-do list.

With that said, let's dive into Trello's Meeting Planner template and explore how it can help us streamline our favorite occupational pastime... meetings!

Meeting planner

It's likely that when you attend meetings, you take notes on a Google document, your phone, or a physical notepad. However, have you ever considered using Trello for this purpose? While Trello is primarily known as a task management tool, it can also be a powerful tool for keeping track of meeting agendas, notes, and action items. In this section, we'll explore how you can use Trello to streamline your meeting notes and keep everyone on the same page.

Take a look at this Weekly Team Meetings template from the Trello template gallery (`trello.com/templates/team-management/weekly-team-meetings-GDz7Wd53`):

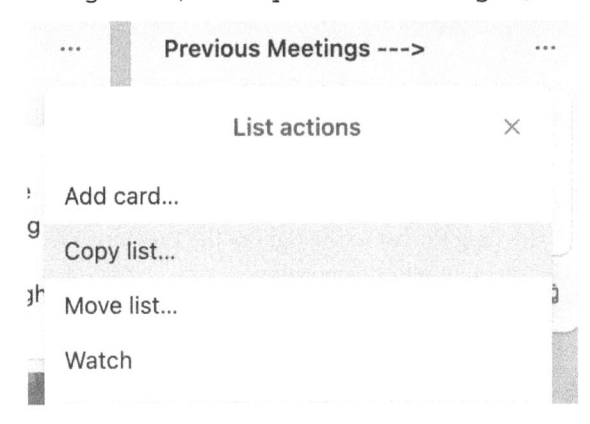

Figure 5.11 – Weekly Team Meetings template board structure

Board structure

In this board, each list represents an instance of a meeting. This makes it easy to find notes and action items from previous meetings so that anything that's discussed isn't forgotten in a hidden document somewhere.

The first list on the board is used as a template. Here, you can add any cards that you want to make sure you cover every time your team syncs, such as any metrics to review, or perhaps ask for feedback about anything that can be improved on by your team.

To copy the list, click the ellipses in the top-right corner of the list and select the **Copy list…** action. This will duplicate the list, allowing you to quickly create an agenda for a new meeting:

Figure 5.12 – Copying a list in Trello

Once that meeting is completed, drag the list to the right of the **Previous Meetings** list or select the **Move list** action from the **List** menu to select its position.

Cards are agenda items

Each card in the list represents something that you want to discuss in a meeting. Keep it clear and simple in the card name and use the card's description to add more details about what needs to be discussed specifically.

Assign a member to the card to designate who should lead the discussion for an item. This also gives that member an alert and some time to prepare before the meeting:

Figure 5.13 – Sample agenda item card

You can use labels to indicate the category an agenda item falls under or during a meeting to clarify the status of that item. For instance, you could have a label to indicate if something needs further discussion, requires action, or if it's just a communication update.

Speaking of requiring action, checklists work well in this type of board because each agenda item will typically have some form of action, even if it's just to "close the loop." You can use checklists to assign an action item, as well as designate an owner and a due date for those items.

Now that you've improved your meetings with Trello, let's take a look at one more common Trello template that will help you communicate with your users.

Product roadmap

Many teams also use Trello for sharing their product roadmap. You can think of this as having a public to-do list. Although it might feel intimidating to share your team's tasks and objectives with the world, many companies are doing this to help their users gain confidence in the direction of the product and understand a company's priorities. Follow along with the Product Roadmap Template: `trello.com/templates/product-management/product-roadmap-template-%7C-trello-FrbAJsbH`. It can be seen in the following screenshot:

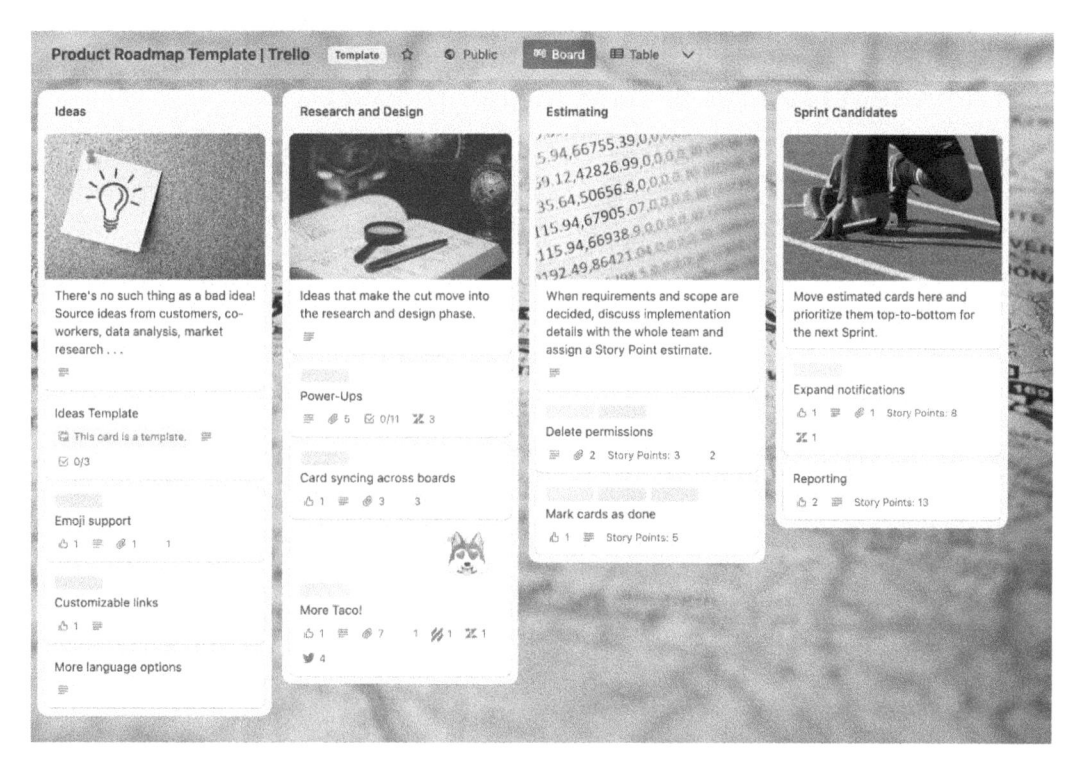

Figure 5.14 – Product Roadmap Template board structure

Board structure

The lists in this board show the steps a feature goes through from being an idea to what is being worked on. Users (or other stakeholders, such as teammates in a company) can submit ideas for features, request bug fixes, or ask something else of the team. Think of the **Ideas** list as a wishlist. Anything can go on that list, but it doesn't mean you need to work on it.

First, the card moves to the next list to help you better understand what the issue might entail and what needs to be done. For example, if someone asked for a chat feature in your product, you might move this card to the **Research and Design** list to do some digging into if this is a common request from users, or just one a one off-request. You might also dig into what implementing a chat feature would look like – are there already tools in place for this or would you need to build something?

The card moves to the **Estimating** list once you've effectively researched the task and what it entails and defined how much effort it would take to complete. I like to think of this as making the research process more tangible and being able to assign a specific value for effort, such as **Story Points**. These are estimated numbers that represent the amount of effort involved in a task.

Finally, any issues that you've planned to work on might move into the **Sprint Candidates** list to be queued up in the developers' workflows. You could add additional lists after these existing ones to represent if the issue is being worked on and when it's finally available for users.

Cards represent features or bugs in your product

Each card represents a part of your product that can be updated or impacted. For instance, you might have a card for implementing a chat feature or for fixing a UI bug that causes text to wrap incorrectly on screen, or maybe you want to be able to customize the appearance of links:

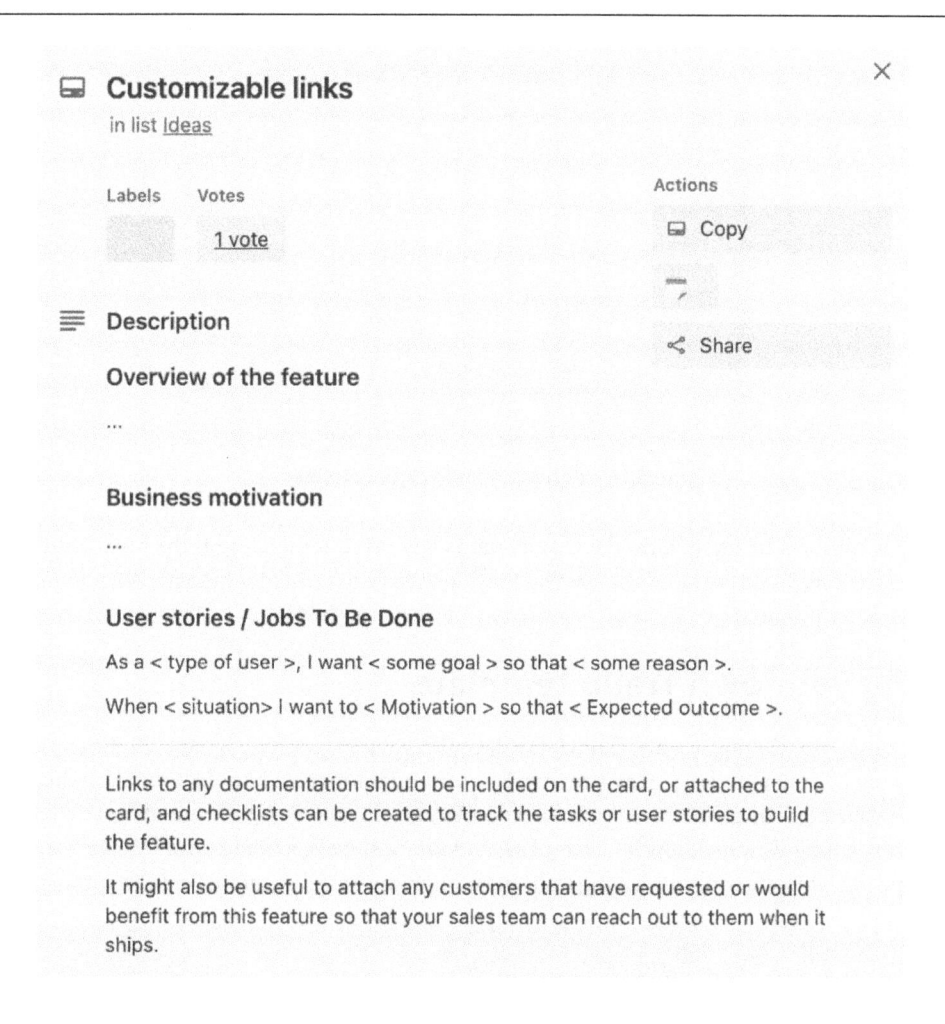

> **Customizable links**
> in list Ideas
>
> Labels   Votes
>   1 vote
>
> Actions
> 🖥 Copy
> ↗
> ⤴ Share
>
> ≡ Description
>
> **Overview of the feature**
>
> ...
>
> **Business motivation**
>
> ...
>
> **User stories / Jobs To Be Done**
>
> As a < type of user >, I want < some goal > so that < some reason >.
>
> When < situation> I want to < Motivation > so that < Expected outcome >.
>
> Links to any documentation should be included on the card, or attached to the card, and checklists can be created to track the tasks or user stories to build the feature.
>
> It might also be useful to attach any customers that have requested or would benefit from this feature so that your sales team can reach out to them when it ships.

Figure 5.15 – Description of a feature request

Descriptions and attachments are very useful in this board because you will need to describe the feature or bug in as much detail as possible to effectively scope out what effort will be involved in fixing it. Make sure you include an overview of the request, how it will help the business, and details about what needs to be done.

Card templates are ideal for this board because including those details in the description is important. Once you've created a card, you can turn it into a template by clicking the **Make template** button via the card actions menu, just under the **Automation** section on the right-hand side of the card. Once you've made a card a template, anyone can create a card in the same format by clicking the template icon at the bottom of a list when adding a card, just after the **Add a card** text:

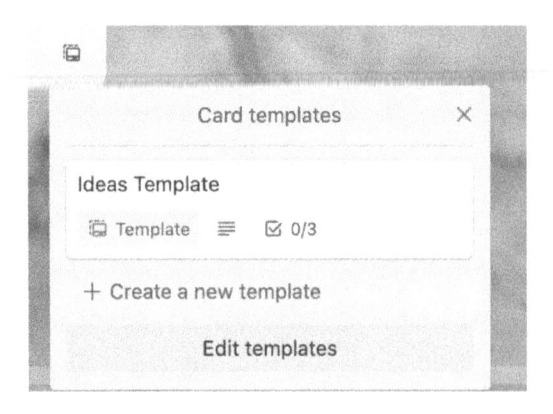

Figure 5.16 – Accessing Trello card templates

Clicking that icon will bring up a modal that contains any saved templates on the board, allowing users to create a card in the same format so that they don't have to remember exactly what to include in the card's description.

Creating your own Trello template

As you customize these templates and build boards, you might want to share them with the world and create your own Trello templates! Any be copied, so you might make a board a template when you want to be explicit this board is meant to be copied and customized. Template boards have a banner across the top, letting viewers know it's a template, and they also have a bold button so that users can quickly copy the template, without having to hunt through the board menu to find the copy action

Figure 5.17 – Banner on template boards

Fortunately, it's super easy to make a board a template.

Once you've created your amazing board to share, click the ellipses in the top-right corner of the board to open the menu. Click **More** and then choose the **Make template** action:

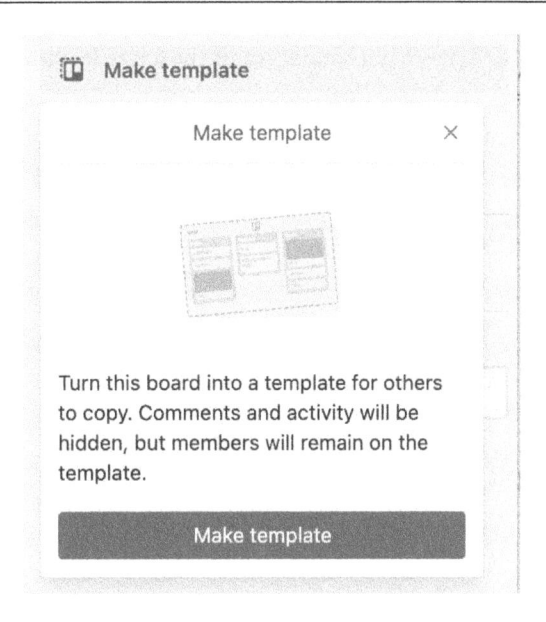

Figure 5.18 – Make template

This tells you a little more about what making a template entails. It will hide comments and activities but keep members, cards, lists, labels, and everything else to maintain the core makeup of the board. Click the **Make template** button to confirm this.

After, you'll be taken to the **About this template** panel, which looks exactly like **About the board**. It will populate with any board descriptions you've previously set, but you can easily change this by clicking **Edit**:

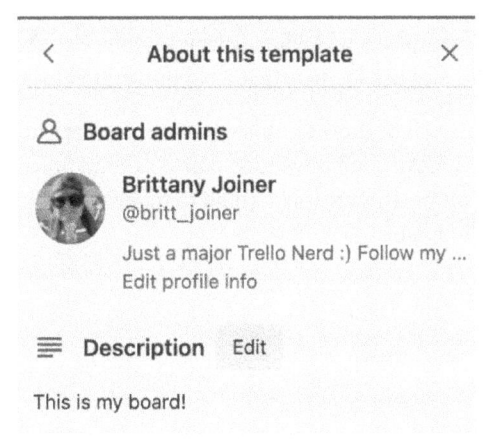

Figure 5.19 – Template description

You'll also notice that your board now has a banner across the top to let visitors know it's a template that they can easily copy.

If you accidentally created a template and would rather it not be a template, you can go back to the menu, click **More**, and choose the **Convert to board** option:

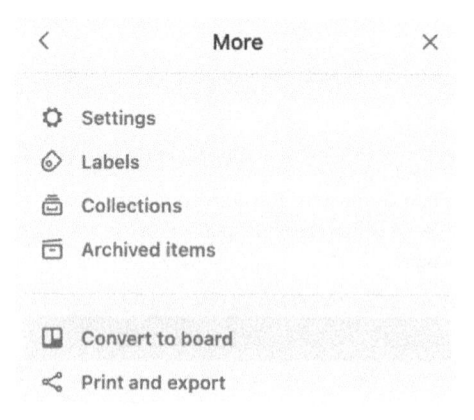

Figure 5.20 – The Convert to board option in the board menu

This will turn your board back into a normal board and will remove the banner at the top.

Summary

In this chapter, we explored four common use cases of Trello and looked at template boards to help you get started. You don't even have to build anything from scratch! At this point, you should be comfortable with searching for templates in Trello's template gallery so that you can get inspiration about various ways to use Trello and use formats that have proven to be effective for teams.

Of course, you can still customize all of these templates so that they're your own and improve them as you go. You know the rules, so now, you know how to break them! Speaking of rules, it's time that we start learning how to create automation rules in Trello to make our new workflows more efficient. This is what we'll do in the next chapter.

Part 2 – Automation in Trello

In this part, we'll dive deep into Trello automation. Buckle up because it's a lot, but don't worry – on your first read, you'll be inspired to learn everything that's possible with Trello's suite of automation tools, from how to start automation to exploring the various kinds of actions that can be automated. This part is great for ongoing reference because there is a wealth of step-by-step instructions and tips and tricks to make Trello do (some of) your work for you.

This part has the following chapters:

- Chapter 6, Initiating Trello Automations
- Chapter 7, Common Automation Actions
- Chapter 8, Advanced Actions
- Chapter 9, Building Automation with Triggers
- Chapter 10, Date-Based Automations

6

Initiating Trello Automations

By this point, you're probably using Trello frequently and are familiar with updating cards, completing checklists, moving cards around, and getting work done in Trello.

Now, we're going to talk about how to automate all of those actions so keeping up with your work doesn't turn into its own full-time job. This chapter will show you the different types of events that we can implement automation workflows for .

You'll learn about the following:

- How to know when you're ready for automation
- Where to find Trello's automation library
- Types of events that can trigger automation

Trello is a collaboration tool that assists in managing tasks, but it does not actually do all of the managing for you. However, there is a solution—automation. By automating certain tasks, Trello can take care of tedious work, freeing up your time to focus on other important tasks. Let's explore automation and see how it can make our work with Trello more efficient.

Getting ready to automate

I want to give a quick word of caution about automation: **don't start automating right away**. Figure out your workflows and how you want to use Trello with your team first. Only once you have a solid workflow and notice recurring patterns are you ready to start automating.

When are you ready to automate?

How do you know when you're ready to automate? You'll know you're ready when you can explain what your workflow looks like in terms like this:

"When a new card is added to the board, then I add myself to the card and make it due in seven days."

"When a card is due this week, then I move it to the Due This Week list."

If you can describe your workflow by using When (or If) ... Then statements, then you're ready. That's because the way automation works is based on two key events: **triggers** and **actions**.

> **Exercise**
> Grab a pen and paper or your favorite digital drawing tool. Try to draw out the way you use your Trello boards, or write out as many "When, then" statements you can think of. This will be helpful as you keep reading because you'll make connections between what types of automation you might use.

Triggers

A **trigger** is an event that happens that starts your automation. This is the "When" statement in your workflow, such as "When a card is added to a board" or "When a card is due."

It's called a trigger because it triggers everything else! Think about a string of dominos. When the first one is pushed, then a bunch of others fall. Automation is just like that – everything starts with one domino: a trigger.

In Trello, a trigger is a specific event that serves as the starting point for your automation. This event could be something such as the creation of a new card, the movement of a card to a particular list, or the addition of a label to a card. Once the trigger occurs, it sets off the automated action or sequence of actions that you have designated.

This isn't just a Trello thing—it's an automation principle.

You can make multiple things happen after the trigger. These are called **actions**.

Actions

Actions are what happen *after* a trigger. They're the "then" statements in your workflow.

You can add multiple actions after a trigger. For instance, you can add a label to a card **and** post a comment **and** change the due date—all within one automation!

We'll discuss actions in *Chapter 7* and in *Chapter 8*, but for now, just know that this is what comes after your triggers and are the things that actually do the automating. But they can only happen if you tell them when to work, which is why we must start with triggers.

Now let's explore the triggers that are available in Trello and when you might use them! Buckle up, because it's a lot—but we'll go through them together, and you don't have to memorize them all. I'll even provide real-world examples of how you might use each one to make them more digestible.

Accessing triggers

We'll talk more in *Chapter 9* about how to tie triggers and actions together and actually build automation workflows in Trello, but for now, if you want to follow along as you read through the types of triggers and actions, you can view them by clicking **Automation** in the top toolbar of any Trello board:

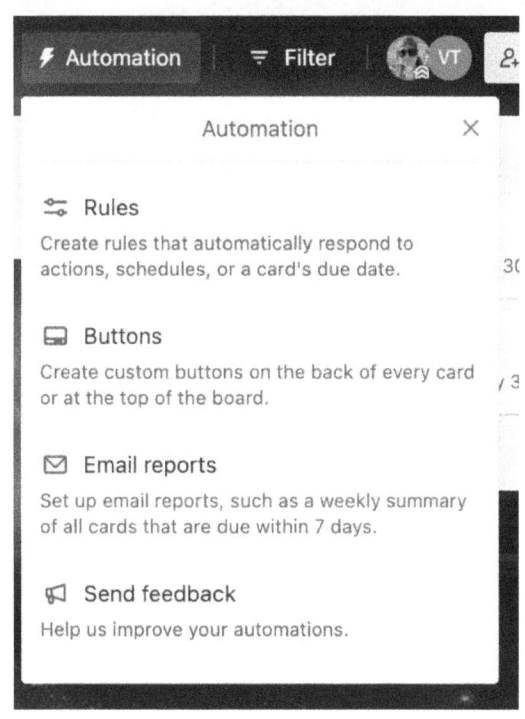

Figure 6.1 – Automation menu from Trello toolbar

In the modal that appears, you'll see various automation types. Most of the standard triggers are found in **Rules**, so we'll go through those triggers in this section. In *Chapter 9*, we'll talk about bringing triggers and actions together to create complete automations, and in *Chapter 10*, we'll explore a few additional trigger options that are available only in the **Calendar** and **Due Date** sections.

Click the first option, **Rules**, which opens the **Automation** overlay. Next, select the button at the top right that says **Create rule**.

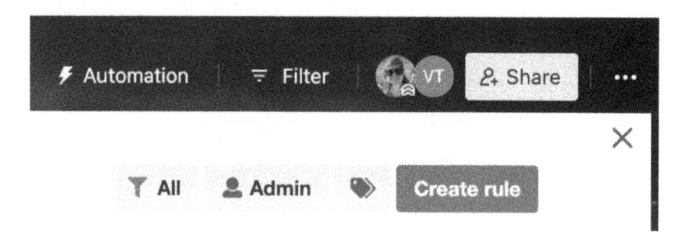

Figure 6.2 – Create rule button in the Automation section

Every rule starts with a trigger. Click the + **Add Trigger** button and you'll see a list of trigger options and tabs describing different sections of cards and boards to watch for events.

Figure 6.3 – Tabs showing trigger options

There's no need to take any action here. Feel free to leave this page open as we follow along. Each section is named after a different tab in the trigger options.

Pro tip – advanced mode

If you want to see even more options for automation, toggle the switch at the far right side of the trigger tabs to turn on the advanced automation features. You'll know this is turned on when the toggle turns blue instead of gray. This gives you more options for filtering triggers so that you can be more specific about the types of cards these triggers will apply to. For instance, you can specify when a card is added to the board *and* the name contains the word "task." Or you can say when a card is moved into a list *and* @moonie is a member of the card. Click the filter icon to explore these options. You'll also notice there's a person icon at the end of each trigger, allowing you to specify whether you want the trigger to fire when you or a specific person or anyone performs the trigger event.

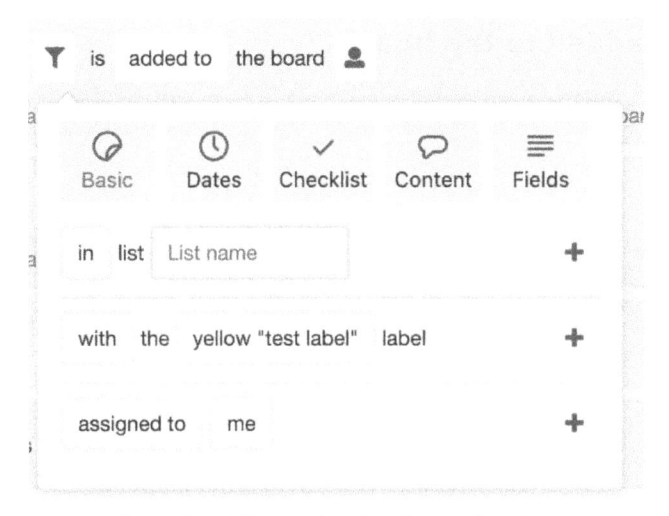

Figure 6.4 – Filter options in advanced options

Now let's look at the first section of triggers for when a card moves.

Card move

When you want to start an automation based on a card being added to a board or list or being moved around the board, these are the triggers you'll use. Let's look at each of the triggers and talk through some real-world use cases.

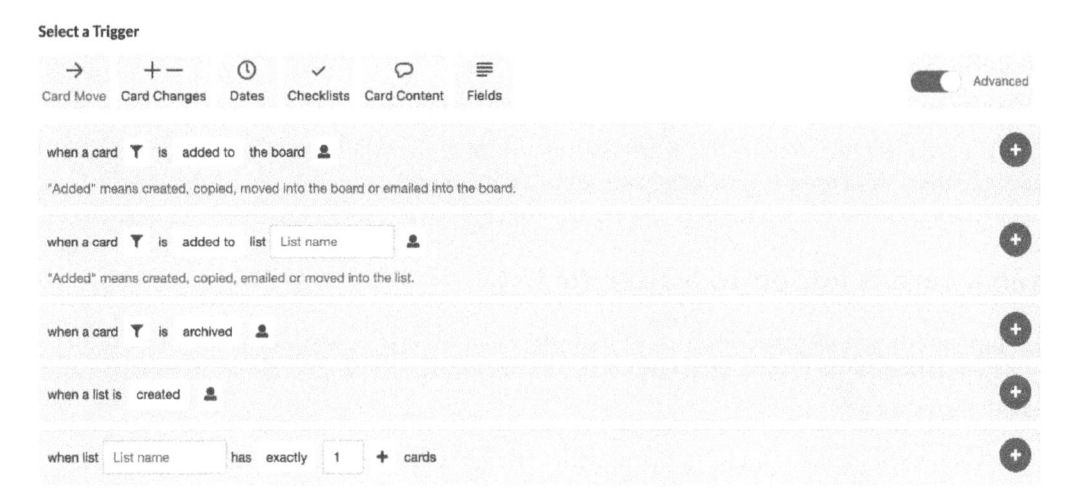

Figure 6.5 – Card move trigger events

These are under the first section because it typically deals with new cards or lists being created or moved into the current board.

When a card is added to the board

This triggers whenever a card is added to the board. You can be specific about *how* a card was added to the board.

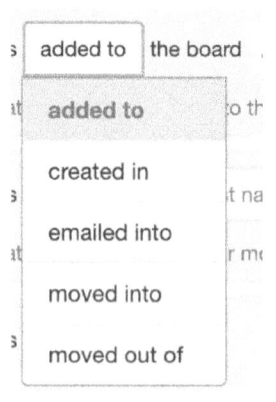

Figure 6.6 – Drop-down options of card movements

For instance, if you're only interested in cards that were emailed into the board, selecting that option from the dropdown will limit the trigger to fire only in that case. **created in** cards will only trigger when a new card is made inside the board. **moved into** triggers when a card was created on a different board and moved into the current one. However, if you want to know about all cards that are added to this board, select the **added to** option.

> **Real-world example**
>
> When a card is added to the board, add @funmanandy to the card.
>
> This is a great way to make sure that when tasks are added to your plate, by you or others, you're aware of them. It's a great way to keep your to-do list organized.

When a card is added to a specific list

This trigger watches for cards added to a list that you define. This is a good way of keeping track of cards moving throughout your workflow. It's helpful to assign specific people or due dates based on which list the card moves to.

Note that you have similar options to the previous trigger, so you can be specific about how the card moved.

> **Real-world example**
>
> When a card is moved into the **Review** list, comment with **@jimmytalksjira it's time to review this task!**.
>
> This is a great way to let colleagues know when a task is ready for them without having to manually alert them.

When a card is archived/unarchived

If you want to trigger something to occur when a card is archived or unarchived (brought back into the board), this is the trigger you need.

Admittedly, I don't tend to use this one frequently, but it can be helpful if you're worried about losing cards and want to be aware if something was accidentally archived.

> **Real-world example**
>
> When a card is archived, send an email to email@test.com with the subject **A card has been archived!**.
>
> This is helpful for alerting you when something has been archived, as there are no native notifications for this in Trello.

When a list is created/renamed/archived/unarchived

You can use this trigger when a list is created, but there are also a few hidden options. Click **created** to see other list actions that can serve as triggers.

Figure 6.7 – List trigger events

Like archiving cards, these actions can be helpful if you have new Trello users on your board and want to be aware of inadvertent changes. Also, if you want live updates when your board is being updated, this is a great way to get a stream of emails with the list changes.

> **Real-world example**
>
> When a list is created, send an email to info@test.com with the subject **A new list named {listname} has been created!**.
>
> This is helpful to alert you of changes to your board as they happen so you're able to revert any unintended edits to your board.

Automation variables

Did you notice that I used {listname} inside that rule? It's because Trello automation allows you to access details about the place an automation is happening, allowing you to make your automation very smart and customized (dynamic, if you will) for the situation. In this example, the email subject will contain the name of the new list every time a new one is created. This prevents you from having to open Trello and make a guess at what new list was added.

Using variables is a great way to make your automation 10x more powerful, but it can be intimidating at first. When you're ready to learn about them, visit support.atlassian.com/trello/docs/butler-variables/ and learn about all the information you can access. As we go through the chapter, you'll see some examples of this anytime some text is written in curly brackets, like this { }.

When a list has a specific number or range of cards

This trigger watches for the number of cards in a list and can perform an action when the desired criteria are met. It's not just for a specific number—click **exactly** and see more options.

Figure 6.8 – List card count options

Set the trigger to monitor whether you have more or fewer than a desired number of cards in a list. Clicking the plus icon allows you to set a range, such as more than 5 cards and less than 10 cards.

> **Real-world example**
>
> When the **To Do** list has more than 10 cards, sort the cards in the list by due date.
>
> This is helpful for prioritizing tasks. When you have more than 10 cards in a list, it will sort them so the ones due soonest rise to the top.

We just learned all about the ways you can interact with cards that move around. Now let's look at all the triggers we have available for when certain changes happen to a card. This one is also a doozy, so grab yourself some coffee.

Card changes

Many automation workflows relate to something changing inside a card, whether it's someone being removed from the card, adding an attachment, or perhaps a label being added. Trello can watch for just about any change you can imagine in a card.

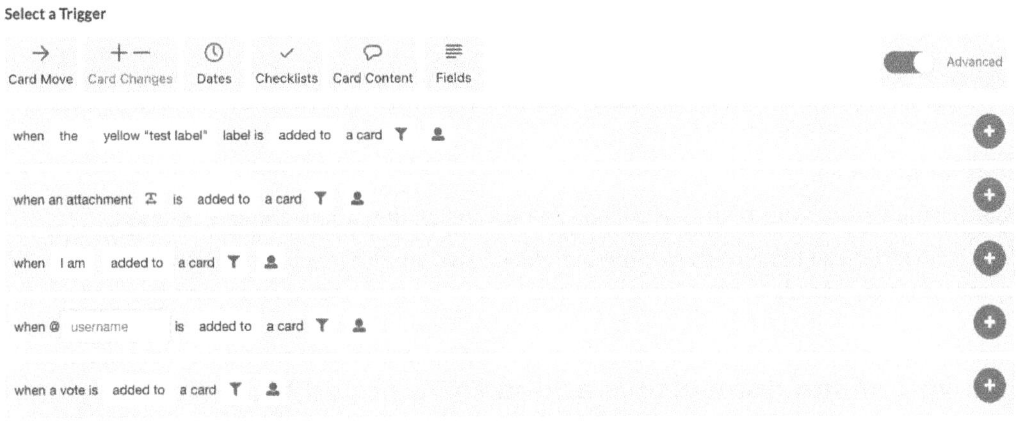

Figure 6.9 – Card changes trigger events

These are some of the most common card changes. If you are looking for something but don't see it here (such as due dates or checklists), then don't panic, because they're probably just part of another trigger tab!

When a specific (or any) label is added to a card

Trigger an action to happen based on when a label is added to a card, or when any label at all is added. Remember, you can use your **filter** settings if you want to be more specific, such as only on cards that have a red label AND are assigned to you.

> **Real-world example**
> When a green label is added to a card, move it to the **Done** list.
> This gives you a quick way to "complete" a card by adding a label rather than dragging a card.

When an attachment is added/removed

You can specify triggers based on when attachments are added to a card, and you can even specify attachments that do or don't contain certain words, phrases, letters, or numbers in the name, by selecting the text icon in the trigger.

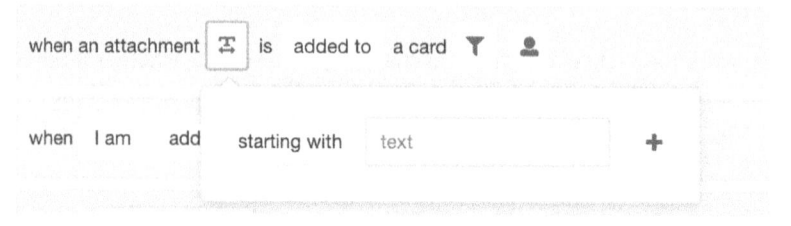

Figure 6.10 – Text filter for attachment triggers

> **Real-world example**
> When a file starting with **Invoice** is added to a card, assign the card to **@andyg_finance**.
> This is helpful for automatically tagging individuals that are relevant to a card when specific types of files are added.

When you or someone else is added to/removed from a card

Use this trigger if you want something to happen when someone is added to a card. This is purely checking whether either you or anyone else is added to or removed from a card, not specific users. If you want triggers for specific people that aren't yourself, you'll need to look at the next trigger.

> **Real-world example**
> When someone is added to a card, move the card to the **Assigned** list.
> This is useful for saving a click when someone joins a card. Instead of joining and dragging a card over, the move to another list will happen automatically, allowing you to quickly tell which cards have been claimed and not.

When a specific user is added to/removed from a card

This is perfect if you need to get more specific about the people being added to the card. For instance, maybe there are certain types of things that need to happen if someone from design is added to a card instead of someone from product.

> **Real-world example**
>
> When **@lane-design** is added to a card, add the **Designer** checklist to the card.
>
> This is useful for adding specific process checklists to a card at each stage of the workflow.

When a vote is added to/removed from a card

Trello enables advanced features on boards via their **Power-Up directory** One special Power-Up, called the Voting Power-Up and built by Trello themselves, adds the functionality for users to vote on cards in the board. If your board is public, voters don't even have to be members of your board. This can be useful for getting user feedback on a product roadmap or prioritizing content for a blog! It's also one of the few Power-Ups that is incorporated into automation as well. We'll talk about this more in *Chapter 11*, but for now, just know it's available in automation.

> **Real-world example**
>
> When a vote is added to a card, sort the `{cardlistname}` list from most votes to least votes.
>
> This automation helps you see the most popular cards and will sort them automatically after the data (number of votes on a card) changes.

That's a lot of things you can trigger based on card changes. Hopefully, by this point, you're starting to think of some activities that are part of your workflow that you might incorporate as triggers, but we're only getting started. Now it's time to talk about dates.

Dates

Although we've been through card changes, did you know there are still so many more changes that can happen to a card? Let's tackle dates in this section—specifically, start and due dates (we'll get more into custom field dates later in this chapter).

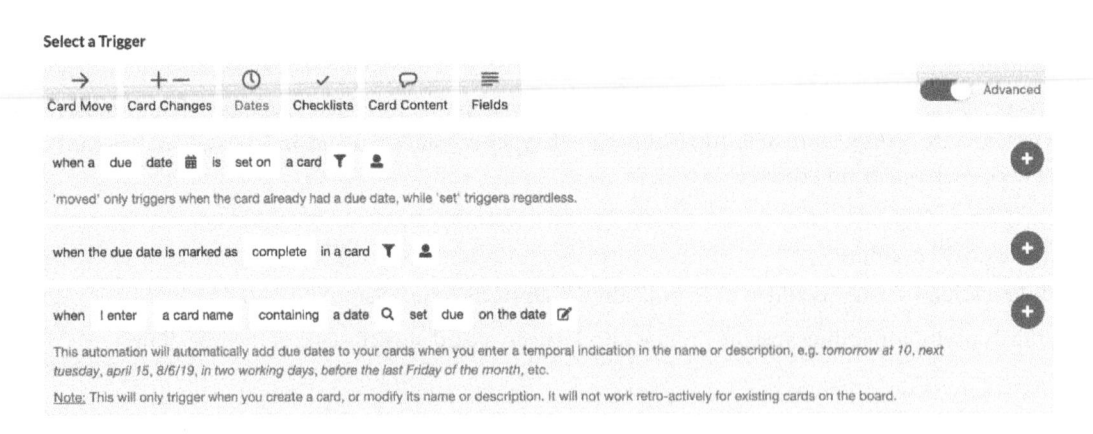

Figure 6.11 – Dates trigger events

Date triggers are when something changes with the due or start date on a card. There are a couple of different options here, but you'll notice there's nothing for *when a card is due*. We'll cover those triggers in *Chapter 10*, when we talk about date-based automation. But for now, we're sticking with the automation triggers available under the **Rules** section.

When a start/due date is set on a card

If you want to trigger an action to happen when a start or due date is added to a card, then this is what you're looking for. As usual, you can click the filter button to be even more specific. This trigger is helpful for clarifying cards in your board that have been scheduled.

> **Real-world example**
>
> When a due date is added to a card, add the card to the **Scheduled** list.
>
> This automation is helpful for queuing up cards into a specific list when they've been assigned deadlines, helping you prioritize the most important upcoming tasks.

When the due date is marked complete/incomplete

This trigger is helpful if you want something to happen when a task is "done," or when someone unchecks the due date of a completed card. This one *only* applies to the due date as a start date isn't a field that can be marked as complete or not.

> **Real-world example**
>
> When a due date is marked complete, move a card to the **Done** list.
>
> This automation saves you a step for completing a card. Simply checking the due date will also move the card to the completed list, so you don't have to do both!

When you or someone else enters a card name containing a date, set the due date

This might not make a lot of sense until you see it in action, but when you set this rule, it will take any type of date (such as a number or even the word **Monday**) in the card's title or description and use that to set the due date of the card.

```
when  I enter  a card name  containing  a date  Q  set  due  on the date
```
This automation will automatically add due dates to your cards when you enter a temporal indication in the name or description, e.g. *tomorrow at 10*, *next tuesday, april 15, 8/6/19, in two working days, before the last Friday of the month,* etc.

Note: This will only trigger when you create a card, or modify its name or description. It will not work retro-actively for existing cards on the board.

Figure 6.12 – Trigger action under the Dates section that sets the due date from the name or description

For example, if you create a card named **Email client on Tuesday**, it will apply the upcoming Tuesday as the due date for a card. If you type a specific date, such as **Email client on April 25th**, it will set that date—in this case, April 25th—as the due date!

Click the pencil icon after the name and Trello will remove the date from the card name.

This rule is unlike any other rule because it contains both a trigger and an action. If you just click the + icon at the end of the rule and save, you won't need to add anything else to it because it already contains both the trigger (when a card has a date in it) and the action (set the due date).

> **Real-world example**
>
> When I type a date into a card name, set that as the due date.
>
> This lets you set the due date of a card when creating it. This means when you create a card named **Email client on Tuesday**, it will then set the due date to the upcoming Tuesday and rename the card to **Email client**.

Now you're a due date trigger expert. Let's move on to checklists.

Checklists

We already talked about checklists in *Chapter 3*, but now it's time to talk about how to automate them. There are a lot of options for these subtasks!

Figure 6.13 – Checklist trigger events

At the time of writing, Trello has recently enabled automation to watch for a due date being set on a checklist item. But there is no trigger available for when a member is assigned to a checklist item.

When a specific checklist is added to/removed from a card

Triggers occur when a checklist is added to any card (or specific cards if you add a filter to it). You will need to specify the checklist in this rule. You cannot choose any checklist, so keep this in mind.

> Real-world example
>
> When the **Monthly Report** checklist is added to a card, set a due date for the last working day of the month.
>
> This is helpful for recurring actions that need to be added to a checklist and completed at a specific time.

When a checklist is completed/made incomplete in a card

Use this if you want something to happen when a checklist is completed, such as sending an email notification or a comment. It can also be helpful to indicate if a checklist is made incomplete. This happens when something is added to it that has not been checked off or a completed item is unchecked.

This does not require specifying a checklist, although you can. Alternatively, leave it to watch any or all checklists.

> **Real-world example**
>
> When all checklists are completed, move the card to the **Done** list.
>
> This rule is helpful if you use checklists regularly because it will make a whole card completed automatically when you have finished the checklists inside a card.

When an item is checked/unchecked

This trigger once again gives you the option to be specific, or to watch any items on a checklist. This trigger lets you fire an action when an item is completed or unchecked. This is helpful if you're connecting cards and checklist items.

> **Real-world example**
>
> When an item is checked, find a card with the same name and move it to the **Done** list.
>
> This is a useful rule when you are using a single card to keep track of other cards as a checklist item. This helps keep them in sync.

When a due date is set on/removed from an item

This trigger watches for due dates being set on items. At the time of writing, it's a new feature as automation for item due dates used to be difficult at best and nonexistent at worst. Just like due date triggers, keep in mind that this is only watching for a due date being set or removed and is not watching for the current date's relationship to that date.

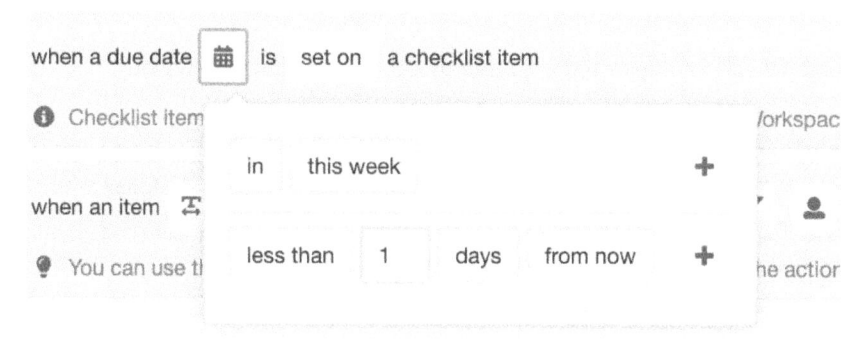

Figure 6.14 – Additional date options for checklist items

Click the calendar icon to view more options for the types of due dates you want to monitor, such as ones that are set for the next month, or the next day. This can prevent unnecessary triggers from subtasks that are too far out in the future.

> **Real-world example**
>
> When a due date in this month is set on a checklist item, move the card to the **This Month** list.
>
> This rule is useful for organizing cards in your board to help you prioritize cards that have upcoming deadlines.

When an item is added to/removed from a checklist

This is like when a checklist is added, but now we're looking at items inside of it. This is a trigger for when any item is added to a checklist.

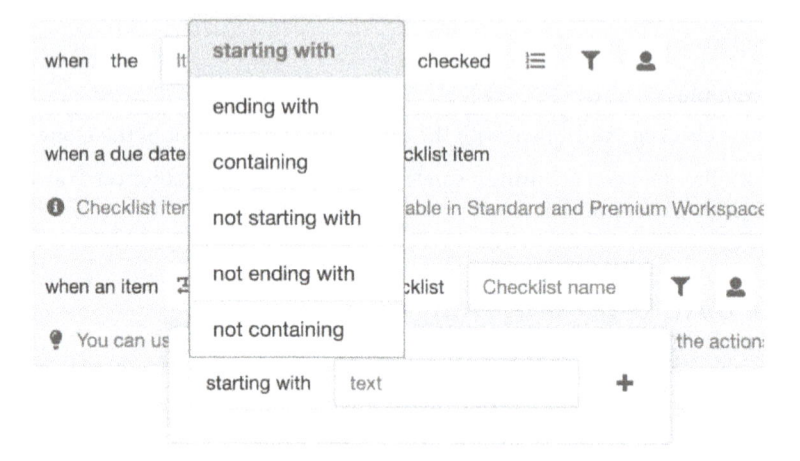

Figure 6.15 – Text filtering options on checklist items

Click the **T** button if you want to be more specific about the type of item to watch.

> **Real-world example**
>
> When an item containing "design" is added to a checklist, add **@nanun-designer** to the card.
>
> This rule is useful if there are specific roles and tasks that members of your team consistently do.

Thought that T for containing/starting with/ending with/ text in a card was cool, eh? Get excited for the next section, which is about card contents. It's all about using text criteria in card names and descriptions to trigger automation.

Card content

If you want to trigger certain actions based on words or characters that are contained in a card, this is the area you'll do that in.

Card content   123

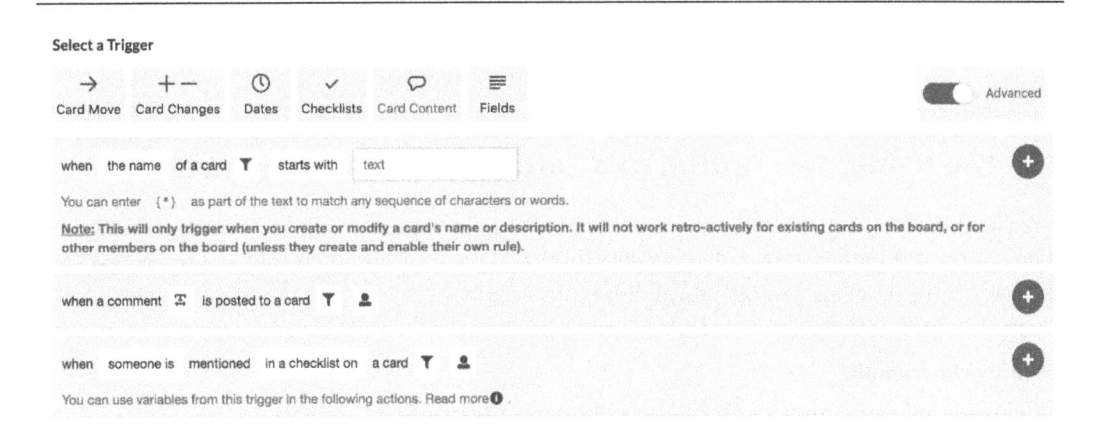

Figure 6.16 – Card content trigger events

If you can't think of any reasons you want to use this, just keep it tucked away in the back of your head as an option. I thought I'd never need these types of triggers, but I recently started to use them on my meal planning board to add labels (such as *produce*, *dairy*, or *meat*) to items on my grocery shopping list, making it easy to sort my shopping list by sections of the grocery store.

Advanced pro-tip

This is extremely advanced and not for the faint of heart. Consider yourself warned. If you want to include multiple criteria in your text filter, such as card name contains `milk` or `creamer`, there isn't a button to click for that. You'll need to use `regex` in the text field and write your own code for "or". It looks like this: `regex:/.*(salt|Salt|oil|Oil|water|Water).*/`.

Figure 6.17 – Example of using regex in automation

If that feels too advanced, don't worry—you might never need it. But now you know it's here and possible if you do!

When the name/description of a card contains specific text

Just like we did with the items in the previous section, you can trigger actions to happen when cards contain certain text in the name or description. This has the same settings where you can say "starts with," "ends with," "contains," or *not* one of those things.

> **Real-world example**
>
> When the card name contains **Q1**, create a due date of March 31st.
>
> This rule is useful for creating relative due dates on cards by using the title, especially if it's a vague or undefined term that wouldn't be recognized with other triggers.

When a comment is posted to a card

This is the same as the name/description, but this one looks for text inside comments.

> **Real-world example**
>
> When a comment containing the word urgent is posted to a card, add the red **High Priority** label.
>
> This is useful for making important tasks more clearly visible and helping them stand out on your board.

When a person is mentioned in a card

This checks the card for someone mentioned. You might use this to create an action for adding the person to the card to ensure important cards don't get ignored because someone missed a comment.

Figure 6.18 – Options for locations to watch for mentions

Trello watches a few sections of a card for mentions, and you can specify which one you're interested in watching. If you want to check all of them, you'll need to make three different rules since there's no way to combine all three.

> **Real-world example**
>
> When someone is mentioned in a comment, add them to the card.
>
> This is useful if the people you tag in comments tend to be stakeholders of a project and will likely want to receive other notifications about activity on a task.

Feeling a little overwhelmed? You don't have to remember all of these. Your goal right now is to just get familiar with all these sections to understand what you can work with and know what's available. One more section to go, and we'll be done with the standard trigger options. Let's talk about triggers for when something changes on custom fields.

Fields

The ability to trigger custom fields is only available on boards that have custom fields (makes sense, right?) and you can only activate custom fields on Trello Standard and higher plans.

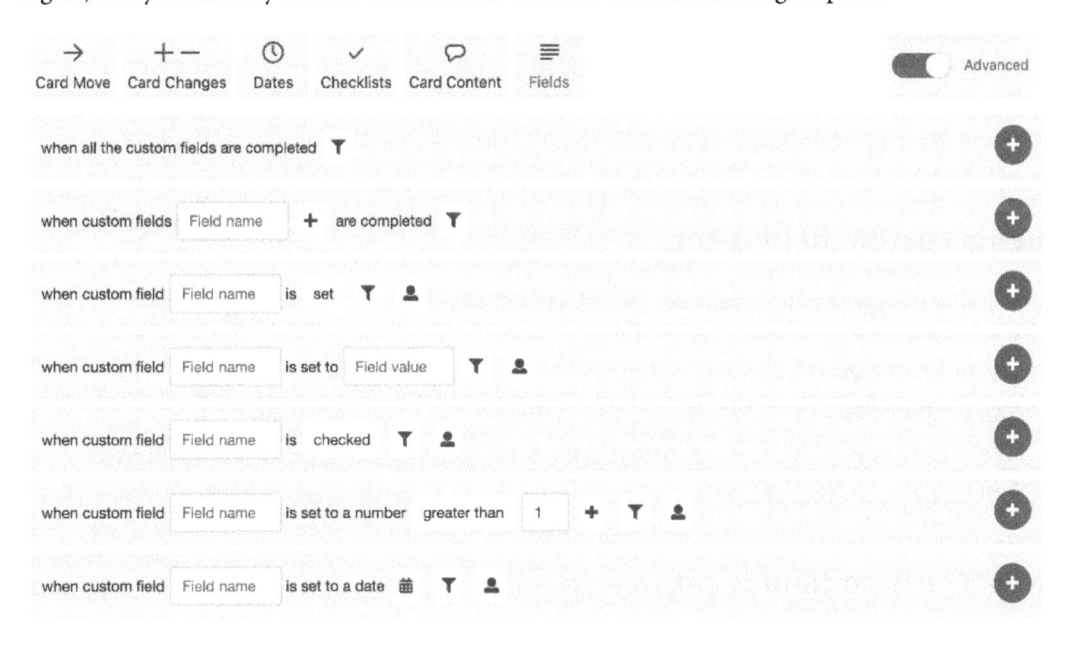

Figure 6.19 – Fields trigger events

If you don't use custom fields, feel free to skip this section and come back to it later if you start using them. They're quite helpful for advanced automation because as you'll see, there are a lot of triggers for watching them!

When all custom fields are completed

If you only have one custom field, this will trigger when that field is filled in. If you have multiple fields, it will trigger only when *all* of them are filled in.

> **Real-world example**
>
> When custom fields are completed, move the card to the **Ready to Use** list.
>
> This rule is useful for creating a sort of "form validation" type of workflow that moves a card to the next stage when you have all the information ready to work on a card.

When custom fields are completed

This is the same as the previous one, but only looking at a specific field being completed. You can add multiple to this rule by clicking the + icon next to the field.

> **Real-world example**
>
> When the **Name** and **department** custom fields are completed, assign **@britt_the_heir** to the card.
>
> This is helpful for creating owners when you have the necessary info to start working on a task.

When a custom field is set

This is similar to a custom field being completed, but lets you only specify one custom field.

> **Real-world example**
>
> When the **birthday** custom field is set, set the card due date to the same date.
>
> This specific rule is useful if you are using Trello as a CRM and want to get reminders to reach out to someone on their birthday.

When a custom field is set to a specific value

This checks when a custom field has a specific value—so, not just that it's set but that it matches what you're looking for.

> **Real-world example**
>
> When the **Department** custom field is set to `Design`, add **@venus** to the card.
>
> This rule is useful to assign owners to a card based on the department it might belong to, which you can select from a dropdown field.

When a checkbox custom field is checked/unchecked

Custom fields come in multiple shapes and sizes, one of which can be a checkbox. This trigger lets you set criteria based on whether a specific checkbox custom field is checked or unchecked.

> **Real-world example**
>
> When the **Approved** custom field is checked, post a comment to the card saying `@card this has been approved`.
>
> This rule allows you to use fields to indicate details about the status of a project and communicate that to the next team member without needing to manually create a comment and alert everyone.

When a number custom field is set to a specific number/range of numbers

Another custom field type is numbers. You can use this trigger to make certain actions happen based on the value of the numbers in a custom field.

> **Real-world example**
>
> When the **Age** custom field is greater than 13 and less than 20, add the "teenager" label.
>
> This is useful if you have specific data that you need to group. It's another example of relating custom field information to other fields on a card.

When a date custom field is set

Another type of custom field is the date field. You have access to start and due dates on a card whether or not you have custom fields enabled on your board. But if you need more date fields, you can create them with custom fields. Then, you can use this trigger to monitor what happens with them.

> **Real-world example**
>
> When a custom date field **Close date**, is set, move the card to the **Won** list.
>
> Similar to due dates, this is a useful automation to indicate the status of something by the existence of a date field.

Summary

You've done it! Now you know about all the options available as event triggers! Hopefully, you're starting to see what's possible and feeling confident about where you might start implementing automation in your boards.

Next, we'll learn about actions so you can see what you can do based on these triggers! You've probably already gotten some ideas about what's possible from the real-world examples, but we're just getting started.

7
Common Automation Actions

It's now time to talk about what happens after you create triggers. Since you know your options for starting an automation workflow, let's talk about the types of *actions* you can actually automate! We'll start by covering the most used and basic ones.

In this chapter, you'll learn how to automate activities such as the following:

- Moving cards to other boards or lists
- Adding members or labels
- Adjusting due dates
- Creating checklists or comments

That's just a few... let's dive in so you can see what I mean. We'll start with where to find these actions.

Accessing automation actions

You access actions in the same way you do triggers—through the **Automation** button that appears at the top toolbar of any Trello board. Click it, then select **Buttons** from the menu that appears.

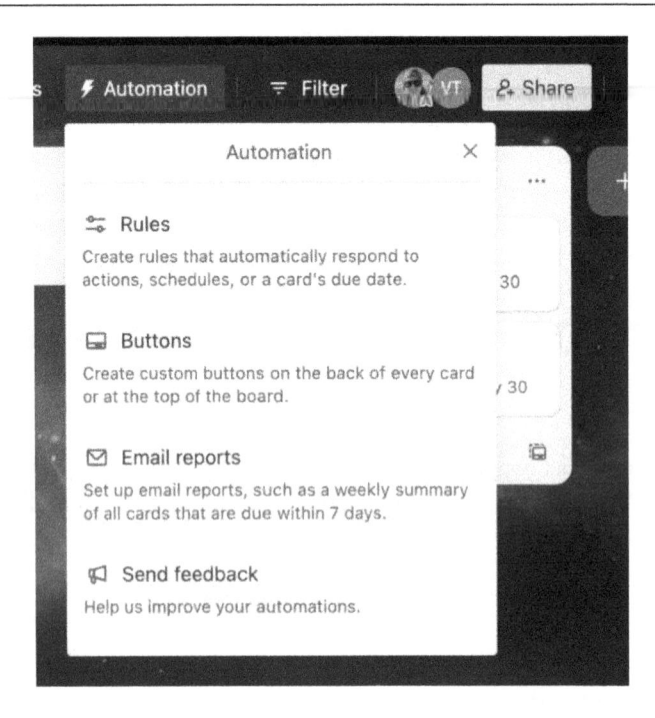

Figure 7.1 – Automation modal

We'll talk more about buttons in *Chapter 9*, but for now, just know that this is a manual way to start an automation, so it's the quickest way to view all the available actions.

From the **Card Buttons** modal, click the blue **Create custom button** option in the top-right corner. Click the + **Add Action** button.

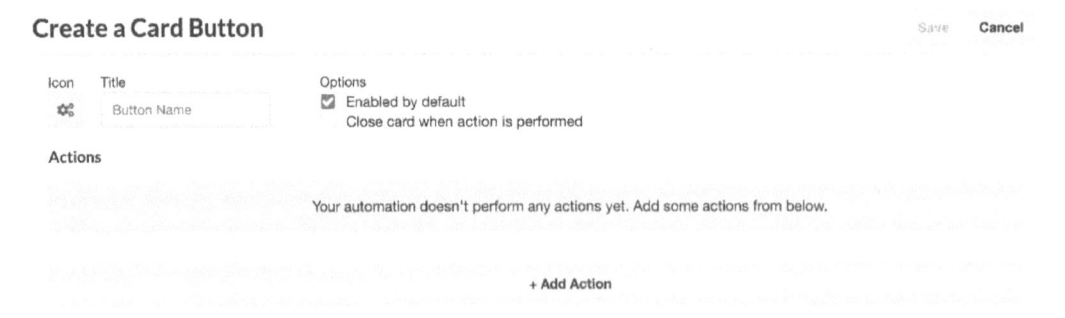

Figure 7.2 – Card button automation options

This brings up a menu of actions that we can automate. Feel free to follow along from here for the rest of the chapter as we go through the different actions available in each section.

I've organized all this info so you can have access to it and quickly find it when you need it, but no one remembers these things off the top of their head (not even me!). The more you play around with it, the more comfortable you'll get, and you'll start remembering what you can and can't do. Let's kick this off by talking about the move actions in your Trello toolbox.

Move

The first type of action you see relates to moving a card around the board, or even to another board. If you want to change the location of a card, the **move** set of actions is most helpful.

Figure 7.3 – Move actions

These kinds of automation actions make it seamless to have your cards in the right place on the board for your workflows. Rather than manually dragging a card around, you can set the criteria for when a card moves to the next stage, such as a checklist being completed, and have it occur instantly.

If you're operating out of multiple boards, this is incredibly useful. You might have one board that collects tasks before assigning them to specific teams or projects, so being able to quickly go from one board to another is essential.

There are only a few options here but there are some nuances to each one, so read closely.

Move/copy the card to the top/bottom of the list

This one is sneaky—if you're looking for the option to copy a card when something is created, this is the one you want! Click on **move** and you'll see the copy option appear. This action lets you simply move (or copy) a card to another list. (You can even clarify whether you want it added to the top or bottom.) Click the board icon at the end and you can specify a list that is on another board. (Note: these other boards do not have to be in the same workspace! They just have to be boards that you're part of!)

> **Real-world example**
>
> When a card is assigned to me, move it to the top of the **Brittany working** list.
>
> This is useful for keeping all of your own cards in one list automatically, making it easy for you to find your tasks without using any filters.

Move the card to the top/bottom of the current list

This is the same as the previous option, but rather than specifying another list, it will perform the action based on the list the current card is in.

> **Real-world example**
>
> When a red **urgent** label is applied to a card, move it to the top of the list.
>
> This is helpful for prioritizing cards and helping the most urgent ones rise to the top.

Archive/unarchive the card

This does exactly what it says! You can archive a card, or unarchive it if it's been archived.

> **Real-world example**
>
> When a card is moved to the **Done** list, archive the card.
>
> This is great for keeping your board clean and making sure you only see the things that need your attention.

Next up, let's talk about another common automation type—adding and removing attributes to cards.

Add/Remove

These actions are for making changes to cards, specifically adding/removing all sorts of elements, such as labels, stickers, links, and event text. A lot of automation tends to fall into this category, so keep an eye out!

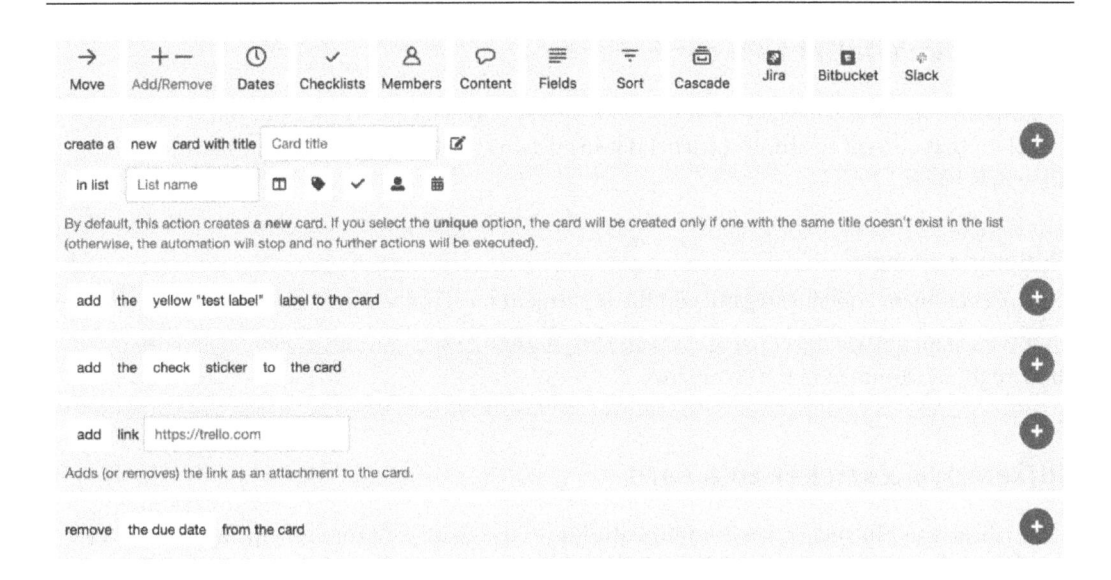

Figure 7.4 – Add/Remove actions

If you're making changes to cards that don't necessarily have their own sections (such as due dates, members, or links), you'll find this section most helpful. It's also a great place to go when you want to create a specific kind of card with checklists, dates, members, and more. For example, maybe you have a board for request ads. You could create a button that uses the **create a new card** action to create a templated card with all the fields set to your preferences, all with the click of a button!

Let's start from the top and work our way down.

Create a new/unique card

Don't get this confused with copying or moving—this creates a brand-new card! You can define just about anything you want with this new card. Though only the title and specific list are required, you can include a description by clicking the pencil icon. The rest is optional, but if you prefer, you can add labels, checklists, or due dates, and assign members. This is great for making a templated card type or creating recurring cards.

> **Real-world example**
>
> Every day, create a new card for the day with today's habits checklist.
>
> This is helpful for generating a new card every day, and has more options and control than the Card Repeater Power-Up.

Add/remove a label to a card

You can specify whether you want to add or remove a specific label to a card. You can choose from any label on that current board. If the label doesn't exist yet, refer to *Chapter 2* for instructions on creating new labels.

> **Real-world example**
>
> When a comment contains **urgent**, add the red **urgent** label to the card.
>
> This is great for quickly categorizing cards and helping ensure you don't miss anything important that might be skimmed in the comments.

Add/remove a sticker to a card

Just like labels, you can add stickers! Admittedly, I don't use these a lot (or ever) in automation, but I can see how they might be useful if you want to style your board and make the robots do it instead of yourself.

> **Real-world example**
>
> When a vote is added to a card, add a **checkmark** sticker to the card.
>
> Okay, maybe this is just a style thing, but it still gives your cards a way to stand out and sometimes that helps you take action on them!

Add/remove a link

If you want to add an attachment to a card, such as a link to an article or a file, you can add that with this action. You can even make the automation advanced enough to find another card and add the link there, rather than the original card, which is helpful for keeping related cards up to date.

> **Real-world example**
>
> When a label is added to the **Invoicing** list, add a link to the invoice template file on Google Drive.
>
> This is incredibly helpful to prevent spending time looking for templates or files in Google Drive, and there's no need to take multiple steps after tagging a card.

Remove (just about anything) from the card

You can remove the due date, the start date, the cover image, all the labels, all the members, or all the checklists from a card. This is great if you need to reset a card! Click the **the due date** option to see a dropdown of additional items.

the due date
the start date
the cover image
all the labels
all the stickers
all the checklists
all the members

remove   the due date   from the card

Figure 7.5 – Due date options

If you want to remove multiple elements, select one, then click the blue plus button at the end of the row, and then rinse and repeat until you've selected all the elements you want to remove.

> **Real-world example**
>
> When a card is moved into the "backlog" list, remove all members from the card.
>
> This is a great way to "reset" a card. You could also add an action that removes the due date and sends a comment to everyone on the card letting them know that for whatever reason, this task has been deprioritized.

Now it's *time* to talk about *dates*. Get it? 😀

Dates

Let's make some automation happen with dates!

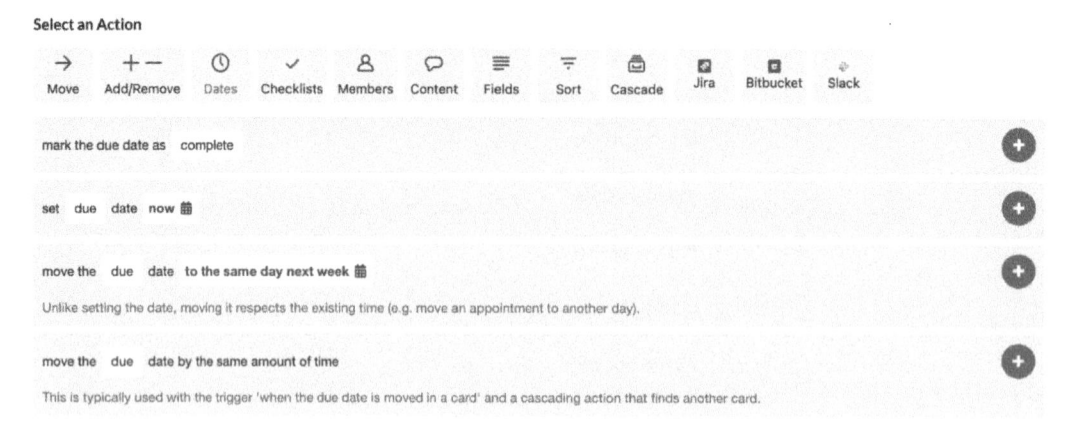

Figure 7.6 – Date actions

If you have a process that involves setting, changing, or completing due dates, this is the section you want to pay attention to. Well, of course you do, because many of us use due dates in Trello to surface the most time-sensitive tasks and make sure we're moving through our projects at the right pace.

However, dates are never static. When was the last time you had a project or task that actually stuck to its intended schedule? Even as I write this book, we've had to adjust the deadlines for drafts and edits throughout this whole process. These automations make setting and shifting due dates easy and allow you to focus on doing the work.

Let's dive in.

Mark a due date as complete/incomplete

You can check off a due date as done, or uncheck it if it's already checked off.

> **Real-world example**
>
> When a card is moved to **Done**, mark the due date as complete.
>
> And a bonus one!
>
> When a comment is added to a card in the **Done** list, mark the due date as incomplete.
>
> These help manage the date field by other properties on the card. The second example is a great way to "reopen" a card if something changes.

Set the due/start date to ___

The world is basically your oyster here.

No, really... you've got a ton of options from setting it to be right away, to a certain number of hours in the future, to an upcoming day of the week, or a specific date or day of this current month, or this year! You can even match it to a date in a custom field.

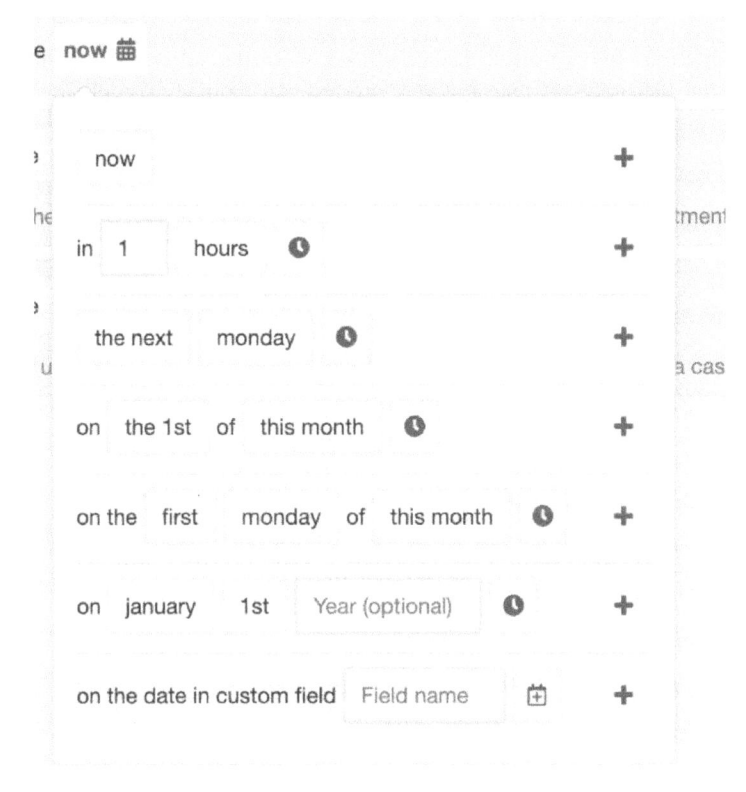

Figure 7.7 – Date setting options

Clicking the clock icon allows you to set a specific time if you have a preference. Click the + button at the end when you've selected your desired time.

> **Real-world example**
> When a card name contains **this week** in the title, set the due date to the upcoming Friday.
> This is a quick way to set the date of a card as it's created, or by renaming it.

Move the due/start date to _

This is similar to the previous one, but with this action, you can shift the date based on a relative time frame from the current date.

> **Real-world example**
>
> When a card button is clicked, **Snooze card** set the due date to the same day next week.
>
> I use this rule sometimes to deprioritize tasks that I know won't get done this week. There's no use leaving it on my plate to distract me and make me feel bad about not completing everything I planned earlier in the week when I was younger and more full of life.

Move the due/start date by the same amount of time

This one's a bit of an advanced maneuver and is usually paired with another action that looks for another card and *then* moves the due date by the same amount of time as specified in the previous step.

> **Real-world example**
>
> When a due date changes on a card with the **orange Brittany Project** label, find other cards with the orange **Brittany Project** label and move the due date by the same amount of time.
>
> This is excellent for managing card dependencies that all relate to the same project. If a project due date is pushed back a week, you might have several (or many) cards that also need to be adjusted. By grouping them together with a label, custom field, or some other attribute, it's easy to quickly adjust everything at once with this rule.

You've time traveled and moved around with dates, so now let's move on to checklist actions.

Checklist actions

The next set of elements that you can automate are checklists, which are subtasks inside of your Trello cards.

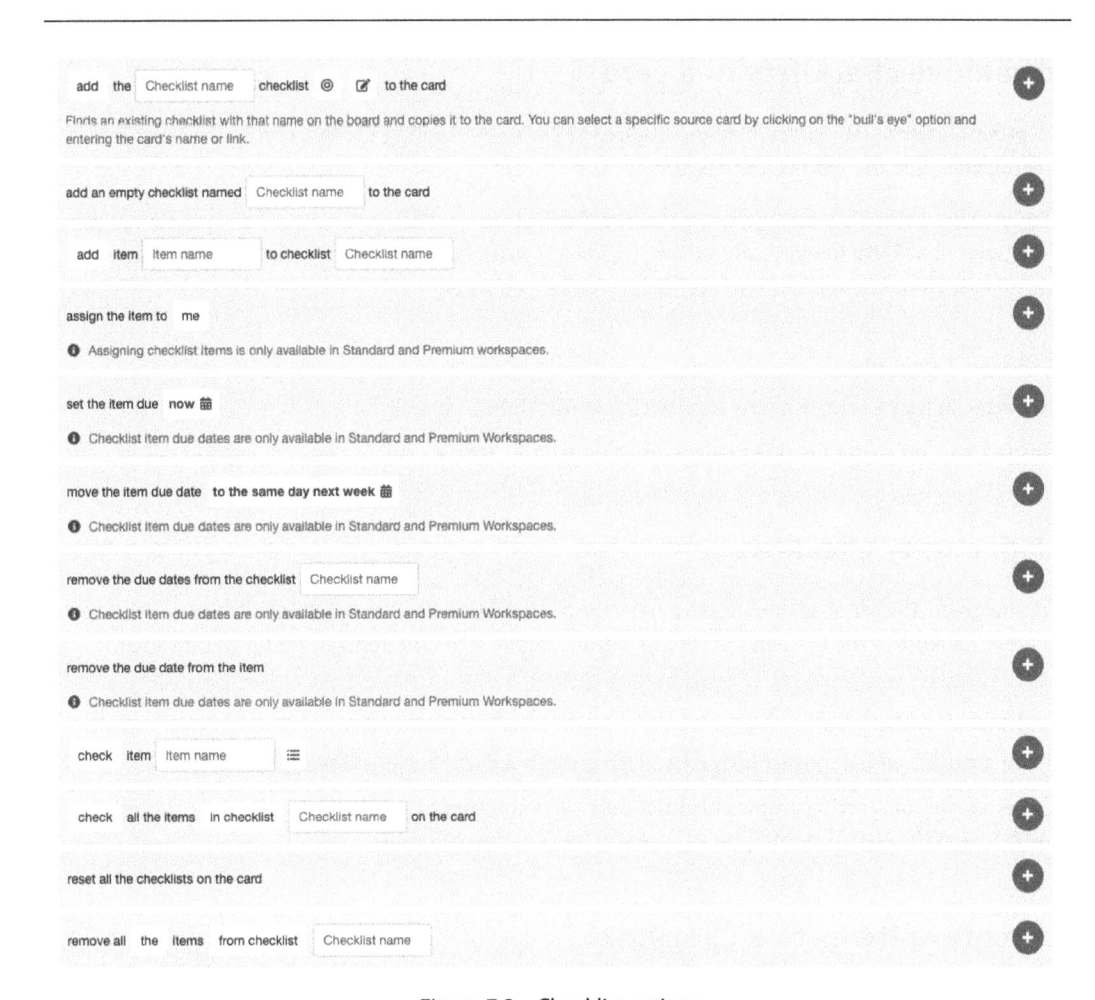

Figure 7.8 – Checklist actions

- add the `Checklist name` checklist ⊙ ✎ to the card
  - Finds an existing checklist with that name on the board and copies it to the card. You can select a specific source card by clicking on the "bull's eye" option and entering the card's name or link.
- add an empty checklist named `Checklist name` to the card
- add item `Item name` to checklist `Checklist name`
- assign the item to `me`
  - Assigning checklist items is only available in Standard and Premium workspaces.
- set the item due `now` 📅
  - Checklist item due dates are only available in Standard and Premium Workspaces.
- move the item due date `to the same day next week` 📅
  - Checklist item due dates are only available in Standard and Premium Workspaces.
- remove the due dates from the checklist `Checklist name`
  - Checklist item due dates are only available in Standard and Premium Workspaces.
- remove the due date from the item
  - Checklist item due dates are only available in Standard and Premium Workspaces.
- check item `Item name` ≡
- check `all the items` in checklist `Checklist name` on the card
- reset all the checklists on the card
- remove all the items from checklist `Checklist name`

Figure 7.8 – Checklist actions

We learned about checklists in *Chapter 3*, and they're one of my favorite parts of Trello. As someone recently diagnosed with ADHD, I've learned that breaking tasks into smaller bites and making clear action items make it easier for me to get started on something, and easier to finish. Plus, it helps me ensure I don't forget any important steps along the way.

While that's all good and well, it means nothing if it becomes another thing to do to manage those subtasks. That's why checklist automation is helpful, whether it's automatically adding a checklist for standard tasks that I have, such as cleaning my kitchen, or moving the due date when life happens and things get delayed.

There are a lot of options here. Instead of feeling overwhelmed, just remember you don't need to learn them all now—it simply means there's more you can do with them if you one day decide to!

Add/remove checklists to a card

This is probably the most common action applied to cards. By clicking the **target** icon you can define an existing checklist that you want to add.

I find this works well with creating a template card that has the checklist you plan to use for automation. That way, you don't have to worry about copying over a partially completed checklist or anything and it's easy to edit from one place if you ever want to make changes.

> Real-world example
>
> Every day at 6 a.m., create a new card with a **Daily Habits** checklist.
>
> This is great for giving me one place to check my daily habits.

Add an empty checklist

This is effectively the same as the "create a new checklist" action you can click inside a card. You can add a new checklist to the card and then add actions below it to add items to that new checklist.

> Real-world example
>
> When a card is added to the **Design** list, create a new checklist called **Design Tasks**.
>
> This is useful for starting a new checklist on a card automatically. Note that this rule doesn't add items to the checklist, but you can use the next action to do that.

Add/remove items to a checklist

You can add/remove items from a checklist on a card. Just specify the name of the checklist you want to add it to, and if it doesn't already exist, then it will create that checklist.

> Real-world example
>
> When a red urgent label is added to a card, add a checklist item for **follow up on the case with customer**.
>
> This is helpful for dynamically updating items in a checklist based on other activities in the card.

Assigning the item to someone

If you have Trello Standard or higher, you will have advanced checklists, which let you assign due dates and members to items in a checklist. When someone is added to a checklist item, that task shows up on their **Home** page under **Your Items**.

You can also incorporate more automation to organize these subtasks in other ways, such as every time someone is added to a subtask, creating a card with that task and a link to the card as a new card on another board.

> Real-world example
>
> When a checklist item is added to **Course checklist**, assign Robin.
>
> This is useful if you tend to have the same people dedicated to specific tasks. It saves you the step of adding them after creating the task.

Set the item due date

Similar to being able to add members, if you're on Trello Standard or higher, you can add due dates to checklist items. This action lets you set the date of a task and gives you similar options to what we saw with date actions. Clicking **now** opens a modal with more date customization options, similar to what you see in the **Dates** section.

> Real-world example
>
> When a checklist item is added to the **Daily** checklist, set the due date to today.
>
> This saves the step of assigning due dates to items when you can logically define when they'd be due.

Move the item due date

Like shifting the due dates of cards, you can shift the due dates of the checklist items inside a card. You have the same options, such as shifting to the same time, by a certain number of days, or to a relative or absolute time.

How you use this will depend on your use case, but it's helpful to know which options are available.

> Real-world example
>
> When a card is moved to the **Next Week** list, find each item in the checklist and move it to the same day next week.
>
> Just like with card due date automation, this action is useful when you have multiple subtasks due on the same day and need to shift to the next week.

Remove the due dates from the checklist

This action allows you to specify a checklist that you want to remove dates from. For instance, you might use this if you want to clear all of the dates from multiple checklist items rather than just a single item.

> **Real-world example**
>
> When a due date is removed from a card, remove due dates from the **Initial Steps** checklist.
>
> Use this rule when you find yourself having to remove due dates from checklist items after a task is deprioritized and moved back to the backlog (or starter list).

Remove the due date from the item

This is like the previous action, but if you don't want to remove the due dates for all checklist items, you'll need to use this with a trigger that specifies which one.

> **Real-world example**
>
> When someone is added to an item, remove the due date from the item.
>
> This is helpful if you use dates as reminders to follow up on a card and assign them. Once someone else is assigned, they can create a new due date if they prefer.

Check/uncheck an item

This action allows you to check off (mark as complete) or uncheck a specific item. You can specify which checklist it falls under by clicking the list icon next to it. This is often most useful when you're trying to sync cards and checklists so that if a card with a task name that matches a checklist item name is moved to a completed list, you can check the item with the name off a checklist in the main card.

> **Real-world example**
>
> When a "submitted" label is applied, check the submit item in the **Process** checklist.
>
> Use this rule with care—you'll need to make sure the text matches what you set! But if you are consistent with text, it's a great way to check off items when they're incorporated with other steps you're already taking.

Check/uncheck all the times in a/all checklist(s)

This is just like it sounds! It checks off (or unchecks) everything in either a specific checklist or all the checklists on the card. This is most useful if you get bothered by incomplete checklists and sometimes you just finish multiple things and then ship a card over to the **Done** list.

> **Real-world example**
>
> When a card is moved to **Done**, check all the items in all the checklists.
>
> I use this one all the time because sometimes I get so engrossed in doing the thing that I realize I've completed all the checklist items and don't want to have to check them off one by one. *(Although sometimes it is kinda satisfying to do that.* 😄*)*

Reset all the checklists on a card

If you're using a checklist from another card and it copies over that checklist with some tasks completed and some not, this is a great way to go ahead and clean up that checklist and start over from scratch.

Again, I generally prefer to have a designated card with a clean checklist that I use to reference checklists in automation. I just find this cleaner and it prevents grabbing half-used checklists. It also makes it easy to add or remove items. But you don't have to do that, and if you'd rather just reference the name of a checklist and not specify a card it's on, then you can use this rule to add a checklist and reset it.

> **Real-world example**
>
> When a card is moved to **Design**, add the **Designer** checklist and reset all the checklists.
>
> This is most helpful if you're using the same checklist across multiple cards and not specifying the checklist from a template card, which ensures the checklist is always starting off as incomplete. With this rule, you can add a checklist and even if it imports a partially completed one, it will reset it for the current card.

Remove items from checklists

You can remove all items or complete or incomplete items from all checklists or a specific checklist. There are a lot of ways you can go about this, but I would mostly group this under the checklist clean-up section. Click **the** before **items** to view a dropdown with additional options for specifying the types of items to remove.

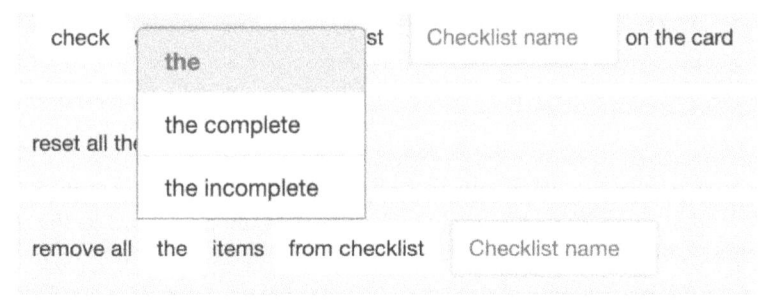

Figure 7.9 – Options for types of checklist items

You can also select **from checklist** to have the action remove the qualifying items from all checklists on a card.

> **Real-world use case**
>
> When a card is due within a day, remove all completed items from all checklists.
>
> This is helpful for prioritizing exactly what needs to be done so you can focus on only the remaining tasks and make your checklists less cluttered. Just make sure to take time to celebrate the things you've already done!

You're a checklist automation expert now! Next up, let's look at what we can automate with members and people in our boards.

Member actions

Member actions are incredibly helpful because assigning a person to a card makes it easy to filter cards and determine who gets notifications about a card. It's also a great way to track capacity and workload management.

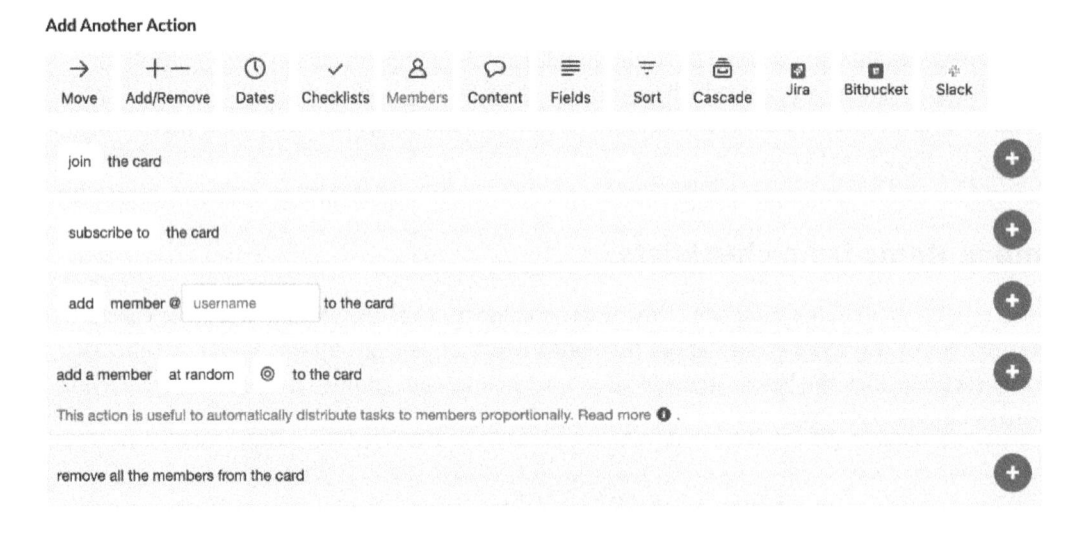

Figure 7.10 – Member actions

Since card members are tied to so many other aspects of Trello, such as filters, views, and, perhaps most importantly, notifications, it's important to make sure the right people are on the right cards at all times. If you think about it, you probably have a pretty systematic way of adding people to your cards, no matter how you use Trello.

For instance, you might have your designer take over the card when it moves to a certain stage in your marketing board, or you might have your product manager assigned to any newly added cards to evaluate their importance. Once you determine a system for who gets what, you can save yourself time each week by avoiding the manual process of opening a card, clicking on members, thinking about who it's for, and then clicking on their name.

Even if you're the only person on the board, you might still want to assign items to yourself for notifications or integrations with other apps.

Join/leave a card

This action is for just you, the one setting it up. So, if you want to automatically join a card (or leave a card) based on certain criteria, this is the action you want to use.

> **Real-world example**
>
> When a card is due in the next five days, join the card.
>
> This ensures you're aware of cards that are due soon, even if you don't have a filter in place or a view that highlights upcoming cards.

Subscribe/unsubscribe to a card

Subscribing to a card is the same as "watching" a card. This means your avatar won't show up on the card and you won't be an official "member" of the card, but you'll still get notifications about activity on the card. We learned about **watching** in *Chapter 2*.

Keep in mind, this rule also applies to just you. You can't subscribe for other folks, so if other people on your team want this rule, they'll need to set it up themselves. Maybe you should lend them a copy of this book with this page earmarked!

> **Real-world example**
>
> When a card is added to the board with the yellow "interesting" label, subscribe to the card.
>
> This is a quick way to watch a card, and by tying it to a label, you'll remember why you wanted to watch the card.

Add/remove a specific user to a card

If you want to add (or remove) specific users to a card, this is how you do it. They must be members of the board! Don't worry if you can't remember exactly what their username is, because when you click the member box, all of your members will show up as options in a dropdown.

Figure 7.11 – Member drop-down options

Just click the one you want, and you'll be ready to go.

> **Real-world example**
>
> When a card is moved to the **Design** list, add @melman to the card.
>
> This is useful for assigning specific people to a card when they're involved in only parts of a card. You can also add a rule that removes them when the card moves to the next list.

Add a member at random/in turn to a card

If you have multiple people that you want to fairly assign to cards, you can use this option to either randomly pick someone or assign people evenly and in order (in turn). This is much better than trying to build out the steps to make this happen, so having it as a command is fantastic. It's great if you have a whole team of people that can do something, so you don't want to assign it to just one person every time.

Figure 7.12 – Define a card to choose members from

If you only want to pool assignments to a few members instead of everyone on a board, create a card with those members and then click the target icon to link to that card.

> **Real-world example**
>
> When a new card is added to a board, add a member from the **Sales Team** card in turn to a card.
>
> This is useful when you have a group of people that could be assigned to a card to ensure their assignment is rotated evenly.

Remove all the members from a card

This does exactly what it says—removes all the members from a card. This is really handy if you need to reset a card that you've copied, or if you have a trigger that takes a card back to the beginning of a workflow.

> **Real-world example**
>
> When the **reset** label is added to a card, move it to the **Backlog** list and remove all members from a card.
>
> Just like with due dates and checklists, there might be scenarios when you need to reset a card. Use this rule to clear all members if a task has been deprioritized or needs re-assignment.

Content actions

Content actions are all about changing the text you interact with inside cards, such as the card title, description, and comments. You can even send emails to yourself, which is a great way to customize notifications.

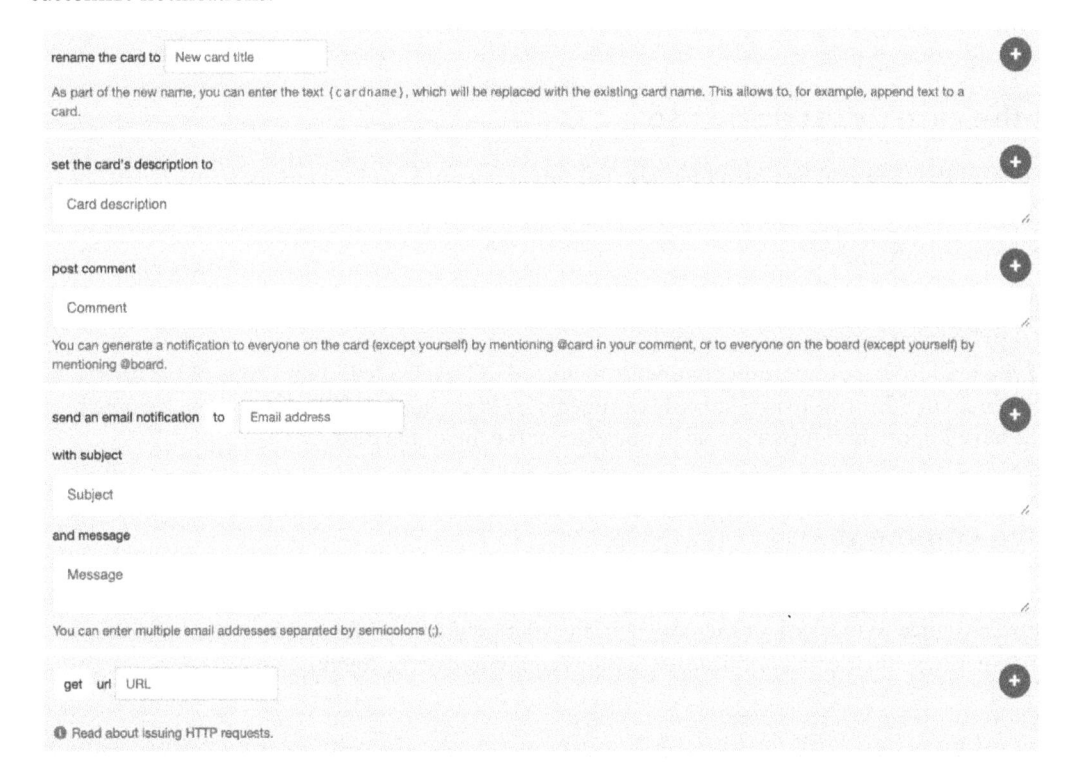

Figure 7.13 – Content actions

I don't use these sections every day, but when I do, they're extremely useful. The power behind these actions is that you can complete your workflow based entirely on context from the item itself.

Instead of stringing automations together based on other actions, you can make Trello perform specific actions that are relevant to what's happening in the details of a card, such as the name, description, or comments, and carry on those actions to the text of the card, altering the meaning behind it and creating a log of information.

Let's dive into some examples to see what I mean.

Rename the card to ___

This allows you to rename a card, which is helpful if you're trying to sync info from another card, or if you want to add text to the name, such as `Ready to Go : {cardname}`, and it will keep the old card name, but include the new text with it.

> **Real-world example**
>
> When the **help** label is added to a card, rename the card to **NEEDS ADDRESSING: {cardname}**
>
> This is another way of making important cards more visible.

Set the card's description to ___

This is just like renaming the title of the card, but this applies to a card's description.

> **Real-world example**
>
> When a comment is added to the card by me, set the card's description to `{carddescription}` , `{commenttext}`.
>
> If you tend to share important comments that need to be included in the scope of the card, you could use this rule to append only comments from you to the card's description, keeping the most important information all in one place at the top of the card.

Post a comment

This adds a comment to the card, which is a great way to send notifications because anyone watching the card, assigned to the card, or mentioned in the comment will get the notification (including an email if they have their email notifications settings configured accordingly).

> **Real-world example**
>
> When the **urgent** label is added to a card, post the `@board this card needs urgent attention!` comment.
>
> This is a quick way to tag everyone on the board and make them aware of something that's urgent. Selecting a label, moving a card, or even clicking a button is much faster than typing a comment out, and it's definitely faster than copying a card link and posting a Slack message!

Send an email notification to __

Even though sending a comment will trigger an email notification, if you only want the email and don't need the content documented on the card, or if you just want to make sure everyone sees regardless of their notification settings, you can send an email notification with this action. You can trigger it to send it to a specific email address (regardless of whether they're a Trello user or not) or send an email to everyone on the card or everyone on the board.

You can then specify the content of the subject and message. This is where knowing **automation variables** is most handy because that's how you can reference the specific card and details about it inside the body of the email.

> **Real-world example**
>
> When a new card is added to the board, send an email notification to every member of the board with the subject **New card : {cardname}** and the message **A new card has been added to the board! View it here {cardlink}**
>
> If you have trouble getting people on your team to check Trello, try using this action to send email notifications. You can even do this for cards people are not subscribed to, which is a perfect way to help more people get on board—literally.

Get/post/put to URL

If you have an API endpoint that can receive and store data, then you can use this rule to get data from that API or send data to it. This is pretty advanced stuff, but if you want to integrate with another tool, this is likely what you'll want to use.

You'll need to be familiar with the API you're working with and what's returned to be able to best use this, but essentially you can reference whatever is returned in your next step. You can learn more about HTTP requests with automation in the official docs here: `support.atlassian.com/trello/docs/issuing-http-requests/`.

> **Real-world example**
>
> When a card is moved into the **Get data** list, get the URL `https://api.thecatapi.com/v1/images/search?breed_ids=beng&include_breeds=true` and post `{httpresponse.image}` as a comment on the card.
>
> *You know, in case you want to put images of cats as comments on your cards. Who doesn't?*

Summary

We've covered so much ground, and these are just the "basic" actions you can automate with Trello. You can now move cards around, add or remove attributes such as labels or links, adjust due dates, create checklists, add members, and more.

You'll never remember all of these off the top of your head, and that's totally okay. Even I have to open up the **Automation** section sometimes to remember everything that is possible. At first, it's also not always intuitive which sections you'll find the actions in, but the more you use them, the more familiar they'll become.

But if you thought that was all, we're only getting started. You can still automate even more actions in Trello, so in the next chapter, we'll talk through some advanced automation actions.

8
Advanced Actions

We've already covered a lot of ground and you are hopefully feeling extremely inspired by how much you can do in Trello. But for some workflows, you'll need to use even more than basic automation actions. For instance, maybe you can't find an action that suits what you need for counting how many cards have been through a workflow, or you need to find a similar card and make an update on *that* card.

In this chapter, you'll learn about more advanced actions such as the following:

- Clearing and setting custom field values
- Sorting lists by attributes such as dates, labels, or fields
- Finding one or more cards and performing actions
- Sending Slack messages with Trello

Now, grab some coffee because there's a lot to go through here!

Field actions

If you want to do any automation of updating or clearing custom fields, this is your section!

> **Custom fields only available for Trello Standard or higher plans**
> If you aren't using them, you can skip right past this section and come back one day when you need it. But if you are using custom fields (or if you aren't but you've thought about it), you have a lot of options for automating those fields, so let's dive in!

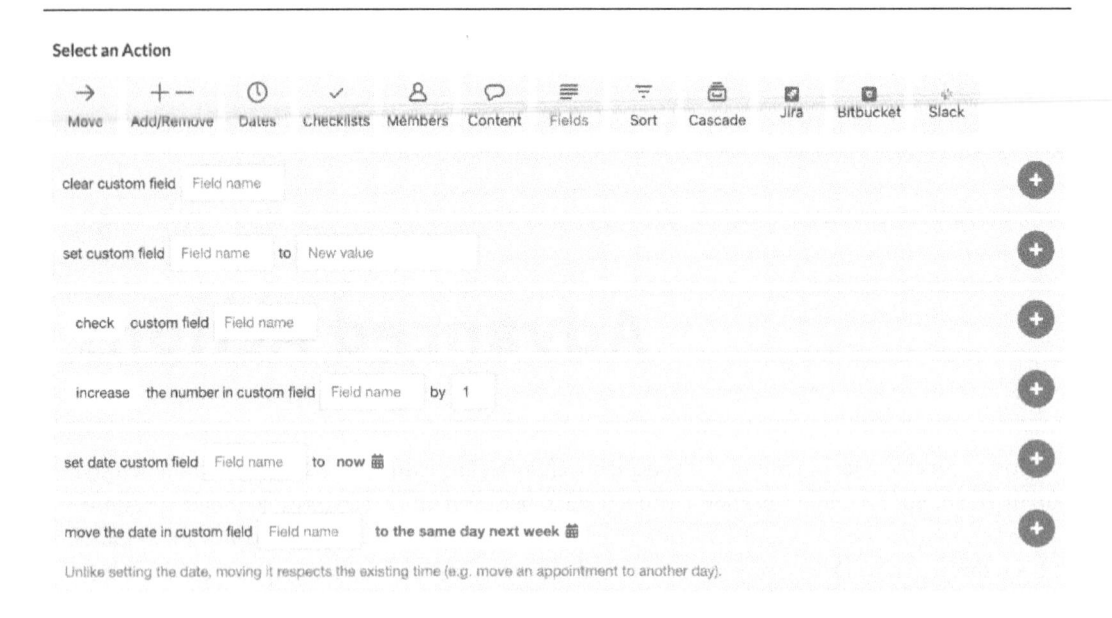

Figure 8.1 – Field actions

In *Chapter 3*, we learned about how powerful custom fields were, and we didn't even talk about automation! While they're pretty nifty just sitting around on cards, the real potency comes from being able to tie automations to them.

If you think your use case is so unique that Trello probably can't handle it, then I'd say you probably haven't used custom fields to their full potential. Although we've discussed a lot of actions for dates, members, checklists, and more, custom field actions allow you to do almost everything else. So, if you were disappointed to not find something in the previous rules, then buckle up because you can find a way to make it work with custom fields. You might just have to get a bit creative!

Clear custom field __

Pick a custom field and clear it—great for when you need to reset a card.

> **Real-world example**
> When a card is moved to **Backlog**, clear custom field **Prioritized**.
> Clearing custom fields is helpful for resetting a card, such as when it's deprioritized.

Set custom field __ to ___

Use this to update a custom field to a specific value. You can make it a single, static value that will apply every time. Or you can make it dynamic by using **automation variables**. For instance, you can set a custom field to be the current date, the current list name, or anything else!

> Real-world example
>
> When a card is added to the board, set custom field **Type** to {**cardlistname**}.
>
> This is a great rule for keeping track of where a card originated. I use this in my recipe board to keep track of the type of meal a recipe falls under (like Meatless, Quick, or New). I'll queue up meals to make in my **Meal Plan** list, and then when I'm done, I use another automation rule to move the card back to its meal type list, by referencing the value in that Type custom field.

Check/uncheck custom field

If you're using a checkbox custom field, this will allow you to set it to "true" or "false" (checked or unchecked).

> Real-world example
>
> When a card is moved to **Ready for Review** list, check the custom field **Drafted**.
>
> Some people prefer using custom fields instead of checklists, which is understandable as they are at the top of the card, and for a while, there were more options for automating custom fields than checklist items.

Increase/decrease the number in custom field __ by __

If you have a number type custom field, you can use this rule to adjust that number by specific increments. This is useful if you want to count the number of times something happens, as every time that thing happens, you can increase the number of a card by one.

> Real-world example
>
> When a comment is added to a card, increase the number in custom field **Comments** number by 1.
>
> This rule is specifically helpful if you want to keep a log of the number of comments on a card. Perhaps your team could agree that if a card reaches 20 comments, it's time to have a quick sync to discuss to make a decision together. This automation would make it easy to quickly count comments, and you could even add another automation that notified you when that custom field reaches 20 (or whatever number you set).

Set date custom field ___ to ___

This is the automation for date fields. You can set it to a variety of options, very similar to what you've seen in the **Dates** automation section.

> **Real-world example**
>
> When a card is moved to **Done**, set the date for **Completed Date** to **Now**.
>
> While you could set the due date, using a custom field for tracking the completed date allows you to see actual versus estimated dates.

Move the date in custom field ___ to ___

If you want to edit a custom field date to change by a certain increment when something happens, you'll use this trigger. This can be similar to setting the date field in the previous one but gives you a few additional options by letting you set the date in relation to the existing date.

> **Real-world example**
>
> When the snooze button is clicked on a card, move the custom field **Draft Due Date** to the same day next week.
>
> Similar to due date automation, this is helpful for "snoozing" a card because, you know—life happens! Trello isn't judging you. Taco just wants to help!

And that's a wrap on custom fields automation! This is a handy way to automate a lot of things because if you can't find the automation somewhere else, you might be able to build everything you need by creating a custom field and setting your automation through that!

Now, let's talk about sorting cards.

Sort actions

We all like a little bit of order, so sorting actions give you options to clean up your cards. Sorting works by list, so if you want to sort your entire board, you'll need to add an action for each list. Get excited though, because you have a lot more sorting options here than you do with the actions inside a list.

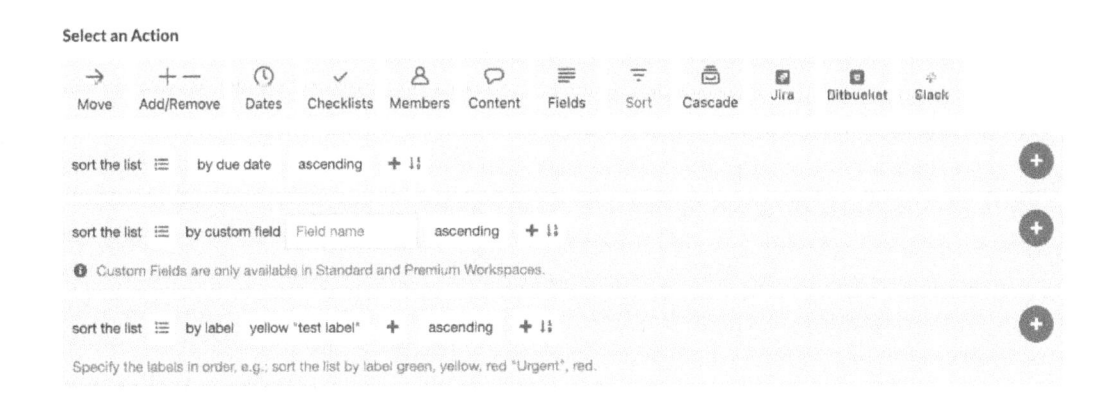

Figure 8.2 – Sort actions

For folks who prefer their cards in a specific order, I don't think I'm being dramatic when I say that this section is going to be life-changing for you. These actions help you organize cards in lists by what matters most to you, whether it's due dates, custom field values, or even labels. While you can manually sort a list by clicking the ellipses at the top of a list, the options there are actually a bit more limited than the automation options. Specifically, there's no option to sort by labels. That's where automation shines!

If you've ever sorted data in a spreadsheet, this is similar. Sorting will group cards by the attributes you define and in the order you'd like. Let's dive into the specifics!

Sort list by ___

You have virtually any option you can think of for sorting a list. This action gives you a way to sort by date, title, votes, age, and time in the list. I like to think of this as my "quantifiable" sort. What I mean by that is, it's clear what order it should be in (alphabetically, newest to oldest, etc.)

Choose a specific list to perform the sort on by clicking the bullet list icon, but if you don't select that, by default, it will perform the sort on the list on the trigger card's list.

Figure 8.3 – Options for criteria to sort lists by

If you click the + button at the end, you can sort your cards even further within that criteria. (Think, sort by date, then by custom fields, then by label, etc.)

> **Real-world example**
>
> Every Monday, sort cards in **To Do** by due date descending.
>
> Because the last thing you want to do on a Monday morning is figure out what's the most important thing to start on for the week.

Sort by custom field ___

If you have custom fields on your board, you can sort by those.

You have all the same options I described in the previous sort of action. You can specify a list to perform it on and more sort layers within the initial sort.

> **Real-world example**
>
> When a card is added to **Review**, sort the **Review** list by custom field **Draft Completed Date**.
>
> This rule is another great way to prioritize cards that are using dates other than due dates, allowing the most important ones to rise to the top.

Sort by label __

This sort action gives you the option to sort your cards by labels. You'll have to specify the order of the labels that you want them sorted in since there's no default ascending or descending order of colors. Click the + button after a label name to specify the order of labels, like this:

Figure 8.4 – Sorting by multiple labels

Once again, you can drill down further and sort within those groups.

> **Real-world example**
>
> When a card is added to **Shopping List**, sort by green **Produce** label, red **Meat** label, and blue **Dairy** label.
>
> I literally use this on my shopping list (along with some automation that assigns those labels based on the name of the card), and it's the closest thing I've found to being able to make a map of the most efficient route around the grocery store (which, by the way, I think is a fantastic app idea. You're welcome!).

Now, let's look at cascading, which (for my spreadsheet nerds) is basically the VLOOKUP of Trello automation. ☺

Cascade actions

I assume you're reading this book because you want to deep dive into all things Trello. But there's a ton of value in the automation we've talked about already (and will continue discovering), so even if you never touch this section, you can still build really powerful automation in your boards.

So just pause, reflect on what you've learned, and grab another cup of coffee (or a nice bourbon if you're head is spinning already!). You don't have to remember all of this. Just take the next few minutes to absorb and see all that's possible within the world of Trello automation. And if you want to skip this and come back later, I'll be here!

When you click the **Cascade** section, the first thing you see is a very useful callout that explains why you might use this section of actions.

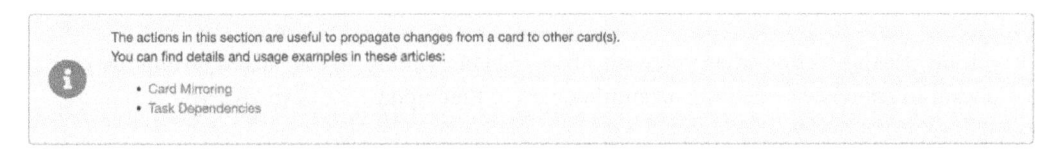

Figure 8.5 – Description of when to use Cascade actions

158 Advanced Actions

The actions in this section are useful for interacting with multiple cards and allowing changes in one card to propagate to another card.

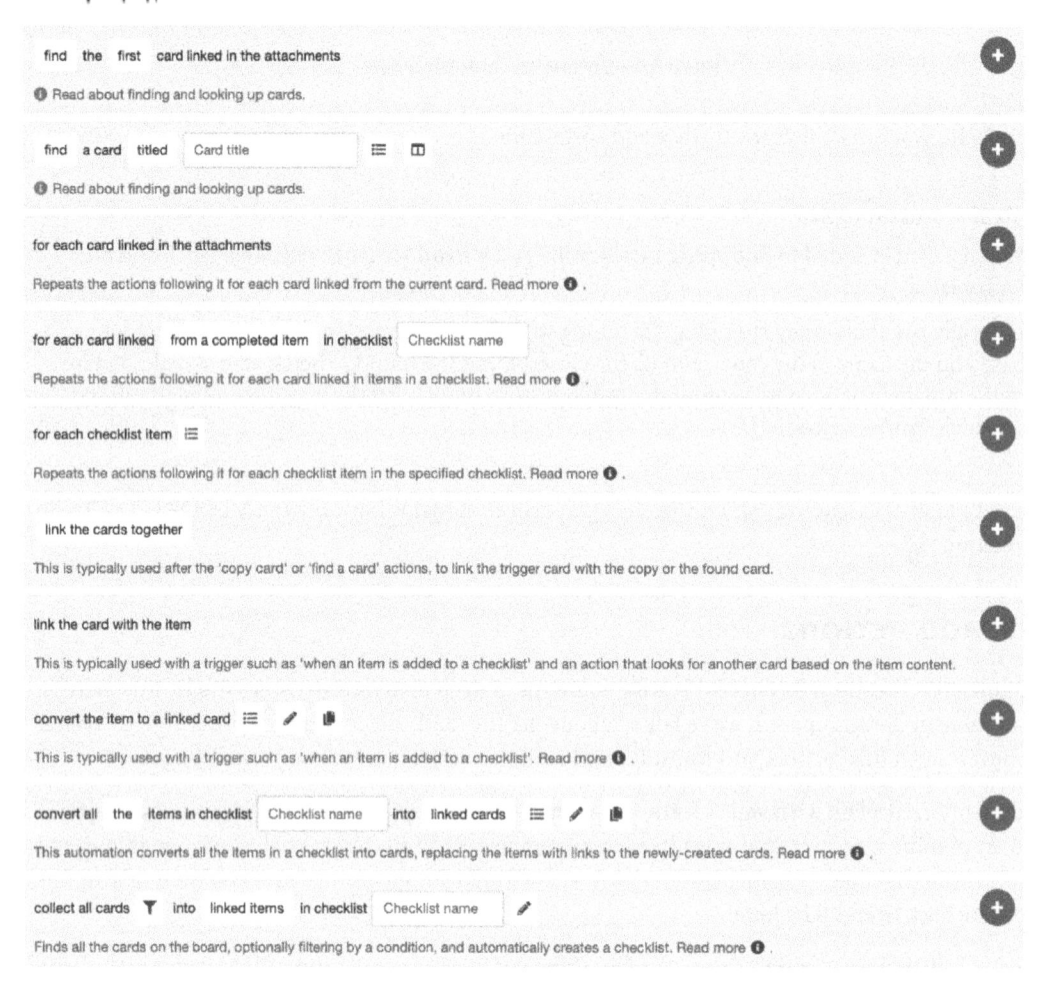

Figure 8.6 – Cascade actions

You'll typically use this section when you want a trigger in one card to take an action on another card or if you want to reference something on another card to then update the original card.

Find/lookup the first/last card linked in the attachments

Let's first talk about the difference between find and lookup. The automation docs explain it well, but here's the gist: **find** will find an attached card and then perform the next actions on that found card, and **lookup** will find an attached card and then retain info from that found card but continue to perform the actions based on the *trigger* card.

This action is never going to be a final step. Rather, you'll add another action afterward specifying what to perform on the specified card.

> **Real-world example**
>
> When a card is added to the **In Progress** list, find the first card linked in the attachments and add a comment **This card is In Progress**.
>
> This is a great way for handling dependent tasks without having to manually keep their status in sync.

Find/lookup a card titled/with link

Similar to the previous one, it looks for another card but, instead of looking through card attachments, it looks for another card with a specific name (you can search across specific lists and boards) or at a specific URL.

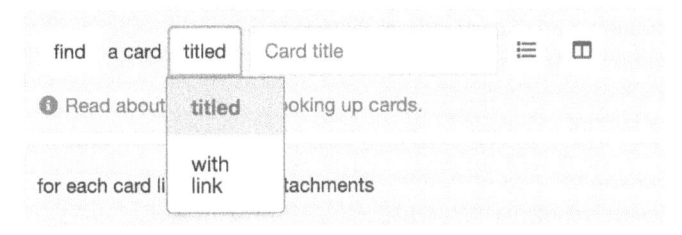

Figure 8.7 – Options for finding a card through name or link

> **All cards have their own URL**
>
> You can find it by going to a card and selecting what's in your URL bar at the top. It will look something like this: `https://trello.com/c/qs4WlF6N/393-wednesday-mar-9-2022-daily`.

This is helpful when you want to perform actions based on related cards and not the initial card that was triggered.

> **Real-world example**
>
> When a card is added to the **In Progress** list, find the card titled **Currently Working** and add a checklist item with {**triggercardname**}.
>
> Like the previous rule, this one helps you keep track of cards inside of another card. So meta!

For each card linked in the attachments

Use this to perform an action for every card in the attachments, not just the first or last one. This is useful when you have one card tracking several tasks from related cards and you would like them to stay in sync.

> **Real-world example**
>
> When a card is moved to **Done**, for each card linked in the attachments, add the green **completed** label.
>
> Use this rule if you want to take your automation to the next level and not just keep your related cards in sync but also perform additional actions on top of status. It's also great if you have a different way of handling the completed status for subtask cards.

For each card linked from an item in checklist

This is a powerful cascading action that ties a checklist item to a card, allowing you to have a single card that references other cards and tracks their progress. It can then find the card linked to the checklist item and apply whatever automation you want to it.

> **Real-world example**
>
> When checklist **ToDo** is completed, for each card linked from an item in checklist **ToDo**, move the card to **Done**.
>
> This is specifically helpful for keeping cards in sync with checklist items that are dependent cards.

For each checklist item

This iterates through an action for every item in a checklist of a card. You can provide a specific checklist by clicking the **numbered list** icon. Otherwise, it will apply to every checklist item on the card.

> **Real-world example**
>
> When clicking the **Convert list to cards** button, for each checklist item, convert the item to a linked card.
>
> If you sometimes think you want a checklist but then decide you actually want those items as their own cards, this rule makes it easy to convert rather than manually clicking through each one.

Link/unlink the cards together

As it says in the rule itself…

This is typically used after the **copy card** or **find a card** actions to link the trigger card with the copy or the found card.

Hopefully, you can see from the first couple of sections in this lesson how helpful it can be to link cards together, so this is where the magic starts. This is particularly useful if you're trying to sync activities from cards across multiple boards.

> Real-world example
>
> When a card is created on the **Marketing** board, copy the card to the **All Activities** board and link the cards together.
>
> This rule is helpful for duplicating cards and attaching them to each other. Note that this won't sync them. For instance, if you make a change on one card, it won't be reflected on the other. It just means the cards will be attached to each other and easier to reference.

Link the card with the item

Trello provides more helpful notes inside this rule.

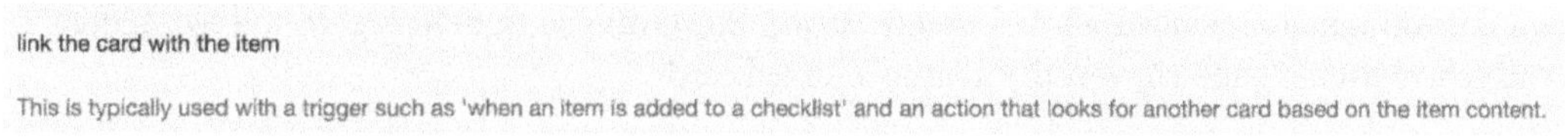

link the card with the item

This is typically used with a trigger such as 'when an item is added to a checklist' and an action that looks for another card based on the item content.

Figure 8.8 – Explanation of use for linking card with item

If you're trying to link cards with checklist items, similar to the previous steps, rather than linking whole cards, you can simply link items in a checklist with other cards.

> Real-world example
>
> When an item is added to a checklist, look up the card with the title {**checklistitemname**} and link the card with the item.
>
> This is helpful if you've already made a card and now want to make a checklist that references that specific card without having to open each existing card and copy the link.

Convert the item to a linked card

There is a bunch of customization options in here, but the gist of this action is that it takes a checklist item and then turns it into its own card.

You can specify a few different things, such as the following:

- The list you want the linked card to be created in
- The pattern you want your card to be named (doesn't have to just be the item name)
- What copies over from the original card the checklist item is on (labels or members, or both!)

> **Real-world example**
>
> When a checklist item is added to a card assigned to me, convert the item to a linked card in list **Brittany's projects**.
>
> I prefer to operate in cards instead of checklist items for my own tasks but sometimes get assigned individual items on another checklist. This automation lets everyone have the best of both worlds, operating out of a checklist *and* a card.

Convert items in a checklist to cards/linked cards

You're probably getting tired of seeing all these options at this point, but believe it or not, they all have nuances that people have requested, which makes the functionality of how they perform quite different!

This one converts specific items (or all of them) in a checklist that you specify to new cards or linked cards. Similar to our previous actions, the difference is that you can watch for completed or incomplete ones. Or if you want to reference all the checklist items, this saves you from having to add two actions for each checklist item and convert the item to a linked card.

And you get the same options as before with defining the list, specifying a pattern, and copying over labels and members.

> **Real-world example**
>
> When a card is due in 7 days, convert all the unchecked items in a checklist to cards on the **This Week** list.
>
> This rule is great for using checklists to determine all the important steps for a project, and then creating cards for them that can easily be worked on as a task is due. I sometimes prefer this method because it allows me to use lists to show the status of all the individual tasks and add comments on specific items instead of having to keep everything in one card.

Collect all the cards into linked items/links/items in checklist

Okay, stick with me—last one!

This one's pretty cool. This action searches for all the cards that fit your criteria (click the filter to see all the options we've become familiar with in our other actions).

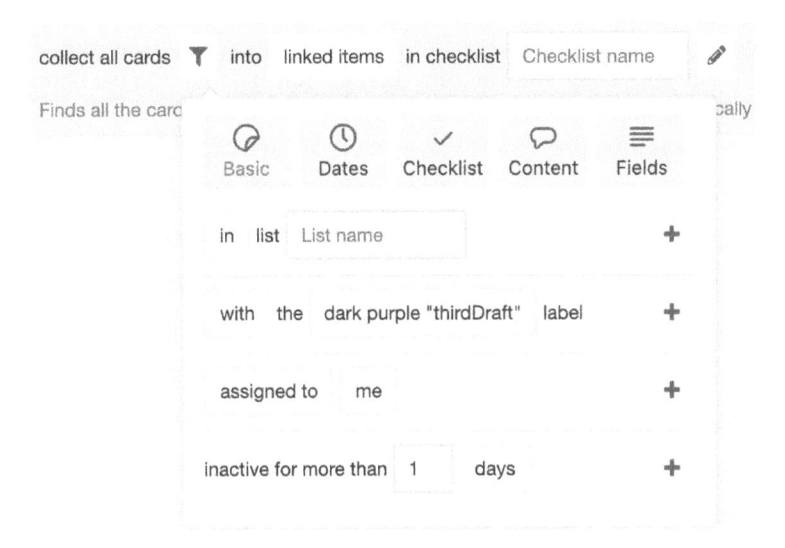

Figure 8.9 – Filter menu options

It then takes the cards it finds on the board and combines them in a checklist for you. As it sets them up in the checklist, it can create them in one of three ways:

- Linked items (checklist item that links to the original card it came from and the card itself with a link back to the card with this newly created checklist)
- Links (straight links to the card with no title info)
- Items (just the text of the card name without any link to the original card it came from)

> **Real-world example**
>
> Every Monday, collect all cards assigned to me with a due date in less than 7 days into linked items in checklist **Rodney Tasks**.
>
> If I preferred to work on checklists instead of cards, I could use this rule to make a single checklist of all the things I need to do, rather than an assortment of cards.

For the final section of automation actions, we're going to talk about non-Trello tools. Trello doesn't offer native automation tools for a lot of integrations, but there are a few exceptions that we'll discuss.

Other tool actions

To combine Trello with other tools through automation, you'll often need to use third-party automation software, such as Zapier. But there are a few tools you can build automation for within Trello's automation suite.

Before creating the automations, you'll need to connect the tools you want to use in the **App automations** section in your Trello **Automation** settings. You can find it in the bottom left-hand side of the automation menu.

Figure 8.10 –Additional automation settings

As much as I love Trello, even I understand that not everything can be done in Trello. While I wish everyone would use Trello, sometimes people prefer Jira. And Trello isn't meant for code management and handling pull requests. And while I can communicate about tasks via Trello comments, there are still a lot of reasons I need to use Slack.

Rather than pretending you can do everything in Trello, automation helps you find the best workflow to make all your tools work together as effortlessly as possible. Let's start with Trello's big brother.

Jira

You won't be shocked to know that since Atlassian owns Trello, the first tool they offer robust internal automation with is Jira, another Atlassian tool. Jira is a popular project management tool used for issue tracking, agile project management, and software development.

Other tool actions   165

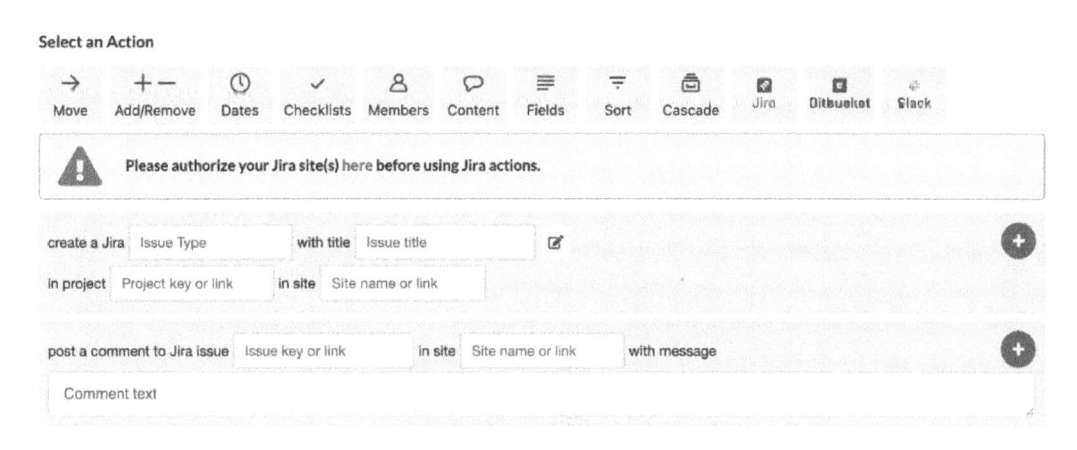

Figure 8.11 – Jira actions

Atlassian owns Trello and Jira, so thankfully, there are some great ways to keep them synced together. Although there are tools out there that are more robust for complete mirroring, if you just need info from Trello pushed to Jira, this should do the job.

There are two available actions:

- One is used to create a Jira issue. You'll need to specify the issue type and title, as well as the Jira instance you want the issue created in.
- The other action is to post a comment to a Jira issue that already exists.

You can use **automation variables** to reference the Jira instance or issue from data on the Trello card, such as a custom field or name of the card.

> **Real-world example**
>
> When a card is added to the **Send to Dev Team** list, create a Jira issue with title {**cardname**} in the project **Requests** in the site **Dev Team**.
>
> This is helpful when your team works in Trello but you have another team that works in Jira. ☺ We can't all be perfect I guess.

Bitbucket

Atlassian also owns Bitbucket, which is a web-based version control repository hosting service used for source code management, allowing teams to collaborate on code and track changes. It's similar to GitHub (I just know someone is going to throw rocks at me for saying that.).

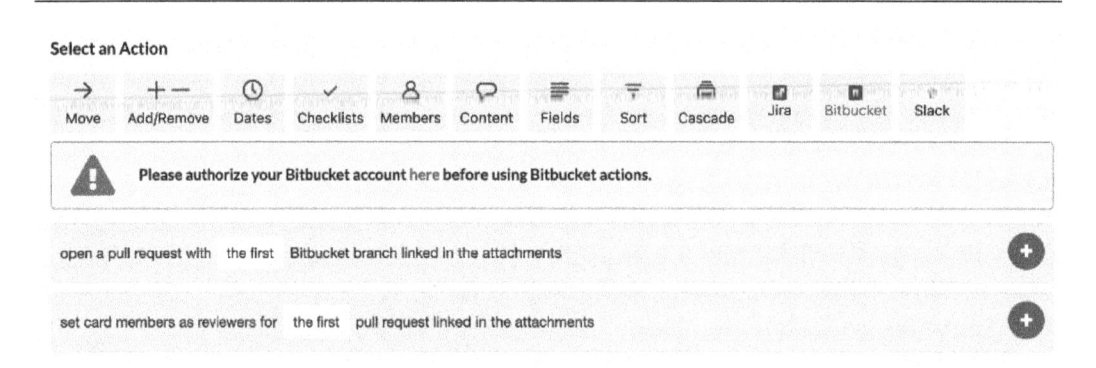

Figure 8.12 – Bitbucket actions

If you want to integrate Trello with Bitbucket, you have a few actions here. You can open a pull request or set card members as reviewers.

> **Real-world example**
>
> When a card is added to the **Ready for QA** list, open a pull request with the first Bitbucket branch linked in the attachments.
>
> This is helpful if your team is using Bitbucket. You can go straight from an issue in Trello to PR in Bitbucket and even tie the two together!

Slack

The final tool that can be easily automated with internal automation options is Slack. Slack is an instant messaging and team collaboration tool that enables real-time communication, file sharing, and integration with other applications.

Many teams, such as my own, use Trello for project management and Slack for communication.

There's one action for Slack, which is posting a message. This is great for sending notifications to keep your team updated on tasks, even if they're not inside Trello.

Other tool actions   167

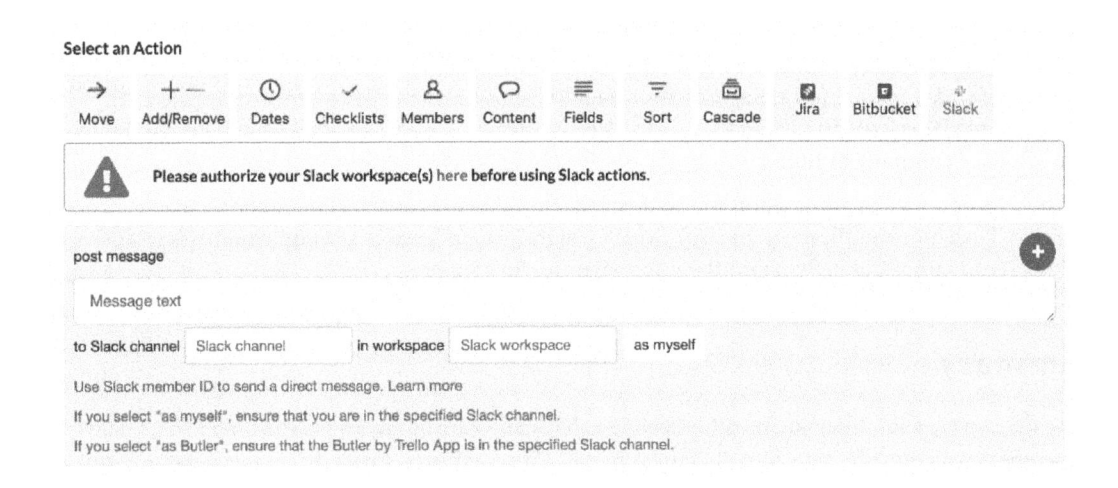

Figure 8.13 – Slack actions

You can craft a specific message that will send every time it's triggered, such as `a card was just added to your board!`, or you can make the message more specific by referencing automation variables from the trigger. For instance, you can say `{cardname} was added to your board`.

You'll need to specify what channel you want it posted in and what workspace if you have multiple connections. (Again, you could use automation variables here if you wanted to—for instance, if you have a custom field called `Comms` and a dropdown of Slack channels, you could set the channel on the card and then reference `{{%Comms}}` for the channel and it will grab that data from the card.)

You can even set the message to come from you or you can allow it to come from Butler* to make it clear that you're putting the robots to work!

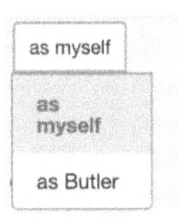

Figure 8.14 – Options for Slack message sender in automation

*Butler is the former name of the suite of automation tools in Trello.

> **Real-world example**
>
> When a card is moved to **Done**, post a message saying, `{cardname} was completed by {cardmemberfullnames}`. 🎉 `Well done team!` to Slack channel **team** in workspace **company** as Butler.
>
> This is another great automation to use if your team is having trouble remembering to check Trello. Push more notifications to Slack, which will make it easier to have your teammates jump into Trello rather than relying on them to remember to go there.

Summary

Wow, that covers a lot. I bet you're either feeling exhausted or inspired…or maybe both! That's okay! Remember—you don't have to actually remember all of these things. Instead, you just want to get to know the foundation so you can come back and find them when you wonder, "Is it possible for cards to be checklist items and stay in sync?" Spoiler, the answer is *yes*, if you pair together a lot of these actions.

In the next chapter, we're going to talk about how you can bring triggers and actions together to form workflows for your automation.

9
Building Automation with Triggers

We learned about triggers that can start automation workflows in *Chapter 6*. We then learned about actions that can follow those triggers to complete various tasks in our cards and boards in *Chapter 7* and *8*. Now it's time to bring everything together and see how we use both parts to make automation actually happen.

While rules are simple enough—pick a trigger and string as many actions together as you want—I haven't even shown you every single possible trigger you can use, because as you head to different sections of automation, new ones unlock! That's what this chapter is for: to show you how to put the rubber to the road and use the knowledge you have to build the workflows that you need to work efficiently in Trello.

Here's what you'll learn how to do in this chapter:

- Tie triggers and actions together with rules
- Use buttons on your boards to trigger automation workflows
- Add buttons to your cards for starting an automation sequence

No matter what you do in Trello, you're probably going to want to automate some of those activities, so this chapter is extremely important. If you're spending all your time organizing items in Trello, assigning members, creating due dates, and moving cards between lists… then you're not saving any time; you've just created another job for yourself to move things around in places!

You know how it's easier to rewrite your checklist on another piece of paper than it is to actually, you know, do the task? It's easy to feel productive when you're organizing your workflow, but anytime you spend doing that takes away from the time you could be spending doing your actual work.

That's why automation is essential—so you can make Trello *work for you*, rather than the other way around. If you've been thinking you don't need automation, this chapter will bring everything together to help you simplify your workflows so that all the tedious moving of cards and setting of fields doesn't detract you from the tasks at hand.

This is where it gets fun, so let's jump in!

Accessing Automation

If you're reading through the chapters in order, you've seen this already in the previous chapters, but here's a quick recap in case you're skipping around.

To access Trello's amazing automation features, click the **Automation** button in the top toolbar of any Trello board.

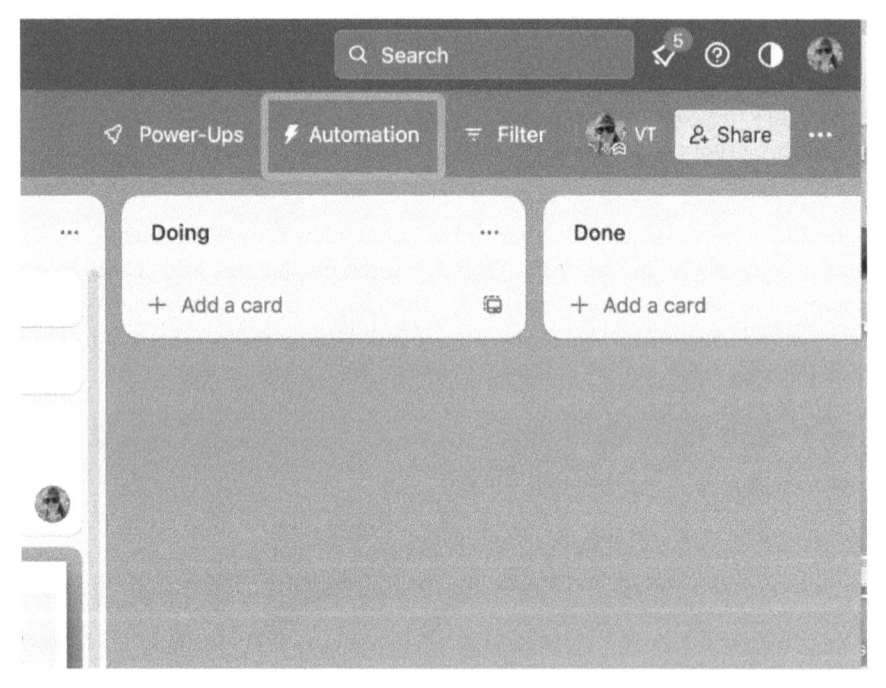

Figure 9.1 – Automation button in board toolbar

This opens a menu with a few of the types of automation. Click any of the options that appear to open a full modal with the entire set of automation categories on the left side.

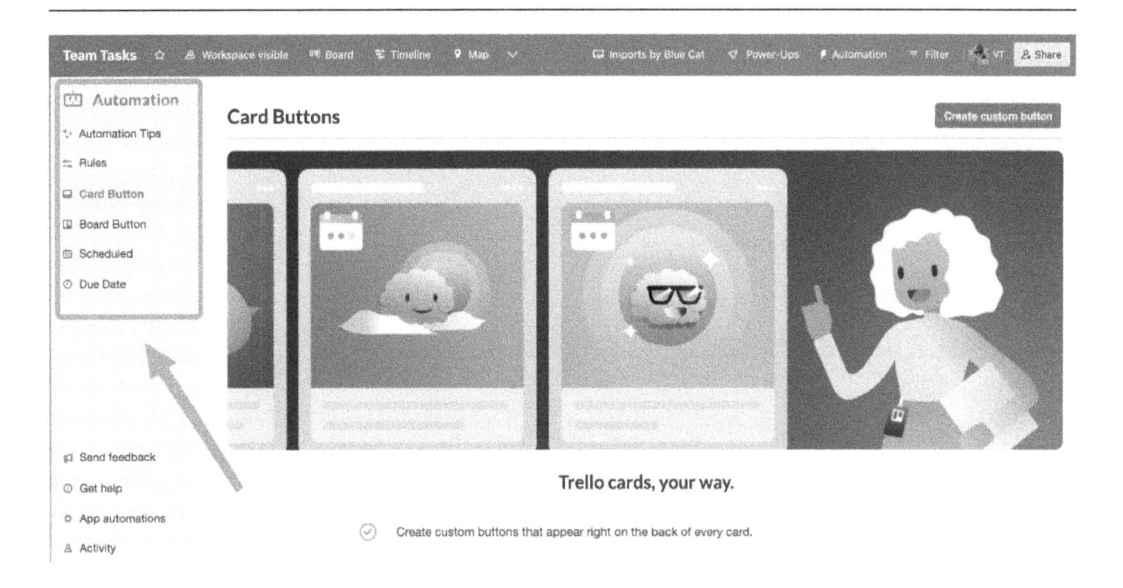

Figure 9.2 – Automation sections in the left-side panel

Throughout this chapter, we'll review each of those categories of automation. As you get to a section, click that category name in the left side panel so you can follow along. Let's start with the first one at the top, just after **Automation Tips**.

Rules

Rules simply combine the triggers and actions we've already discussed. *Chapter 6* showed the possible triggers that can be set for events. You'll find all of these triggers in this section, and you can then string to any number of actions.

Remember the examples such as "When a card is added to the board, set the due date to seven days from now"? You'd set that type of automation up here because it's watching for an activity that happens on the board (such as a new card being added).

Rules might be the most common type of automation—as you might expect, because I wrote an entire chapter about the triggers that live in the **Rules** section!

> **When to use rule automation**
>
> If you want automation to happen based on something else happening in a card or on the board, you'll probably want to use rules. Go back to the "When this happens… then that…" statements about your workflow. If your "When" has a specific action that occurs, such as a label being added, a card being moved, or a field being set or changed, then you'll want to use rules.
>
> If you can't find a trigger that suits the action you're thinking of, don't despair! You can still manually trigger the action with buttons or set it to happen at a regular occurrence with scheduled automation, but we're getting ahead of ourselves.

Creating a rule

Think about what you want to automate. You have all the triggers and all the actions at your disposal. Let's make a rule together.

We'll make a rule that every time a new card is added to the board, you are added to the card and a due date is set for seven days from now.

Sound like a lot? Don't worry, it's easy!

Make sure **Rules** is selected on the left-side panel of your automation modal, and then click **Create rule** in the top right.

Figure 9.3 – Create rule button

Then, you'll be prompted to add a trigger by using the **+ Add Trigger** button. Click that, and you'll see a menu appear with all the available triggers.

For our example, we want to trigger an action when a card is added to the board. Click the + button at the end of the row, next to the first trigger, to add it to our rule.

Rules | 173

Create a Rule

Select a Trigger

Card Move | Card Changes | Dates | Checklists | Card Content | Fields | Advanced

when a card ▼ is added to the board 👤

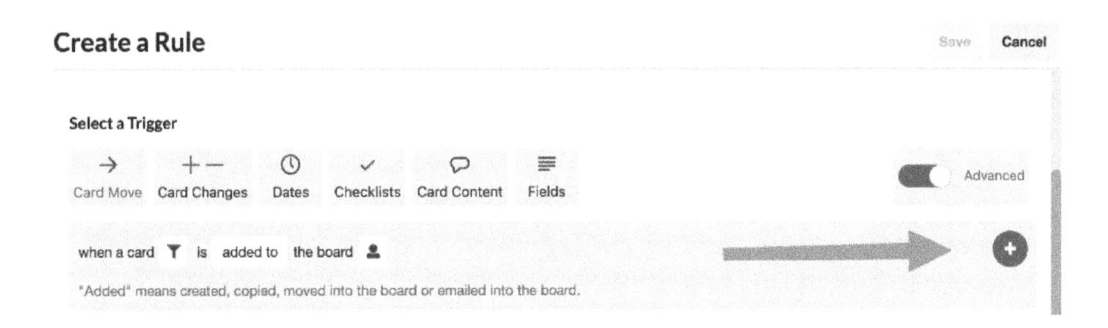

"Added" means created, copied, moved into the board or emailed into the board.

Figure 9.4 – Use the +/plus button to add a trigger or rule to the automation

If you want to be more specific and only trigger this rule on cards added to a specific list or that have certain labels or other attributes, click the filter icon. We won't need that for now, but just keep that in mind if you need it in the future.

Scroll up and you'll see that trigger has been added, and the sections below have changed to actions.

Create a Rule

Trigger

when a card is added to the board

Actions

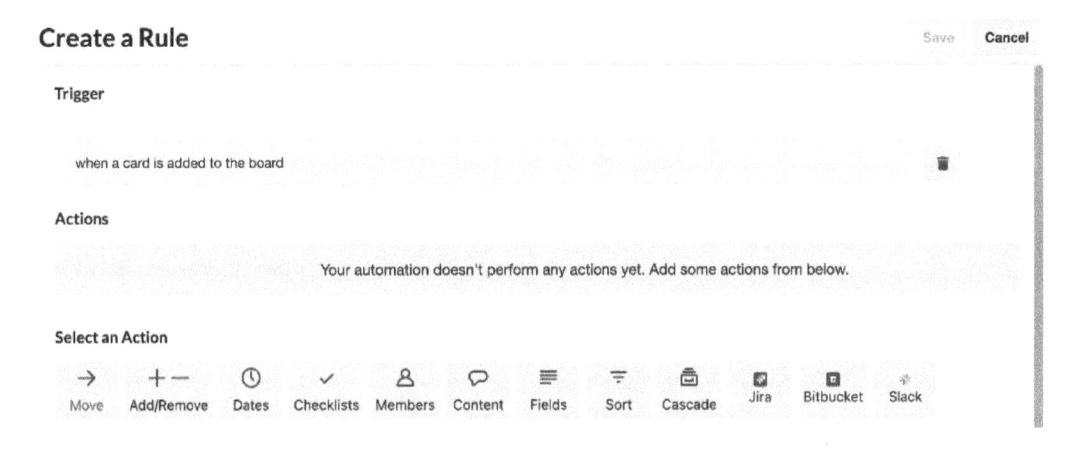

Your automation doesn't perform any actions yet. Add some actions from below.

Select an Action

Move | Add/Remove | Dates | Checklists | Members | Content | Fields | Sort | Cascade | Jira | Bitbucket | Slack

Figure 9.5 – Steps in automation

If you accidentally added the wrong trigger, click the trash icon next to the trigger to remove it and try again.

But ours is looking correct, so we're good to go. Now it's time to pick out our actions.

Let's start with the action for adding ourselves to the card. This way, we get notifications about anything that happens on that card, and it will show up in any filters we apply and any workspace views looking for cards that belong to us.

174 Building Automation with Triggers

To do this, click the **Members** tab, and select the very first action to join the card. Once again, click the + button at the end of the row.

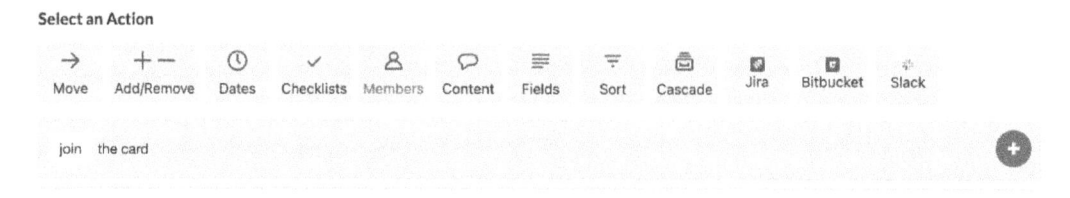

Figure 9.6 – Action for joining the card

Scroll up to confirm this is listed as an action, and then you can stop right there and save the rule, or you can keep going to add more to it. We're overachievers, so we'll keep going.

Head to the **Dates** tab. Look at the second action, which says **set due date now**. Click **now**, and you'll see that you have an assortment of options.

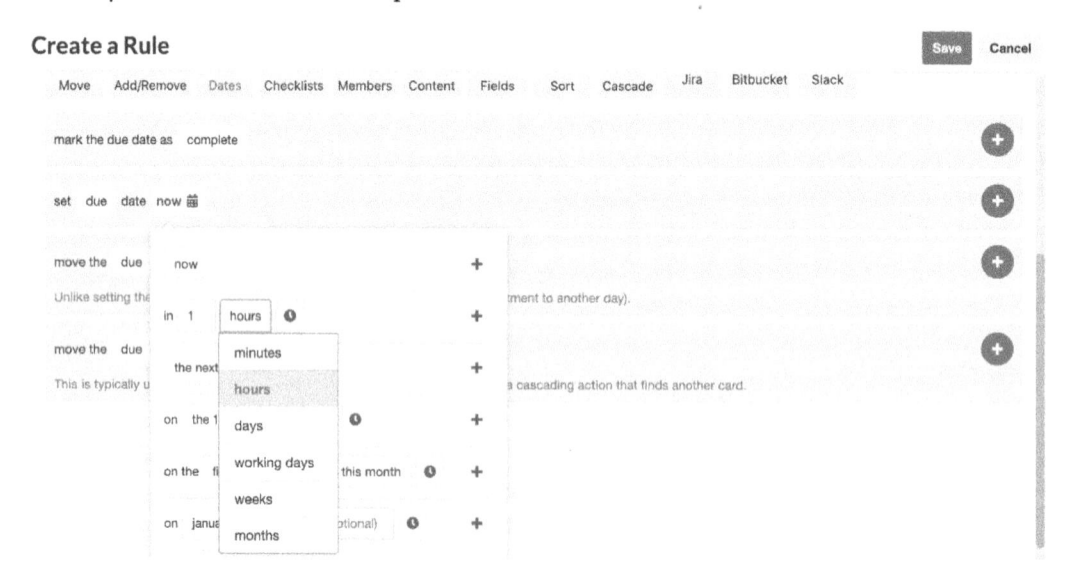

Figure 9.7 – Option for action to set due date on a card

We want to set the card to be due in seven days from the moment it's created; that way, we won't forget about it, and we'll be prompted to take some action on it within a week, even if the action is reassigned to a later date.

Click **hours** in the second row, and you can select another cadence. Change it to **weeks**, and now your card will be due one week (or seven days) from when it was created. Click the + button at the end of the row in the modal.

Finally, don't forget to click the + button at the very end of the row to add this action to the workflow!

Almost done, but there's one more step. Scroll up to confirm the rule looks the way you expect.

Figure 9.8 – Preview of triggers and actions

Make sure the trigger matches your expectations and isn't so broad that it will run often, but also not so narrow that it never runs. You might have to try this rule for a few days to figure it out. Also, make sure the actions are what you intended. When you're ready, click **Save** in the top-right corner.

Enjoy the confetti that sprays across your screen after you save a rule. 🎉 This is one of my favorite parts of Trello!

Testing your rule

You might think you're done at this point, and you could be. But this next step is what sets you apart from an automation rookie. You're going to test the rule because you're a professional and you don't want anything to happen inadvertently.

To test a rule, simply do the action that triggers it. For the rule we made, we triggered it to happen every time a card is added to a board. So, create a new card, and confirm that you're added to the board and the due date is set to one week from the current date.

176 Building Automation with Triggers

Go ahead and try it out. I'll wait.

Figure 9.9 – New fields set on automation when a card is added to a board

Yay, it worked! If it didn't work for you, make sure your rule looks like the screenshot in *Figure 9.8*. If it doesn't, that's an easy fix; you can edit existing rules.

Editing existing automations

If you want to make changes to the rules you've created, head back to the **Rules** section of **Automation** and you'll see a list of the rules you've created. Find the rule you created. If you just created it, it will be at the top.

Figure 9.10 – List of existing rules

Click the pencil icon above the rule, and you'll be back in the editor. You can remove actions and triggers and set them to be whatever you'd like them to be.

For this example, we built this automation to happen for every single card that is created on this board. But after a while, you might find that's happening too often, and you really only want it to happen to cards that are added to a specific list or have your name in the card description. This is where you can adjust the rule by using filters and changing the trigger and/or actions.

> **You can edit all automation this way**
> This isn't just for rules! Any other automation you create can be edited after it's been built by going to its menu from the left-side panel, then clicking the pencil icon next to the rule you want to edit.

Other automation settings

Let's take a moment to explore the other buttons near the pencil, as they each help you be as efficient as possible with your automation.

Figure 9.11 – Options for editing existing automations

The **tag icon** to the left of the pencil allows you to label automations and group them. Notice the filter button to the top right above all automations that says **All** at the top. Clicking that gives you options to show only automations that fit the specified criteria, such as a tag.

The **copy icon** on the automation menu is for copying. This duplicates a rule, which can be helpful if you need the same set of actions to occur with multiple triggers. As of 2022, there's no way to apply OR triggering, for example, "when a card is added to the **To Do** list" OR "when a card is added to the **Doing** list," so the copy button is helpful to duplicate a rule and just swap out the trigger.

The **trash icon** is for deleting a rule, but if you want to stop a rule from running, I recommend unchecking the **Enabled on this board** field below the rule. This stops the rule from being executed on the board but keeps it saved so you can turn it back on later.

Lastly, we have the **light bulb icon**. This opens a log so you can see when the rule was run and any errors that happened with it. I don't use this much, except for when something doesn't work the way I expected and I need to debug.

There is one more button at the end that is powerful – it allows you to take the current rule and add it to another board. This is incredibly useful if you have a series of boards that serve the same purpose and need to use similar automation.

I hope I get the chance to write an updated edition of the book one day and report that Trello has made it much easier to bulk apply automation to other boards or share automation with others for them to add to their own boards, but for now, this is the best way to do it. You can share libraries of commands, which share a group of tagged commands with others in your workspace, but this is only available for Trello Standard and Premium workspaces, and it only shares with folks within your workspace, so it's not helpful if you're building automations for other teams or clients. Also, buttons can't be shared, but the Trello docs state that they plan to include them at some point. See here for reference: `support.atlassian.com/trello/docs/working-with-command-libraries/`.

You could spend forever playing with rules, but it's time to move on to the next type of automation.

Button automation

Sometimes you can't quite put your finger on when you need to trigger automation. For instance, maybe it's not *every* time a card is moved to another list, just sometimes. Or maybe you don't always want to convert all the checklist items to cards, but you also don't want to have to manually do it for each item either.

This is where buttons come in handy. You can add buttons to your cards and your board so that you decide when the automation happens, and then Trello takes over from there.

> #### When to use button automation
> Use buttons when you have a series of actions you want to automate but there are no consistent criteria for when you need it triggered. Or use it when you just prefer to have the control of clicking a button to make a series of actions happen! I know some people who use card buttons to move a card to another list, even though you can drag it or select the **Move** action on a card.
>
> This can be useful if you're trying to limit the **command runs** you perform. All Trello plans have access to the same automation features, but each plan offers a different volume of the number of times an automation can run.
>
> Buttons also make a nice aesthetic on a card and can be great for instructing newbies on what needs to happen next on a card.

Trello offers two kinds of button automation: card and board. Let's start with the card button.

Card buttons

Card buttons are used for automation that you want to perform on, well, a card! This button will appear on every card on your board and will perform the associated actions on that specific card.

Let's make a card button that removes the members and due dates from a card, and then moves it to our **Backlog** list. This is helpful for "resetting" a card, which you might need to do if a task has been deprioritized or a project moves to another team.

Creating a card button

To create a card button, go to the **Card Button** section of the **Automation** menu on the left-side panel.

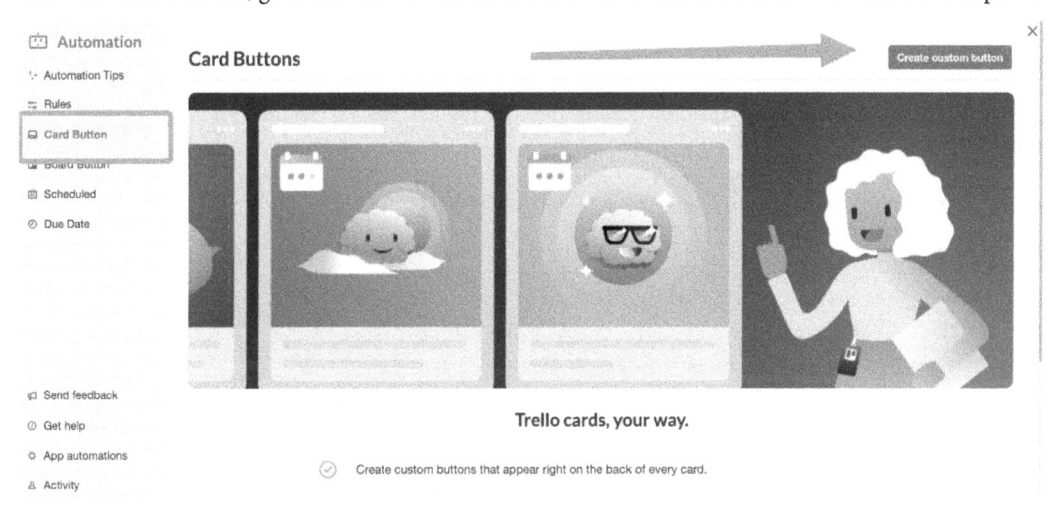

Figure 9.12 – Card Button automation section

From there, click the button that says **Create custom button** in the top-right corner.

You'll start off with the most fun and important task… coming up with a name for your button and selecting a related icon!

Figure 9.13 – Card button title and settings

I try to give the button a name that is clear and concise about what's happening. Good luck. This is the hardest part 😊 I'm going to call this one Reset card.

After you've picked a name and icon, confirm the options. By default, the buttons will be enabled, but you can turn that off so the button does not show up for everyone and needs to be added by individuals. You can also check the option to close the card once the actions have been completed. I tend to leave these settings as is. When I'm making a card button, I tend to want everyone on the board to access it, and sometimes I still want to do things on the card after the action has been completed. (Also, I can easily close a card by pressing the *esc* key on my keyboard.)

Next, you'll click + **Add Action** and then string together the actions we became so familiar with in *Chapter 7* and *8*.

Since we're removing info from the card, we'll go to the **Add/Remove** tab.

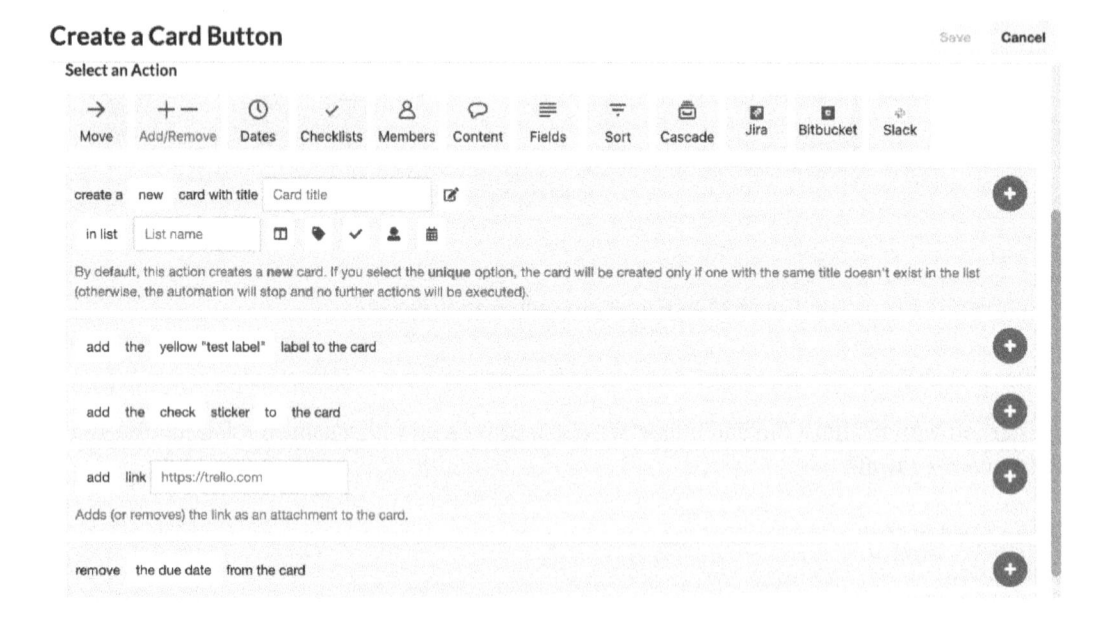

Figure 9.14 – Add/Remove actions available for card button

Select the + button at the end of the final row to add it to our list of actions. Scroll up and you'll see the action listed above the sections. Scroll back down and click **the due date** to see a dropdown appear with other options.

Figure 9.15 – Removal options for an action in a card button

Click **all the members** and then once again click the + button at the end of the row. Scroll up and you should see both actions above the tabs.

Let's add one more action that moves the card to the Backlog list. Click the **Move** tab. Click the **List name** field in the first action. Choose the **Backlog** list from the dropdown (or another list on your board that you'd prefer to move the card to).

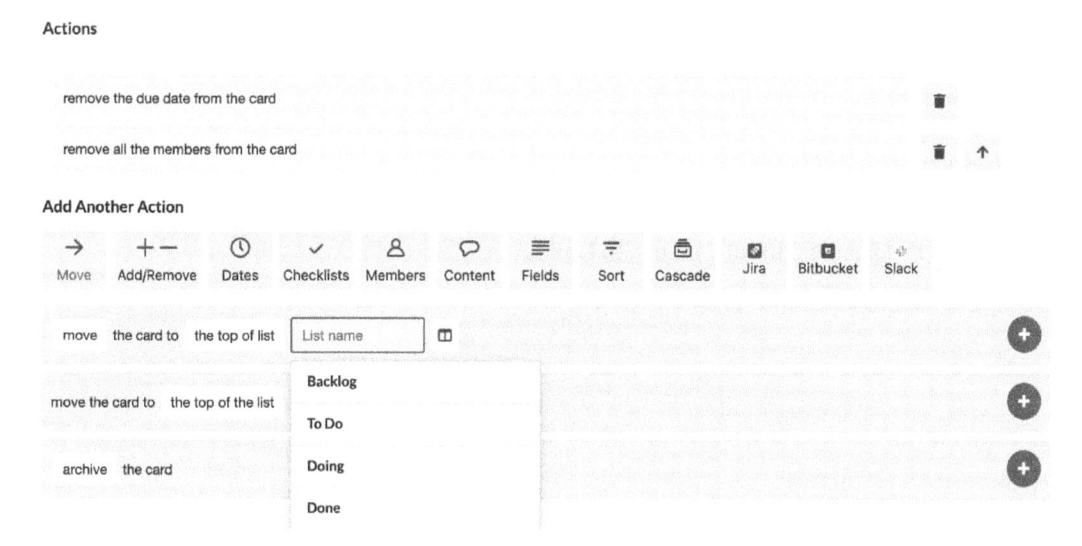

Figure 9.16 – Card button Move action options

Click the + button at the end of the row to add the action, and then scroll up to see all the actions. You did it!

Figure 9.17 – Preview of actions for card button

Click the **Save** button in the top right. Enjoy the magical confetti that sprays across your screen. Now, let's test the button!

Testing your card button

Head to a card on your board that has members and due dates. I'm going to use the card we automated with a rule that I added. It's currently on my **To Do** list.

Look at the new fancy button on our card!

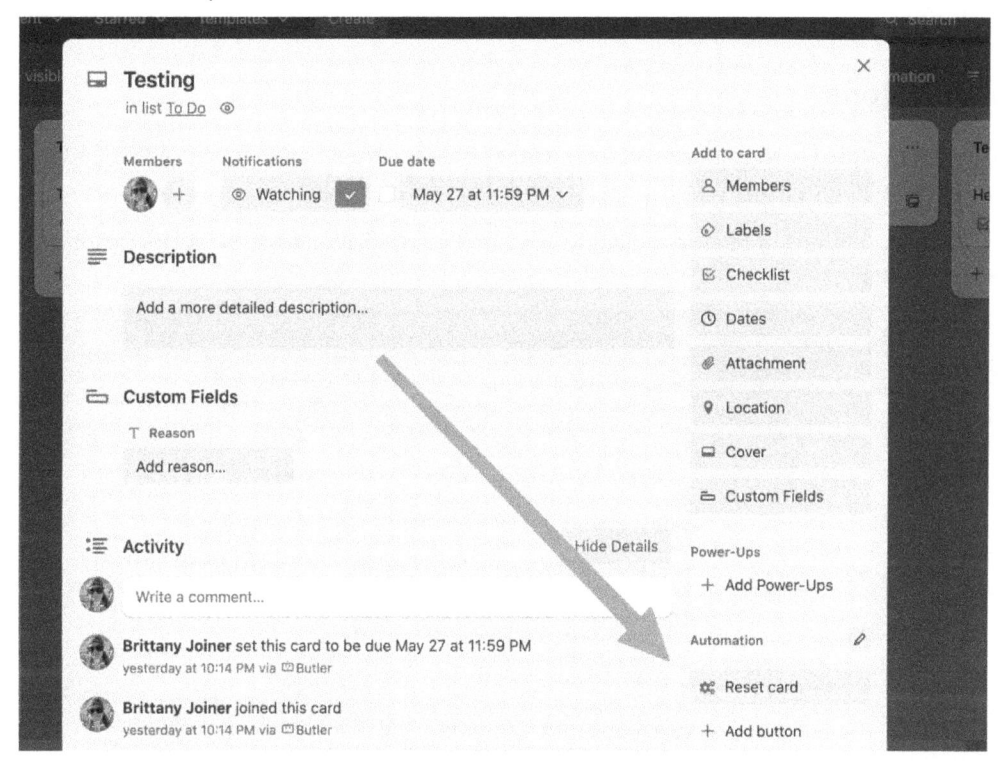

Figure 9.18 – Where to view card buttons on a card

Don't see it right away? Check on the right side below the **Add to card** and **Power-Ups** sections. Click the button and watch the members and due date be removed, and the card moves to the list specified in our rule.

A handy notification appears in the bottom right to let you know what is happening when you press the button. This is helpful for teammates, or even a refresher for yourself if you can't remember what you told a button to do.

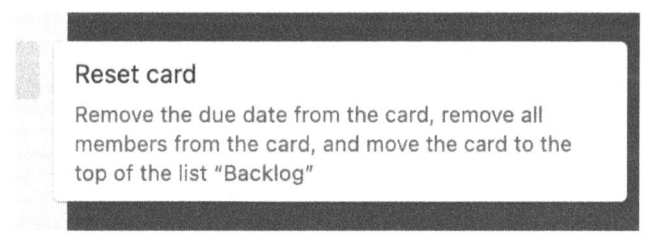

Figure 9.19 – Toast notification explaining the card button

You're a card button expert now! But that's not all the buttons Trello offers. You can also add buttons to your board.

Board buttons

Board buttons are used to trigger automation from the board level, not a specific card level. I find this particularly helpful for sorting lists or creating templated cards for requests.

You'll find these buttons in the top toolbar of your Trello board, alongside the **Automation** and **Power-Ups** buttons.

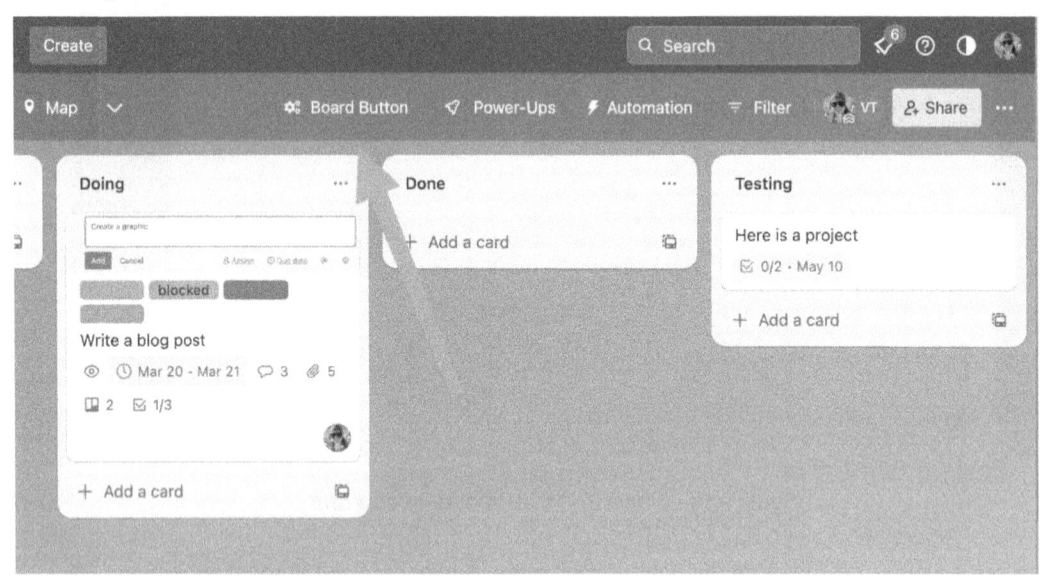

Figure 9.20 – Board button placement in the top toolbar

There are a few additional actions available in board buttons because of the nature of them being a board-level automation. For example, under the **Sort** section, there's an action for shuffling cards in a list you define.

The **Move Cards** section also offers some fun new actions to play with. You can build some useful workflows here, such as a button that plans your week for you by moving all the cards with certain criteria to your **This Week** list, or even randomly picking cards from your Backlog list to ensure you aren't just picking favorites.

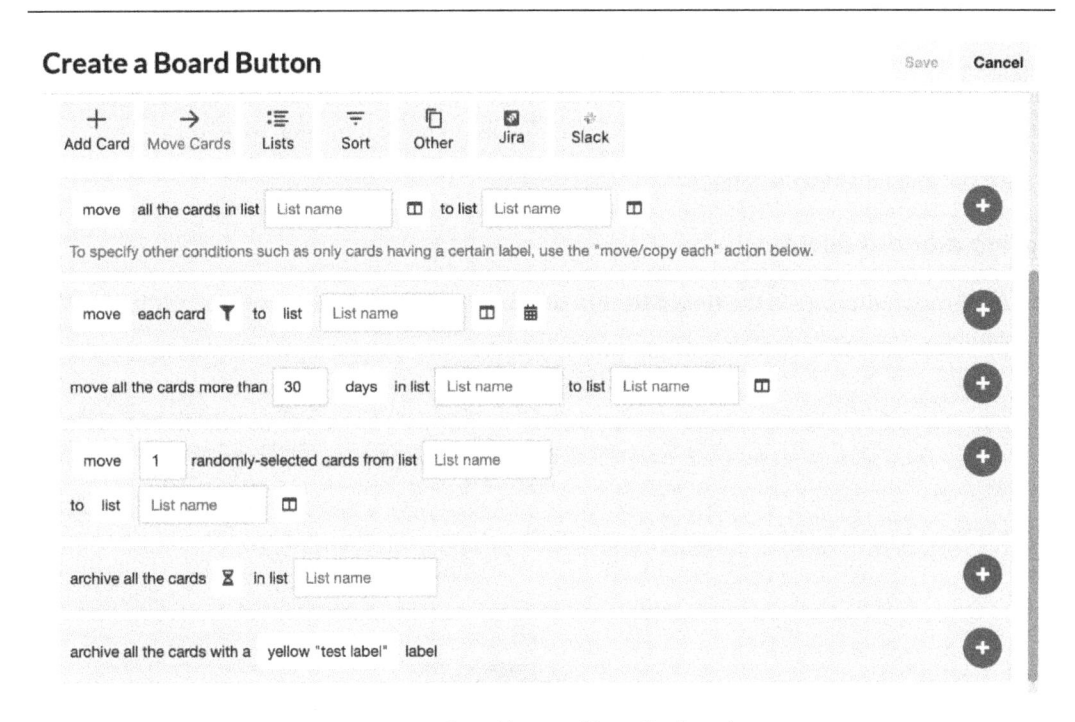

Figure 9.21 – Board button Move Cards actions

I like combining **Move Cards** actions with **Lists** actions for weekly board cleanup. Head to the **Lists** section and check out the actions there allowing you to create lists, rename them, move them, or even sort them!

Figure 9.22 – Board button list actions

These work great when combined with **automation variables**. For example, you can create a board button that creates a new list with the current week number, moves all your done cards to that list, and then randomly picks three cards from your Backlog list to move into your ToDo list.

Let's try it out and build that together!

Creating a board button

To create a board button, go to the **Board Button** section of the **Automation** menu on the left hand side panel.

Figure 9.23 – Board button automation section

Just like with card buttons, you get to start with the fun part of coming up with a name and icon. Then decide whether you want the button to be enabled by default. I tend to leave this as is, just like with cards. I'll call this button `New week`, and I'll use a calendar icon because that's fun.

Next, click **+ Add Action** to see all the actions available. First, we need to make a list of all the tasks we completed this week currently sitting on the **Done** list. I want this newest name to mention the week number so I can use lists to sort when tasks were completed. To do this, I'll use the `{weeknumber}` automation variable, which will dynamically name the list the current week number.

Figure 9.24 – Board button Lists action example

Depending on when you run this rule, you might want to use {lastweeknumber} if you are running this at the beginning of a week and want to create a list showing what you worked on the previous week. You can learn more about the options for automation variables in the Trello documentation: support.atlassian.com/trello/docs/butler-variables/.

Click the icon with numbers and arrows to choose where this newly created list will be placed. I want it to go to the end of the board on the far right, so I'll specify that by selecting the + icon next to **in the bottom position**.

Figure 9.25 – Card button creates list options

Finally, click the + icon at the end of the row to add the action to the workflow. Next, head to the **Move Cards** section, because we want to move all the cards in the **Done** list to the newly created list. To do this, we'll use the very first action. Click the first **List name** field to select the **Done** list (or whatever list you define as your "completed" list in your board).

In the second list field, type {weeknumber}, or {lastweeknumber} if you used that in the earlier rule. This should be the same as the new list you created.

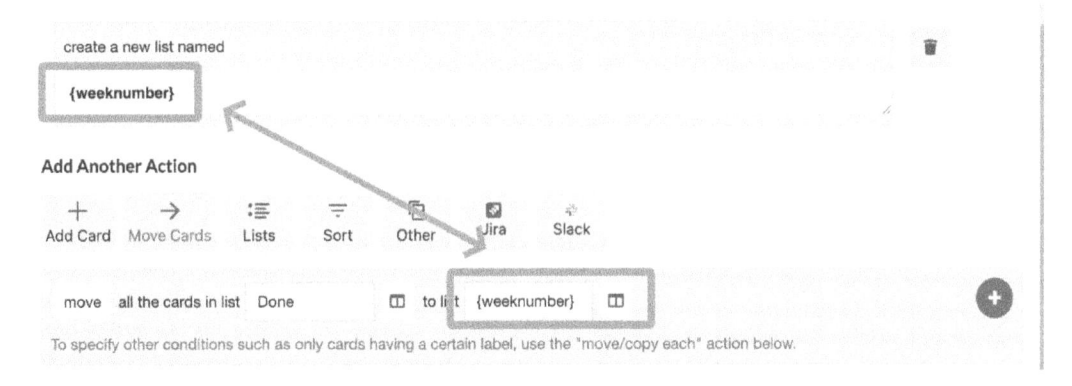

Figure 9.26 – Variables for new list and moving cards to list should match

Click the + button at the end of the row to add the action to your workflow.

The hard part is done! Let's just add one more action for picking cards from our Backlog list. Scroll down to the **move 1 randomly-selected cards from list** rule. I like to use the randomly selected one sometimes because I struggle with prioritizing and I tend to forget about cards in my Backlog. So, assuming I have a list of things with equal importance, this is a fun way to make Trello decide which things I should work on and save my brain power for something else.

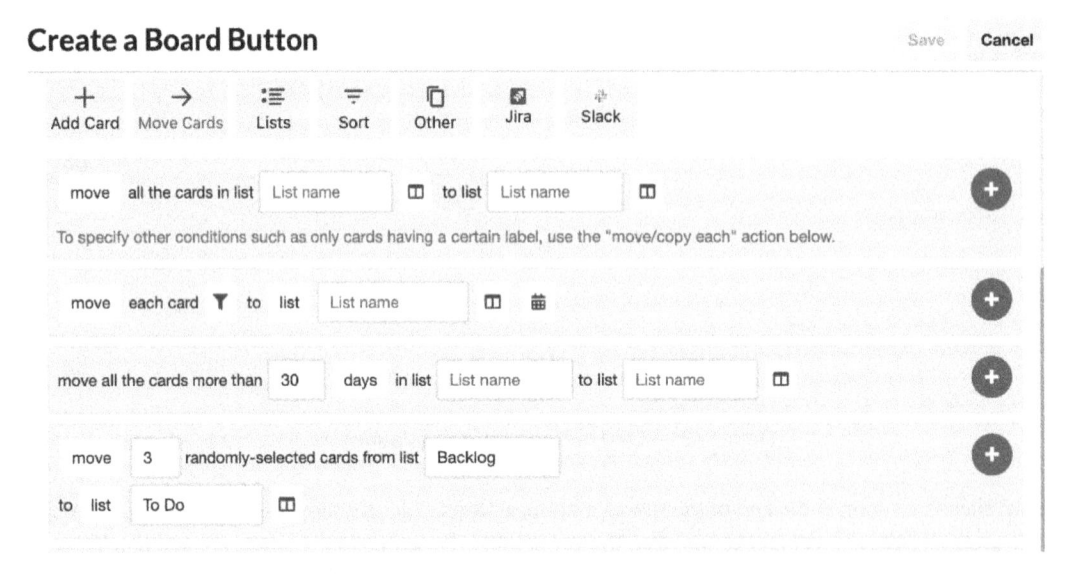

Figure 9.27 – Board button move random cards action

Change the **1** to a **3** and click the first **List name** field to select your Backlog list. Next, click the second **List name** field to choose the **To Do** list that you want to move the cards to. If you want these cards moved to the top of the list (or the bottom), clicking the **list** button before the second **List name** field opens a dropdown to choose the placement.

Click the + button at the end of the row and scroll up to confirm you have all your actions. It should look like this.

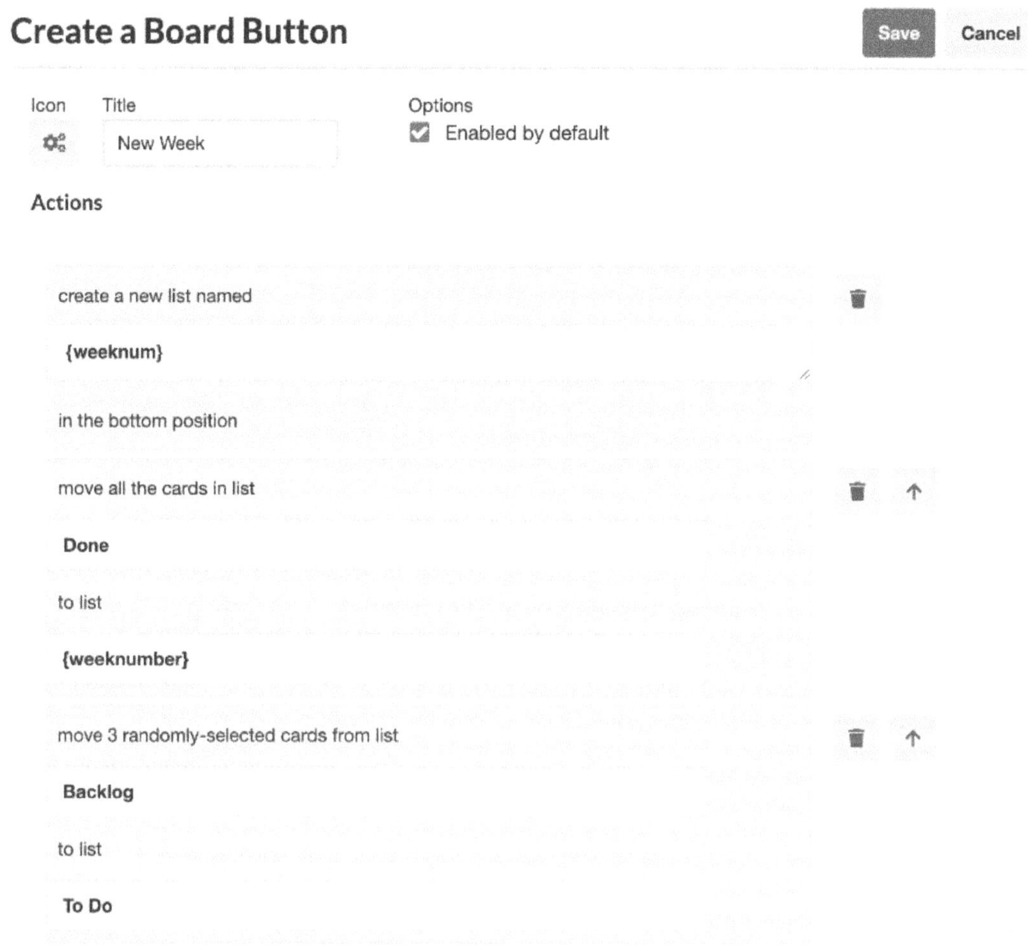

Create a Board Button

Icon **Title**
⚙ New Week

Options
☑ Enabled by default

Actions

create a new list named

{weeknum}

in the bottom position

move all the cards in list

Done

to list

{weeknumber}

move 3 randomly-selected cards from list

Backlog

to list

To Do

Figure 9.28 – Card button create list options

Now click the **Save** button in the top right and let's go try out our button!

Testing your board button

After saving your button, close out of the **Automation** modal and you'll see your new button above the lists in your board's toolbar.

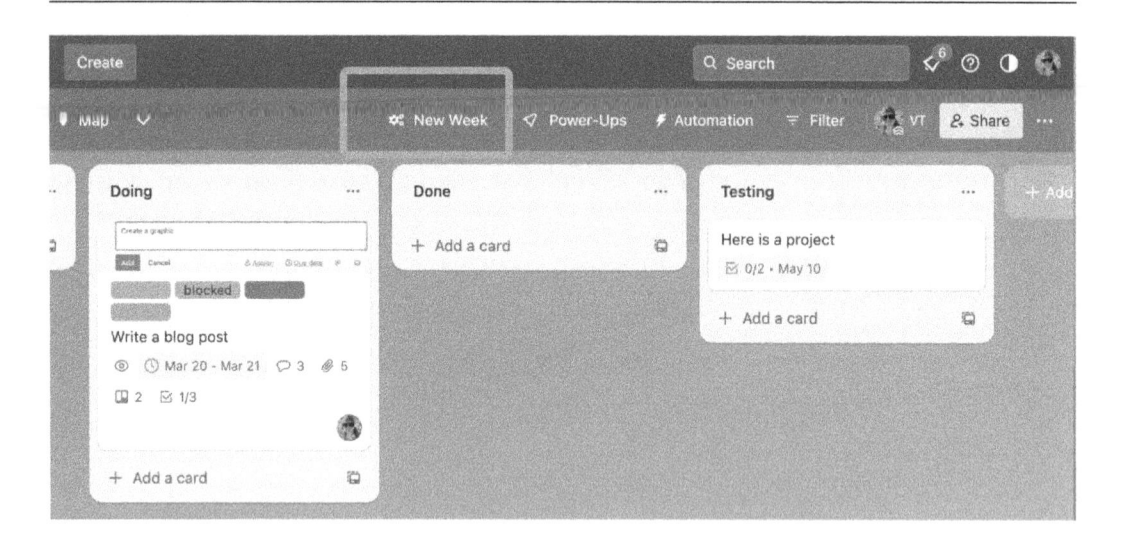

Figure 9.29 – Newly created button appearing in board toolbar

Click the **New Week** button and watch the magic happen! A notification bar appears at the bottom of the screen to show the automation is running.

Figure 9.30 – Lower-banner notification to show progress during Board Button runs

When it's finished, you'll be able to click to see the details. I don't do this every time, but it's helpful for debugging in case anything didn't work as expected.

Now your week is organized and planned, with a click! Isn't that magical? But what if we could do all of this… without even a click? I feel like that's a great segue to talk about scheduled automation.

Summary

Wow, I hope you're treating yourself to a relaxing beverage of your choice after making it through this chapter. We covered so much ground, and if you followed along with me, you built several automations for your workflows that will help you surface important and urgent tasks, organize and prepare your work for the next week, and clean up cards for you.

There are a few more triggers that I want to show you, so let's head to the next chapter to talk about date-based automation in Trello.

10
Date-Based Automation

While you can trigger automations to occur when certain things happen with triggers, and you can manually make them happen with buttons, there are two other ways you can trigger automations, both of which are related to dates. We'll dive into how they work in this chapter.

Here's what you'll learn in this chapter:

- Automation for creating a new card each day
- Testing your date automations
- Automation for joining a card when it's due

Just like in the other chapters, you may not use these every day, so there's no need to obsess over every detail if this is your first time learning about them. Get comfortable with what's available and come back to re-read this chapter whenever you want to dive deeper into how to set these up.

Scheduled automation

So, you get it – there's a lot you can do with Trello automation, and buttons are great for when you want to manually trigger something. But what about the trigger of time?

Scheduled automation is Trello's version of telling specific actions to happen at a recurring interval, such as daily, weekly, monthly… or just about any time you can think of.

> **When to use scheduled automation**
> Use scheduled automation when you have processes that you do every day or week, such as creating daily reminder cards or moving cards between lists at the start or end of a week. If you explain your workflow in Trello and catch yourself saying "Every Monday morning, I…," then that's a cue that you should probably automate it with scheduled automation!

192   Date-Based Automation

Because of the nature of scheduled automation, we need more triggers than we've seen so far. Let's see what we can find. From the **Automation** modal, make sure you're on the **Scheduled** section in the left-hand side panel:

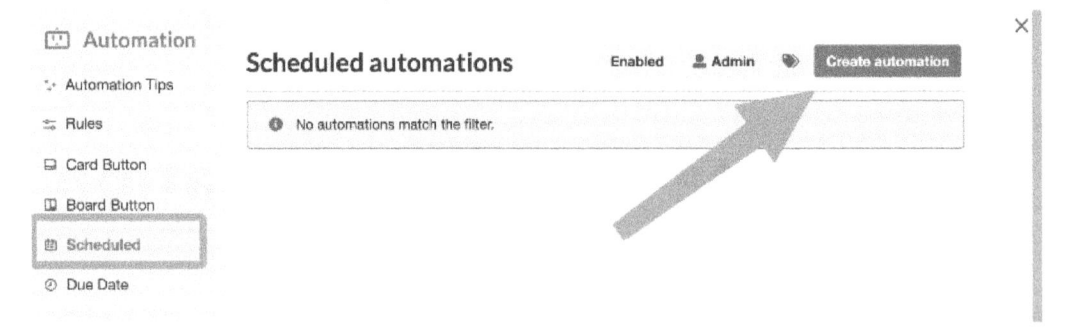

Figure 10.1 – The Scheduled automations section

Click the **Create automation** button in the top right, then click **+ Add Trigger**.

You might think you've seen all of this before, but lo and behold, new trigger options will appear!

New triggers for schedule automation

Because we are in the **Scheduled** section, we get some special triggers. These are different than the ones we reviewed in *Chapter 6*:

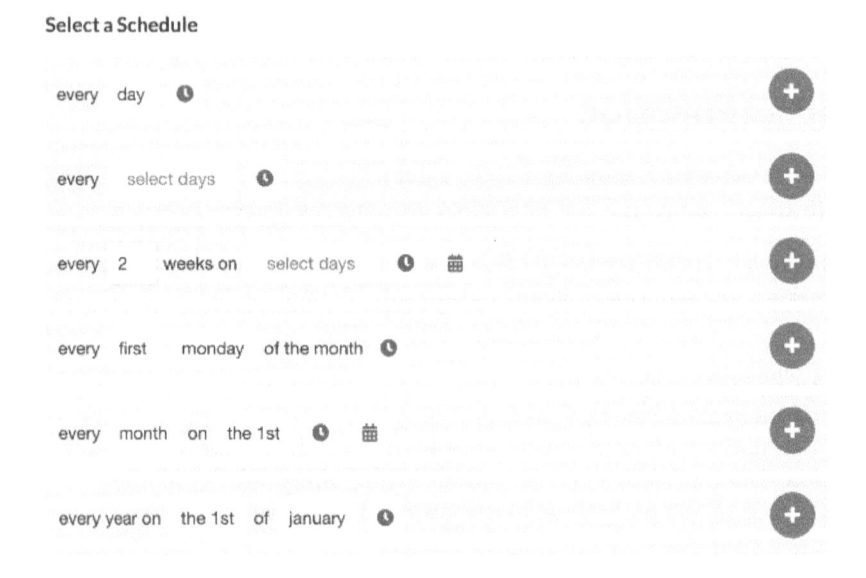

Figure 10.2 – Scheduled automations trigger options

You get the idea – there's a variety of customizations you can make with each one; just click through the options and explore them. One of my favorite parts about this kind of automation is that you can set something to happen every day, or every weekday, which is helpful if you want to do things such as assign leads or create recurring cards for reminders to do things such as "clear out work email inbox" on every day except weekends:

Select a Schedule

every day

every day
       weekday

every 2 weeks on select days

Figure 10.3 – Every day/weekday trigger options

You can also select multiple days by choosing every Monday, Wednesday, and Friday in one trigger, rather than needing to create three separate rules for each day:

every monday ✖ wednesday ✖ friday ✖

every tuesday
       thursday

every saturday
       sunday

Figure 10.4 – Multi-day trigger option

The **clock** icon after each trigger is used to specify a time if needed. After setting some actions, you can use the **calendar** icon to choose the date the automation will start. For instance, you can create an automation that happens every two weeks starting next week (rather than waiting two weeks from when you trigger it).

Creating a scheduled automation

While we're in the **Scheduled** section, let's create an automation that cleans up our week for us every Saturday so that when we come to work on Monday morning, everything is ready to go. This automation has the same actions we just built for our Board Button, but we'll use a scheduled trigger to make it happen so that we don't have to click anything.

Choose **saturday** from the dropdown for the **every select days trigger**:

Figure 10.5 – Selecting a day for recurring automation

After choosing **saturday**, click the + button at the end of the row.

You will see all the actions we had in the Board Button automation, so let's grab the same actions we used in our last rule. We'll add a **Lists** action for creating a list with {weeknumber} added to the bottom of the board and then a **Move Cards** action to move all the cards in the **Done** list to the newly created {weeknumber} list. Finally, we'll add another action to move three randomly selected cards from the **Backlog** list to the **To Do** list.

If you're following along, your scheduled rule should look like this:

Create a scheduled automation

Trigger

every saturday

Actions

create a new list named

{weeknumber}

in the bottom position

move all the cards in list

Done

to list

{weeknumber}

move 3 randomly-selected cards from list

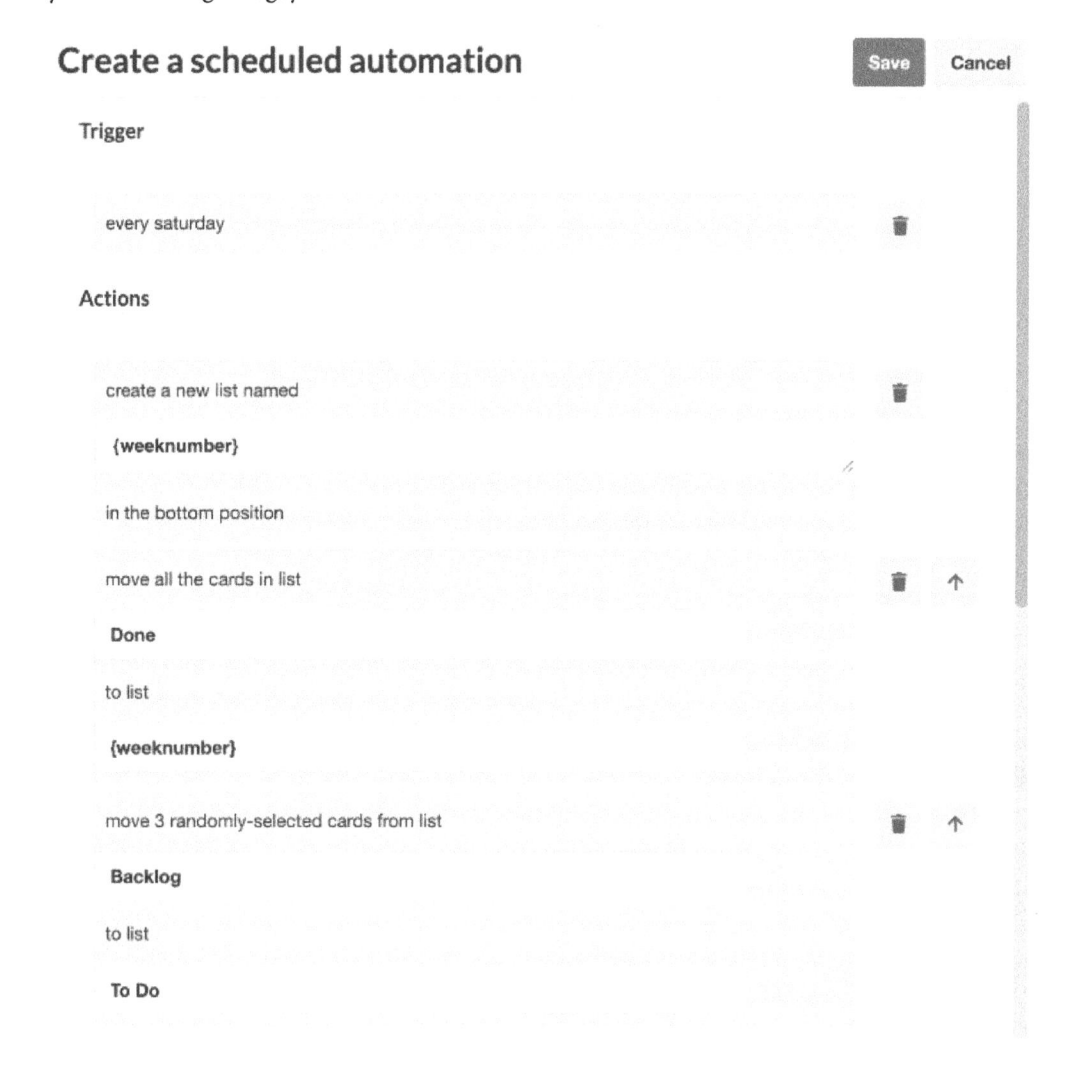

Backlog

to list

To Do

Figure 10.6 – Preview of a scheduled trigger and its actions

Click **Save** in the top-right corner to get that dopamine hit from the confetti spraying across your screen and the satisfaction of knowing that you don't even have to push a button to have your week set up for you.

Testing your scheduled automation

You might be wondering how you'll test out your new rule since you can't just enforce your trigger and suddenly make it Saturday (although that would be nice).

Thankfully, Trello has a way for you to pretend it's Saturday, or whatever day/time you have set up in your trigger:

Figure 10.7 – Rocketship icon for testing scheduled automations

From the **Scheduled automations** menu, find the rule you want to test; you'll see a new icon above your rule! Upon clicking the rocketship icon, Trello will execute your actions as if the day/time trigger has just happened, allowing you to be sure the desired actions take place and you're happy with your rule.

If you're not, click the pencil icon and tweak your rule until it does what you'd like. Sometimes, it takes some experimentation – no matter how good you are at Trello automation!

There's one more set of special triggers that we need to discuss before I can present you with your Ph.D. in Trello automation. Let's talk about **Due Date** automation since it's well *overdue*. 😄

Due date automation

We've almost covered all the ground regarding Trello automation, but if you've been following along, you might have noticed there's one more section we haven't discussed yet. Let's talk about **Due date** automation.

> **When to use Due date automation**
>
> You'll use **Due date** automation if you have specific actions that you need to happen concerning a card that's due. If you felt that the date triggers in **Rules** were pretty limited, you'll be happy to know you have some additional triggers here. The difference is that these relate more to monitoring the relation of the current day to a due date, whereas **Rules** focus more on changes in the fields, regardless of their relation to the current scope of time.

Because we need to automate based on time, some new triggers are available. Let's explore them!

Start by making sure you're in the **Due Date** section of the **Automation** modal:

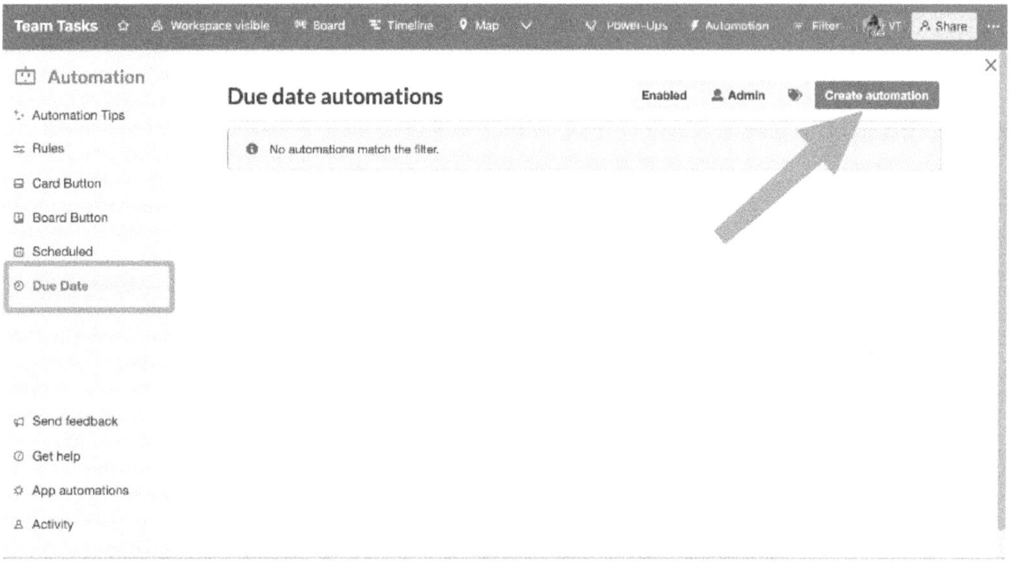

Figure 10.8 – The Due date automations section

Click the **Create automation** button in the top right, then click **+ Add Trigger**. Once again, we have a whole new world of trigger options to explore.

New triggers for Due date automation

These new triggers all focus on monitoring the due dates of cards and the current day/time's relation to that.

A banner inside this section offers some sage advice that I'll highlight as well because it's important to know. If you apply a new automation for moving all cards due in the next seven days to the **This Week** list, for example, you might be wondering why your cards didn't move after you saved them. That's because these automations *do not work retroactively* and will not find cards that are due within seven days and then move them. The automation will look for the current date and any cards due today, plus seven days after, for each day. So, if you don't see your cards move suddenly, that doesn't mean your automation is broken. It just means you'll need to manually find those cards and move them.

> **Pro tip – use a Board Button for any cards you want to retroactively apply this rule to**
> You can use a board button to move any card with a due date in the next seven days to a specific list. This means you can still use automation and don't have to do anything manually!

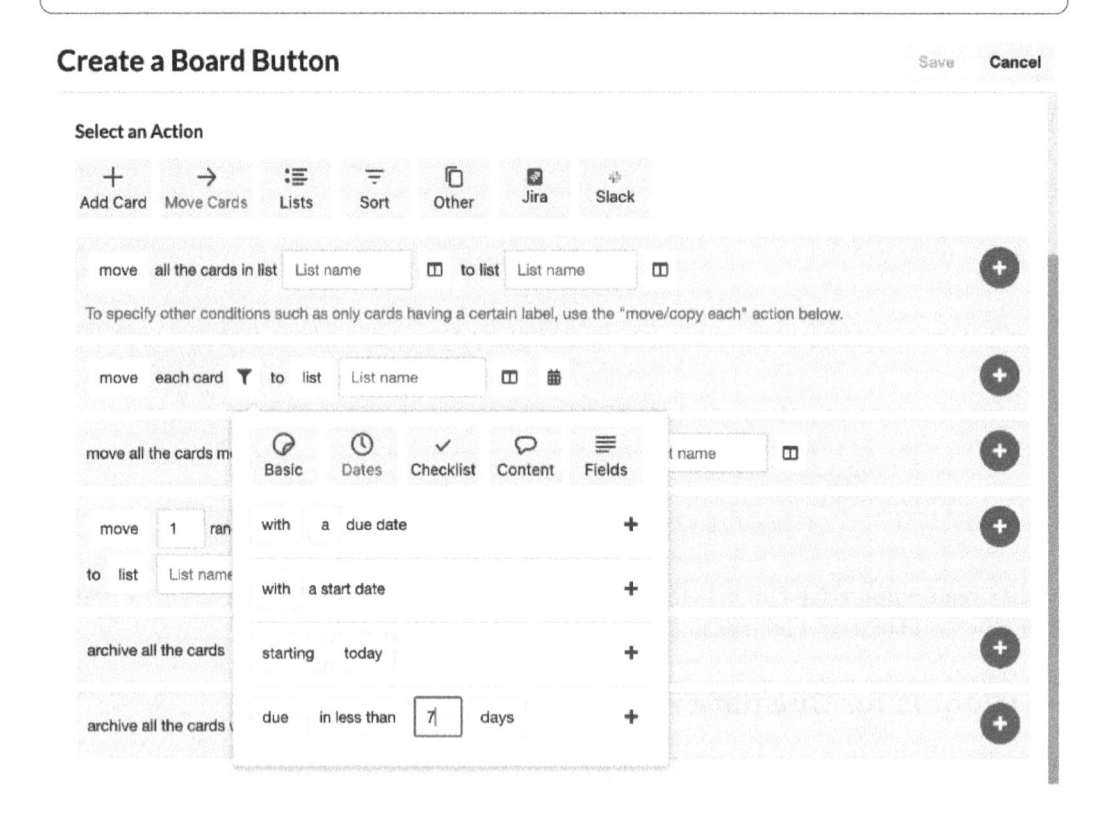

Figure 10.9 – Action to retroactively move cards with due dates

Now that we've got that warning out of the way, let's talk about the actions that are available to us:

Due date automation   199

Create a due date automation   Save   Cancel

Trigger

Your automation doesn't have a trigger yet. Select a trigger for the automation below.

> ⚠ **Due date triggers are not retroactive.**
> For example, if you enter an automation that says *2 days before a card is due, …*, this will not trigger for cards that are already due in 2 days or less.
> It will trigger the moment a card becomes due in 2 days through the passage of time, starting from the moment the automation is entered.

Select a Due Date Trigger

                                                                                    Advanced

the moment   a card   ▼   is due   ➕

2   days   before   a card   ▼   is due 🕐   ➕

on the   monday   before   a card   ▼   is due 🕐   ➕

Figure 10.10 – Triggers for due date automation

These triggers do exactly what their names suggest. You can set a trigger for the moment a card is due or the beginning of the day it's due. Just like with scheduled automations, you can reference working days. Click on **days** in the **2 days before a card is due** trigger to see your options. Here, you can choose from **days**, **working days**, or **hours**. Unfortunately, working hours are not an option:

2   days   before   a card   ▼   is due 🕐

    days
on the
    working days
    hours

Figure 10.11 – Options for a due date trigger

You can also click **before** in some triggers to see more options, such as **after**, **of the week**, and **of the week before**, which helps you prioritize cards for each day of the week:

Figure 10.12 – Options for customizing days relative to the due date

I prefer to use these triggers for flagging cards that are due soon to help me make sure I don't miss anything important, as well as to escalate cards that are past due.

Creating a due date automation

If you want to see all the cards that are due for the current week each Monday morning, you can create an automation that assigns you cards the Monday of the week they're due if they have a **p1** label. Let's walk through how to do that.

From the **Select a Due Date trigger** section, go to the trigger that starts with **on the monday before**. Click **before** to open a dropdown and select **the week**. Click the **filter** icon to show more advanced options:

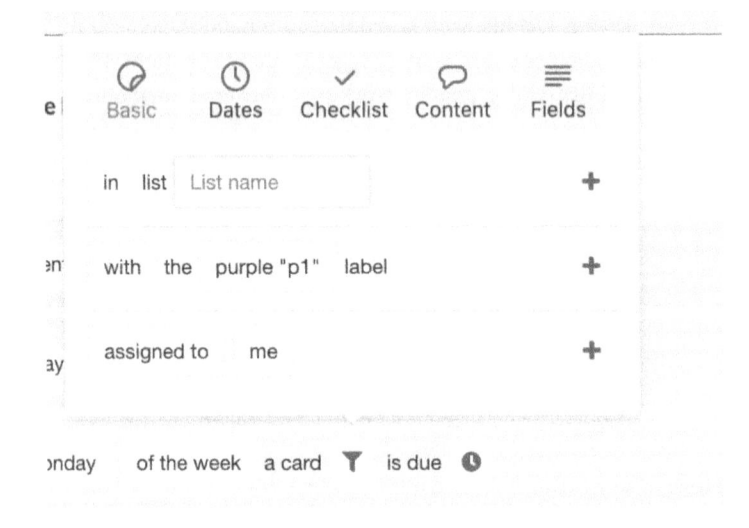

Figure 10.13 – Filter options for narrowing trigger criteria

This is where we'll choose to filter with cards that have the purple **p1** label. Click the + icon next to the label filter, then click the + button at the end of the row to add the whole trigger to your automation.

Next, go to the **Members** section of **Actions** and click the + icon at the end of the row for the **join the card** rule.

You can add more actions to this, such as one for sending you an email reminder with details of the card, updating a custom field to show that you've got it queued up for the week, editing the description with templated information about the project, or adding a checklist for a development process.

The options are endless! When you've got everything you need, scroll up to ensure the automation looks like you expect. It should look like this if you have stuck with our example and not added any additional actions:

Figure 10.14 – Previewing a trigger and its actions

After clicking the **Save** button in the top-right corner, you'll be ready to roll. That confetti spraying across the screen never gets old, does it!?

Testing a due date automation

The best way to test a **due date** automation is to create or find an existing card and set a due date that would fall within the trigger criteria. For instance, if you choose the moment a card is due, you can set the due date to be 1 minute from the current time and see if your automation runs.

If you choose to automate the **day of** or **monday before** trigger, this is a bit tricker. What I prefer to do is create my actions as a board button and confirm that they work as desired there. If the actions do what I expect, I can build a **due date** automation and trust it to work in the same way. Trello has never let me down when it comes to telling me when a card is due, so I'll trust that these triggers will keep working!

You're pretty much a **due date** automation wizard at this point, so I hope you keep practicing and find tons of uses for these in your workflows.

Summary

You're basically a Trello wizard at this point! You can automate so many things, and you can make them happen at specific intervals or prioritize automations when you need them to happen based on due dates.

Keep playing around with automation – this is what lets you build applications for your workflows inside Trello, with no code needed. I've worked with several clients who can take automation principles inside Trello and create systems that manage their companies' operations virtually on autopilot.

You can build anything you need! If you're ever stuck or need help, reach out in the *Trello* section of the Atlassian Community: `community.atlassian.com/t5/Trello/ct-p/trello`. In the next chapter, we'll talk about expanding the wonderful world of Trello with Power-Ups!

Part 3 – Power Up Your Boards

In the final part, we'll discuss add-ons for your Trello boards called Power-Ups. You'll learn about some of the most common ones that cover a variety of use cases, and we'll help you make your boards work as effectively as possible. We'll even discuss reporting Power-Ups to help you make sense of the data in your Trello boards so that you have everything you need to be successful!

This part has the following chapters:

- Chapter 11, Power-Ups Built by Trello
- Chapter 12, General-Use Power-Ups
- Chapter 13, Syncing Info between Boards and Tools
- Chapter 14, Reporting in Trello

11
Power-Ups Built by Trello

At this point, we've covered most of the default functionality of Trello, which is already pretty powerful. But this is just the core of Trello! Your boards can go to the next level when you layer add-ons, called Power-Ups.

In this chapter, we'll talk about what Power-Ups are and how they can supercharge your board. We'll review some specific Power-Ups Trello has made that add amazing functionality to your board for free. You'll be able to do things such as the following:

- Integrate Trello with other apps you use every day, such as Slack
- Visually indicate how many cards are in a list and change the color if it's more than a set amount
- Create and display a how-to guide your colleagues can read when they visit your board
- Allow board members, or even non-board members, to vote on cards and then sort those cards by the most votes

We'll also discuss a few other Trello-made Power-Ups that you might be interested in. Before we dive into specifics, we need to talk about what Power-Ups are and where to find them.

> **The best Power-ups are what works best for you**
>
> Over the next couple of chapters, we'll be discussing Power-Ups. People always ask: "What are the best Power-Ups to use?" If you've come here hoping I'll answer that question for you, I hate to disappoint, but that's something that only you or someone who deeply knows your workflows can best answer.
>
> While the number of boards a Power-Up has been added to is a way to see which ones are most popular (or more often, which ones have been around longer), there is no ideal Power-Up toolbox set for every single person. Use these chapters as an opportunity to get familiar with searching for and interacting with Power-Ups and understanding what they're capable of. Then, use them if they work for you, or explore the Power-Up directory to see whether there's anything better that might fit your workflow.

What are Power-Ups?

Power-Ups are add-ons that provide more functionality or styling to boards and cards. They enhance productivity, collaboration, and organization by adding new features or fields, or aggregating information from other sources. There are over 300 Power-Ups available, so no matter what you'd like to do in Trello, you can probably find a Power-Up to help.

Many people use Power-Ups to integrate Trello with other apps they use, such as Slack or GitHub. Power-Ups offer a seamless way to sync information without needing to jump between multiple places. You'll see more examples of this in the *Power-Ups for Integrations* section.

Aside from integrating with other tools, people use Power-Ups when they're looking for specific features they want in their boards that they can't natively do. For example, if you're doing reporting or time tracking, you'll find Power-Ups that can help Trello work even better for your use case.

Power-Ups are free to add to your board, and you can add as many as you like. But for some third-party Power-Ups (ones not made by Trello), you'll be charged a fee by the developer. These prices can vary from a couple of dollars a year to $20 a month (or more in some cases). Most Power-Ups offer a free trial period so you can make sure it's what you want before you're asked to pay for it. And don't worry—you're never charged by merely adding them to your board. Every Power-Up is slightly different, but for paid Power-Ups, you'll be asked to create an account and select a subscription.

Power-Ups can be added to a board by any member of the board and can be customized to suit the specific needs of the board or project. Now let's talk about where to find Power-Ups and how to add them to your board.

Accessing Power-Ups

To access Power-Ups, click the **Power-Ups** button in the top toolbar of any Trello board.

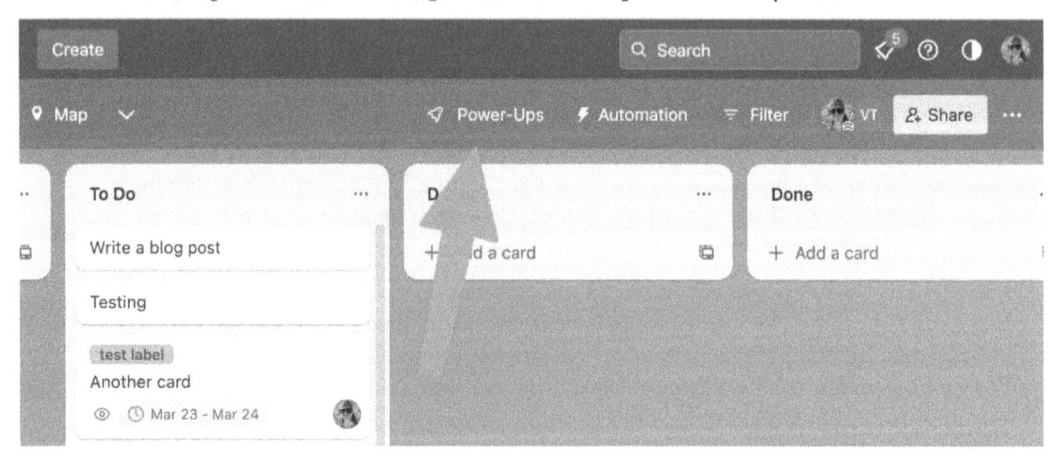

Figure 11.1 – Power-Ups board button

If you have any Power-Ups already added to the board, you'll see them appear in a list with the choice to toggle board button displays, as well as accessing the Power-Up settings. If you haven't added any yet, you'll see an inspiring graphic and an **Add Power-Ups** button.

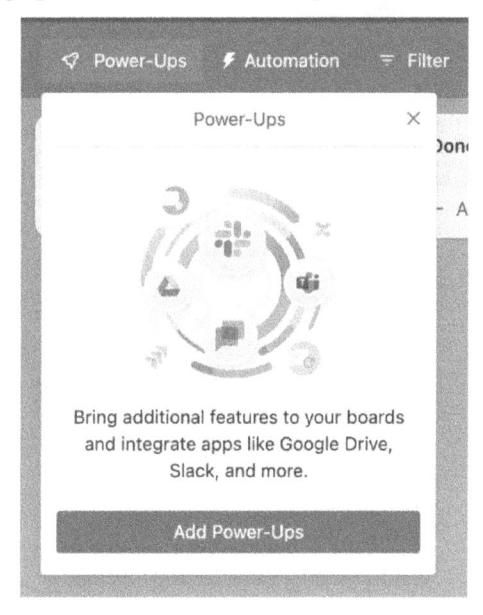

Figure 11.2 – Power-Up modal

Click the button to go to the directory and discover all the Power-Ups you can add to your boards.

I don't recommend going in here and just adding Power-Ups at random. That can get overwhelming, as there are many to choose from! Just like with automation, there is such a thing as too much of a good thing. Having dozens of Power-Ups on your board will slow down performance and add distractions, preventing folks from effectively using your board.

Instead, I recommend looking around to see the options available and then thinking about what makes the most sense in your workflow.

The sections on the left side of the directory (see *Figure 11.3*) will also help you narrow down what Power-Ups might be most useful to you. For instance, you can see which ones are featured and most common, or you can sort by specific use cases or industries.

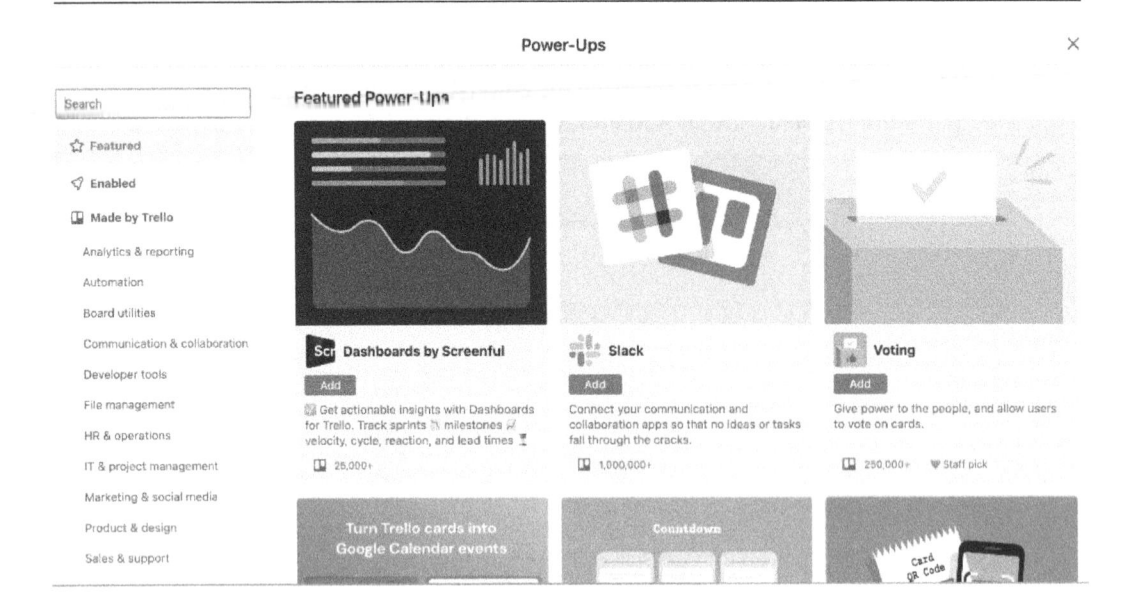

Figure 11.3 – Power-Up directory

If you work in human resources, you might want to check out the **HR & operations** category. If you want to get more data about what is happening on your board, you might want to review the **Analytics & reporting** section.

As you view Power-Ups, you'll see various details about them. Each card shows a logo, the name, a brief description, and the number of boards it's been added to.

Figure 11.4 – Power-Up card

This helps you to understand how popular a Power-Up is and how many people have used it. Featured Power-Ups include a picture that often shows an example of how the Power-Up looks or might be used.

You can add a Power-Up from the card view, but if you want to learn even more, simply click the card.

Figure 11.5 – Power-Up listing

This takes you to the listing, which shows even more detail. Power-Up developers will typically use this section to explain what the Power-Up does, what type of user it's best for, and how it works, often with GIFs and screenshots included. You'll typically see pricing information on here as well if the Power-Up is not free.

You can also find a way to contact the Power-Up developer with the **Contact support** button just below the name at the top. This is helpful if you have questions about the Power-Up or need to troubleshoot anything.

When you're ready to try out a Power-Up, simply click the **Add** button. Every Power-Up is a little bit different, so what happens next will vary by Power-Up. But it will typically include a screen asking you to approve their access to your Trello board, and sign up for or sign in to any third-party accounts or configure any initial settings.

After you've added a Power-Up, you can always access it from your board via the **Power-Ups** button in the top toolbar.

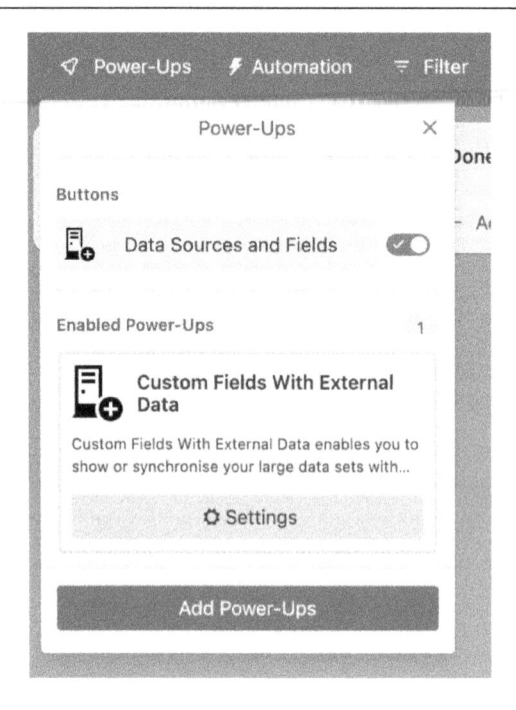

Figure 11.6 – Board Power-Up settings

Clicking the **Settings** button will allow you to remove it, view the listing, or authorize the Power-Up if you didn't do that at setup.

Now let's talk about some specific Power-Ups built by Trello and how you might use them!

Power-Ups for Integrations

One of the most common reasons people use Power-Ups is to send or receive data between Trello and other apps so they can work seamlessly together. Trello has developed many Power-Ups with other tools to make this work as efficiently as possible and help you have all the data you need in one place.

> **Why connect Trello with other apps?**
>
> I'm not naive enough to think that Trello is the only tool you or your team will ever use. Trello's fantastic, but it's not where I'd go to design images or have conversations with my colleagues. Integrating Trello with other apps you use can be helpful to bring all the information you need in a central place, while allowing each tool to serve its own purpose. It can also save you time from having to repeat work by updating multiple tools. If you struggle to keep track of notifications in Trello, sending those updates to Slack or Google Chat will help your team see what's most important in the places that matter.

Tools Trello integrates with easily

If you're curious about the available tools that can be integrated with Trello, the possibilities are endless. In this chapter, I will specifically cover the Power-Ups created by Trello, which are native integrations provided by Trello itself. In the following list, you'll find a comprehensive list of these Power-Ups and examples of how you can utilize them:

- Box, Google Drive, and OneDrive (preview files from these providers directly in your cards)
- Evernote (sync notes between Trello and Evernote)
- Giphy (add GIFs to cards on your board)
- GitHub (preview pull requests and issue info in your cards)
- Google Chat (get Trello notifications via Google Chat)
- Mailchimp (view campaign performance details in a card)
- Salesforce (view case and contact details directly in your cards)
- Slack (get Trello notifications via Slack)
- Twitter (preview Tweets in a card)
- Zendesk (search for tickets and attach them to your cards)

I won't go through every single integration as there are a lot of tools out there, but this gives you an idea of what you can do. If there are any specific tools you're looking to integrate with, search for them in the search box in the top left of the Power-Up directory.

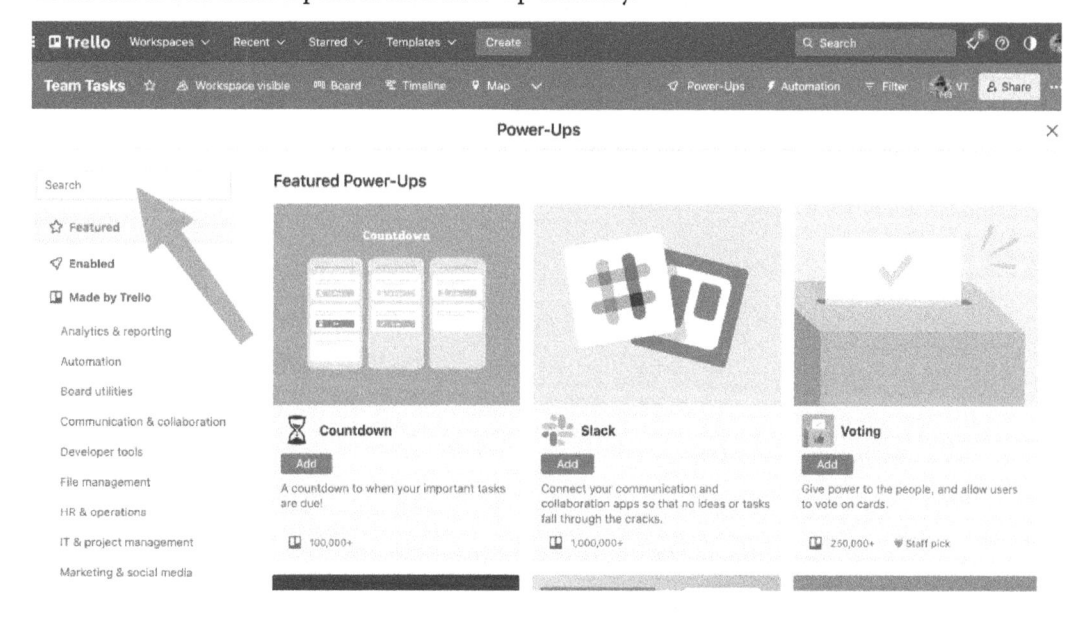

Figure 11.7 – Search field in the Power-Up directory

Let's assume that I work at a tech company and I'm using Trello to organize my marketing team's tasks, but we also communicate via Slack. We'll walk through setting up the Slack Power-Up so that my team can get notifications directly in our internal marketing channel in our company Slack workspace.

Adding the Slack Power-Up

Search for Slack in the top-left search bar and select the first card that appears.

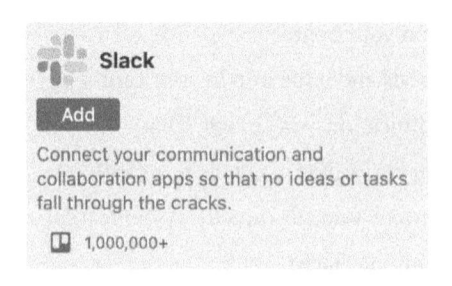

Figure 11.8 – Slack Power-Up card

Click the **Add** button. Immediately, the color and text of the button change. Click the newly created **Settings** button, then click **Edit Power-Up settings**.

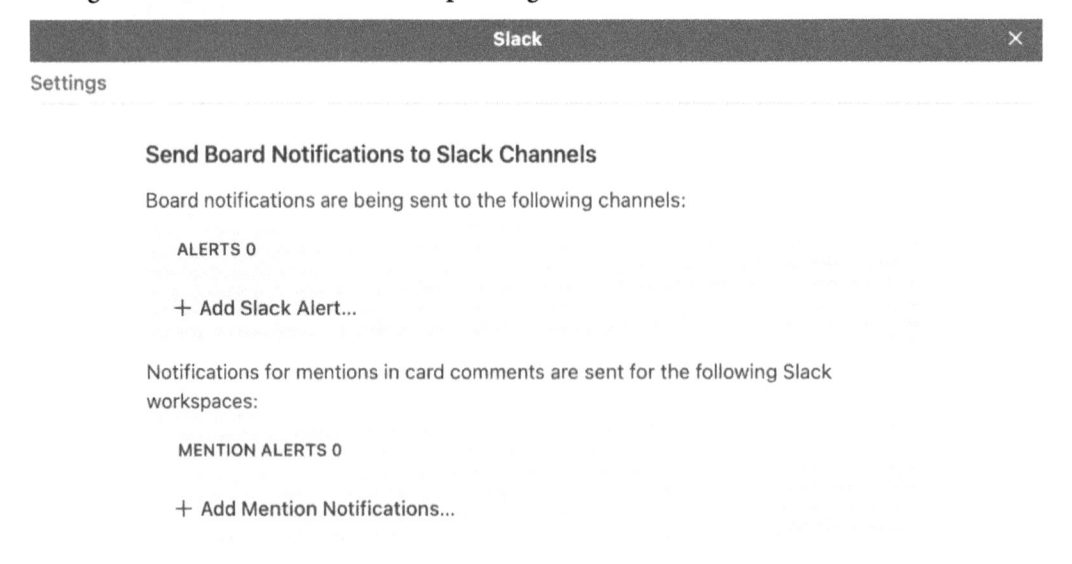

Figure 11.9 – Slack Power-Up settings

Power-Ups for Integrations   213

From here, configure what kind of Trello notifications you want to be shared in Slack. Select the **+ Add Slack Alert...** button under the **ALERTS** section.

Select a Slack workspace, then choose a channel you want notifications to be posted in. To stick with my marketing example, I might set these notifications to go into my **#marketing** channel.

Check the box next to the type of notifications you'd like. I prefer to stick with comments and cards created and moved to a different list.

Slack	✕

Settings / New Alert

First choose a Slack workspace: *

PixieBrix Community

Now choose a channel: *

Select...

Which Trello actions would you like to send to the Slack channel?

Board

☐ Member Added / Removed

☐ Renamed

Lists

☐ Archived / Unarchived

☐ Created

☐ Renamed

Cards

☐ Archived / Unarchived

☐ Attachment Added

☑ Comments

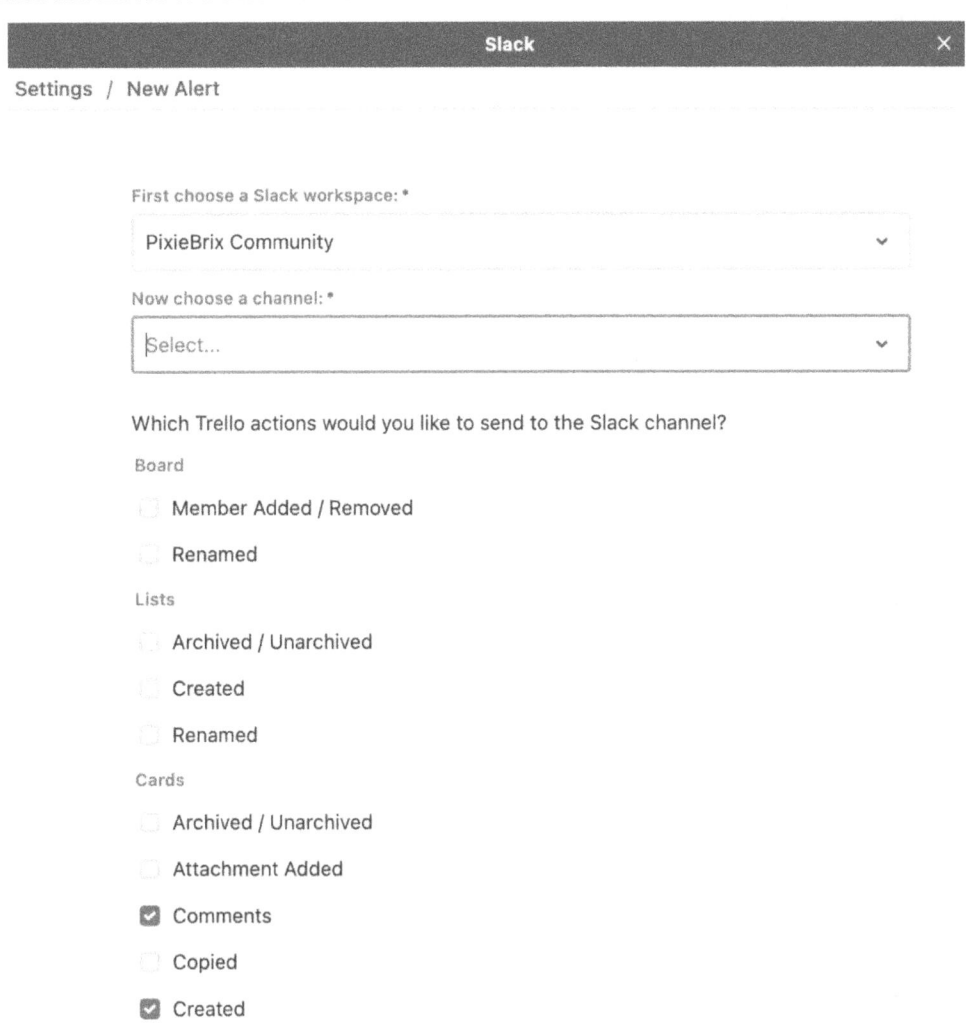

☐ Copied

☑ Created

Figure 11.10 – Slack alert configuration

If you have not connected to your Slack workspace yet, you'll need to do that before selecting channels or other options. Just click **+ Add new Slack workspace** from the drop-down menu and allow the permissions.

Viewing notifications in Slack

Once the workspace is hooked up and you've configured the types of alerts you want, you're ready to get notifications in Slack right away!

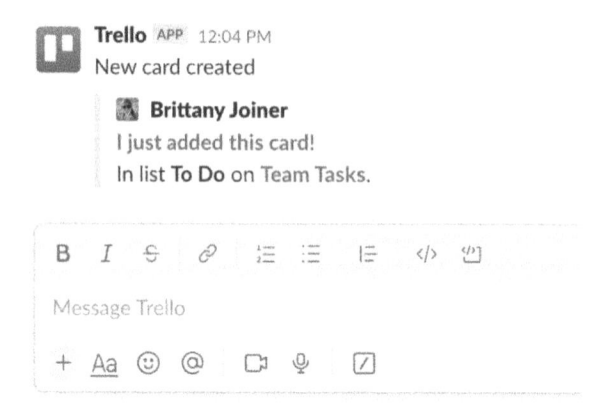

Figure 11.11 – Trello notification in Slack

They'll appear in the channel you specified, and anyone can click the link to go to the card or the board.

You can always change these settings later if you are getting too many or too few notifications in Slack. Remember—you want these notifications to be useful and work for you, not against you; so if it's too noisy and everyone ignores them, you'll want to reduce the volume of notifications.

Speaking of too much going on in your boards, let's talk about List Limits.

List Limits

Have you ever found yourself starting too many things and finishing nothing? I'm guilty of this, especially on my side projects! I have so many ideas and everything sounds fun and exciting, but soon I find myself in the middle of 10 different things, unable to give any one thing the attention it needs.

This happens to many teams at work as well. You've been given mandates from higher-ups, and it seems impossible to get everything done but you keep trying. And at the end of the week, to your surprise, you find that not everything has been completed.

> **Why limit tasks?**
>
> Limiting the amount of work in progress is important because it allows you to focus on completing tasks before moving on to new ones. When I have too many tasks in progress, I lose focus, my productivity decreases, and I'm more likely to make mistakes and forget about deadlines. When you limit the amount of work in progress, you can prioritize tasks, manage your time more effectively, and ultimately achieve better results. Limiting work in progress can also help reduce stress and improve work-life balance, as you are able to complete tasks more efficiently and have more time for other activities.

With the List Limits Power-Up, we can set a limit on the maximum number of cards to be displayed in a specific list. Although this does not prevent us from moving cards to that list, this Power-Up visually changes the display of the list so it's obvious if we've gone over the limit.

Let's pretend I'm managing my development team's work, and I'd only like them to be working on a maximum of five cards at a time. If they want to grab a new feature from the backlog, they can only do that if there are less than five cards already in progress. Here's how we'd set that up with List Limits.

Adding the List Limits Power-Up

To add the List Limits Power-Up, head to the Power-Up directory and search for List Limits in the top left. Choose the first option that appears and click **Add**.

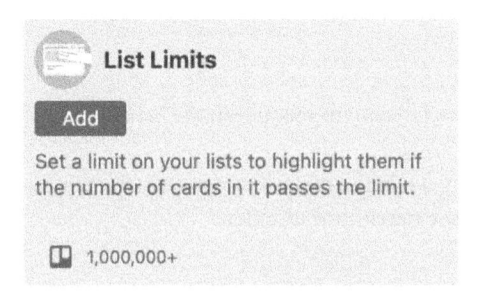

Figure 11.12 – List Limits Power-Up card

Once the button changes to, say, **Settings**, exit out of the Power-Up modal by pressing the *Esc* key on your keyboard or clicking the **X** icon in the top-right corner of your screen. This takes you back to your board.

Configuring List Limits

To use this Power-Up, you'll need to configure the maximum number of cards you'd like in each list on the board. You don't need to set it for every list, but you can if you'd like! Find the list where you'd like to set limits and click the ellipses next to the list name:

Power-Ups Built by Trello

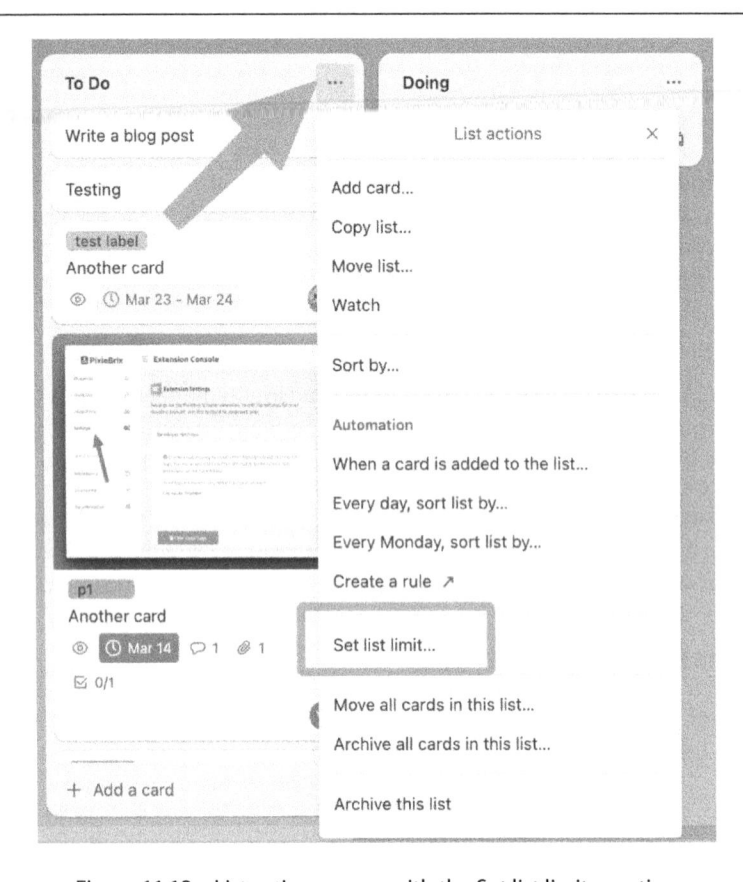

Figure 11.13 – List actions menu with the Set list limit… action

Scroll about two-thirds of the way down the menu that appears, and you should see the **Set list limit…** action. Click that, and then set the maximum number.

Figure 11.14 – Set list limit options

You can type in any number or use the arrows to scroll. For my example, I'll type **2**. Once you've set your number, click **Save**. Alternatively, if you have a limit set already that you'd like to clear, you can just click **Remove**.

Using List Limits

When you configure a list limit, a badge will show at the top of the list with the current number of cards and the maximum number you set.

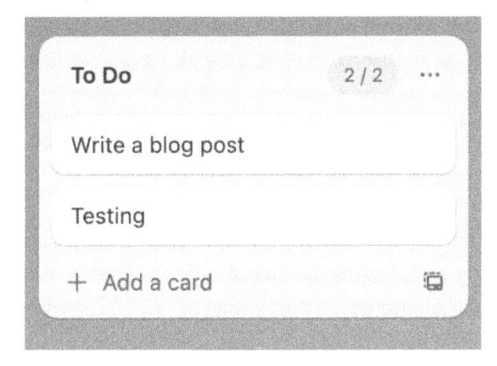

Figure 11.15 – Badge at the top of the list showing the number of cards

If the current number of cards is equal to or less than the maximum, the rest of the list will be displayed normally. However, as soon as there are more cards than the maximum number, the list changes from a gray background to a light-yellow background and the badge at the top is boldened to make it stand out.

Figure 11.16 – Badge boldened and background changed when cards exceed list limit

You can still add cards past the limit and view the count at the top. I find this ideal because sometimes I really do need to make exceptions, and it's more helpful to use the Power-Up as a guideline rather than strictly preventing cards from moving to another list.

Even if you don't need limits, this Power-Up is helpful for counting the number of cards in a list since it always displays that number via the badge at the top. I sometimes use this on lists just to keep track of how many cards I have in case I want to report on it, such as the number of tasks I'm working on this week, or the number of contacts in my **Won** list.

How you choose to utilize limits is entirely up to you and your team. In fact, outlining your intended use of limits is something you can mention in your board's Read Me, which we will discuss in the next section.

Read Me

No matter how clearly you organize your board, folks will still join and feel a bit lost and unsure of how to use the board. Even if you go through the board with your team, it's still nice to have a central place explaining how to use a board and the expectations of board members.

A README is a file in a software project that typically has important information about the project, such as its purpose, how to use it, how to install it, and any dependencies or requirements. It is often the first file a user will read when exploring a new project. This is where the Read Me Power-Up gets its name, as it's the first thing a user sees when they're added to a board if you have this Power-Up.

> **Why add Read Me to Trello boards?**
> Having a short snippet of text that introduces people to a board and walks them through it will increase the likelihood of people using your board and—perhaps even more importantly— help them use it correctly. I recommend using this Power-Up with any board that you have other people working on, or template boards. It's free and easy to configure, so there's no reason not to!

Adding the Read Me Power-Up

If you're working on a support team, you might want to use Read Me to explain to your support engineers how to use your board and ensure everyone understands how to grab tasks.

To add the Read Me Power-Up, head to the Power-Up directory and search for Read Me. Choose the first Power-Up that appears, which looks like this:

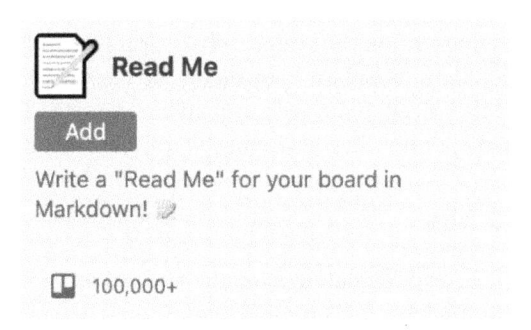

Figure 11.17 – Read Me Power-Up card

Click **Add**, and a popup appears to configure your Read Me. In this section, type up a description of your board. You can format the text with Markdown syntax, which allows you to create headers, bold or italicize text, add images, create bulleted or numbered lists, and more!

Figure 11.18 – Read Me configuration

After you've created your description, you can choose when visitors to your board should see this Read Me. I recommend leaving **Show "Read Me" button on the board** checked so your teammates can quickly access it any time they need. I also recommend checking the **On user's first visit** and **Whenever Read Me is updated** options. Click **Save** when you've completed your configuration.

Previewing the Read Me

To view your Read Me, click the **Read Me** button from the top toolbar of your Trello board. If you didn't check the box to include that button, then simply do the actions you triggered it to show for. (For instance, if you chose to show it every time the board loads, then refresh the page.)

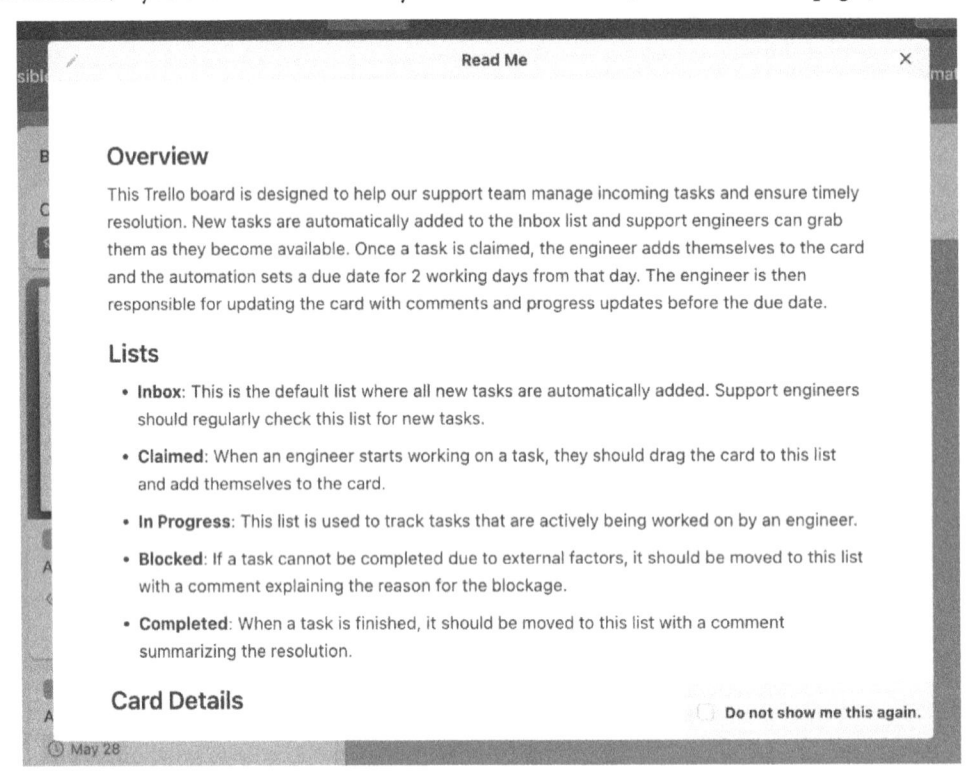

Figure 11.19 – Preview of the Read Me

You should see the description you typed, formatted nicely with Markdown!

Editing the Read Me

When you open the Read Me, you'll also see a pencil icon in the top-right corner. This allows you to go back and edit the Read Me if there's anything you want to change. You can also edit the Read Me by clicking **Edit Power-Up settings** from the Read Me settings in the Power-Up menu.

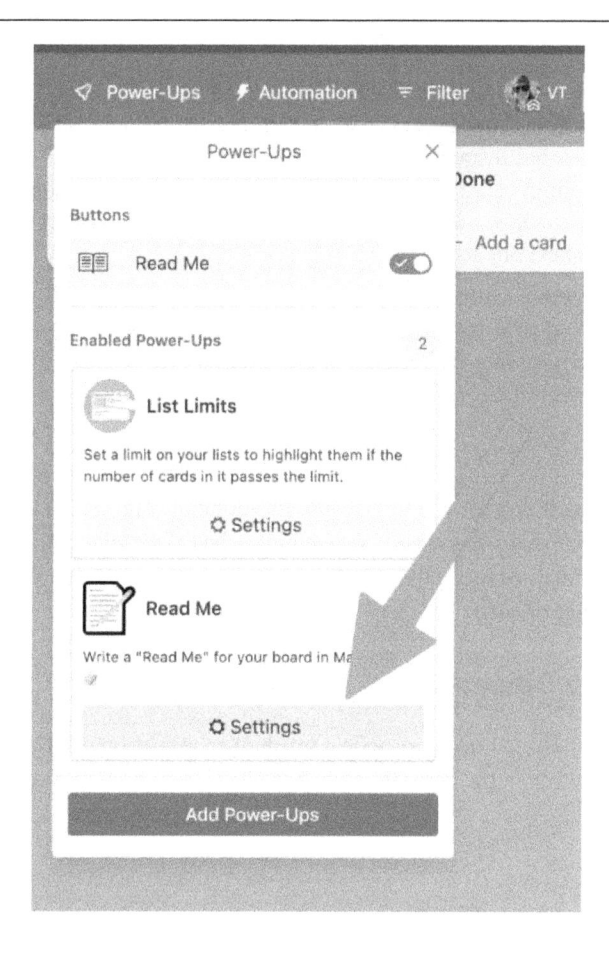

Figure 11.20 – Settings for editing Power-Ups on the board

You'll be able to reopen the modal and change the text or the configuration options and save it.

If you want more ideas for engaging people on your board, you'll be excited to learn about the Voting Power-Up!

Voting

Sometimes you might want to get opinions about what people want to work on or what types of topics are most interesting to folks. Although you might think about just asking someone to join a card if they want to "vote" for something, that adds a lot of unnecessary overhead (such as notifications about activity on the cards and those cards showing up in your filtered lists).

> **Why vote on Trello boards?**
>
> You might want to enable voting features in your Trello board if you want to collect feedback from users or teammates. For instance, if you are a product team, you could use Trello as your roadmap and allow product users to share feature requests and vote on them. This could be useful to allow you to prioritize your backlog and work on only the most requested features that would have the highest impact.
>
> There are many other reasons you might want voting on your board, such as quick polls asking teammates to pick a good time for a meeting, or for prioritizing items in a meeting agenda. It's also a great way to ensure buy-in from the team for tasks you want to accomplish during a project. By doing the tasks that everyone agrees are important, employees will be more likely to complete the tasks.

The Voting Power-Up makes it easy for you to incorporate voting in your Trello boards. This Power-Up adds a button to card actions that allow members (even non-board members) to +1 a card. Each card will show a tally of the number of total votes, and lists have a new action that allows you to sort the cards in a list by the number of votes.

Adding the Voting Power-Up

Let's add the Voting Power-Up to our hypothetical product roadmap board. Head to the Power-Up directory and search for Voting in the top-left search bar. Click the **Add** button on the first Power-Up that appears.

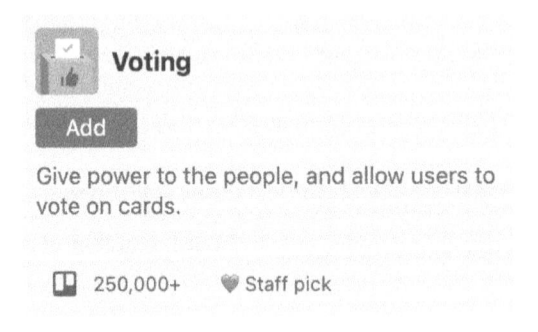

Figure 11.21 – Voting Power-Up card

When it turns into a **Settings** button, your Power-Up is ready to go --no need to configure anything! Close out of the Power-Up directory by pressing the *Esc* key or clicking the **X** icon in the top-right corner, then open any card on your board.

If you do want to configure some other options, click the **Settings** button and you'll be able to configure some options, such as who can vote and whether vote numbers should be visible or hidden. If you want to change these settings later, you can access them from the Power-Up button at the top of the toolbar on your Trello board.

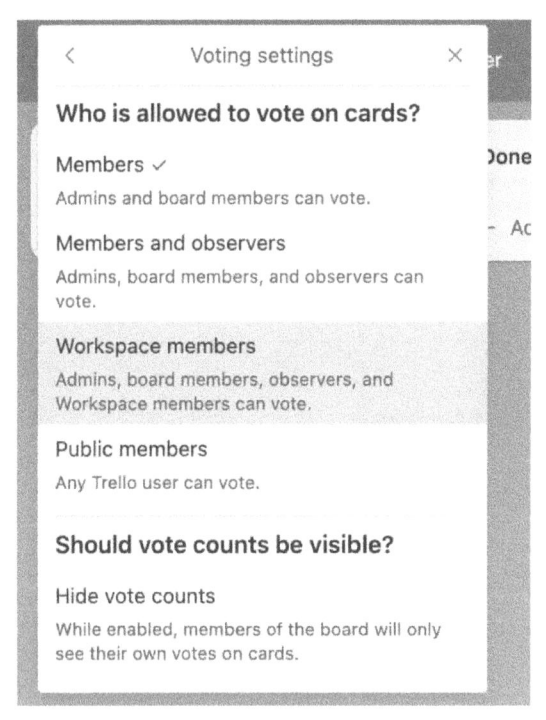

Figure 11.22 – Voting settings

We'll go ahead and change this to **Public members** now because we want to enable any Trello user to be able to vote on our feature requests. This allows our users to vote on cards in our board but not edit any of its content.

Voting on a card

On every card on your Trello board, you'll notice a new button in the **Actions** section at the bottom right, just to the right of the **Activity** section.

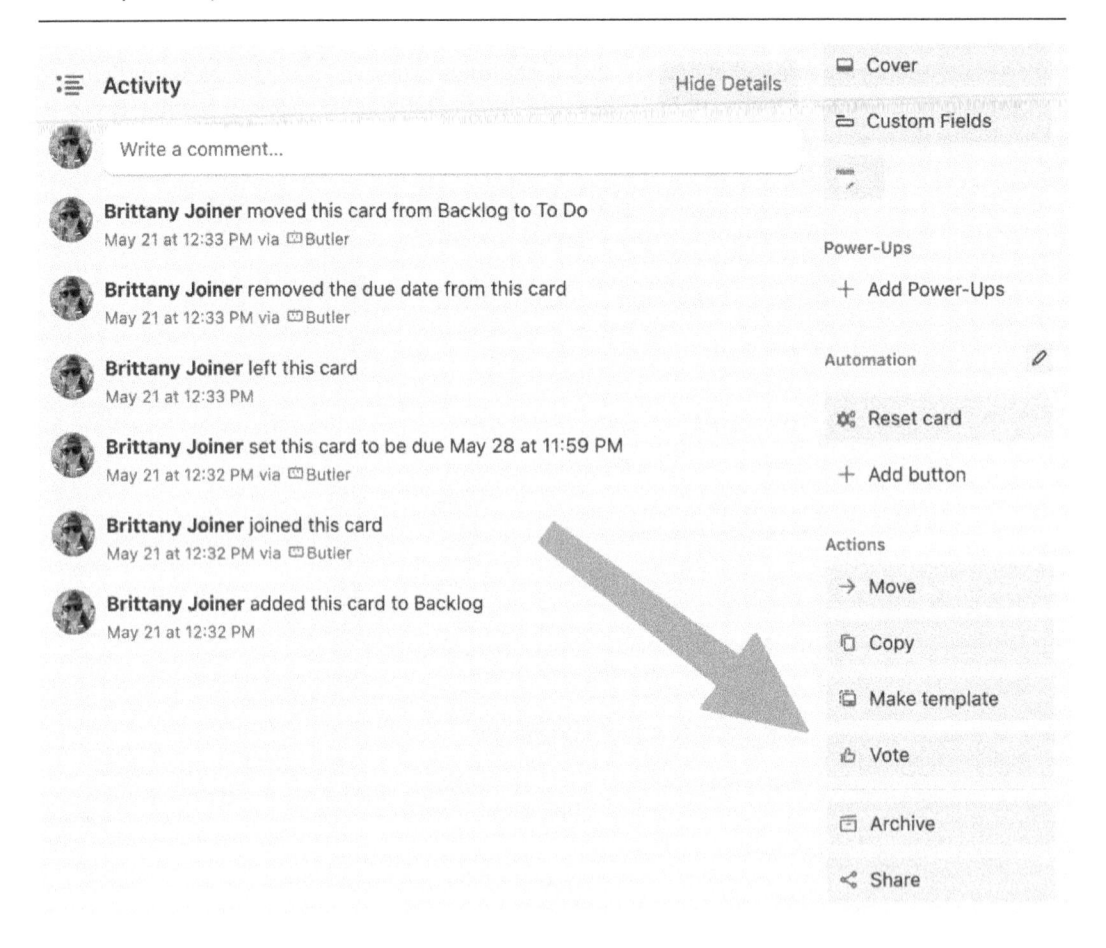

Figure 11.23 – Vote button on a card

Click the **Vote** button and notice a checkmark appears to show that you've voted for the card.

Figure 11.24 – Check on a card after the vote is submitted

If you want to remove your vote, just click **Vote** again.

For each card on the board that has at least one vote, a thumbs-up icon appears on the front of the card displaying the number of votes that card has.

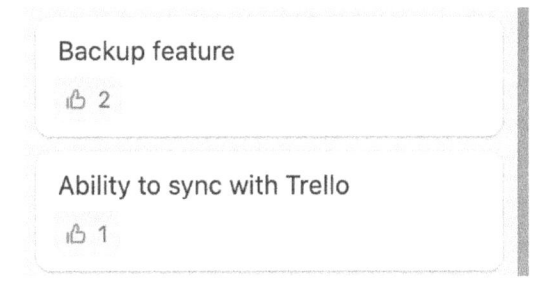

Figure 11.25 – Number of votes appears on the card front

You can also view the number of votes on the back of the card by opening the card and looking just below the card title. This gives us a way to quickly see the popularity of a specific feature request.

Sorting a list by votes

If you want to organize your lists to see the cards that have the most votes rise to the top, click the ellipses next to the list name, and choose the **Sort** option. This opens the sorting options you've seen before, but you'll notice a new option!

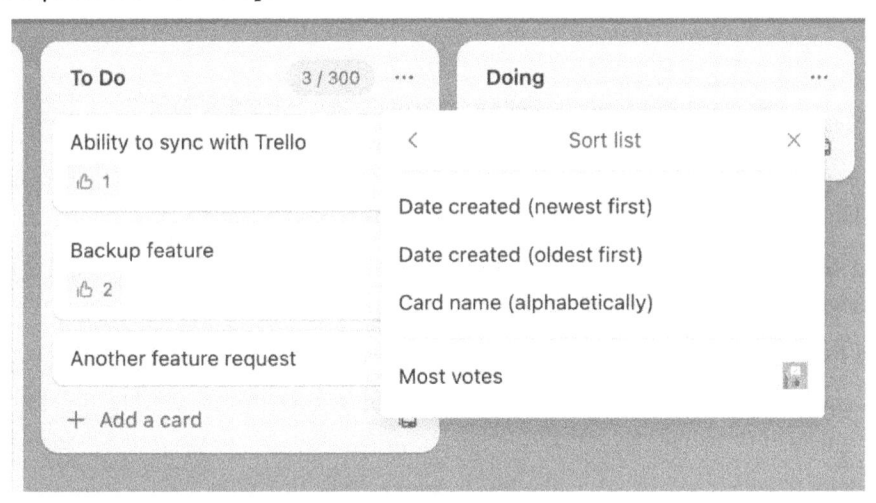

Figure 11.26 – Sorting options with the Voting Power-Up

You can sort by **Most votes**. Choose that option and watch the cards move around to sort the cards by the highest to lowest number of votes. Now you can quickly tell which features you should be prioritizing based on popularity!

Other Trello-made Power-Ups

This book would quickly become a series of encyclopedias if I talked about every Power-Up, and even if I just talked about every Power-Up that Trello has made. I've picked my favorites and some of the most useful ones that apply to some common use cases, but this is just the beginning.

If you want to explore more Trello-made Power-Ups, head to the Power-Up directory and click the **Made by Trello** option on the left-hand side of your screen:

Figure 11.27 – Made by Trello section of the Power-Up directory

Here you'll see some of the Power-Ups we've already talked about as well as several more, such as the following:

- **Card Snooze** (allows you to snooze cards so they disappear from your board and show up again when you want them)
- **Card Repeater** (sets a card to copy itself at specific intervals)
- **Package Tracker** (view shipment tracking information directly on a card by providing the tracking number and service provider)
- **Calendar** (display cards in a calendar if you aren't a Trello Premium user)
- **Dashcards** (mini reporting card that shows a count of cards that meet the filters you set)

Search for these in the directory and view the listing pages to learn more about how to use them and give you ideas and inspiration!

Summary

You've up-leveled your Trello knowledge yet again! In this chapter, we've talked about how Power-Ups give your board superpowers so you can do even more with Trello. Anybody can make Power-Ups, but some of the most popular ones are made by Trello, and we focused on those in this chapter.

We talked about Power-Ups that integrate with your other tools, such as Slack and Google Drive. We also learned how to create structure around your board to count cards in each list and provide limits, as well as how to create documentation on your board so others can use it effectively. We even learned how to turn our Trello board into a feedback-collecting machine with the Voting Power-Up.

If you've never used Power-Ups before and this is your maiden voyage into them, you're well on your way to improving your Trello boards, but you've got so much more to discover. In the next chapter, we'll talk about some more Power-Ups that you might like made by other developers.

12
General-Use Power-Ups

You've already learned about some Power-Ups created by Trello that will help you improve your workflows, but it's time to step outside the internal ecosystem and explore Power-Ups created by others. In this chapter, we'll explore a few Power-Ups that aren't made by Trello but instead are made by other companies and developers. Although I'd have to write a million books to talk about all of them, we'll cover a couple that work well with a handful of use cases and solve the most common challenges I am asked about.

In this chapter, you'll learn about the following topics:

- Approvals for Trello—streamlines your team's review and approval process
- Amazing Fields—adds custom fields to your Trello cards for a more comprehensive overview of your projects
- Bulk Actions—simplifies your workflow by letting you perform actions on multiple cards at once

It's a lot, so let's jump right in!

Approvals for Trello

This Power-Up is useful if you have any approval process as part of your workflow in Trello. For instance, maybe you need to keep track of your content calendar on Trello, and before any content can be published, your manager or other teammates must approve it.

While you can build your own approval system with Trello's custom fields and labels, why not use a Power-Up that gives you everything you need out of the box? That's where Approvals for Trello comes in.

It's a Power-Up built by the AppFox team, the makers of other much-loved apps for Jira, Confluence, and monday.com. Approvals has been added to over 75,000 Trello boards worldwide and is free to use, although there is a paid subscription plan that adds some cool extra features.

> **Why use Approvals?**
>
> Adding an approval process in your workflow can help ensure everyone is on the same page about who is working on what. It eliminates the "I had no idea that was going out!" conversation or the "No one checked with my team!" frustration that can tend to happen when we're all moving fast and (hopefully not) breaking things.

Adding Approvals for Trello to your board

To add the Power-Up, go to the Power-Up directory from the top toolbar of any Trello board by selecting the **Power-Up** button. Click the **Add Power-Ups** button and search for Approvals in the search field on the top left. Click the **Add** button on the first result that appears:

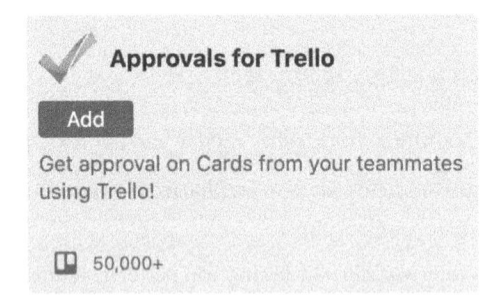

Figure 12.1 – Approvals for Trello card in the Power-Up directory

You'll be prompted to click **Add** again to confirm you understand that this is a third-party Trello Power-Up, made by another developer outside of Trello. Don't worry, though—Power-Ups still go through a rigorous review process, so you can ensure your data and information are safe!

A modal appears explaining how to use Approvals for Trello. Take a moment to review it, and then we'll go through creating an approval together:

Thank you for installing Approvals for Trello!

This guide will help you get up and running in a couple of minutes:

1. Create an Approval

Add Board Members to a Card to get their Approval!

- a. Click on a Card
- b. Click on 'Approval' on the right and select the Approvers

2. View the current approval status

See who's approved and other details.

- a. Open a Card
- b. If an Approval is currently active, you can see the details here
- c. See the status of different approvals directly on the Board.

3. Get Pro to extend the functionality

With Approvals for Trello Pro, you can:

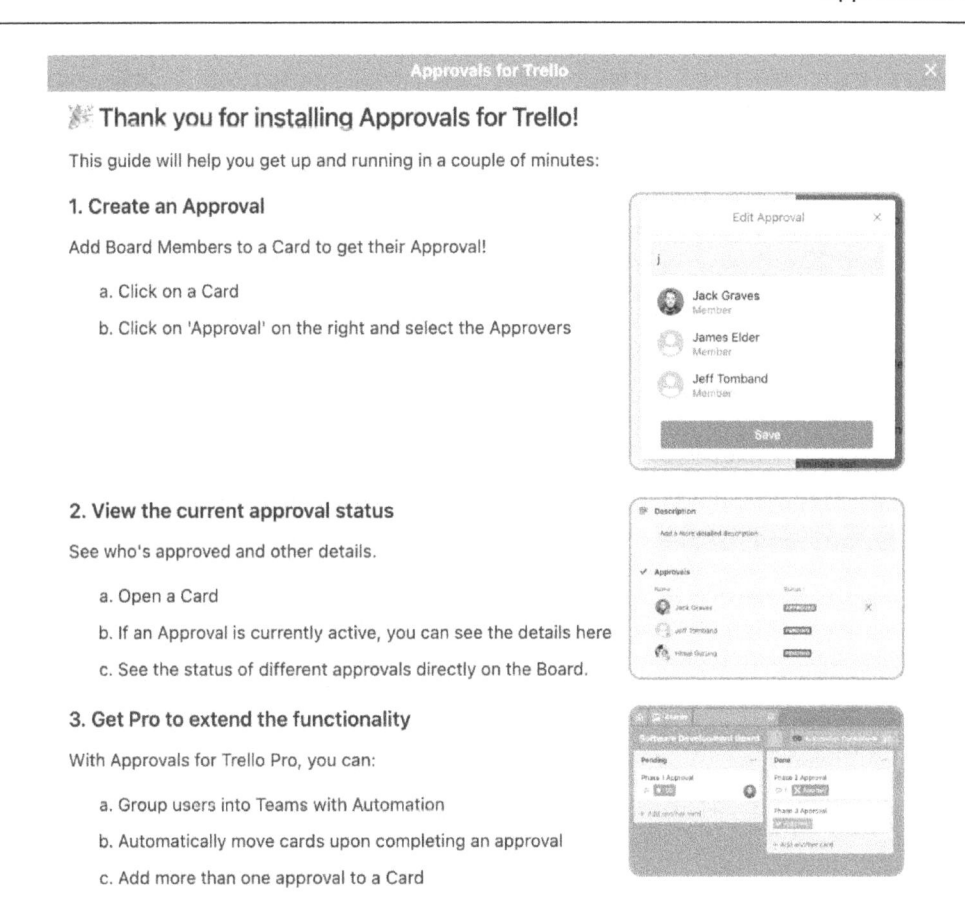

- a. Group users into Teams with Automation
- b. Automatically move cards upon completing an approval
- c. Add more than one approval to a Card

Figure 12.2 – Approvals for Trello welcome flow

Once you're ready, click **Get Started**, then close out of the Power-Ups modal to try it out. We'll walk through an example of creating an approval on cards that are in our **Review** list asking for our Tech Lead to approve the card.

Creating an approval

Every Power-Up is a little bit different, but to use this one, head to any card on your Trello board. Look in the **Power-Up** section just below the **Add to card** section on the right side of any card.

232 | General-Use Power-Ups

I'm going to pick a card in my Review list on my board, but you can choose from any card or list you like:

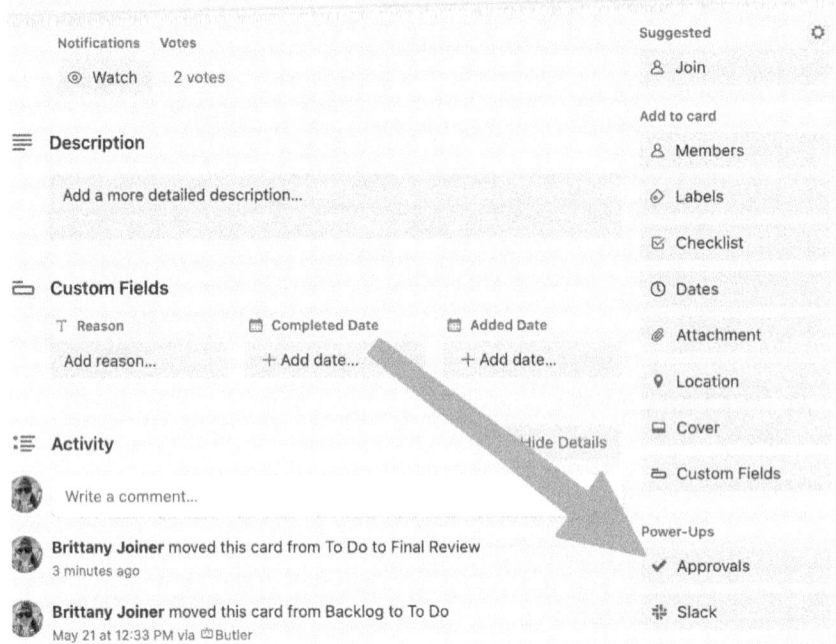

Figure 12.3 – Approvals button on cards

Click on the **Approvals** button, and a modal invites you to start adding approvals. You'll see any existing approvals, but since we're new, it's empty. Click the + button at the bottom.

Pick an approver from the drop-down options, which include all members of the board:

Figure 12.4 – Adding an approver to a card

When you've selected a member, the **Create** button darkens to be clicked. You could select multiple members here if you have multiple people that need to give approval for something. I'm going to leave it to just myself for the sake of the example.

Click **Create** and you've set up your first approval! Now, let's take a look at how this looks in your Trello card. As you can see, it appears below the card description, and any custom fields you've added are above the **Activity and Comments** section:

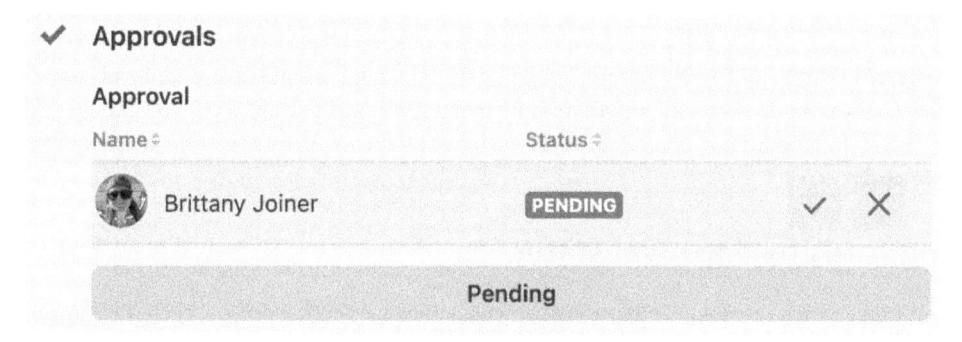

Figure 12.5 – Approvals button on cards

The **Approvals** section in your Trello card clearly displays whose review has been requested and the status of that approval.

Approving or rejecting an approval

If you're the approver, you can click the ✓ or **X** button to approve or reject. If you accidentally click, you can click again to reverse your approval.

Notice that not only do you see the status visualized on the card back but you can also see the status from the card front as well, making it really easy to see at a glance on your Trello board:

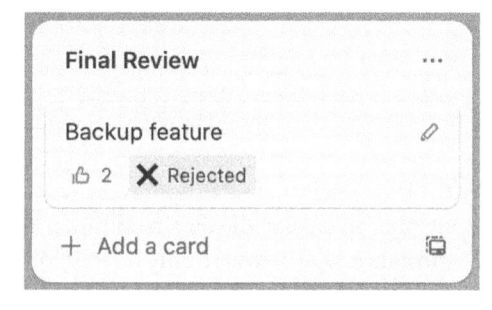

Figure 12.6 – Rejected status on the card front

This makes it easy to quickly identify the approval status of cards across a board.

Of course, you may not want to manually add an approver for every single card if you always need the same people to approve a card. Although there's no way to quickly select multiple cards and set approvers for them, here's what I recommend doing.

Start by creating a card that we can use as an example for any new card added to your Trello board. In my example, I might make a template card for a feature request. Set the approvers on that card. I'll add my Tech Lead as the approver.

Now, whenever I want to add a new feature, I'm going to copy that example card, and it will copy over the approvals. (We can do this with automation by making a board button! Refer to *Chapter 9* for a refresher on creating board buttons.) And there we have it—the approvers have been automatically set for this card!

Viewing cards by approval status

If you want to see which cards you've approved, or which ones are waiting on you, click the **Approvals** button that appears in the top toolbar of your Trello board!

An **Approvals** dashboard will appear at the bottom of your Trello board so that you can easily view your cards by approval status and quickly identify anything that needs your attention:

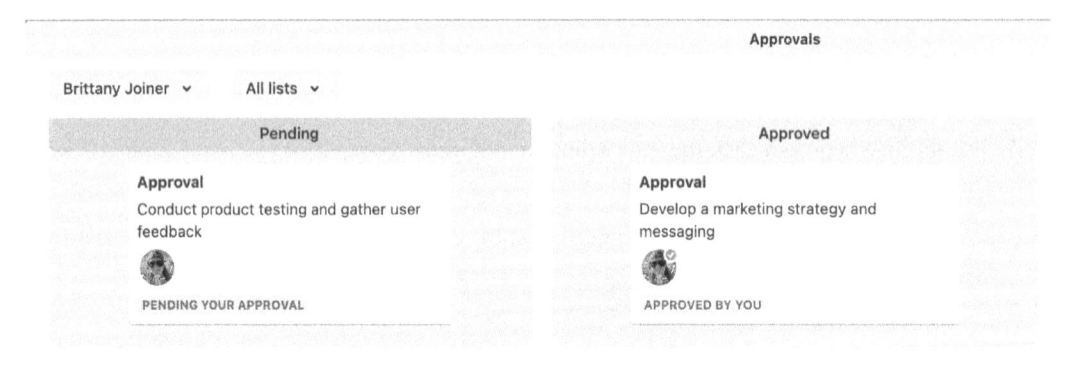

Figure 12.7 – View of cards sorted by approval status

Use the drop-down menus to see the review status of other approvers. Just click your name and select **All members** or another board member to change the displayed cards. You can also click **All lists** to specify which lists to view. For instance, maybe you're only interested in cards that require your review right away, so maybe you want to only show cards that need your review in the QA list rather than every card on the board that will eventually require your approval.

Advanced features

If this sounds good but you want a bit more, you'll be excited to know that the paid (Pro) version includes more features.

Creating an approval group or team

With the Pro plan, you'll have the ability to create an approval team. Let's say you need someone from legal to sign off on something, but you don't need a specific person—just one member of the legal team. You could create a team of five people from legal, and only one of them would need to approve to show a card with an approved state. Now, you can specify a type of approval and how many people you need from that group to approve.

Specifying multiple approvals on a card

Another Pro feature gives you the ability to specify multiple approvals on a card, instead of just one that may contain multiple people. For instance, you might do this if you need someone from legal, someone from infosec, and someone from finance groups to approve a new tool to add to your company's workspace.

Moving cards based on status

Typically, when someone approves a card, it's moved to the next stage in the workflow, and if it's rejected, it might move to a previous stage in the workflow so that a teammate can rework it and request approval again. Rather than having to manually move the card after you see the approval status updated on a card, you can set up automation rules (in **Approval Teams**) that move cards to specific lists once their approval status has changed. If you create an Approval team in the Pro plan, you can select **Move on Approval** or **Move on Rejected**.

Upgrading to Pro

If any of these features sound interesting and you want to upgrade, it's easy to do. To do this, click on the **Approvals** button on the right side of any card, and select the **Get Pro** action at the top:

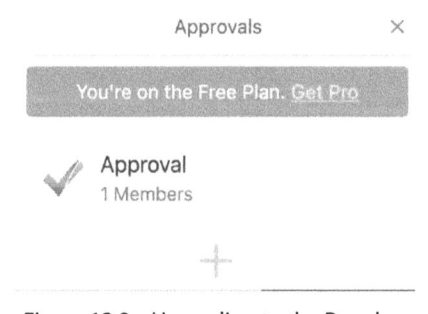

Figure 12.8 – Upgrading to the Pro plan

Now that we've covered approvals, let's talk about other fields you might want to add to your board!

Amazing Fields

Trello's native custom fields are powerful and versatile, but for something called custom fields, you can only "customize" so much. There are only five types of fields and you can't style anything about them, other than the colors of the drop-down options for the drop-down field type or the name of the field. While they're useful for holding data, if you want to type longer notes (or anything more than about 20 characters), the text gets cut off and is hard to read. And hey—they work great for many use cases! But sometimes you just need a little bit more.

Amazing Fields takes custom fields a step further, allowing you to create additional fields on your Trello cards and customize where and how they appear. Amazing Fields is built by the Amazing PowerUps company and has been added to over 100,000 boards! Just as with other Power-Ups, there's a free plan that has plenty of functionality and a Premium version that lets you do even more!

> **Why use Amazing Fields?**
> You'll want to use Amazing Fields when you have additional info you want to add to your boards, such as more dates or more text fields, checkboxes indicating status, or just about any other piece of data that doesn't exist with core Trello card attributes.
>
> Specifically, you'll want to use Amazing Fields instead of Trello's native custom fields when you want to choose how additional fields look, or when you want to want to control the visibility of fields and who can edit them.

Although there's a ton you can do with Amazing Fields, I'll explain how to get set up and create your first field, and then I'll leave you to play around to your heart's content.

I'm going to show you a *very* real-world example because I'm actually using it to write this very book! I'll show you how I use Amazing Fields to keep track of the number of pages I need to write for each chapter, as well as the number of words.

Adding Amazing Fields

To add Amazing Fields to your board, click **Add Power-Ups** from the **Power-Up** button on the top toolbar of any Trello board. When in the directory, search for `Amazing Fields` in the search bar on the top left. You should then see the following:

Figure 12.9 – Amazing Fields card in the Power-Up directory

Click the **Add** button, and then once again, click **Add** to confirm you're aware this is a Power-Up not created by Trello. Immediately, you'll be prompted to connect your Trello account and allow access, and then you're ready to create your fields!

If you close out and go back to your board, you can access this settings page by clicking **Fields** in the top toolbar of the board and then selecting **Settings**:

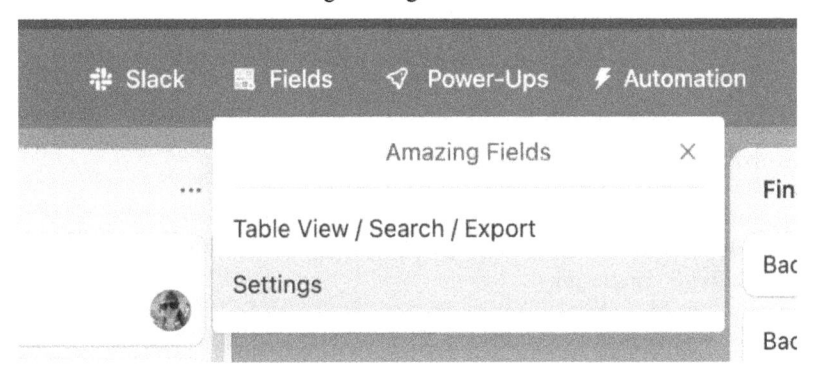

Figure 12.10 – Amazing Fields modal with Settings

Now, let's make a field! Specifically, let's make an *amazing* one. 😁

Creating a field

Start by clicking the **+ Add** button on the left side of the panel, just inside the **Fields** section below the **Settings** section:

Figure 12.11 – Amazing Fields Settings and Fields sidebar

Then, you'll be prompted to choose a type of field. Hover over each one to display more options and see which types of fields you can build:

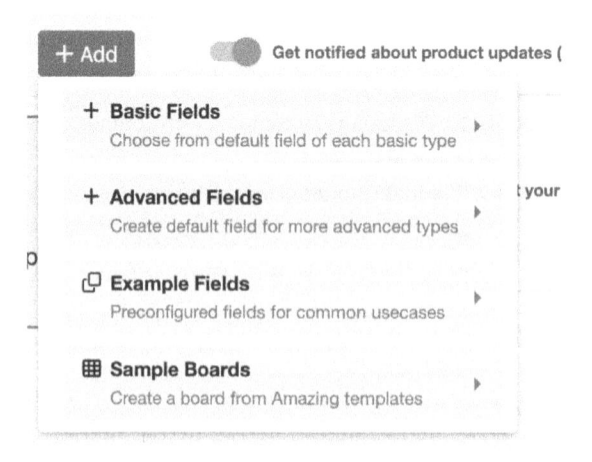

Figure 12.12 – Amazing Fields categories

There's a lot you can do! You're probably expecting basic fields such as text, checkbox, date, numbers, and dropdown, but there are many other field types such as progress bar and card reference, and even fields that organize your fields such as sections headers or tabs.

For my Trello book board, each card is a chapter, and I needed a number field to store the number of pages for that chapter. I clicked on **Basic Fields** and selected **Number Field**. Go ahead and do that to follow along with me!

Now, you're on a page giving you options to configure more than you ever thought possible for your fields. Start by naming your field. You can even give your field an emoji!

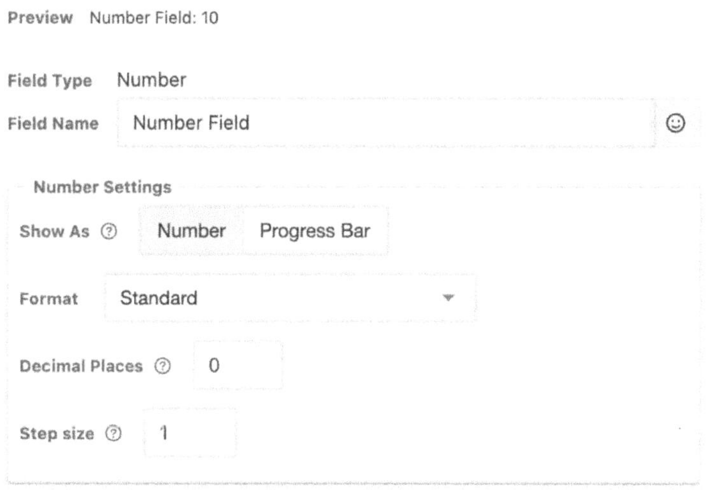

Figure 12.13 – Amazing Fields number configuration options

For numbers, you can set the format of a number, such as a currency or a percentage, and you can choose whether it's displayed as a number or progress bar. Other fields will have other settings in this section. If you chose a drop-down field type, this is where you'd set the options. If you chose a text field, you could choose if you want the text to be single or multiple lines. If it's a checkbox, you can choose from six different ways to style the checkboxes!

We'll leave these settings as is for our **Pages** field. Now, let's look at the **Card Display** options:

Figure 12.14 – Amazing Fields Card Display options

You can choose whether you want to show the field name and/or value (the answer on the front of the card or the view when you are looking at a card on a board with other cards), as well as whether you'd like comments on the card to log when changes are made to a custom field. This is helpful if you need to see when a record changed, who changed it, and what was changed. Lastly, you can choose to hide new fields on a card so that empty values don't clutter your cards.

Next, you can change the way a field is displayed in the **Field Editor Layout** option:

Figure 12.15 – Amazing Fields Field Editor Layout options

You might choose to make it display the full width of the card if it's a long text field and you want to show as much text as possible. This is something you can't do with Trello's native custom fields, and it's extremely helpful for displaying long blocks of text, especially when paired with the **Multiple Line** layout for text fields. You can also specify the location of the label in relation to the field, giving you even more customization options.

For more styling, you can set the **Background Color** option of a card to help it stand out, and you can add conditional logic to specify the background based on the value of the field. You might use this to make a checked box appear green and an unchecked box appear red:

Figure 12.16 – Amazing Fields Background Color options

The next sections of options are only available for Premium subscribers, as shown by the **Supporter Only** badge. Field formulas are great for setting values based on the value of other fields. Although I don't use them for my **Pages** field, I do use them to calculate the value of my **Words** field. Since I know each page should have about 3,500 words on it, my word goal is `Pages * 3,500`, and I can build that formula with Amazing Fields. I can also choose to not show the **Words** field if I haven't set the **Pages** field:

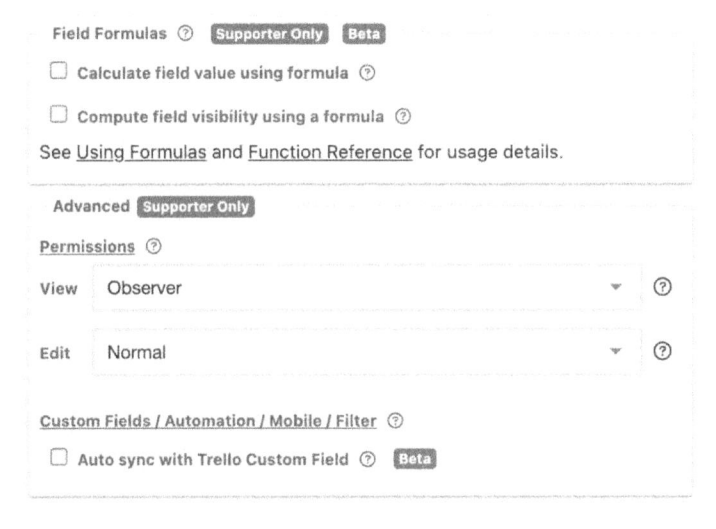

Figure 12.17 – Amazing Fields Field Formulas and Advanced options

The last section is also only for supporters but is extremely useful if you need ultimate control over your fields. In some cases, you may want only your admins to be able to edit these fields, or maybe you even only want them to be able to view them. With these **Permissions** settings, you can control who can see and edit custom fields across the board. This is another limitation of Trello's native custom fields, as anyone on a board can view any values for custom fields.

The very last setting is what I think really makes Amazing Fields more magical than ever because I used to tell people that if you want style, use Amazing Fields, but if you want automation, use Trello's native custom fields. But with this final setting, you don't have to choose!

Why would you ever want both Amazing Fields and custom fields in your board instead of just one? Because Power-Ups don't work on mobile, so if you want to view field values on mobile, you'll need to use Trello's native custom fields. Power-Ups also aren't accessible in Trello's automation suite, so if you want to automate anything with your fields, you'll also need to use custom fields. But as you've been reading this section, you can hopefully see all the benefits that Amazing Fields has over Trello's native custom fields. That's why this setting is awesome. You can have your cake and eat it too. If checked, Amazing Fields will create a custom field for your amazing field and keep it in sync. You can also add the **Amazing Fields for Chrome** extension, which will hide custom fields so that it doesn't show duplicate fields on your cards.

And you're done! No need to click save or anything—your field is saved as you go, and when you're ready to see it in action, just close out of the **X** button at the top right!

Updating a field

Open a card on your board, and you should see your newly created fields just below the **Description** section:

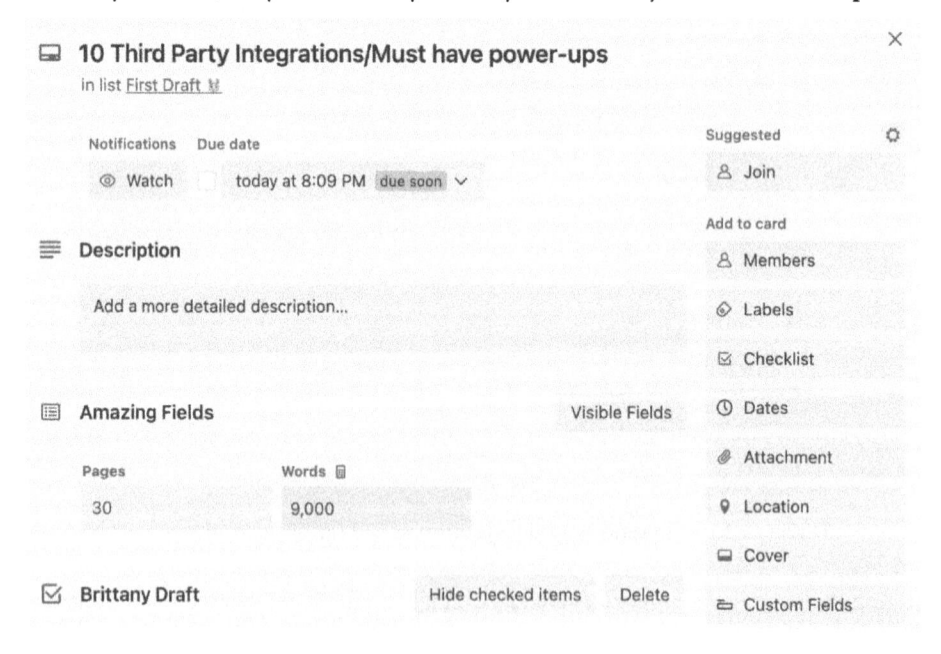

Figure 12.18 – Viewing Amazing Fields on cards

To edit a field, click it and type or select the value, just as you would with native custom fields on your board.

Click the **Visible Fields** button near the top right of the fields if you want to hide fields on a specific card. You might do this if you have some reference or instruction cards that don't require values like other cards on the board do.

Additional features

There is one more thing I want to show you before we close this section. Amazing Fields also offers a board backup feature that copies the board and provides a backup just in case anything changes in the board that you want to revert. To enable this, toggle on the choice from the **Getting Started** page:

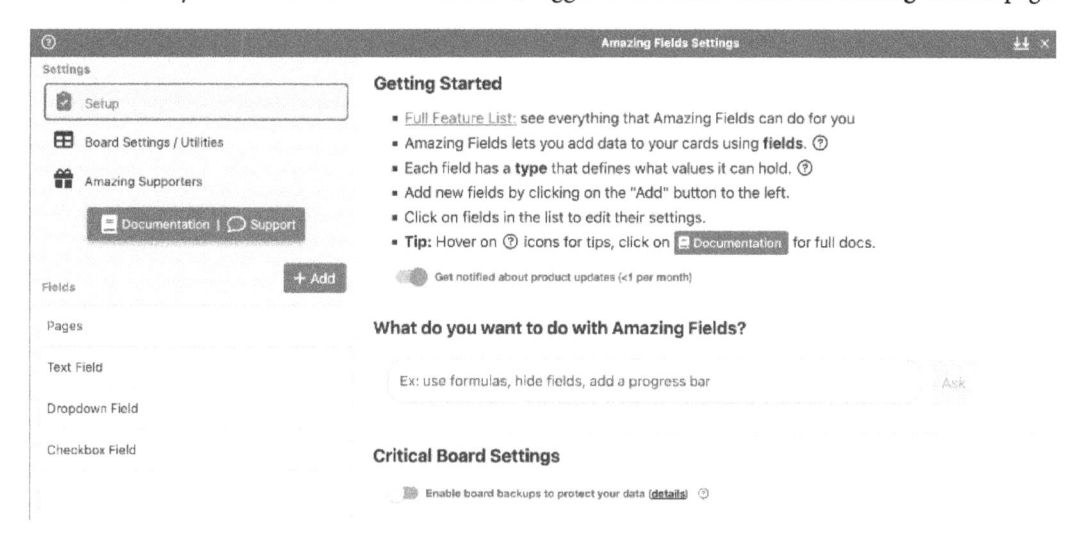

Figure 12.19 – Amazing Fields board backup feature

You can also export a board in case you need to add the data to another tool or in another format. And something else special—you can copy the board configuration, which is important if you want to create multiple boards with these created fields. For my developer friends, you can also access your Amazing Fields data via an API so that you can reference that data in other tools if you'd like. This is great if you work with teams that want to be able to access your project data through other tools.

And one more thing! Amazing Fields even lets you view your cards in a table view, without requiring a Trello Premium plan. To do this, click the **Fields** button in the top toolbar of your board and select the **Table View | Search | Export** option. You'll then see a screen like this:

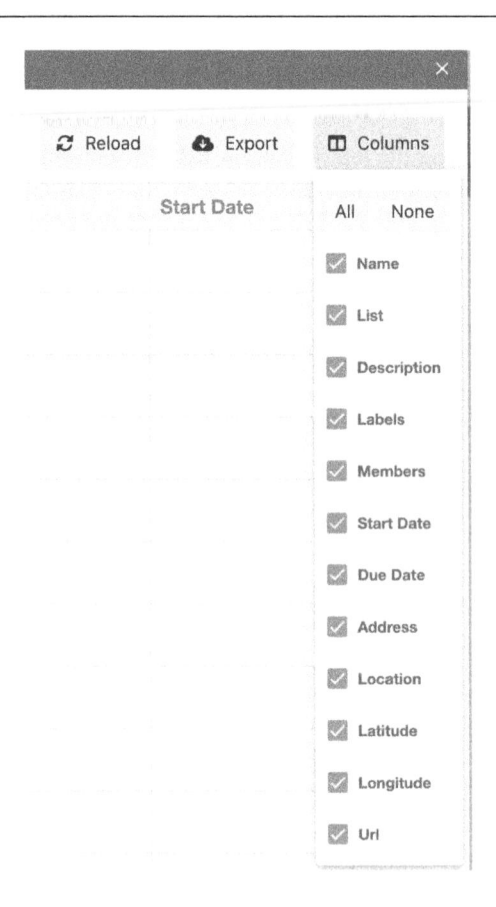

Figure 12.20 – Amazing Fields Table view

Unlike Trello's **Premium Table** view, this view allows you to view cards in a table along with your created fields, and you can control which attributes and fields are shown.

Many more chapters would have to be written to cover everything you can do with Amazing Fields, but thankfully, the Power-Up is very intuitive and you'll learn a lot just by clicking around. You can also reach out to support via the chat in the bottom-right corner of the **Settings** page.

You can do so much with your boards, but before we end this chapter, I need to show you one more thing—how to quickly edit multiple Trello cards!

Bulk Actions

While making changes to any one Trello card isn't all that difficult, making changes to many of them at once can take a while. As of 2022, Trello doesn't natively offer a way to quickly edit multiple cards at once, such as adding members, changing due dates, or removing labels. But this is possible with the Bulk Actions Power-Up!

Bulk Actions is built by AxoApps and has been added to over 100,000 boards! There is a limited free plan that allows actions on a maximum of 5 cards at a time, but you can edit more cards for as little as $1 a month per board.

> **Why use Bulk Actions?**
>
> Whether it's spring cleaning, project dates shifting, or new members added to (or leaving) a team, you'll find there are a lot of situations where you need to quickly make sweeping changes in your board.
>
> It's possible to do all of this manually, but it takes so much time. If you ever find yourself in situations where you have had to quickly move a bunch of cards to another list, update due dates on cards when milestone date changes, or re-assign labels or members to cards, you'll find this Power-Up saves you tons of time.

Let's go through two examples of editing cards. We'll edit a handful of cards to add labels to them since I came up with a new way to organize my cards, and we'll also walk through an example of shifting the due dates on multiple cards when a project changes due dates.

Adding Bulk Actions

Go to the Power-Up directory by clicking on the **Power-Up** button at the top of any Trello board, then clicking **Add Power-Ups**. If you already have a couple of Power-Ups on your board, the **Power-Up** button might be a rocket ship icon instead of the text. When you've arrived at the Power-Up directory, search for Bulk Actions, and click **Add** on the first Power-Up that appears:

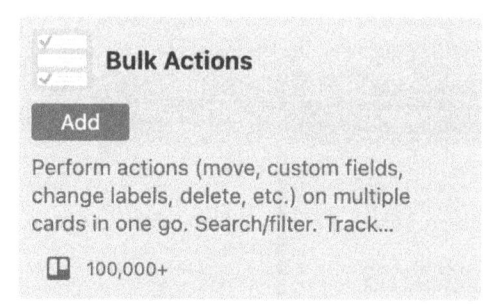

Figure 12.21 – Bulk Actions card in the Power-Up directory

You'll be asked to click **Add** once more to confirm you acknowledge this Power-Up wasn't built by Trello.

You'll see a few intro slides explaining how Bulk Actions works, and then you'll be prompted to sign up for a subscription. You'll then see some information about the premium plans and your free trial:

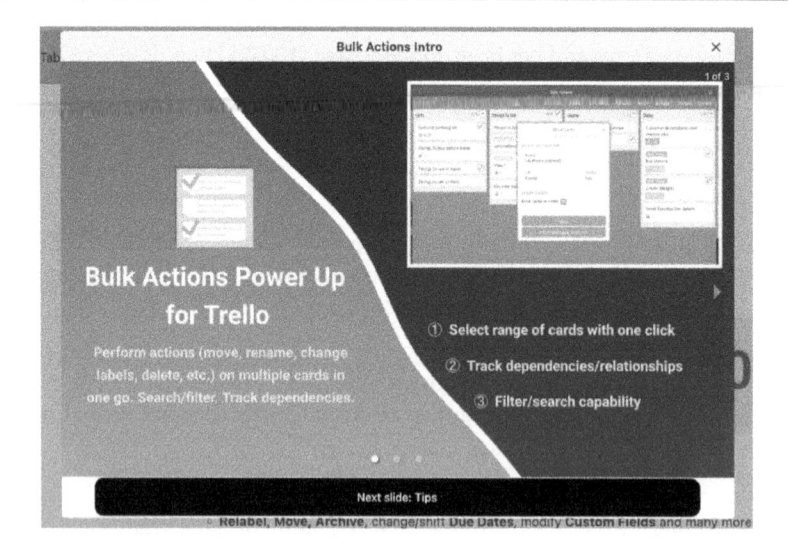

Figure 12.22 – Bulk Actions welcome instructions

You can choose a subscription that pays per board, and you can add a number of boards. This is great if you know you specifically have a couple of boards that you will want to add this to and want your team to have access to bulk editing features. There is a minimum number of licenses, and each plan comes with a free 7-day trial.

Next, you'll need to open the Bulk Actions editor to start choosing cards and making changes. Click the **Bulk Actions** button at the top of your Trello board to see a version of your board with a few additional elements:

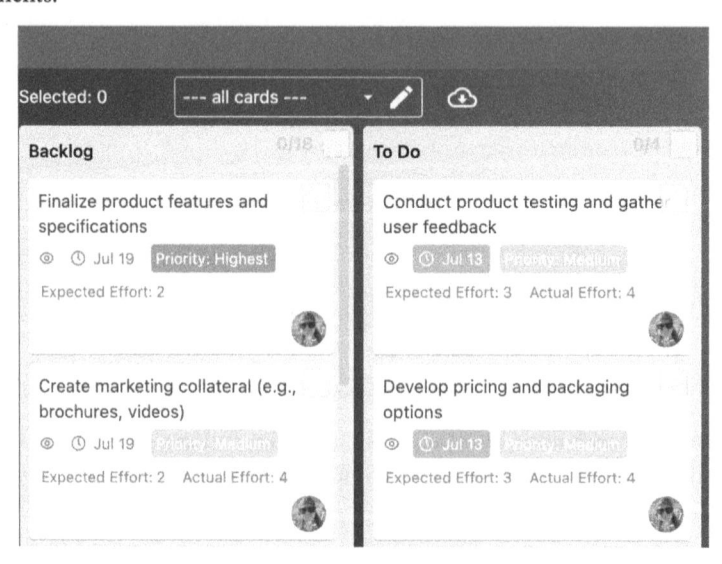

Figure 12.23 – Bulk Actions editing view

Notice on the left that there's a dropdown with a pencil that can be used to filter cards, and there's also a list of actions across the top of the page on the right.

Lastly, you'll notice each card and list has a checkbox on it in the top-right corner. This is how you select cards to change!

Selecting multiple cards to edit

Before you're ready to make changes to cards, you need to select the ones you want to edit. You can do this by manually checking the box on each card, but that can still be a lot of clicking around, so I only do this if there's no clearer way to quickly grab all the cards.

If you want to select all the cards in a list, click the checkbox at the top of the list. If you want to select all the cards on the board, just click the checkbox on each of the lists.

Keep in mind that you can only select a maximum of 80 cards at a time. This can be tough if you have a lot of cards in a list, but there's a handy way to still quickly select a lot of cards. Hover over any card to see what I mean:

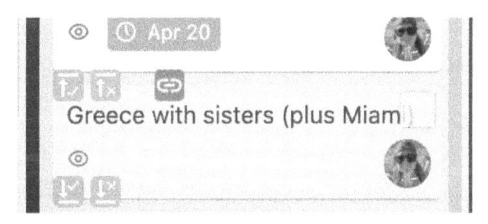

Figure 12.24 – Icons for selecting cards between other cards

You'll see green and gray boxes appear on the left of the card, which allow you to select all cards above or below the current card. This allows you to select a card at the top and then scroll down to quickly grab all the ones in between. You can see how many cards have been selected at the top left of the board.

One more way to quickly grab multiple cards is with the filter. Click on the dropdown that says --- **all cards** --- at the top of your board, next to the pencil icon:

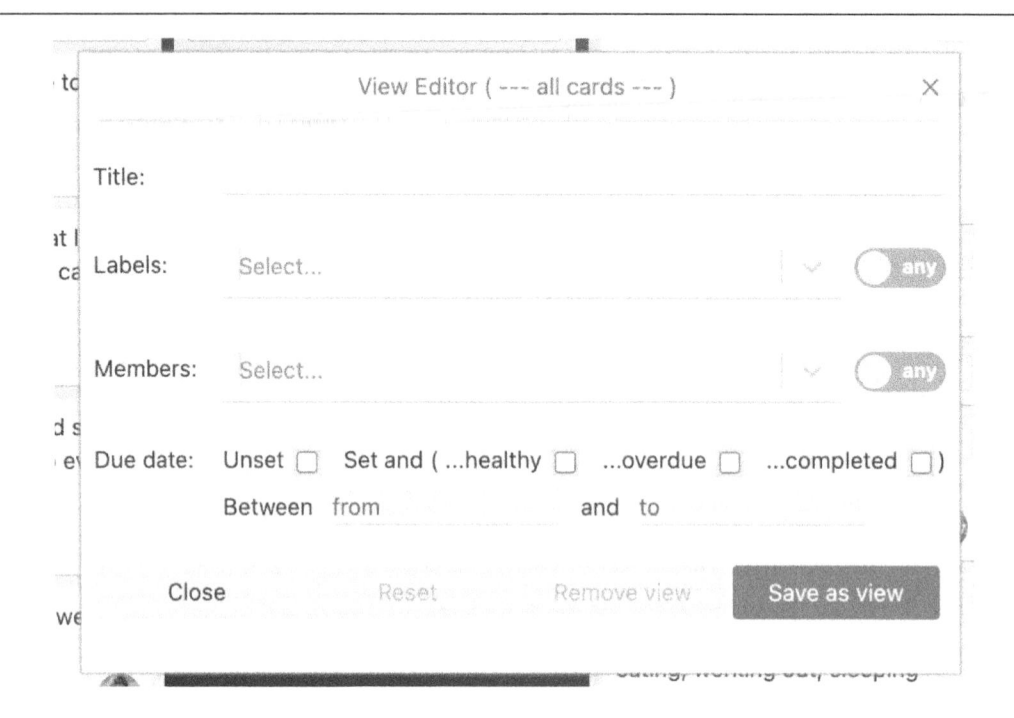

Figure 12.25 – Bulk Actions filter options

This opens a modal that filters the cards that are displayed in the **Bulk Actions** modal. You can filter by labels, members, keywords, or due dates. You can leave the page and the filter will be automatically saved as a draft. However, you can also choose **Save as view** to name it and access multiple filtered views. This shows a filtered version of your board so that you can quickly check the lists to select all the cards.

This is helpful if you know that you want to change all the cards that are assigned to one teammate to another teammate.

Making changes to multiple cards

Now that you know how to select multiple cards, you're ready to apply edits to those cards! Once you've selected the cards you want to change, choose the field you want to change from the top of the board:

Figure 12.26 – Bulk Actions nav bar

We'll start by changing the labels, so we'll click **Relabel**. A modal appears with all of our board's labels. We can now check the labels we want on the cards and remove the checks on the labels we want to remove. If you don't want to make any more changes to those cards, click **Relabel**. I'm going to adjust the due dates, so I'll click **Relabel and keep selection**:

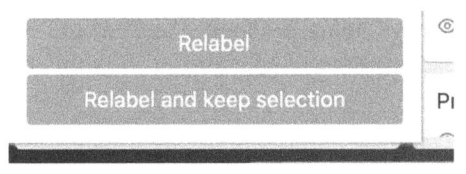

Figure 12.27 – Bulk Actions options for saving changes

Now, your cards have new labels! You can see this in the **Bulk Actions** overlay. Next, let's shift the due date. When you're working on a project and the final due date is pushed back 10 days, that's a real pain because now you must go find all the dependent tasks and click 10 days later for each task. I've always thought there had to be a better way, and sure enough, there is with Bulk Actions.

I chose to keep the selection, so the same cards are still selected, but if you don't want to use these cards, then go ahead and select the cards that relate to the project. You might be wondering—but wait, they are all going to have a different date, so is it really a bulk change? And yes, it is, because you can *shift* dates, which is going to move all the dates by the same amount, rather than to the same date. Click **Due dates** from the top of the board. This opens a modal giving you options for how to change the dates as well as a preview of what those changes will look like:

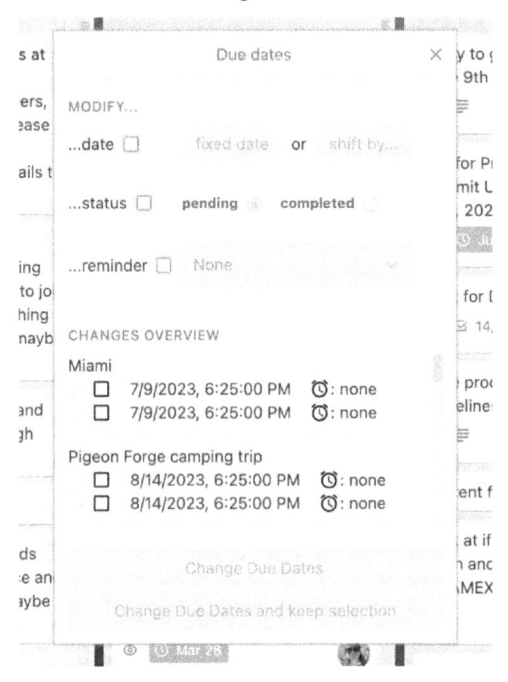

Figure 12.28 – Due date editor

Check the **date** box and then click the **shift by…** option.

You'll then have the option to show how much to shift the date on each card by. You can control shifting by years, months, weeks, days, hours, or minutes, and you can even use negative numbers if you need to shift to an earlier date instead of a later one. Preview the changes and confirm it looks like you'd expect:

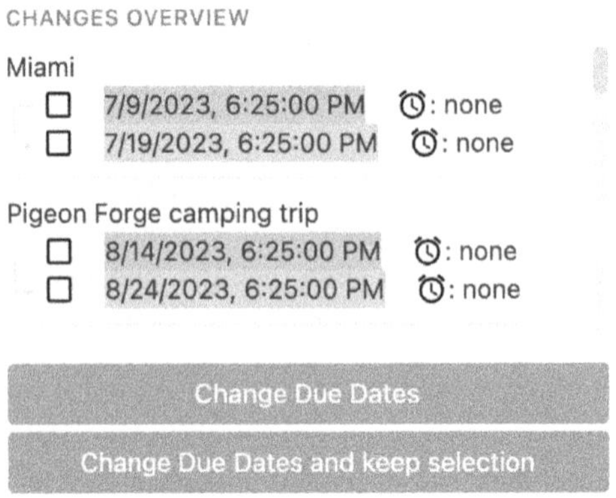

Figure 12.29 – Previewing due date changes

When you're done, click **Change Due Dates**. You know how to shift due dates like magic! Close out of the **Bulk Actions** overlay by clicking the **X** button in the top-right corner, and you'll see your cards on your board have the new due dates.

There are so many other changes you can make to cards with Bulk Actions, including updating custom fields, or archiving or deleting cards. I tend to recommend this Power-Up frequently because it's so useful, no matter how you use Trello.

Summary

I'll say it once more—these are just a couple of the hundreds of Power-Ups that are available. There is no perfect answer to "What are the best Power-Ups for every Trello user?" because everyone uses Trello so differently! But these Power-Ups work well for just about any use case because most involve getting stakeholder approval, adding custom data, and making changes to many cards at once.

Explore the Power-Up directory to learn about Power-Ups for your use case. For instance, if you're managing contacts in your Trello boards, you'll want to use Crmble to add contact fields and pipeline reporting to your board automatically. If you want to build your own app on top of Trello, such as a hiring portal or a blog, you can use a Power-Up such as Hipporello to create apps for your users that let you operate in your Trello boards. Even email has Power-Ups in Trello, such as SendBoard and Cardbox that let you manage your inbox from Trello, perfect for support teams or any team with a shared inbox that needs triaging.

And new Power-Ups are being added all the time! Search the Power-Up directory or post in the Atlassian Community to learn about more Power-Ups and get inspiration for which ones might work best for your boards.

No matter how you use Trello, you'll find these useful to improve your workflows. Now, let's dive into some more Trello Power-Ups that help you get information into your boards and synced with other tools or even other boards!

13
Syncing Info Between Boards and Tools

Unfortunately, we can't get everyone to use Trello (don't worry— I haven't given up trying), and even for those that we can, we can't all operate on the same board! Some of the most common questions I'm asked are how to sync between multiple boards and how to quickly get information in Trello.

Although you can get some syncing capabilities with advanced automation, it's a lot to build and it never works perfectly. But thankfully, there are solutions. In this chapter, we'll explore two Power-Ups that help you solve this challenge and make it work like a dream.

In this chapter, you'll learn about the following:

- How Forms by Blue Cat gathers information from team members and clients in a more organized way to create cards
- How Unito connects different sources of data with your Trello boards for a more integrated workflow

Let's start by talking about how to sync information from info filled out on a web page straight to your Trello board.

Forms by Blue Cat

While templates work great for creating cards, sometimes folks may still be confused about where to put something when creating a card, or what kinds of information are needed before work can begin on a task.

There are also some cases where you may want others to make requests or create cards on your boards, but you don't want them to view or edit cards. Maybe you want your users to be able to request a feature that becomes a task on your dev team's Trello board, but you don't want to add all of your users to your Trello board. That's costly, requires your users to have or create a Trello account, and gives them access to sensitive info in the team's board.

This is where Forms by Blue Cat can help. This Power-Up lets you create a public form that you can embed or share anywhere. On every form submitted, a new card is created with the information from that submission.

This Power-Up is built by Blue Cat, a company that has made many other amazing Power-Ups, including Import to Trello, which allows you to convert a spreadsheet into a Trello board, and perhaps their most famous Power-Up, Blue Cat Reports, which we'll discuss more in *Chapter 14*.

Forms by Blue Cat has been added to over 40,000 boards, including many of my own!

> **Why use Forms by Blue Cat?**
>
> If you want to quickly capture the required information to create new cards or tasks, you might want to use Forms by Blue Cat. It's perfect for defining criteria that need to be answered before adding a task to your board and prevents you from adding something to your board that hasn't been thought out.
>
> It's also great for collecting feedback, information, and files from external users, such as people who aren't part of your board or people who may not even have a Trello account! You can map the form fields to attachments as well as standard and custom Trello fields. I've used Forms to collect subscriber feedback for my own Trello newsletter, and I allow my subscribers to ask me questions about Trello in the "Dear Taco" section of my newsletter. Readers submit questions via Blue Cat forms, which are then queued up in my Trello board so I can keep track of which ones I've answered.

Like many other Power-Ups, Forms by Blue Cat offers a free version, but to get premium features or more volume, you'll need to pay. The free version is very powerful and allows up to 10 submissions per account each month.

Let's go through an example of how I use Forms by Blue Cat to answer my subscribers' questions about Trello!

Adding Forms by Blue Cat

Head to the Power-Up directory by clicking **Add Power-Ups** from the **Power-Up** button in the top toolbar of any board. From there, search for Forms by Blue Cat in the field on the top left.

Figure 10.1 – Forms by Blue Cat card in the Power-Up directory

Click the **Add** button on the Forms by Blue Cat card. You're now ready to create your first form!

Creating a form

If you've just added the Power-Up, you'll be immediately directed to the home page and should see a button called **Create form**. Click that to get started. If you went back to your board after adding the Power-Up, you'll need to click the **Blue Cat Forms** button in the top toolbar of your board.

Once you arrive in the form editor, you can customize your form to suit your use case.

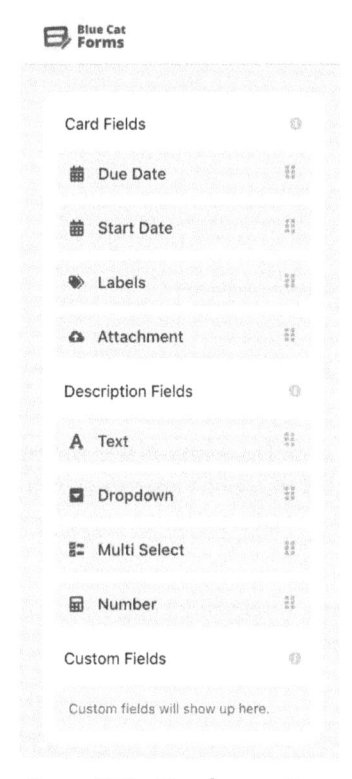

Figure 10.2 – New form options

Start by naming the form something that makes it clear what the form is about. For instance, you might name it **Request a feature** if you're planning to collect feature requests. In my case, I called mine **Dear Taco** because that's the name of my newsletter section where I solicit reader questions and answer them (Shameless plug to subscribe if you haven't already: trello.substack.com/).

Adding and customizing a field

Next, drag the fields from the left-side panel into the middle of the page to create a field with that type. I'll drag a text field first since I want to collect a subscriber's name or nickname to reference in the answer. (It's fun seeing what people submit for this... my current favorite is **How I Trello's #1 Fan!**).

Click the newly added field to configure it.

Figure 10.3 – Field options

We're going to change the field name from **Description Text** to **Name**. I'm also going to update the **Description** field to let folks know that they don't have to actually provide their real name. Give any additional context you want for your field, such as examples or helper text to clarify what a user should put in the field.

Next, adjust the way the field text works by selecting **Long Text** and changing it to a specific type of text that you're expecting, such as **Email Address** or **Short Text** if you want to take up less space.

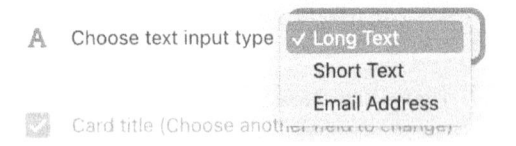

Figure 10.4 – Text input types

By default, the first field added to your form will have the **Card title** field checked since each card must have a name. Once you add more fields, you can select that checkbox in another field to make that field's value the title of the card. In my case, I actually do want to keep the subscriber's moniker as the title, so this is fine.

Next, you'll decide whether this field is optional or required, and finally, you can choose whether you want to apply conditional logic to a field. This will only show this field if the person filling out the form has provided a specific value in another field. For example, if you use this form to collect shipping info, you might only show a **State** field if someone has chosen **United States** in the **Country** field.

The last section shows where the info from that field will be sent when someone fills out the form. You can't change this, but if you want to send information to another section of the card, just choose a different field type. For instance, if you want to map the text to a custom field, look on the left-side panel at the field options and you'll see **Custom Fields** as a field type to drag over. Any responses to that question on the form will be added to that custom field.

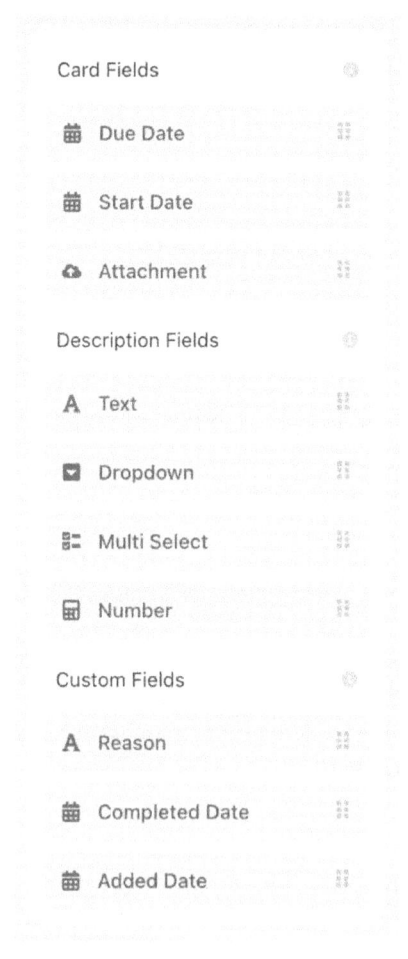

Figure 10.5 – Field types

You can add as many fields as you want to your form. And the best part, you can make those fields map to different parts of the card instead of just the description and custom fields!

Mapping fields to other parts of a card

I like to give folks the opportunity to share screenshots when they ask their Trello questions in case that helps clarify the question. To do this, I just drag over the **Attachment** field type and update the name and description. Just be aware that attachment fields are a paid feature that is only available on Basic and higher Forms by Blue Cat plans.

You can also map form answers to labels or dates. This is helpful if you want to ask users to respond with a date, which will set the due date of the card, or if you want to sort out what type of request it is and allow users to choose from labels.

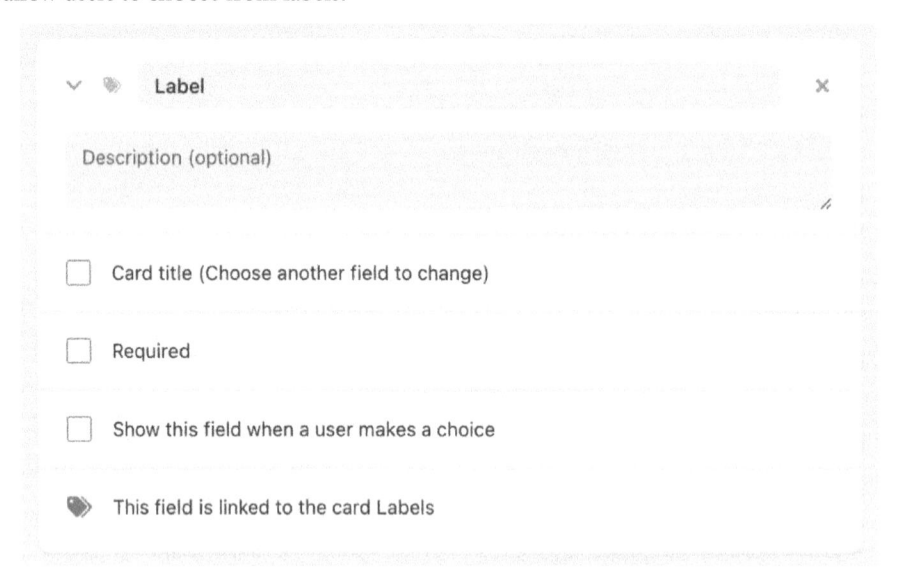

Figure 10.6 – Field options for Forms by Blue Cat

Just keep in mind that if you use labels, this means the options for that question will be all the available labels on the board. You cannot select a subset of labels. If you want to provide a subset, it's better to just use the **Dropdown** or **Multi Select** field type and then use automation rules to update the label based on text inside the card description.

Form settings

After you've added fields, scroll back to the top of the form and click the **More Settings** button next to the form name.

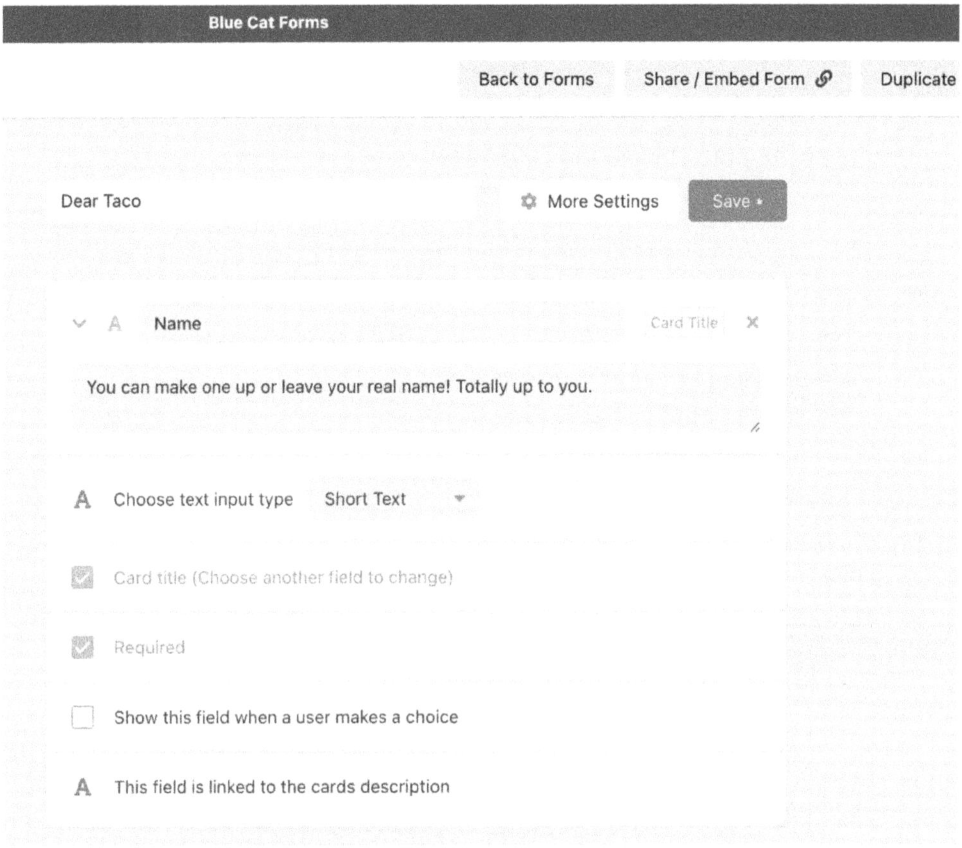

Figure 10.7 – Title and more settings for Blue Cat Forms

This is where you can customize the experience of the entire form, instead of just specific fields. If you want to make your form stand out, you can add custom branding, though this will require you to be part of the Forms by Blue Cat Pro plan.

By default, new responses to the form will create cards in the first list on the board, but if you'd like to change it to another list, just select it from the dropdown.

Syncing Info Between Boards and Tools

To make your form extremely clear, set the introduction and thank you messages. Introduction messages will be shown above the form, while thank you messages will appear after the form is submitted.

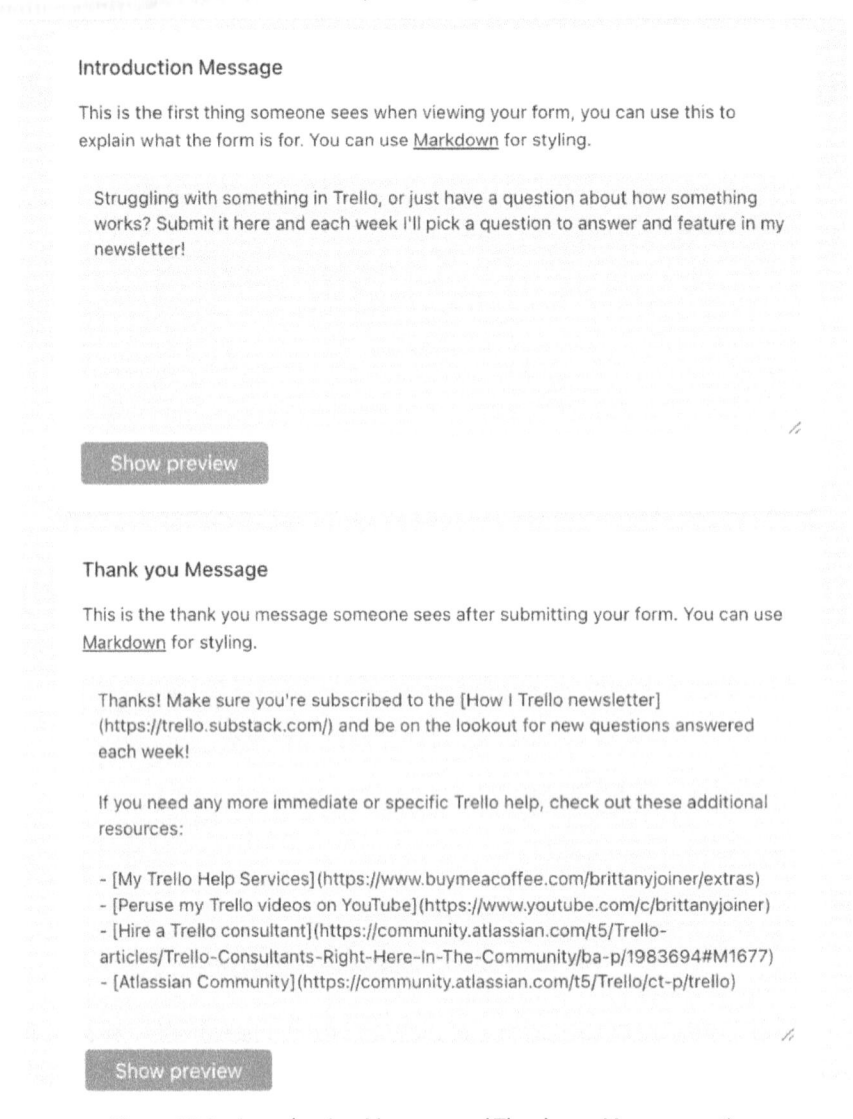

Figure 10.8 – Introduction Message and Thank you Message options

These allow you to give more context to your form so folks can fill it out appropriately. It's also great for giving more information and actions after filling out the form. I use **Thank you Message** to tell my readers about my YouTube channel and also point them to places to get more help with Trello, such as the Atlassian Community.

Lastly, you can change the submitted text to anything else you'd like. It would probably be more fun to change mine to say **Ask Taco!** rather than **Submit**, so I'll go ahead and change that.

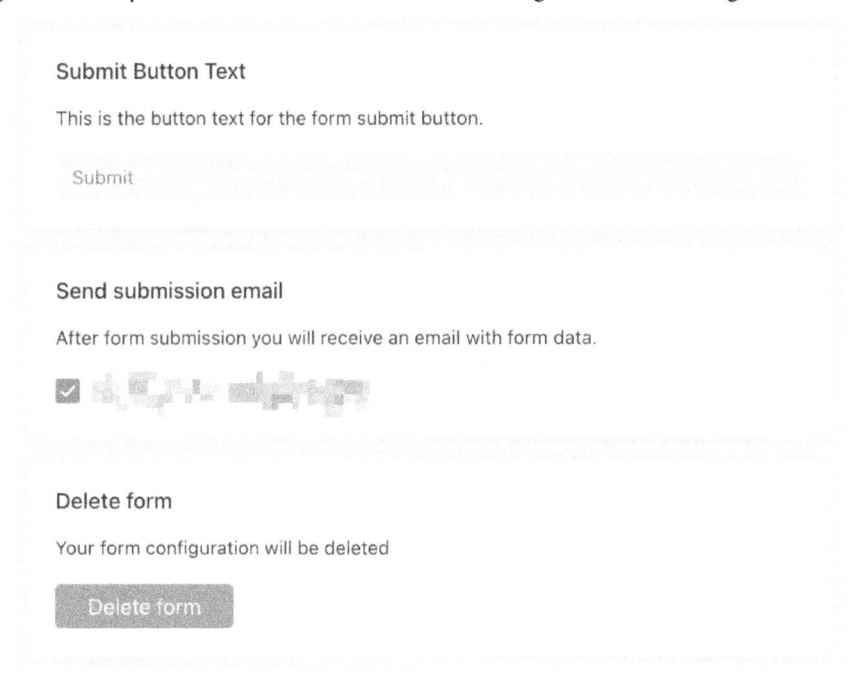

Figure 10.9 – Blue Cat form options

You can also choose to get an email notification when a new response has been submitted. I like to use this as another way to keep track of when requests or submissions have been made.

Once you've added your fields and customized your form options, click **Save** at the top of the page, and you're ready to start sharing your form with the world!

Sharing a form

Each form lives at a special link that anyone can access. They don't even need to have a Trello account! To view this link, click the **Open Form** button in the top-right corner of the form you're viewing or editing.

262 Syncing Info Between Boards and Tools

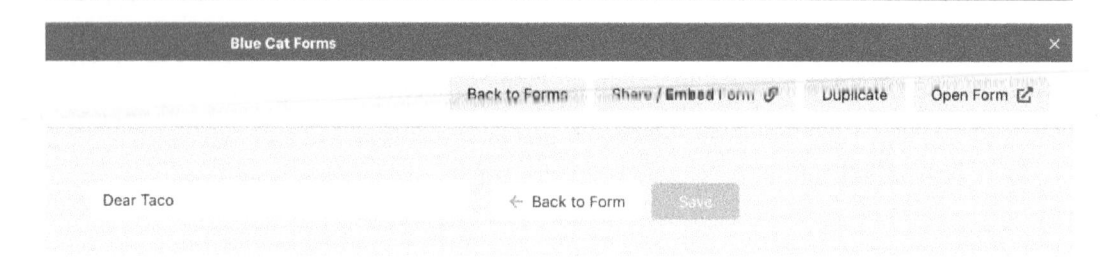

Figure 10.10 – Blue Cat Forms nav bar options

A new tab opens with your form. Double-check that it looks as expected, and if it doesn't, go back to the other tab with the form and make any changes.

Figure 10.11 – Example Blue Cat form

Notice the link in the URL bar. You can copy that link from this page, or you can go back to the form options and select the **Share / Embed Form** button to open a modal with more sharing options, including the link.

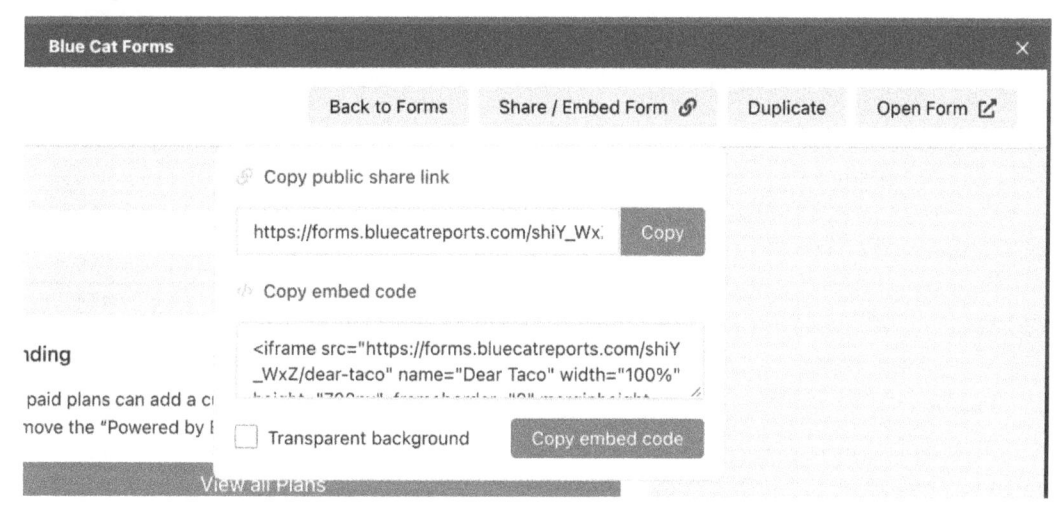

Figure 10.12 – Share options for a Blue Cat form

Copy the link, or use the code snippet to embed the form on your website, or anywhere else that displays iframes.

Testing a form

There's one more thing to do before sharing your form with the world! If you've read the previous chapters, you'll know I'm a big proponent of testing as we go. Let's test out our form.

Go to the share link and fill out the form. After submitting, return to your Trello board and confirm that you have a new card in the list you expected, and that all the information is mapped to the fields you wanted.

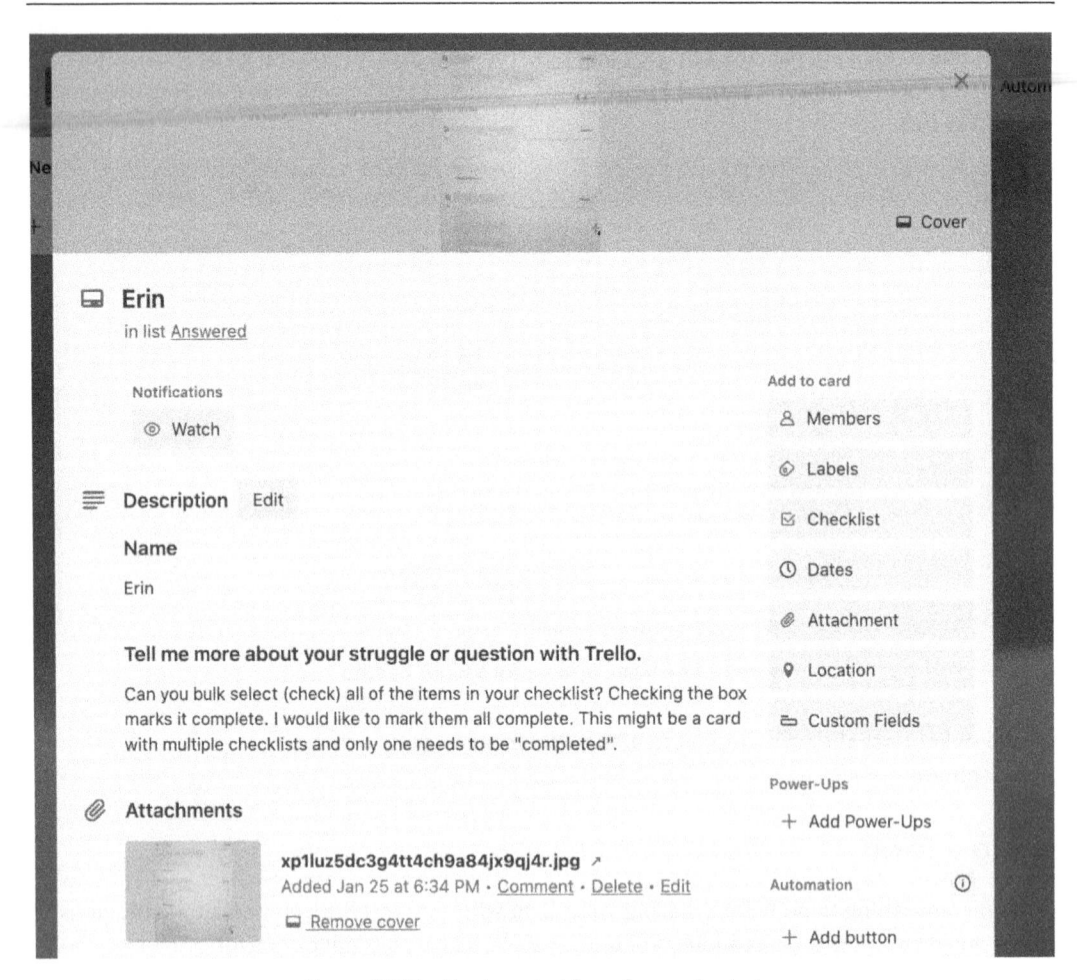

Figure 10.13 – Card created from form submission

If you need to make any changes (now or later), you can always go back to your form by clicking the **Blue Cat Forms** button at the top of your Trello board's toolbar and selecting the edit icon to the right of the form name.

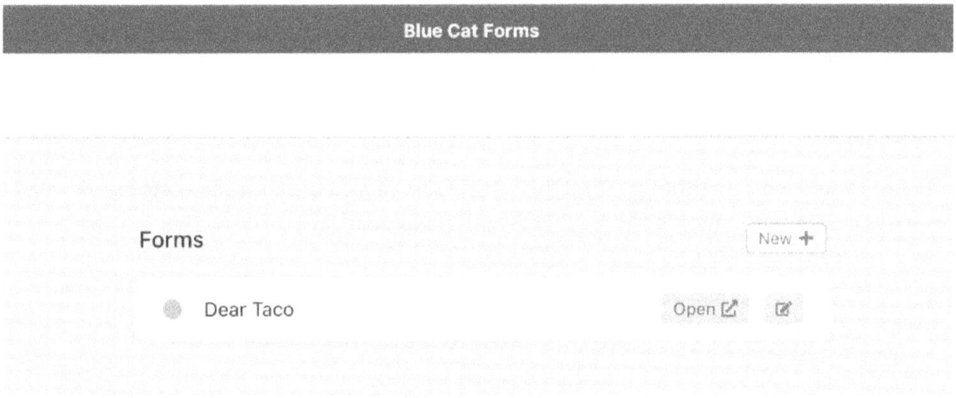

Figure 10.14 – Blue Cat form list

This is also a great place to quickly get the share link for a form.

Now you're ready to share your forms with the world and help get your information into Trello as quickly as possible!

Unito

As much as I want everyone to use Trello, and as much as I've tried, I just can't get everyone in the world on board with it (pun intended). So, you probably won't be able to either (*although if you do, that will make my life easier, so 🙏 thank you in advance*). Even if you could get everyone to use Trello, you'd never be able to get everyone to use the same board. And for that reason, Unito enters the scene to make everyone happy and literally bring everything together.

Unito offers many Power-Ups, but at its core, it is a syncing company that integrates with many tools, such as Trello, GitHub, Monday.com, Asana, Jira, and even Google Sheets, to help you keep all your tasks in sync while allowing everyone to work from their own spaces. It even works to integrate Trello boards with each other!

It's not free, and if I'm being honest, it's not even cheap (at the moment, plans start at $30 a month for basic features and syncing 150 items a month). But you can get a 14-day free trial to test it out and make sure it works for your use case, and if you are looking for a quick and easy way to sync multiple tools or Trello boards with each other, you won't find a better tool or alternative!

> **Why use Unito?**
>
> Unito is a fantastic tool because we will never all work in the same place. Unito lets you keep your tasks in Trello while your engineering team works in GitHub and your product team works in whatever tool they want to; Unito keeps everything updated, regardless of where the change happened. If a label is updated on a card in one Trello board, you can mirror that change on the same card in another board, or even another tool, such as Notion!

There's so much you can do with Unito that I won't be able to cover it all in this chapter. We'll go through an example of connecting Trello and Notion, since that's something I've been exploring lately, and you'll follow a similar process regardless of what you're connecting with Trello, even if it's just another Trello board!

To start using Unito, you can either go directly to their site, or you can find them via the Power-Up directory by searching for Unito, or the tool you want to sync with.

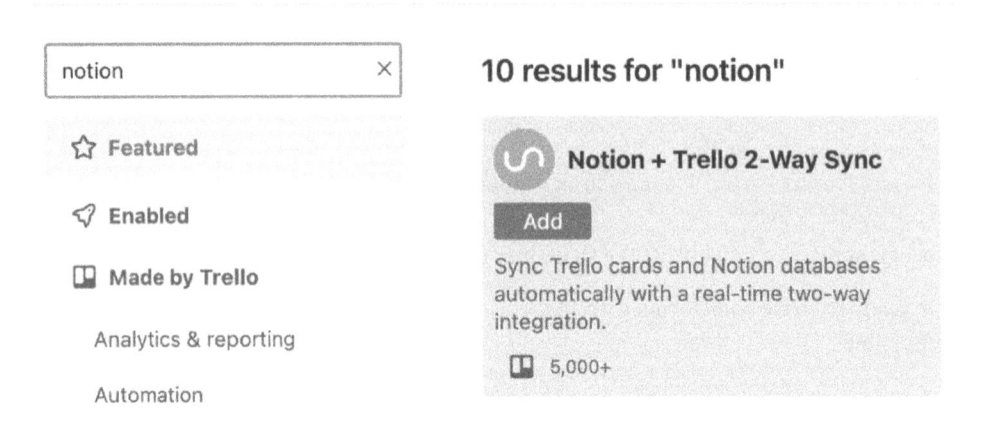

Figure 10.15 – Unito card in the Power-Up directory

I'm searching for Notion since that's what I want to sync with Trello. Once you've added the Power-Up, it's time to create your Unito account and set up your flow!

I prefer to set up Unito flows from their website instead of through their Power-Ups. You can do that too, and it eliminates the need to add the Power-Up to your board. If you want to do this, head to `unito.io/` and create an account. You can even sign up with your Trello account!

Creating a flow

A flow connects two tools together to put them in sync. From the Unito dashboard (the main page you arrive at after logging in or creating an account), click the **+ Create flow** button. Then, you'll be prompted to connect your tools.

Connecting tools

A flow is what connects your tools and keeps data in sync. The first step in creating a flow is connecting the tools you want to be unified.

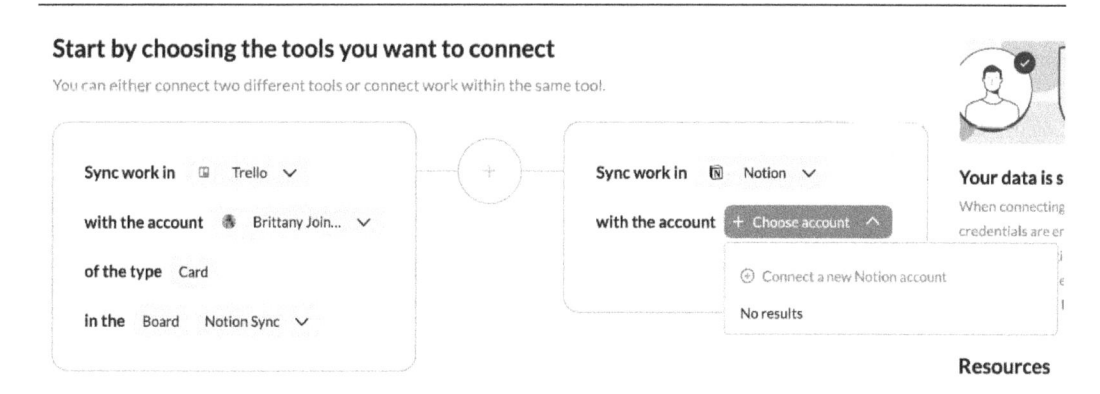

Figure 10.16 – Unito account configuration

This connector is quite easy to use. Just click each dropdown to select the tool, connect an account, and choose which board, project, or database you want to sync, depending on the tool.

I'm choosing a specific Trello board that I want to keep in sync with a Notion database. I've never connected my Notion, so I'm prompted to do so by clicking the **Connect a new Notion account** button from the dropdown.

I'm using Notion as an example, but you can choose from 30+ integrations. See a full list at `unito.io/connectors/`. It's a similar process of connecting your account, giving permissions, and selecting the exact space, such as a repository, board, or project.

For my Trello and Notion sync, this is how my settings look.

Figure 10.17 – Example Unito flow configuration with Trello and Notion

Click the **Confirm** button once everything is configured.

Choosing your flow direction

The next step is configuring the direction we want the cards to sync. You probably want to sync both ways, which means any change that happens in either space reflects in the other.

The next step is configuring the flow direction, which controls where new items get created. In a two-way flow, you'll see new Trello cards automatically created by Unito when you create new rows in Notion and vice versa.

If you only wanted to push work items from one tool to another, you'd create a one-way flow. So, a one-way flow from Trello to Notion would see Unito creating new Notion rows whenever you create a new Trello card. You can still get updates in both tools even with a one-way flow, though! That's because this step only controls where *new* items get created, while any changes in existing items will still be synced in both directions.

If this is the case, you'll just need to change the arrow to point to the direction you *do* want changes to sync.

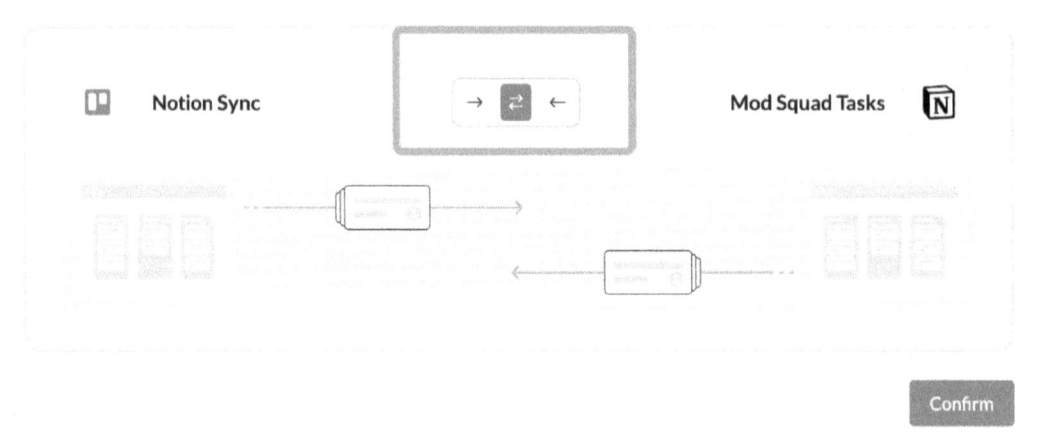

Figure 10.18 – Setting flow direction in Unito

I'd want Unito to create both Trello cards and Notion rows, so I'll leave it with the default bi-directional arrow.

Just click **Confirm** when you're ready to move to the next step. This takes you back to the flow page. Select the **Continue** button on the next part of the configuration.

Choosing what syncs

If this feels like a lot, just keep in mind that for most cases, you can just click through these settings as the default is often what you want! The reason we're going through these step by step is to show you the options you have available in case you want to customize and do something specific.

In this step, you can filter which cards (or issues, pages, or other items depending on the apps you connected) are synced. You might choose to do this if you only want to sync your own cards to another board or tool, instead of all cards.

To do this, you'd click **Add a new rule** to specify that you only want to sync tasks from another project where you're the owner.

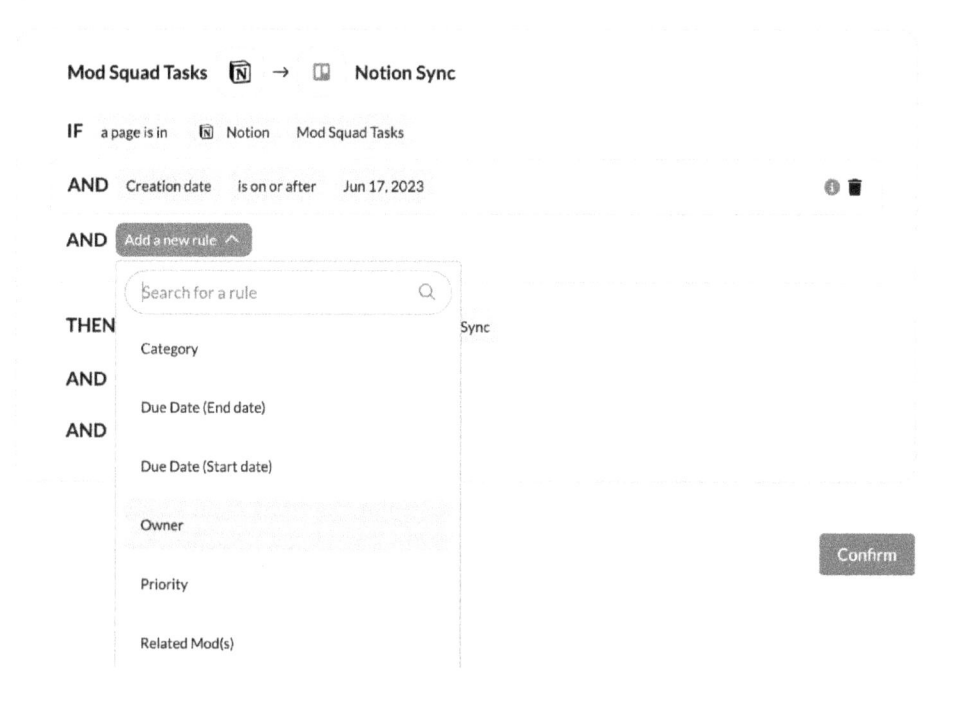

Figure 10.19 – Rules for syncing in Unito

You can also filter by other criteria, such as syncing only cards created at a certain time or with certain labels or attributes.

By default, your flow will only sync cards from the current date onward and will not apply retroactively to previously created cards. If you want it to apply to existing cards, you'll need to click the trash can icon to delete the default creation date filter.

Figure 10.20 – Syncing existing cards in Unito

Once you're good to go, click **Confirm** to move to the next stage, and then click **Continue** once again to specify what information flows between sources.

Specifying what information flows

We're nearly done! I know it seems like a lot of options, but in many cases, you'll never need to jump into Unito again and your tools will work together like magic.

This is the last section to configure because it's where we specify how the different fields relate to each other.

Unito gives you two options: you can use the Auto-map feature, or **Start from scratch** to manually map the fields. In most cases, the Auto-map feature works well and knows exactly which fields should map, so I (and Unito) recommend choosing that option first. You can always customize the mapping afterward if anything is incorrect, but this gives you something to start with. Click **Auto map my fields**.

If it doesn't guess them perfectly, or if you want to change them, you can click the + **Add mapping** button at the top and create a new map between fields. For instance, I want the title of my Trello card to map to sync to my task name in Notion.

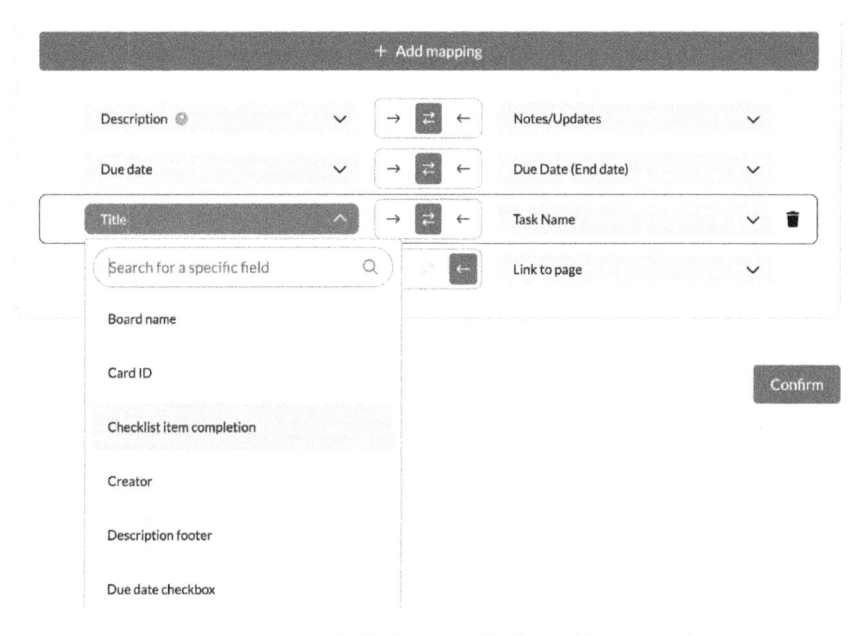

Figure 10.21 – Mapping fields between Trello and Notion with Unito

You can map any other fields you want or remove any mappings by clicking the trash icon at the end of the row. You can also pick the flow direction at the field level here. So, if you only want updates to go in one direction, you can pick a one-way arrow from the source tool to the tool where updates will happen. Usually, you'll want to keep most field mappings two-way, since this is where Unito really shines. Once you're done, click **Confirm**. Then, you're ready to move to the very last step!

Launching your flow

Now it's time to launch your flow and watch the magic unfold. Click **Continue** from the flow setup page, then name your flow and confirm you're ready to start syncing.

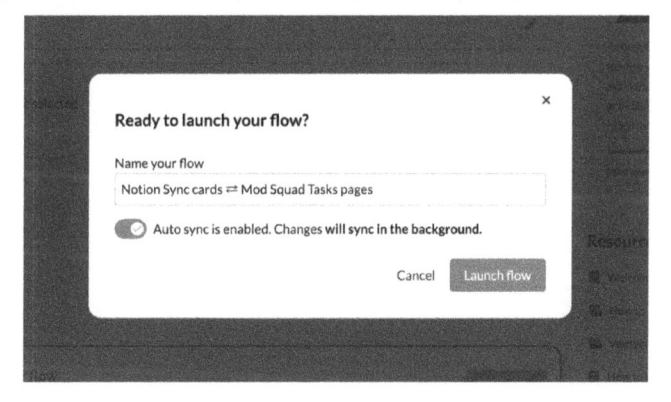

Figure 10.22 – Naming and launching a flow in Unito

Leave auto sync enabled to continuously sync cards. You'd only turn this off if you wanted to do a one-time sync across tools, or manually go into Unito each time you want information to sync.

Click **Launch flow** when you're ready.

You'll see a notification that the syncing is happening! It might take a few minutes, but you should see new cards flowing into your board soon.

Testing a flow

Head to your Trello board and you should see data from your connected source in your board! Now make an update to a card, and check that it's reflected in the other tool or board.

If anything looks off or you need extra help, reach out to the Unito support team by clicking the chat icon in the bottom-right corner of the Unito dashboard.

Now you can make everyone happy and let them work in the tools they work in!

Summary

Wow, Trello Power-Ups are the gift that keeps on giving! Who knew you could do so much with them? And we've only explored a handful so far! Check out Blue Cat Reports' Power-Up directory, which is updated every month with any new free Power-Ups: `bluecatreports.com/free-trello-powerups/`.

Now you can get information into your Trello boards from anywhere, even from people who don't have a Trello account. You can also sync your board with other boards, or even other tools entirely, such as GitHub, Notion, Monday.com, Jira, and Google Sheets.

Now it's time to wrap up our Power-Up journey by discussing the next biggest Trello topic I'm asked about: reporting.

14
Reporting in Trello

You're almost ready to conquer the world with Trello. But I can't leave you without discussing your options for reporting in Trello. There are multiple Power-Ups and tools that are available. In fact, you might use several together. Maybe my next book will be all about reporting in Trello, because it's a very deep topic.

But for now, time is limited and we're coming to the end of this book, so I'm going to touch on the three that I am most familiar with and help you understand how to decide which ones are right for you and your team.

In this chapter, you'll learn how to do the following:

- Build lists with more advanced filtering options
- Create charts showing the progress of a project over a month
- Estimate when a project will be complete based on your team's historical performance

You might expect things like that from a spreadsheet, but now you're about to learn how to do it from Trello, too! Let's start with the easy-to-use yet powerful option that fits most use cases.

Blue Cat Reports

Blue Cat Reports is like Trello tables but way more customizable, and it gives you charts. That's the simplest way to describe it, but it's very powerful.

Remember when we talked about creating workspace tables in Trello views back in *Chapter 4*? While that's pretty cool, it's a bit limited. You can only include up to 20 boards, which works for many people, but others have a lot of boards that they need to combine. Trello views allow you to filter by lists, labels, and due dates, but you can't filter by custom fields, and you also can't even display those fields in the table!

Blue Cat Reports solves this and also gives you the opportunity to make charts to show meaningful trends and information about what's happening in your Trello boards. The best part is that it's really easy to get started with and configure. You don't have to set up any mapping to get started, and you'll go through a helpful list of options that walk you through setting up the chart you need.

> **Who is Blue Cat Reports best for?**
>
> Of course this is just an opinion, so make sure to look at multiple tools and do your own research, but I've found that Blue Cat Reports is best for teams that need a lightweight and quick-to-configure reporting solution. If you want to see what's been completed, what's coming up, create custom tables of cards, and aggregate information about those cards, Blue Cat Reports is going to be great.
>
> For most teams, I actually think Blue Cat Reports is a great fit because it covers most of what you will likely need in terms of reporting, and it's affordable and incredibly easy to use. Seems like a no-brainer for most teams!

One thing to note: even if you're the only person using Blue Cat Reports, you'll be charged for each person in your workspace. Although it might seem strange, if you think about it, it makes sense because Blue Cat Reports is collecting that data from each person's profile and activities in Trello to aggregate the data for you.

Adding reports to your board

From any board, head to the Power-Up directory and search for the Reports by Blue Cat Power-Up. It doesn't matter which board you want to use; you'll be able to choose any board you have access to from inside the Reports by Blue Cat Power-Up. But for now, feel free to stick with the data board that you just made or copied.

Figure 14.1 – Reports by Blue Cat Power-Up card

Once you've added it, head back to your board and click the Blue Cat Reports button in the top toolbar. You'll be prompted to create an account, and then your 7-day free trial will begin.

Let's take a look at what we can do.

Figure 14.2 – Blue Cat Reports home page

From the home screen, there are two buttons with actions. We can create a quick list or a report.

Quick lists

Remember when I mentioned super-advanced Trello tables with more fields and filters than you could imagine? That's what quick lists are! I actually find these to be even more useful than the reports, because I can set a list of criteria and quickly access the specific cards that fit those criteria. It also counts the cards and sums any number fields, such as time spent or expected effort.

You can even look at checklist items across multiple boards and multiple people, which is pretty much impossible to do any other way.

Making a quick list is easy peasy. Click **Create a Quick List**. Blue Cat prompts you to name the list, decide whether you want to show cards or checklist items, and then choose the boards you want to look at. You can select as many as you want.

I'm going to name my list `Product Launch Tasks This Week` and only include that board for now.

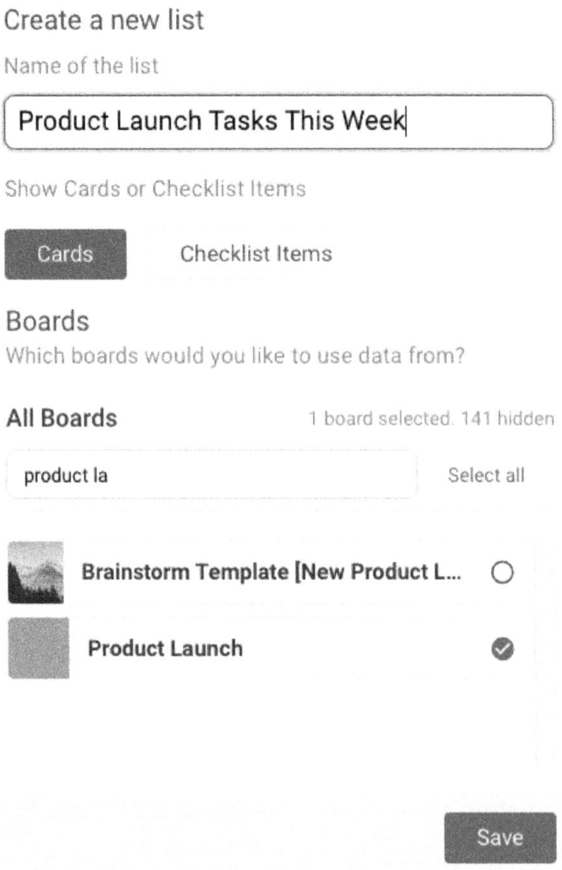

Figure 14.4 – Modal for creating a new quick list

Click **Save**, and now it's time to look at the filters we have! At the start, it's going to pull all the cards from your selected boards. You can see the total number of cards next to the list name.

We want to show tasks that are due this week though, so let's dig into these filters on the left-hand side.

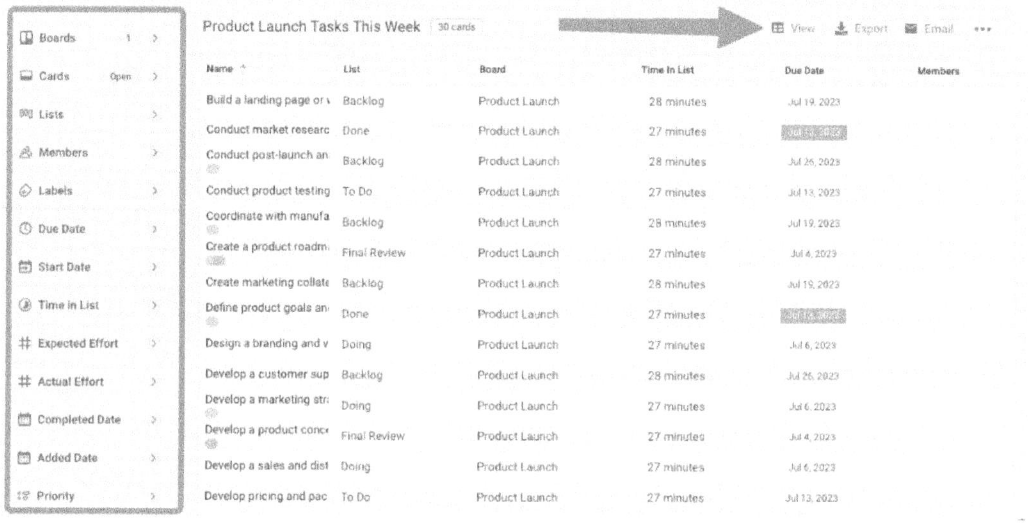

Figure 14.5 – Quick list with filter options and view button highlighted

Head to the **Due Date** section and you'll see your options for date filters, which are more advanced than Trello's native date filter options.

I'm going to click **This week** and then press **Save**. This takes me from 30 cards to just 7 and shows me exactly where I need to focus this week. But we don't have to stop there. I want to see my personal to-do list for the week, so now I'll go to the member filter and click next to my name.

I'll click **Save** and see that we've now narrowed down my list to show my five tasks for the week! I might add one more filter for labels because I don't want to see cards that are blocked at the moment since I can't take action on them.

So, now I can see what tasks I have, but maybe I want to know a bit more about my specific tasks for the week. Click **View** in the top right, above the table, and you'll be able to decide exactly which attributes you want to show for each card.

278 Reporting in Trello

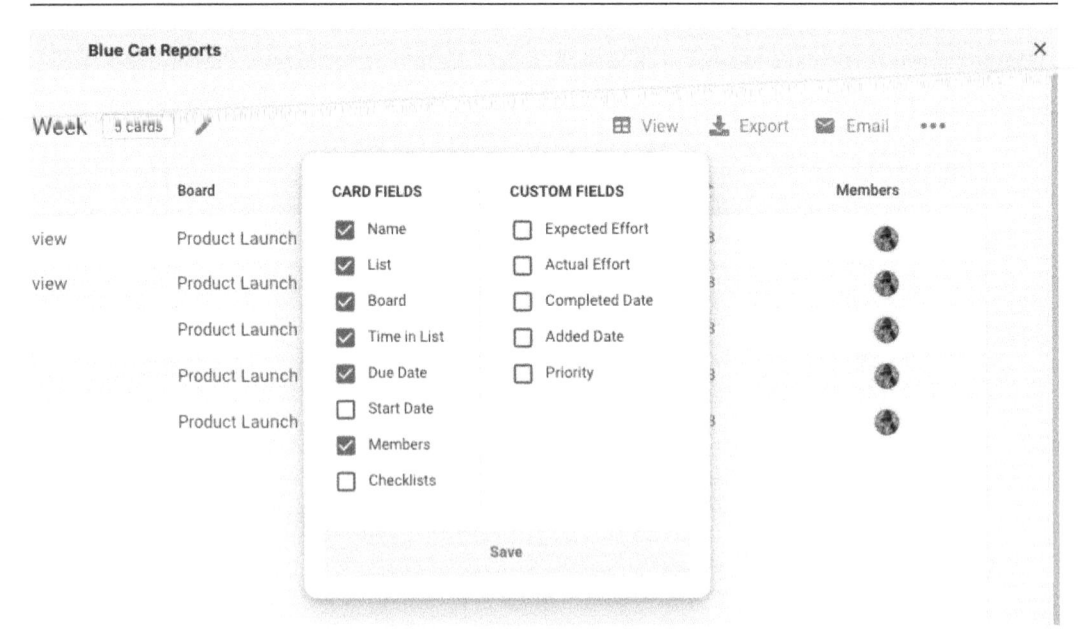

Figure 14.5 – Columns options for quick list table

Notice that you have access to all the core fields in Trello, as you'd expect, such as the list and board, dates and members, and so on. But you can also see **Time in List**, as well as any custom fields you have set. I like to use the **Expected Effort** field that I created because I can see whether I've made a realistic plan for the week, or look back on tasks completed for the previous week and see how much I've accomplished. **Priority** is also helpful to look at so I can determine where to start and focus my time.

Figure 14.6 – Filtered quick list with the sum of fields

I've now got a handy table showing me exactly how my week is going to shape up, and the best part is, each week it will update to check cards for that week. I can sort my table by any one of the fields, such as **Priority**. I can also click on the name of any card to open a new tab with the card. I can even export the board or email it, or I can head to https://app.bluecatreports.com/ and go to the list to get a specific URL that will always take me right to that list.

This is just one way you might use quick lists. You might also create quick lists for the following:

- Seeing what tasks were completed over the past month, sorted by team member
- Creating a list of items from multiple boards that are waiting on review
- Listing all cards that were created in the last month that are tagged as feature requests, along with the estimated effort to complete them
- There are many ways you might use these lists, but we're starting to talk about how much work was completed and looking at the number of tasks with priority, so it's time to head to the reports and get some visuals to answer our questions.

Reports

You'll use reports to display a high-level overview of your projects across one or more boards. It's helpful for showing things like how much work is getting done or seeing if you're allocating tasks evenly between teammates. You can also see how long work takes, identify slow-moving cards and track other trends on your boards. With only a little bit of effort, you can use it to create custom reports like this.

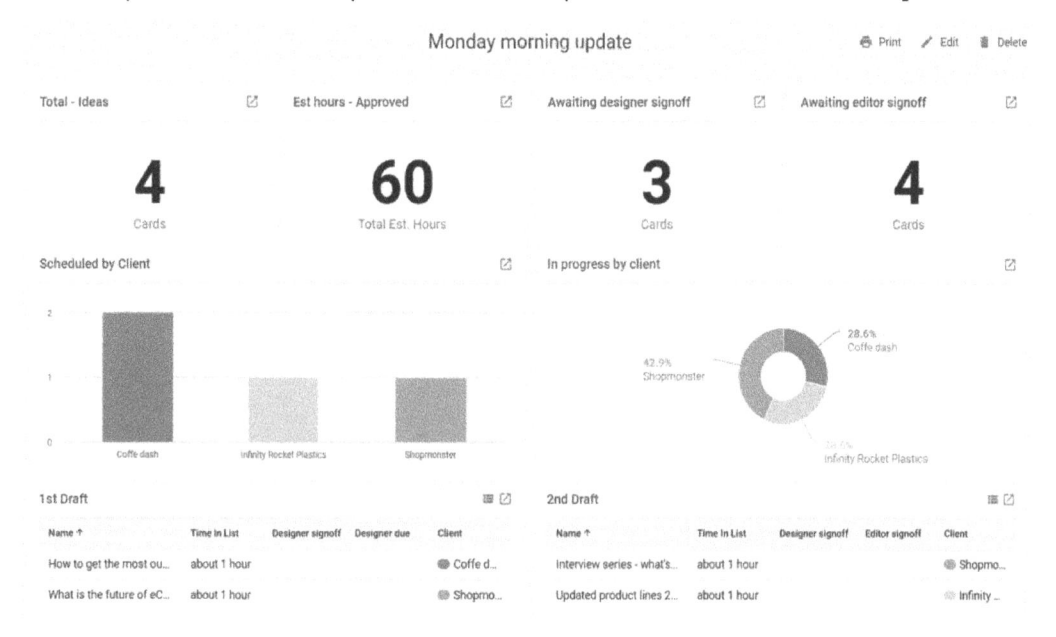

Figure 14.7 – Creating custom reports

Let's go through an example of how to make a simple report showing how much work is getting done and a few different charts we can create to look at that.

Head back to the home page of Blue Cat by clicking the **Home** icon in the top left. Click the button on the right-side panel that says **Create a Report**. You'll be asked to name your report. It is helpful at this point to think about when you would use the report and name it after that, that is, **Monday morning standup** or **Monthly board review**. So if you can think of a sensible name then pick that, or feel free to call it **Test report** if you prefer. Now, click **Save**.

Next, you will need to click **Create chart**. You'll now see various types of charts that you can choose from. This book isn't about charts and task reporting overall, just how to do those things in Trello, so I won't go into much detail here, but you can always ask the Blue Cat reports team or post in the Atlassian Community if you need some help figuring out which chart to use.

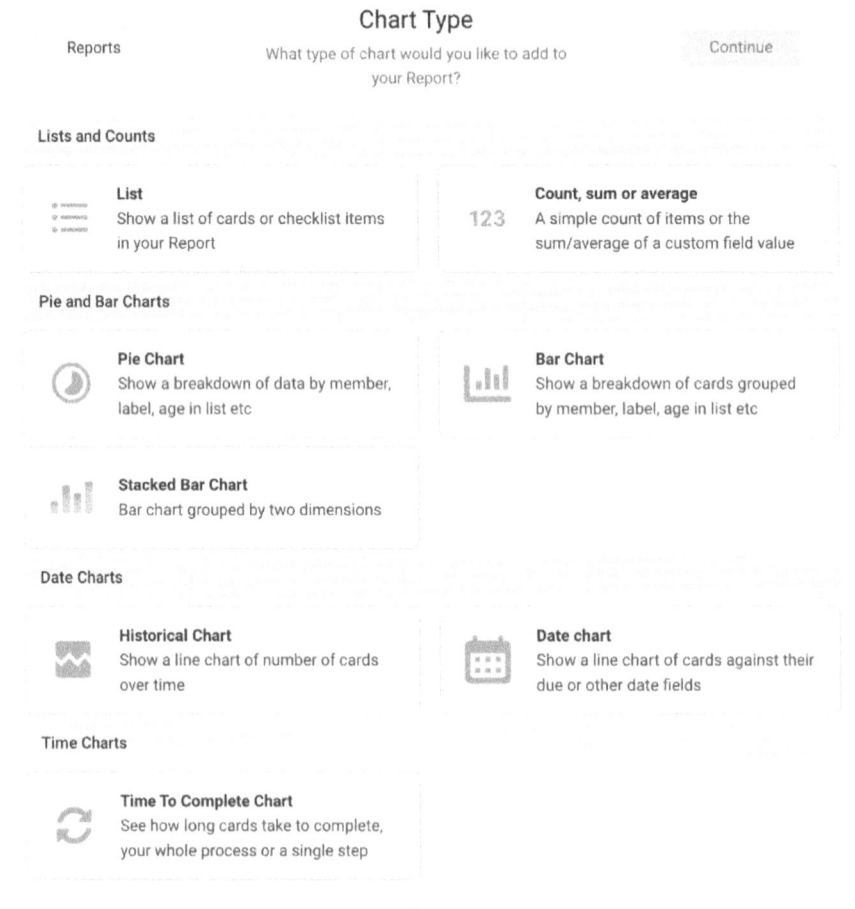

Figure 14.8 – Chart type options

I'm going to choose a **Historical chart**, because I want to show how much work is being completed over time. If you pick the wrong chart, you can click the **Back** button to change or you can edit it later.

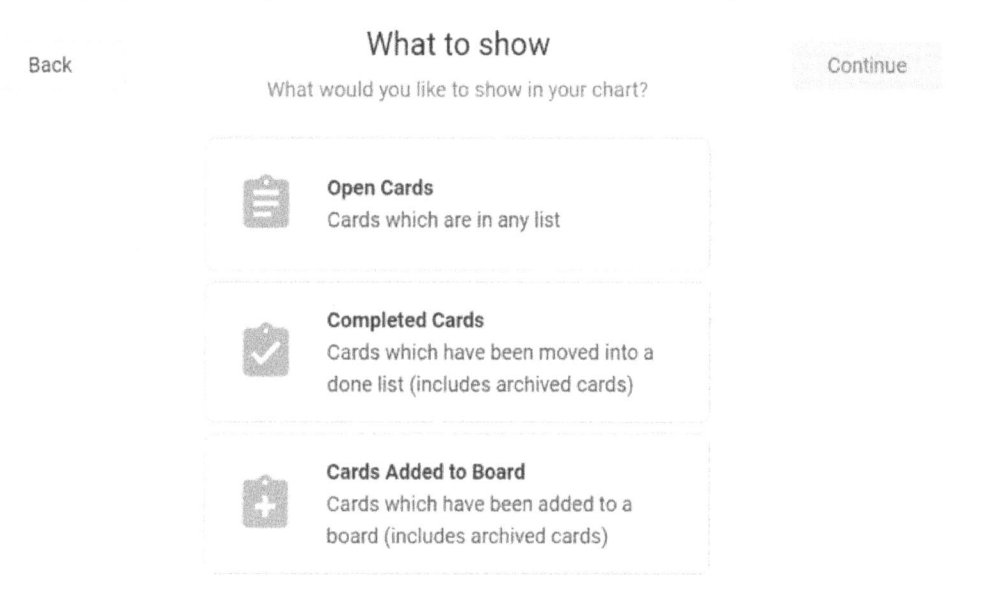

Figure 14.9 – What to show page

After you pick a chart, you'll be walked through a series of questions to help you configure your chart. The questions are very clear, such as **What size do you want your chart?** and **What would you like to show in your chart?** The subtext gives more clarification, such as explaining which cards fit in each option. For instance, you can specify **Open Cards** or **Completed Cards**. Then you'll pick which board(s) you want to look for cards on.

Here we will pick **Completed Cards** as that is what we want to show in this chart. Next, we select the list our cards are moved to once complete, this is how Blue Cat Reports knows a card is completed and when it was completed for your reports.

Reporting in Trello

[Figure 14.10 – Completed lists]

Next, we can select to have a single line for our historical chart to show all the completed cards by date, or multiple lines showing cards completed by member, label, and so on. We will select **None (Single Line)** here.

[Figure 14.11 – Data breakdown]

You can choose from the Member, Label, List, or most of the custom fields you've created.

You'll even get to choose *how* you want to measure what's been completed. This is my favorite feature because I can actually track how much effort I've completed instead of just the volume of cards. Not every card is the same amount of work! Writing a blog post takes a lot longer than sending an email, but each might be just one card. By creating a custom field called **Actual Effort**, I can assign a number to each card that shows the level of effort in the card and then sum (or average) the value for all cards completed in a given time.

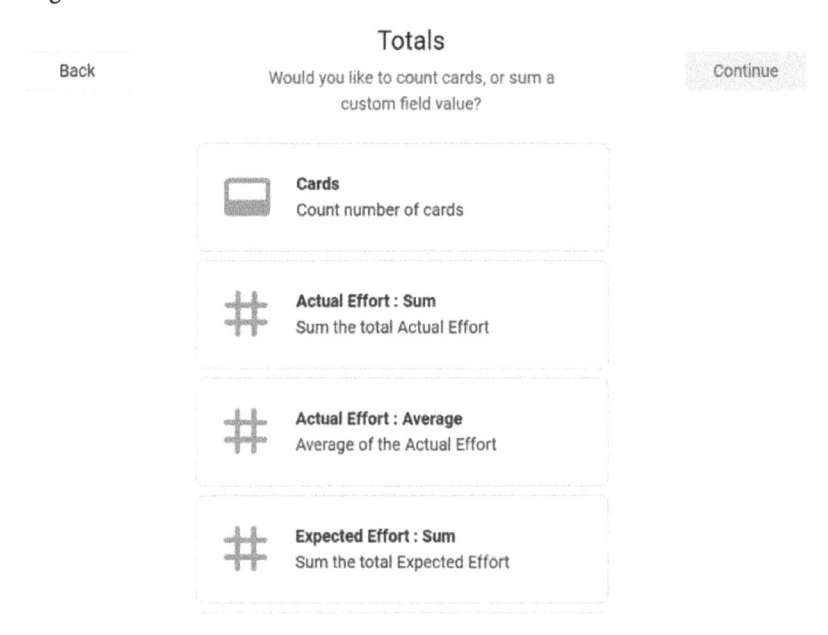

Figure 14.12 – Counting cards or a custom field value

Lastly, you can choose if you want to filter cards by another attribute. We will select **Show All cards** here as we want to show all the completed cards.

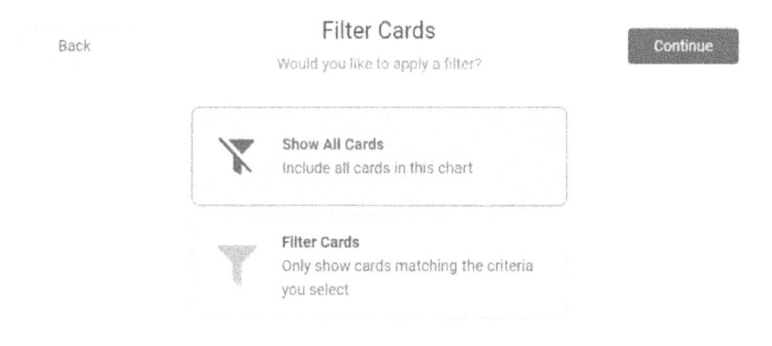

Figure 14.13 – Filter cards

If you were showing open cards (for a chart showing how many cards team members have assigned), you would want to filter by list to include only the lists you cared about. You can add filters for any of your data in Trello as well as Time in List which can be used to find cards spending longer than wanted in any specific list.

Name your chart something like **Cards completed** and click **Save** to view your chart! At first, you will still be in edit mode, click on **Save Report** in the top right to see all the features of your chart.

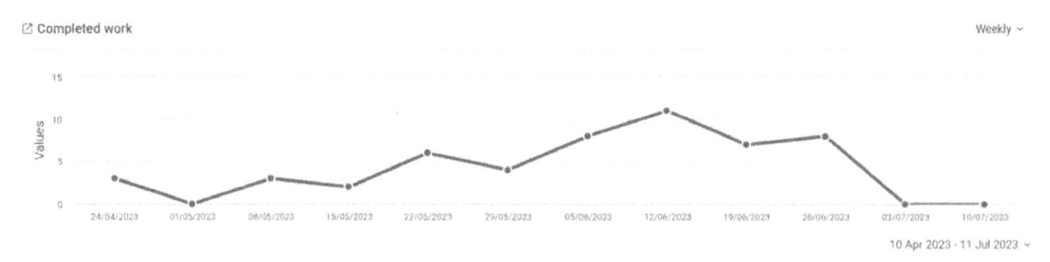

Figure 14.14 - Blue Cat Reports Historical chart of completed cards

You can use the controls on the top and bottom right of the chart to select dates and time periods to display, here we are showing weekly data but can quickly change that to show daily, monthly and so on. You can build as many charts as you want in a report, and in the top left you'll have the option to select the period and exact dates which will apply across all charts on the board to save having to update each chart one by one.

The next step is to add more charts. If you are interested in completed cards you could go through a similar process to add charts for:

- **Cards completed by member**: This is a bar chart with the same settings as the Historical chart, broken down by member.
- **Effort completed by Priority**: This is a bar chart with the same settings again, broken down by the Priority custom field but using the Effort field to generate the Totals rather than the Card counts.
- **How long work takes to complete**: This is a **Time to Complete** chart with the same settings as your Historical chart above.

Here we see an example of an **Effort completed by Priority** bar chart:

Figure 14.15 – Effort completed by Priority bar chart

The bar charts (and most of the charts) can be drilled into by clicking on the title to get additional information. Here we see the drill-down for the **Completed by Member** bar chart. We can filter the data further, see the actual cards completed, and export the data if we needed to.

In the top right of the report, you'll have options as you did in Quick Lists to **Export** and **Email** a report. You'll also be able to **Edit** the report, useful for adding or removing charts and reorganizing the page by dragging charts around.

With Reports, you're now able to answer key questions about your workflow like:

- What's the average time cards are spending in each list?
- Are we spending enough time on high-priority tasks?
- Is the workload balanced evenly among teammates?
- How much work is planned for future weeks?
- Which cards have spent too long in specific lists?
- How many cards are added over time?
- Get all of this emailed to you or anyone on your team on a schedule you define.

And more! Now let's talk about another tool you might use for reporting and also project management.

Placker

While I find Blue Cat Reports is plenty good enough for most use cases, sometimes you need a little bit more, or you need to get data from multiple places, such as Jira boards. To do this, you'll want to try out a more robust tool, such as Placker. I say *more robust* because it offers features such as time tracking and more card data, including estimate-versus-actual fields for budget, effort, and time.

The other benefits of Placker include more project planning tools. You might want to use Placker if you're looking for Gantt charts or more advanced timeline projects.

Placker is also useful if you can't get everyone on your team to use Trello. The teammates who do like to use Trello can easily work inside the app, but others who don't prefer it can easily operate in the Placker app, which reads everything that's needed from Trello boards and offers more views for cards.

It's also nice because if you have 50 people in your Trello boards but only one person who needs to view a dashboard, you can pay for Placker for just that one member and you're not charged for all 50 members. Pretty sweet, as there are generally far fewer people interested in reporting than those that are active in the Trello boards.

> **Who is Placker best for?**
>
> I recommend using Placker if you're working with many stakeholders and multiple projects and you're not just seeking reporting on your Trello cards, but you're also looking for more robust tools for planning projects. Especially if you have multiple projects or different teams in flight, you will appreciate the different views and groups you can set up, while allowing the folks who need it to have everything in one place. You might also be interested in Placker if you're part of a larger enterprise company that wants to use standardized (and customized) dashboards across your teams. Placker allows these teams to create their dashboards that show exactly what is required and then re-use these dashboards across different boards and board groups.
>
> If you're a one-person team, you might find Placker to be a bit more than you need and not worth the configuration time.

While Placker offers some amazing features, the tradeoff is that it's not going to be as quick and easy to set up something like Blue Cat Reports. There's also a lot more buttons and things to click, which can be distracting at best and confusing at worst. But don't worry, it's still painless and you've got a guide (it's me!) to walk you around and help you get the lay of the land.

Plus, you get a free 15-day trial and the team is very helpful and willing to assist, so there's no reason not to try it out!

Getting started

To start using Placker, add the Projects by Placker Power-Up to your board. You can find it by searching in the Power-Up directory for Placker.

Figure 14.16 – Projects by Placker Power-Up card

When the Power-Up is added, the **Placker-sign up** button becomes visible on the board:

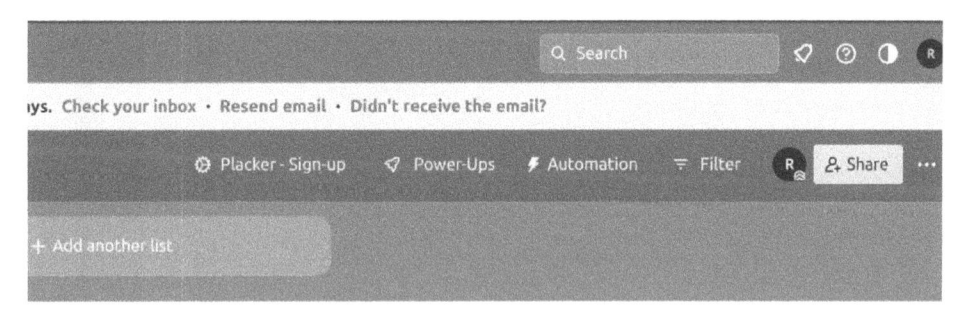

Figure 14.17 – Placker buttons in the toolbar

Click **Placker - Sign-up** from the toolbar and you'll be prompted to accept privacy terms and finish sign-up. After signing up, you'll need to import the boards that you want to use.

When the board is imported into Placker, the Power-Up settings page will be available automatically so you can take the next step in setting up the board: mapping your board.

Mapping a board

Once you connect a board, you'll need to configure some settings about the board to help Placker function best.

You can do this by clicking the **Projects by Placker** button in your toolbar and selecting **Edit Power-Up** settings.

This will open the related Power-Up settings directly and help you set up tracking, calendar, and other relevant settings. You can also copy these from another board, so once you have it set up, you don't have to do it again!

Figure 14.18 – Placker configuration settings

One of the most important settings is progress tracking, which helps Placker understand how you track the status of a task in your board.

Click **Open** next to any of the settings or select another section on the left side panel to adjust more settings. The most important setting is the **Progress tracking** section.

Progress tracking

When you tell us how you track your progress on your board, we will automatically keep track of the actual start and end dates to help you meet your timelines.

○ By hand	○ Label	● List
Manually updating the status attribute in Placker will update the progress dates.	Adding a label to a card will automatically update the status attribute. Updating the status attribute manually will add the corresponding label and update actual dates.	Moving the cards between lists will automatically update the status attribute. And updating the status attribute manually will move the cards between lists.

Progress status

No update	⋮⋮ Completed In Past
No scope	⋮⋮ Next Up ⋮⋮ Backlog
Open	⋮⋮ This Sprint To Do
Started	⋮⋮ In Progress
Paused	
Blocked	⋮⋮ QA ⋮⋮ Blocked
Completed	⋮⋮ Done
Cancelled	

Progress tracking

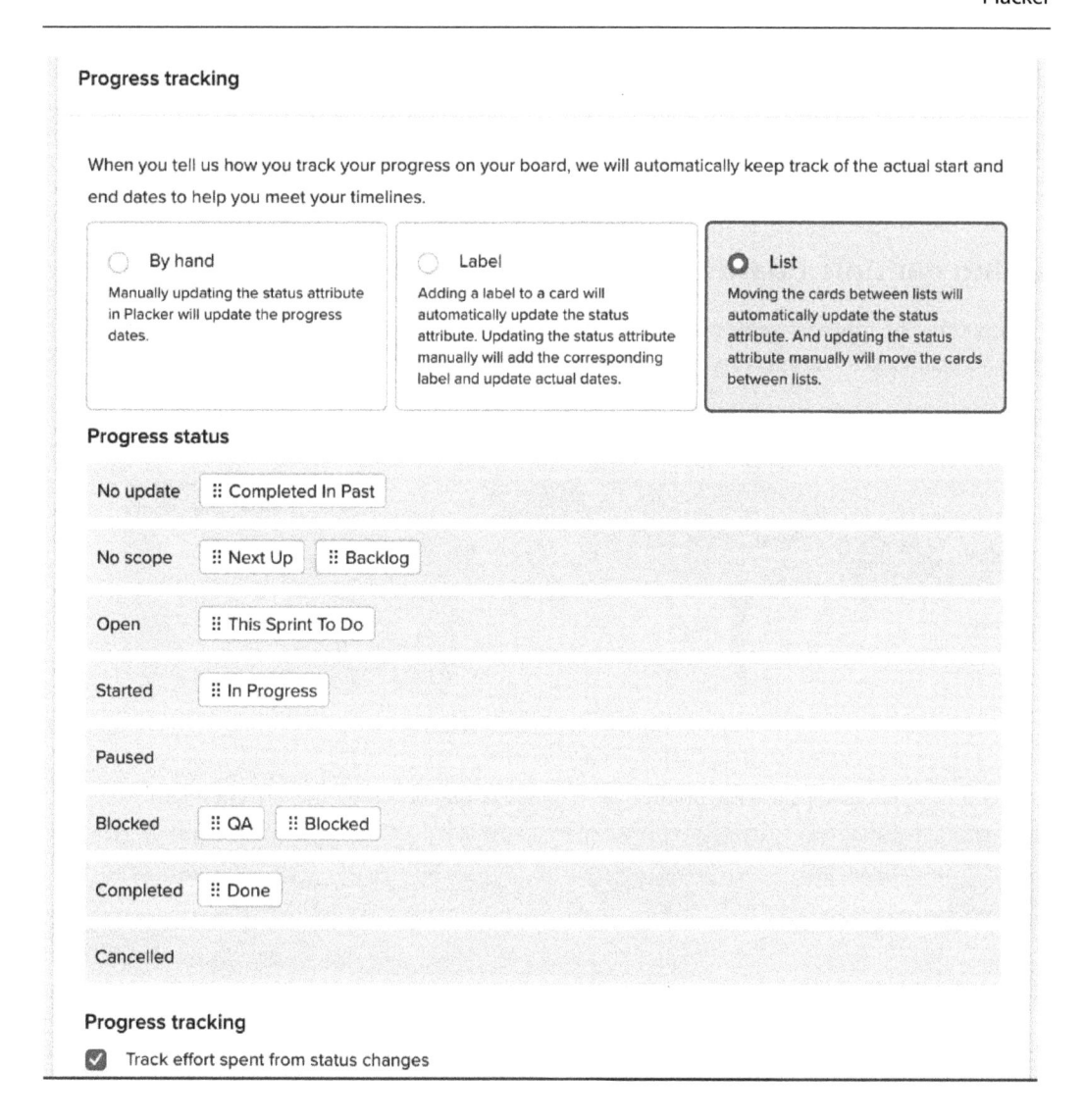

☑ Track effort spent from status changes

Figure 14.19 – Mapping status in Placker

This is how you define a task's status in your board, and, well, show progress on your projects! I like that you can define a task's status in multiple ways. While lists are the method of the more traditional kanban style, many teams will use labels instead to note if something is in progress or completed. Placker lets you choose either way and populates the options below to help you map each list (or label) to the correct stage of your workflow.

I could spend many pages writing about the settings here, but click around and you'll discover all the options. You can always click the chat icon in the bottom-right corner if you need clarification or help setting up.

Now let's combine boards to start seeing the magic!

Viewing multiple boards together

Go to any other boards you want to add to Placker and follow the preceding steps. Now when you want to access Placker features, you'll be able to access those boards as well!

From any board that you've added Placker to, click one of the view options in the toolbar. I'll choose **Board** for now.

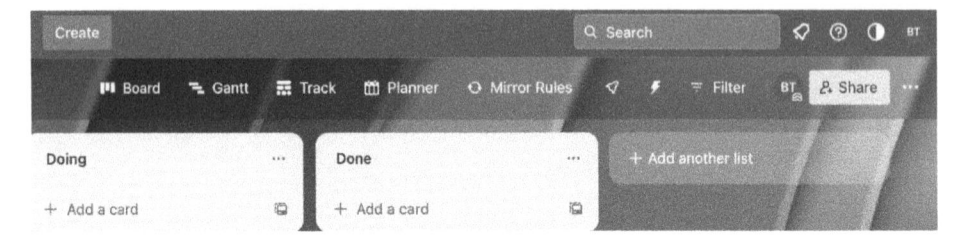

Figure 14.20 – Placker view buttons

You'll see a new modal appear with another view; **Scope** at the top shows the current board.

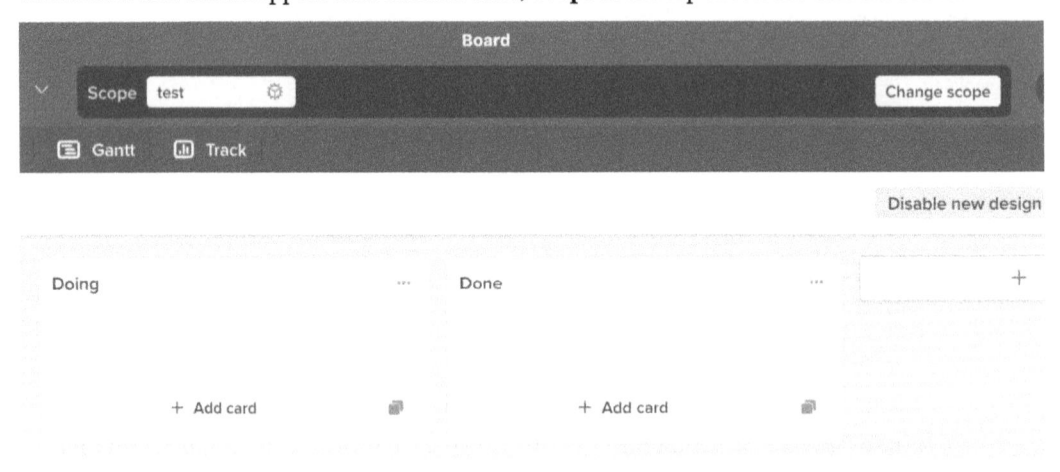

Figure 14.21 – Setting the scope for Placker views

To add more boards to the project, click the **Scope** bar and you'll be able to choose more boards, and you'll see the option to import more boards if you'd like. You can also click **Add view** in the top left to create a group of boards if you plan to frequently reference them together.

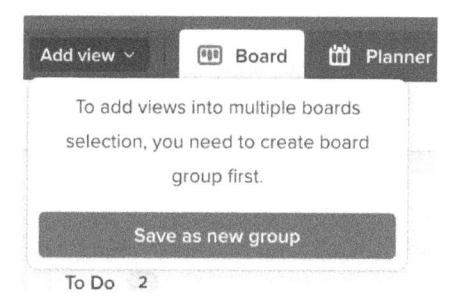

Figure 14.22 – Saving a group of boards in Placker

You can now view your cards grouped together in multiple ways. For instance, check out this view that combines all of the boards I use at PixieBrix for keeping track of my tasks.

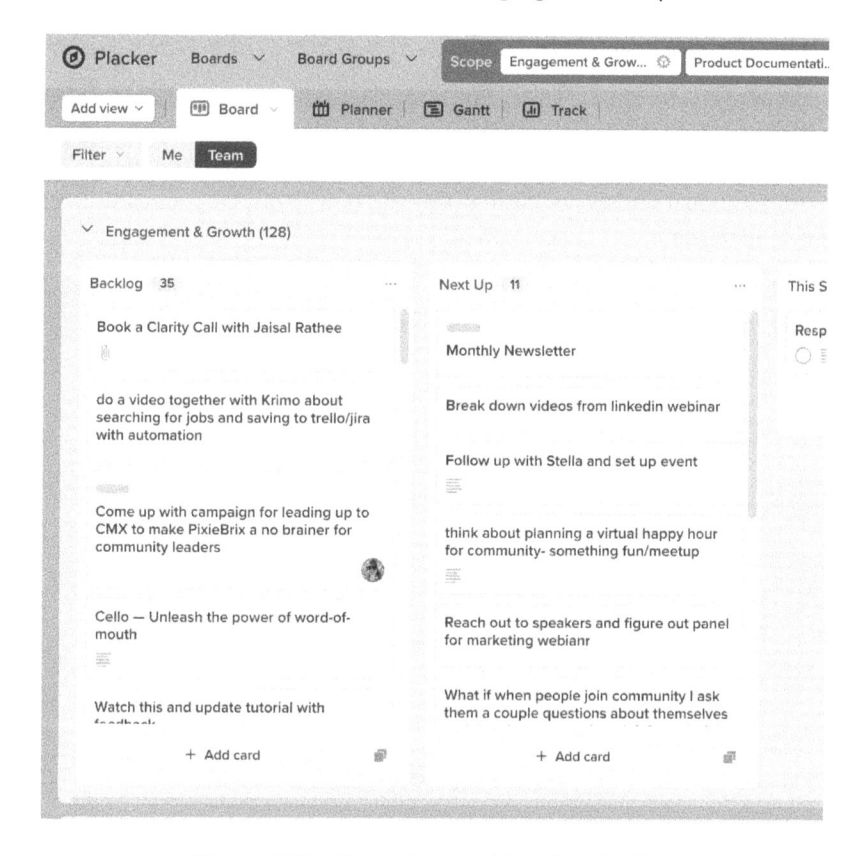

Figure 14.23 – View of grouped boards in Placker

If I don't want to see a board, I can just click the arrow next to the name and minimize it. The real magic comes from this top navigation bar with multiple options for viewing the content.

Reporting in Trello

If I want to see all of these tasks together on one board, I'll click **Combined** from the top left.

Figure 14.24 – Layout options for Placker views

This will add the lists from all the boards into one big board (and it's even smart enough to combine lists if they have the same name, such as **In Progress**).

I also have the option to change my view based on what I'm prioritizing, such as planning projects and getting an overview of the week, or vertically grouping each list by criteria such as member or priority. And finally, I can create swim lanes that display cards in a horizontal grouping. Within each of these layouts are additional settings for customizing the view to display your cards in exactly the way that's most helpful to you.

You can also add filters on the left side of the top bar to narrow down the cards that are displayed. These filters are way more advanced than Trello's native filters.

Figure 14.25 – Filter options in Placker views

Not only can you pick cards that meet certain criteria, but you can hide cards that also meet certain criteria. For instance, I can show all cards except ones that have a due date more than a week away, or except ones that don't have any label. Just start typing and you'll be able to find the attribute you want and create a filter. You can also quickly filter to just see your own cards (there's even a button for this at the top of the board, before you click into the filter).

Default attributes for reporting

When you open a card from the Placker modal, you'll see a lot more fields than you get in Trello. This is helpful when you need more advanced reporting because you can assign many attributes to a card, such as planned and actual dates, estimated budget, progress on a card, priority, and more!

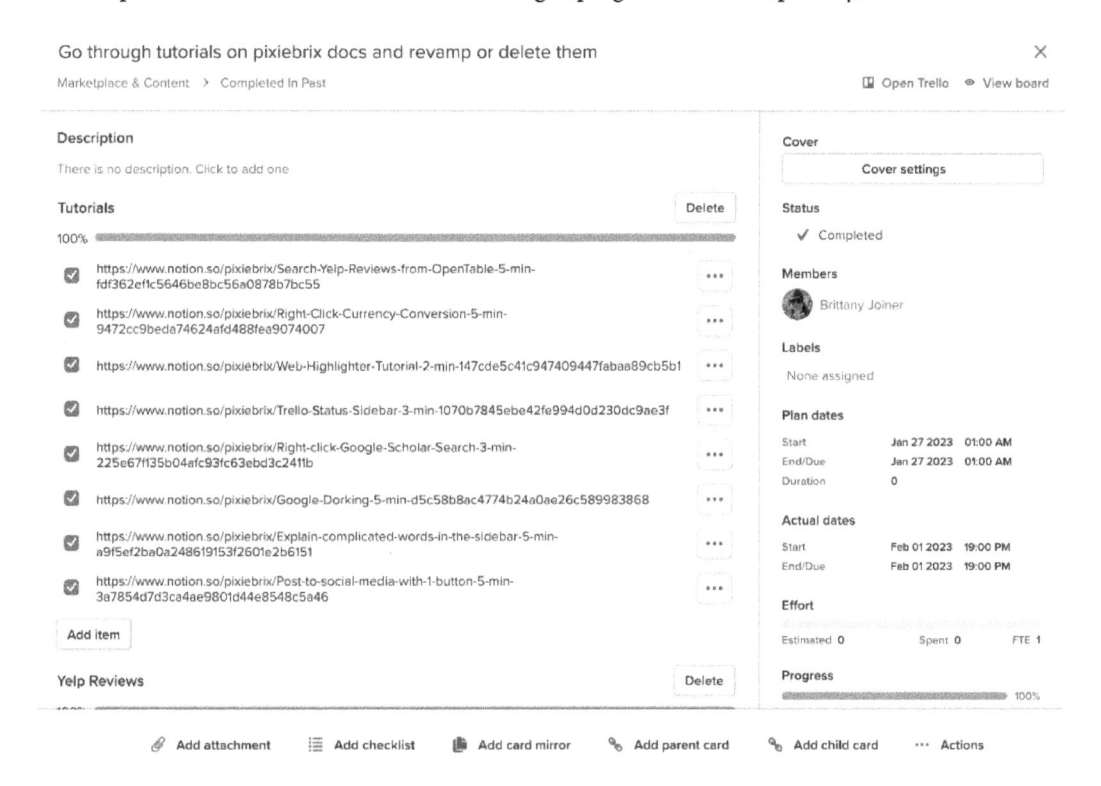

Figure 14.26 – Viewing Trello cards in Placker

Of course, you can access your custom Trello fields here too, and you can create custom attributes that are only shown in Placker if there's anything you want to show up here but not in your boards on Trello.

It's possible to create custom fields in Trello for all of these items, but with Placker, they're just there out of the box. Plus, without needing to create any special automation, you can set special effects on cards, such as relationships to other cards or mirroring other cards.

You even have the opportunity to create child cards from checklist items with one click, making it easy to establish relationships between tasks and subtasks.

Adding widgets and reports

Now it's time to combine all the data and organization you have seen here into a nice chart that gives you information about your projects. To access your reporting options click the **Track** button at the top of your Trello board, or from Placker, just click **Add view** and choose **Track**.

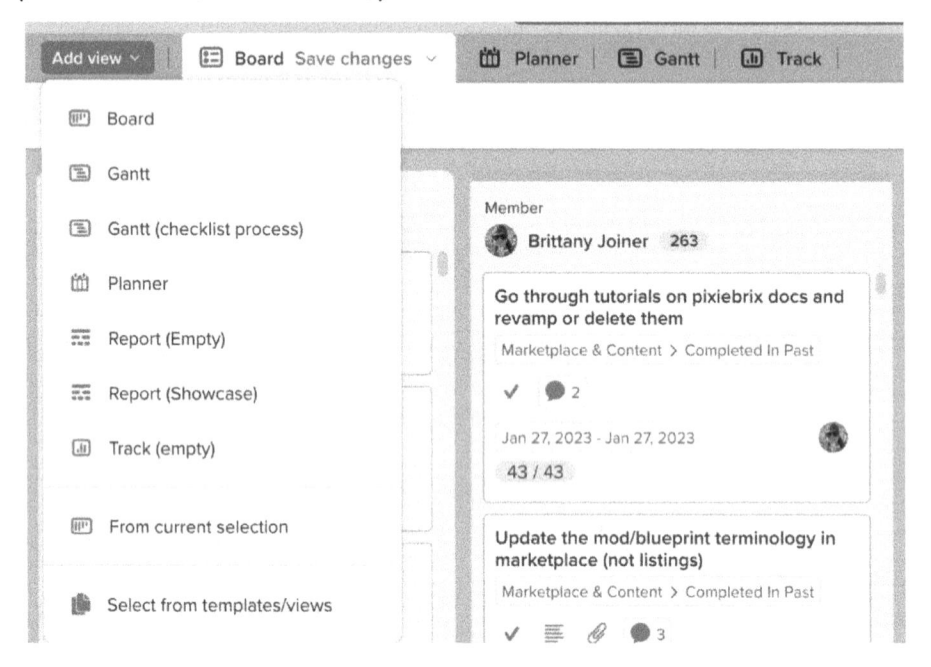

Figure 14.27 – Placker view options

By default, you've already got a report with some charts about what's happening in your boards without configuring anything at all!

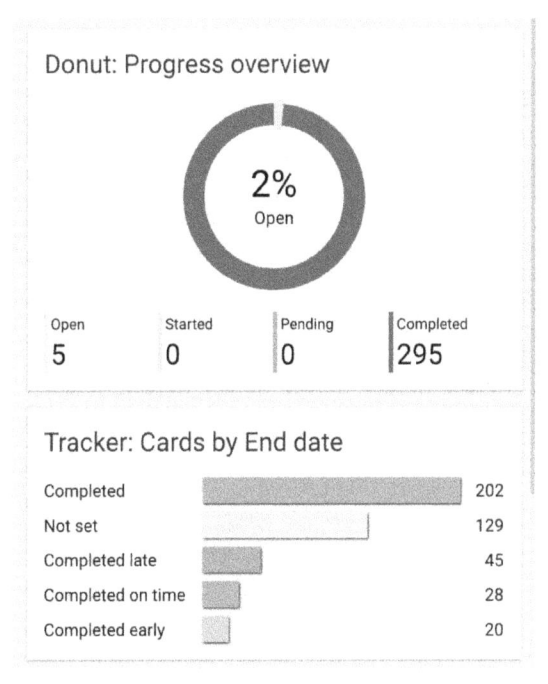

Donut: Progress overview

2%
Open

Open	Started	Pending	Completed
5	0	0	295

Tracker: Cards by End date

Completed	202
Not set	129
Completed late	45
Completed on time	28
Completed early	20

Figure 14.28 – Sample charts built by default in Placker

You can see the status of your cards, and even check their progress based on their end date! This quickly shows whether your team is effective at completing tasks (and on time), or whether you might be starting a lot of things and finishing a few.

There's even a pivot table showing each member's cards aggregated by status across multiple boards, helpful for being able to quickly see how a team is progressing through tasks for the period.

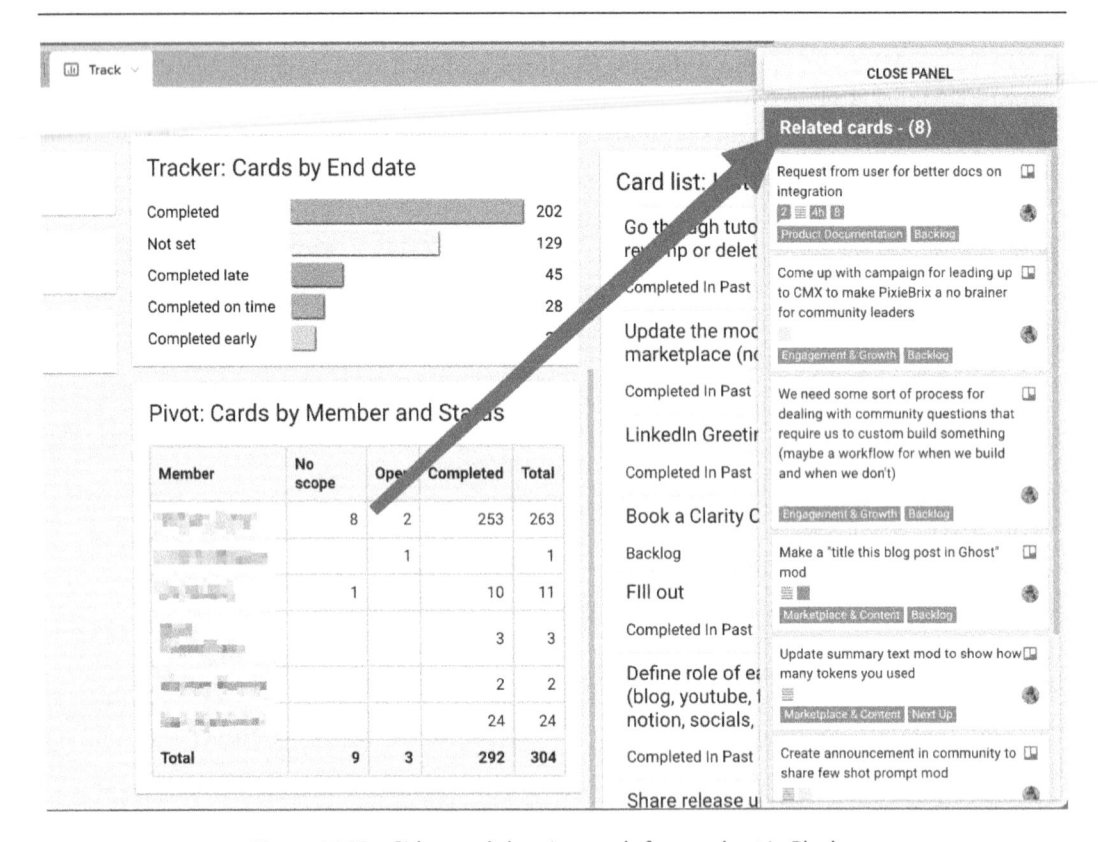

Figure 14.29 – Side panel showing cards from a chart in Placker

Even better, you can click any number in the table to open a side panel that shows the cards related to that metric, giving you the ability to quickly zoom in on your team's tasks quickly.

While all of this is helpful, let's assume you want to add your own chart to this view. Click **EDIT** in the top-right corner to show a menu of options. You'll be able to copy or delete the page from here or change the layout and add widgets. That's what we'll do, so click **Edit layout & widgets**.

Figure 14.30 – Navigation bar on Track view in Placker

At the moment, this report is displayed in three panels, but if you only want two, you can clean it up by clicking **REMOVE AREA**. I am going to remove the first panel, since it's mostly instructions, so now that the middle panel takes up 2/3 of the page and has some more room to breathe.

Now, click **ADD WIDGET** to get some more data in there. Configuring a widget can be a bit tricky. Makes sense, right? With great power comes great responsibility.

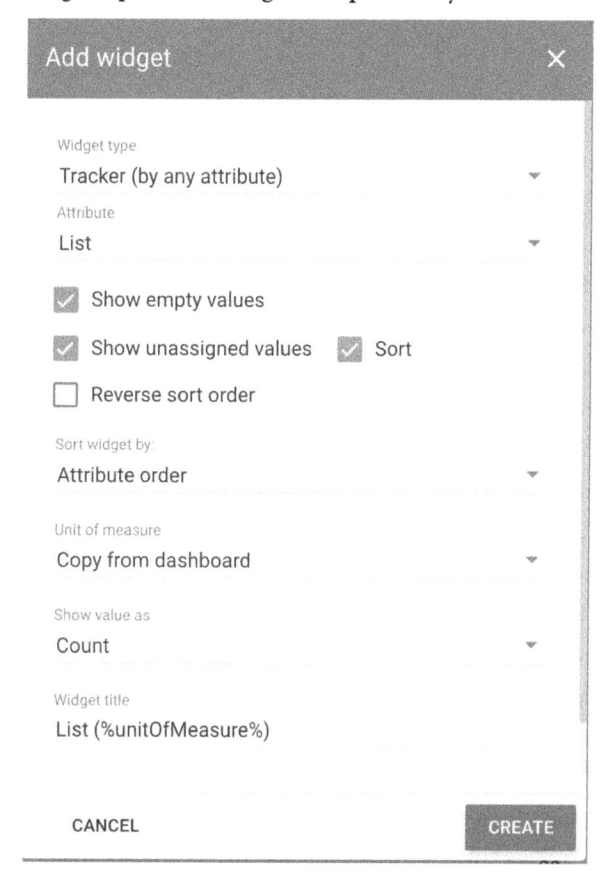

Figure 14.31 – Widget options for a chart in Placker

It will take you some time to get familiar with the different options. Scroll through the **Widget type** options to see what's available, but in many cases, you'll probably just stick with the first one, **Tracker (by any attribute)**.

Next, you can select the attribute (part of the card) you want to observe. Let's say we want to track our custom **Priority** field and check that we've been primarily completing cards with high priority. Just like with other reporting tools, I can define what we want to count, whether it's the number of cards or the sum of the effort involved.

I'll now go back up to the top left and select **FILTER & SETTINGS**, which opens the same filter we saw on the board view. From here, I'll select cards that have been completed, and ta-dah 🎉 my chart at the bottom now shows my cards completed by priority!

Sort by Priority		EDIT
High		75
Low		11
Medium		18
Unassigned		193

Figure 14.32 – Chart of tasks sorted by priority in Placker

Looks like of the cards that have priority assigned, we are completing the high-priority ones! But we still have some work to do with making sure we actually assign priority to cards.

There's still a lot more you could discover in Placker, so make sure to take time to click around and connect with their team as you go through your 15-day trial.

Screenful

It's time to review one more reporting tool for your team. This one is called Screenful and what makes it special from the others (in my opinion) is that it's a good hybrid of advanced reporting options with ease of use.

You'll see many of the same reporting features you've seen in other tools. Screenful also allows you to create charts and aggregate data then group it by other attributes (such as members or labels). But where Screenful shines is by supplying so many charts, reports, and insights right out of the box, without needing to configure anything. And they're beautiful!

As soon as you connect your boards, you'll be able to view charts showing you how many open cards you have, how many cards you complete each week, and even a forecasted project completion date! All of this, just by connecting your boards and confirming the lists!

> **Who is Screenful best for?**
>
> There's no single perfect tool for everyone, so it really depends on what you need out of a reporting tool. If you need to quickly answer questions about your workflow or if you have less technical users who don't have time or skills to configure reports, Screenful is a perfect fit because you'll get most of what you need right out of the box, or with very little customization.
>
> You also might prefer Screenful if you're concerned about beautiful visuals for your shared charts and reports. While the other tools I've used are manageable and look nice enough, I prefer the appearance of the Screenful charts more than the others.

Of course, with everything there are tradeoffs, and for Screenful the tradeoff is price. Although they don't charge by user, their lowest plan starts at $49 a month, and that's only for two custom reports and doesn't include all features, such as custom branding or scheduled reports. This tool also won't work well for you if you use labels instead of lists to track the status of tasks. I don't think it's impossible to track status by labels in Screenful, but it would likely require a lot more configuration.

Getting started

Screenful is another one that you can add via Power-Up, but you can also just go directly to their site at https://screenful.com/. Once there, create an account, and you'll be prompted to connect to an account (such as a Trello account!) and then select the boards you want to connect.

I'll connect my Trello account and select a couple of related boards, and then click **Next**. I can always go back later and add more if I want. Screenful will guess which lists relate to which status.

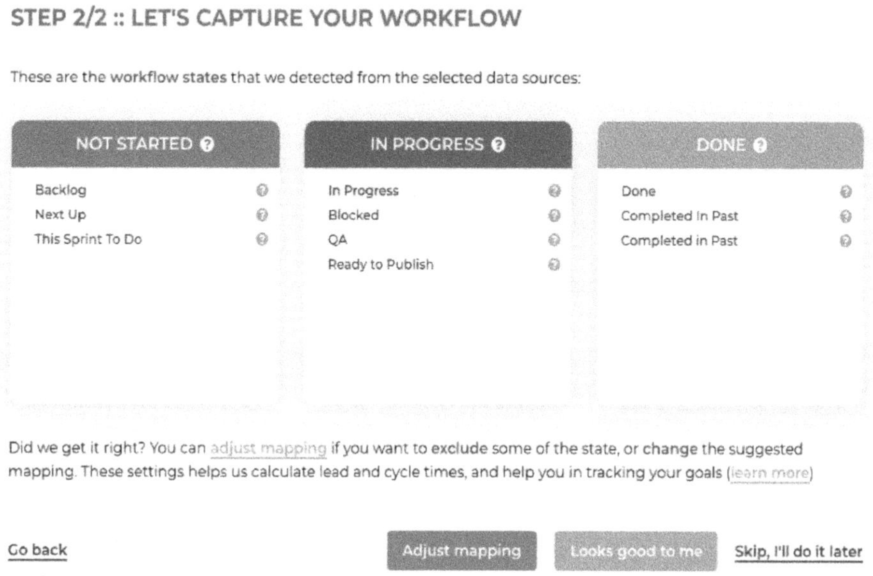

Figure 14.33 – Mapping workflow stages in Screenful

It's pretty good at guessing! But if you need to adjust, you can click **Adjust mapping**. But this will only let you exclude lists or move them between stages.

Insights

Once you've connected your boards, you land on the **Insights** tab, where you can start analyzing data from your cards right away, just by scrolling through the page.

You'll first see a summary of how many cards are in all your boards that have not been completed. These are your open tasks. This can be helpful as it's effectively the quantity of your to-do list. It will never be zero, but having a high number of open cards can make a project feel impossible.

Next, you'll see those open (non-completed) cards broken down by label. This can help you identify if there are any specific types of tasks that have not been completed yet. For instance, if you're a marketing team and you see a lot of cards with a "content" label, you might need to hire another content writer.

Figure 14.34 – Grouping options for charts in Screenful Insights

But aside from just label, you can group by any number of things, such as who the card is assigned to, custom fields on the card, its state, and more. These give valuable insights about those aspects of your funnel because you can identify any gaps and see where you're over- or under-indexing.

You can also compare this information over time.

Figure 14.35 – OPEN ITEMS TREND chart in Screenful

Viewing open cards over a period can help you see if you're consistently having the same amount open or if they're trending down. For one-time projects, such as a feature release or a product launch, you should see this decrease as you complete more items each week. If it's going up, you might be adding more tasks than you can reasonably complete, which it looks like I might be doing!

By default, this chart shows the last three months, but you can select other periods from the dropdown in the top right above the chart.

Lastly, you can have it all with a chart that combines the trends with groupings by label, member, priority, or other attributes.

If you want to filter any of this data, just click **Set filter** in the top-right corner of the board. You'll have the options to filter the data by any fields and to only show cards with a certain label, giving you the ability to micro-analyze a specific type of task's activity.

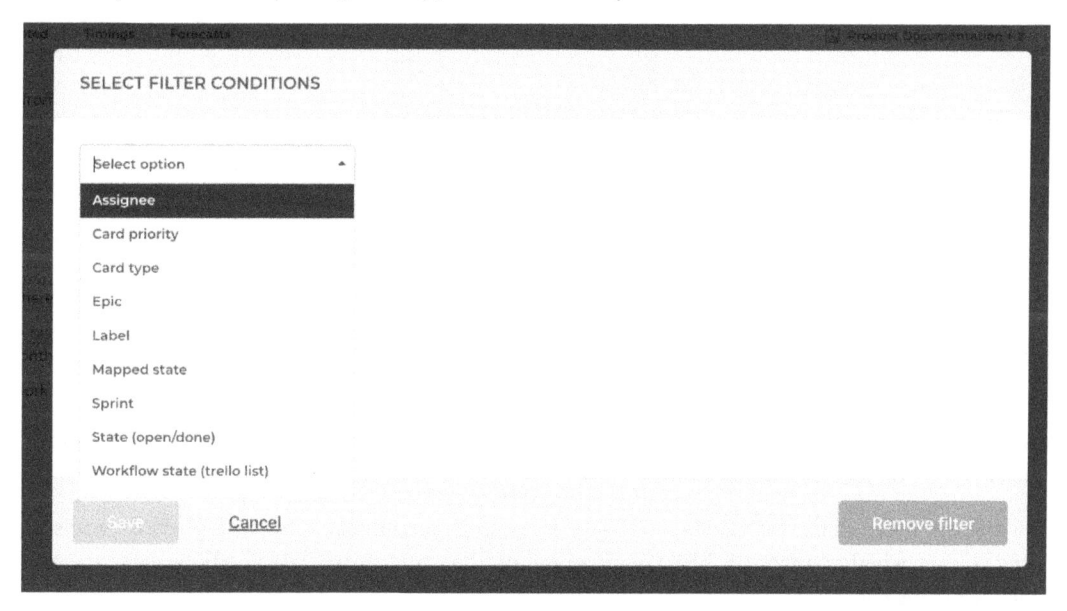

Figure 14.36 – Filter options in Screenful

My favorite part about Screenful is that all of this comes out of the box. We've already learned bits about our workflow without having to do anything more than connect our board.

Figure 14.37 – Navigation and sections in Screenful

Check the sections at the top, just below the **INSIGHTS** tab. You'll see more tabs that you can look through, all as part of the **INSIGHTS** section. Click **Completed** and you'll see similar charts to what you saw in **Open items**, but instead showing the data about cards that have been completed.

You'll start by seeing a table of tasks recently completed, and clicking on one will take you directly to the Trello card. This is a good way to quickly recap what your team has done in the last week for retrospectives.

Next, you'll see a chart showing you how much work is completed over periods. Can you tell that I've been on vacation?

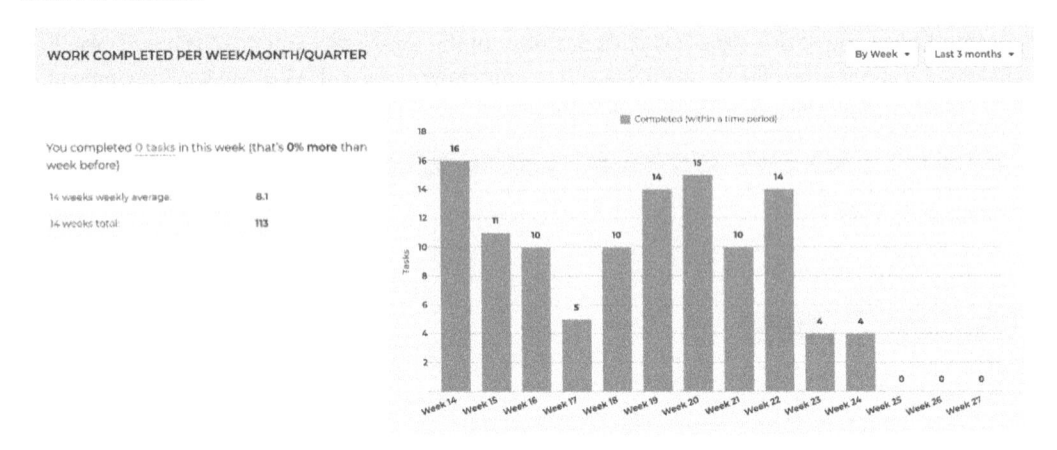

Figure 14.38 – Chart showing trends of work completed weekly

You can change the cadence to see monthly, weekly, or quarterly, and you can change the time period to span a longer or shorter amount of time.

Below this are more charts for viewing this data grouped by attributes such as members or labels, helping you see whether anyone is being overworked on the team or isn't carrying their weight and might need some coaching.

My favorite chart shows cards created versus completed.

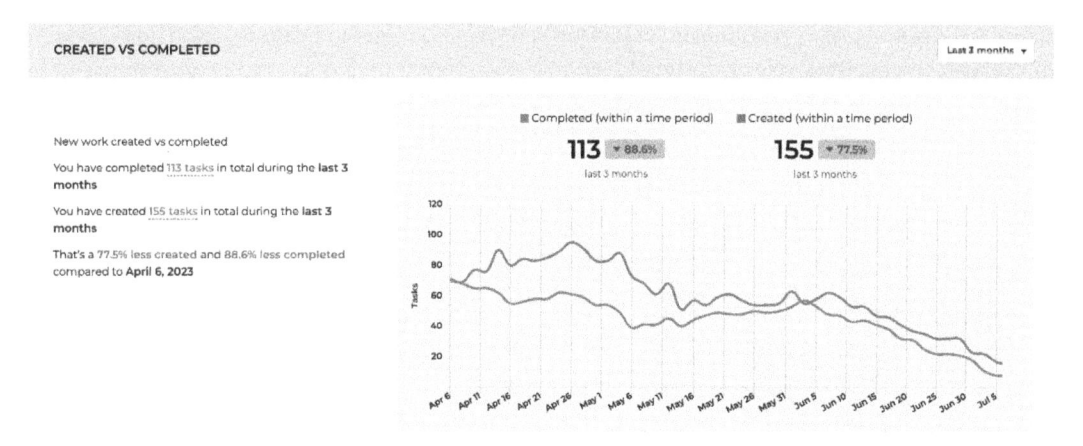

Figure 14.39 – Chart showing the volume of cards created versus completed

I love this chart because it shows why I can never seem to complete my to-do list...for every card I complete, I'm adding at least one more card to my list! (This also explains why I have so many cards open!)

Next, head to the **Timings** tab and you'll learn more about how cards move through your workflow. I won't go into detail here as most of these charts are well explained, but my favorite one is this chart that shows how long cards sit in an **In Progress** state.

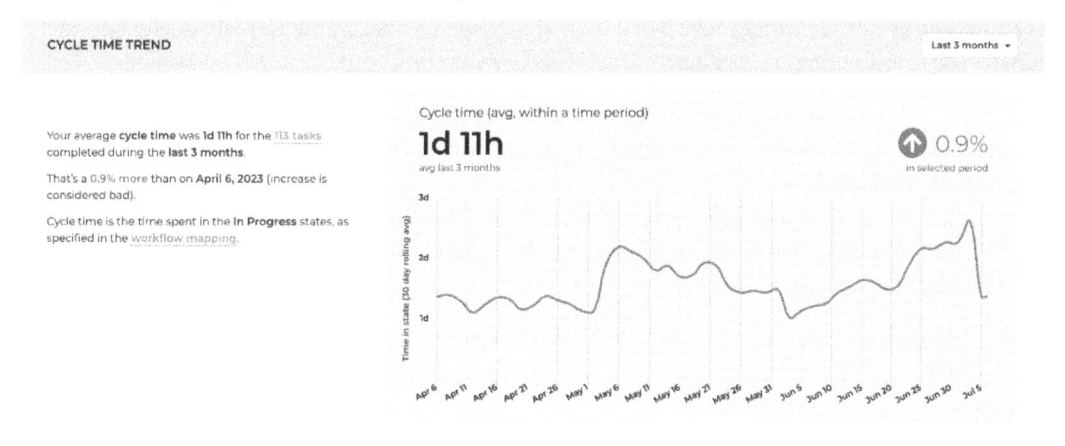

Figure 14.40 – Chart showing how long cards spend in progress

This takes the average time of cards that are sitting in your **In Progress** lists so you can see how long it's taking tasks to be completed. If you see long cycle times here, it could mean you have some bottlenecks and need to investigate what might be taking so long to move cards through your workflow.

Lastly, we'll look briefly at the **Forecasts** tab.

This section helps you make projections and estimates about your projects and tasks based on how you've been working. You can track velocity history to see how much your team is doing each week historically.

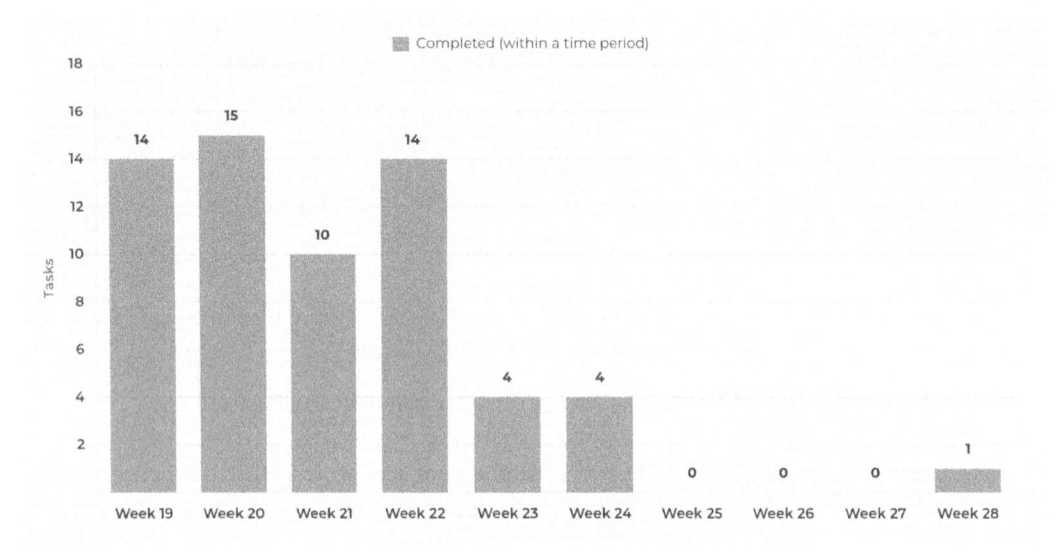

Figure 14.41 – Chart showing weekly velocity trends

Make sure you're not planning more work than your team has been able to realistically handle, otherwise you're just setting yourself up to never complete your tasks and constantly move things over.

If you keep scrolling, you'll see more charts that give you a date to predict when your project will be completed. There are two ways to estimate – one assumes no new work is added, and the other assumes work is added. You can also adjust the velocity to be optimistic or pessimistic to help you have a range. I like these charts because they're great to show to a pesky management team that keeps extending the scope of a project. You now have an actual chart to show them how adding more tasks as you go delays the date significantly.

Now, just in case you'd like even more info, let's head to **CHARTS** and see what we can build.

CHARTS

The **INSIGHTS** section shows prebuilt reports with charts, but for those who have a specific vision of what you're looking for, or you just want to dive even deeper, the **CHARTS** tab lets you explore a bit more to get the info you are looking for.

Click **+ADD NEW CHART** in the top right. Just like the other tools we've shown, you'll get several types of charts to work with. But rather than these just being the standard types, such as bar, pie, and so on, there are some prebuilt charts that are already configured.

Figure 14.42 – Prebuilt chart options in Screenful

Scroll through the list before making a blank one, because the data you're looking for might already be an existing chart that you can add and then customize! If it's close, click the chart and then click **Configure Chart** in the top right to let you make any changes to show exactly the data you're looking for.

Figure 14.43 – Unit options for effort in Screenful charts

For instance, maybe not all my cards are created equal in size and I actually want to track card size instead of just the number of cards. I can change the unit to make it fit my data model more accurately.

Once I'm ready, I can click **Create chart** at the bottom right and view my data. While simply viewing the chart is useful, I can do even more from the toolbar just above the chart on the right side.

Figure 14.44 – Chart settings and options in Screenful

I can change the time this chart reflects to make reports more dynamic and serve multiple purposes. If I want others to view this chart, I can use the **Share** options to either embed it in another page or send the link (or even make it a public link that anyone can access, no Screenful or Trello account needed!)

Use **Chart settings** to style the chart, and if you need to make any changes to the data or the way it's organized, simply click **Edit chart**. The three dots provide more options, such as changing the filter, duplicating the chart, exporting, deleting, or adding to a report, which feels like the perfect segue to head to the next Screenful section called **REPORTS**.

REPORTS

Charts are individual, well, charts that show you a specific visualization for your data. But you need to piece multiple together to tell a whole story, and that's where reports come in. Click **REPORTS** in the navigation bar at the top.

By default, Screenful has already created one report for you called **Weekly velocity**. Click the name to explore. You'll see a series of charts pieced together to give you a weekly summary and help you see how you're trending over time.

Weekly velocity

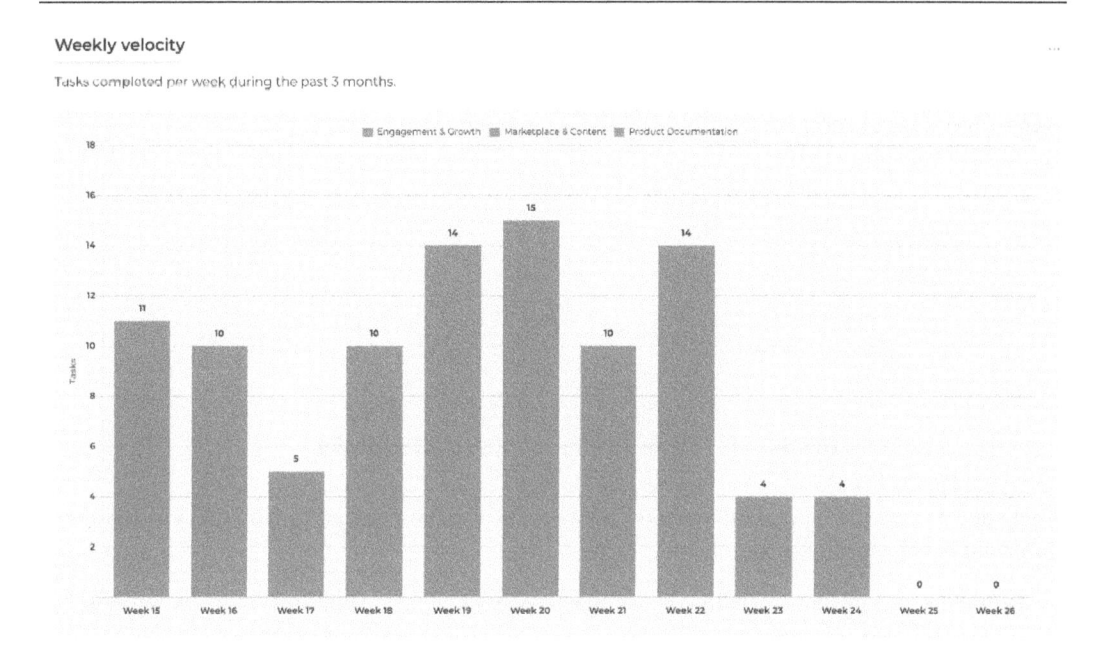

Tasks completed per week during the past 3 months.

Figure 14.45 – Weekly velocity chart split by board

You can edit any of the charts by clicking the three dots in the top-right corner. You'll have options for editing or styling the chart, and you can apply a filter.

If you want to edit the layout of the report, click **Edit Report** in the top-right corner to move things around or add more charts or elements.

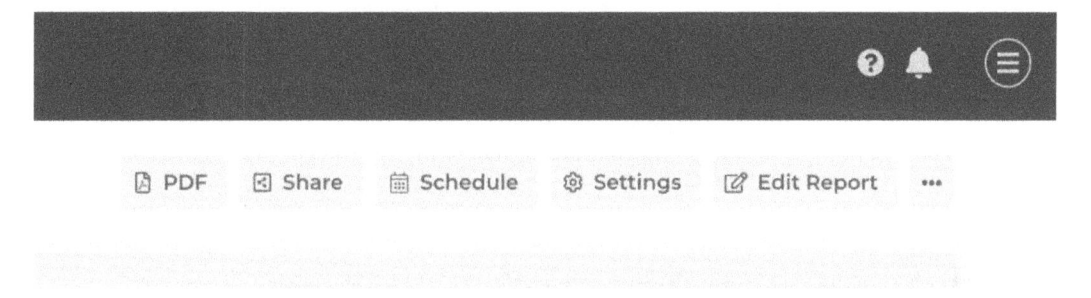

Figure 14.46 – Report settings and options in Screenful

You'll also see similar options to **CHARTS**, where you can share an entire report, or style the report by clicking **Settings**. You can even add your logo to the report if you'd like!

308   Reporting in Trello

But there is one other important action I want to call out...you can schedule this report. That means that you can make any report save the data on a regular interval, allowing you to access previous versions if you want to compare week over week, for instance.

Report	Weekly Report
Frequency	Weekly
Day	Monday
Time	09:00 America/New_York (UTC -05:00)

Figure 14.47 – Report scheduling options in Screenful

Not only does it save these previous versions, but you can also have Screenful send them to specific users, or post a message in Slack.

Click **REPORTS** once again to go to the reports home page, and you'll see the **+ ADD NEW REPORT** button in the top right.

New blank report   Weekly report

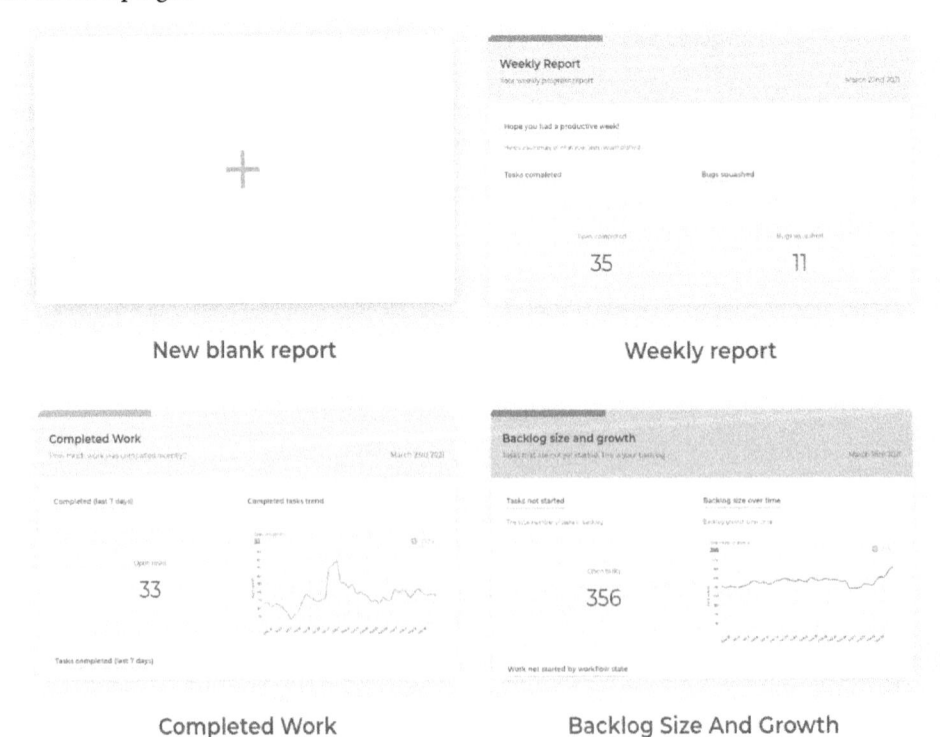

Completed Work   Backlog Size And Growth

Figure 14.48 – Prebuilt reports in Screenful

Just like charts, you can select from a prebuilt template for reports and then customize specific elements and charts, which is definitely the easiest way to go about it. But if you can't find something that looks like what you want, you can select **New blank report** to build out what you're looking for from scratch.

Clicking the + button on an existing report or **ADD CHART** on a new report will open a modal to choose any charts you've built, or build a new one.

I like to think of charts as a puzzle piece and reports are the final product that you can only see when all the pieces are lined up together. Then, insights turn that into actionable information to improve your workflows.

Screenful is a great reporting tool if you need something more advanced and customizable, but it also gives you something to work with out of the box. It doesn't really involve task management and planning, but it excels at making an easy interface for getting started with reporting and quickly getting valuable information about your projects.

Summary

Here we are at the end of the chapter, and hopefully you've read through all of these options and have an idea of which tool might be the right fit for you. If you want something that covers most use cases and is easy to use and affordable, you might want to go with Blue Cat Reports!

If you need something that incorporates custom attributes and planning tools as well as advanced reporting, you might want to use Placker. And if you want something advanced reporting that's beautiful and easy to configure, you might choose Screenful.

There's no right answer as to which one is *best*, but they all offer free trials, so take them all for a spin and play around to see which ones work best with your workflows. If you have any questions, reach out to their support teams.

Wow, it feels almost surreal writing the last few sentences of this book. We've been on quite a journey together. Think about when we started and you learned about the components of Trello, all the way to learning how to automate and make Trello work for you, and finally to adding integrations that make Trello even more powerful and basically a standalone app for handling task management and reporting.

You've come so far, and I hope you're happy with your Trello setup and comfortable enough to tweak it as you go. If you ever need a hand, you know where to reach me, and in case I haven't said it enough, I'll say it once more...head to the Trello section of the Atlassian Community to meet other Trello enthusiasts, get inspiration, and learn how to do even more cool things with Trello.

Index

A

actions 108
activity details
 adding, to Trello card 40
Add/Remove actions 132-135
alternative board views
 accessing 72, 73
Amazing Fields 236
 adding 236, 237
 additional features 243, 244
 creating 238-242
 updating 242, 243
 using 236
Approvals for Trello 229, 230
 adding, to board 230, 231
 advanced features 235
 approval, approving 233, 234
 approval, creating 231-233
 approval, rejecting 233, 234
 cards, viewing by approval status 234
 need for, using 230
Approvals for Trello, advanced features
 approval group or team, creating 235
 cards, moving based on status 235
 multiple approvals, specifying on card 235
 upgrading, to Pro plan 235, 236
attachments 45
 inline attachments 51, 52
 items, attaching to card 45
 need, for using 45
automation 107
 accessing 170, 171
automation actions
 accessing 129-131
automation variables 149, 153, 165, 186
 reference link 187

B

Bitbucket 165
Blue Cat forms 253, 254
 adding 254
 creating 255
 field, adding 255-257
 field, customizing 255-257
 fields, mapping to other parts of card 258
 setting 259-261
 sharing 261-263
 testing 263-265
 using 254

Blue Cat Reports 273, 274
   adding, to board 274, 275
   chart type, options 280
   example 279-285
   Quick List, creating 275-278

board buttons 184-186
   creating 186-189
   testing 189, 190

board menu 15
   additional settings 18
   archived items 19
   background 16, 17
   closing 23
   collections 18
   copying 21
   description 15, 16
   email address 19, 20
   exporting 22
   stickers 17
   template 21
   watching 20

boards, Trello 9
   creating 9
   home page 10
   top toolbar options 10

Bulk Actions 244, 245
   adding 245-247
   changes, making to multiple cards 248-250
   multiple cards, selecting to edit 247, 248
   using 245

button automation 178
   board buttons 184-186
   card buttons 178
   using 178

C

calendar 75, 76
   cadence, changing 76
   card, adding 77
   dates, editing on card 77
   Power-Ups, suing 78, 79
   syncing with 78

card 27
   locations, setting 60, 61

card buttons 178
   creating 179-182
   testing 182-184

card changes
   trigger events 115-117

card content
   trigger events 122-125

card covers 61
   adding 62, 63
   need, for using 62

card front 30
   quick actions 42, 43

card move
   trigger events 111-114

card views
   card back 30
   card front 30

cascade actions 157, 158
   card, linking with item 161
   cards, collecting into linked items/links/items in checklist 162
   cards, linking/unlinking 161
   card titled with link, find/lookup 159
   find/lookup, first/last card linked in attachments 158, 159

item, converting in checklist to cards/linked cards 162
item, converting to linked card 161, 162
using, for each card linked from item in checklist 160
using, for each card linked in attachments 160
using, for each checklist item 160

checklist 57
actions 138-144
adding 57, 58
advanced checklists 58
items, viewing 59
need, for using 57
progress, viewing 59, 60
trigger events 119-122

comments
adding, to Trello card 39, 40
using 39

content actions 147-149

copy icon 177

cross-team project management 94
board structure 95
cards, representing objectives 95, 96

custom fields 52
creating 53-56
need, for using 52
setting 56

D

Dashboard view 73
existing tile, editing 75
tile, adding 74, 75

dates
actions 136-138
creating 34

due date 34
due date, adding 34-36
start date 34
start date, using 34-36
trigger events 117-119
using 34

descriptions, Trello cards
editing 31
using 31

Due Date automation 196, 197
creating 200, 201
testing 201
trigger options 197-200
using 196

F

field actions 151, 152
custom field, checking/unchecking 153
custom field, clearing 152
custom field, setting 153
date custom field, setting 154
date, moving in custom field 154
increase/decrease number, in custom field 153

fields
trigger events 125-127

filters 67, 68
dimensions 69
logic, using 71
removing 72

filters, dimensions
due dates 70
keywords 69
labels 70
members 69

H

HTTP requests, with automation
   reference link 149

I

inline attachments 51, 52
items, attaching to card 45
   cloud drives 50
   computer files 46-48
   link 51
   Trello boards 49
   Trello cards 49

J

Jira 164

L

labels
   creating 32-34
   descriptions, editing 31
   editing 32, 33
   using 32
light bulb icon 177
link cards 64
   disabling 65
   reference link 52, 64
List Limits 214, 215
   configuring 215-217
   using 217, 218
List Limits Power-Up
   adding 215
lists 23, 24
   actions, for cards 26
   archive 27
   card, adding 24, 25
   cards, sorting 26
   copy option 25
   move option 25
   watch option 25, 26
locations 60
   need, for using 60
   setting, on card 60, 61

M

maps 81-83
   location data, setting on card 83
   new card, adding 83
meeting planner 97-99
   board structure 97
   cards, as agenda items 98
member actions 144-147
members, Trello cards
   adding 37
   using 37
move actions 131, 132

P

Placker 286
   attributes for reporting 293
   benefits 286
   board, mapping 287-289
   multiple boards, viewing 290-293
   reports, adding 294-297
   widgets, adding 294-297
   working with 287
Power-Ups 206
   accessing 206-210
   examples 211
   integrating 210
   integrating, made by Trello 211, 212

notifications, viewing in Slack 214
Slack Power-Up, adding 212-214
product roadmap 99
board structure 100
cards, representing features or bugs 100, 101

R

README 218
Read Me Power-Up
adding 218-220
editing 220, 221
previewing 220
rules 171
automations, editing 176
automation settings 177, 178
creating 172-175
testing 175, 176

S

scheduled automation 191, 192
creating 194-196
trigger options 192, 193
using 191
Screenful 298
CHARTS tab 304-306
Insights tab 299-304
REPORTS tab 306-309
URL 299
working with 299
Slack 166, 167
Slack Power-Up
adding 212-214
sort actions 154, 155
list by date, sorting 155

sorting, by custom field 156
sorting, by labels 156
Story Points 100

T

table 80
card or list, adding 81
cards, editing 80, 81
tag icon 177
tiles 74
timeline
card, adding 80
dimension, adding 79
Power-Ups, suing 79
tool actions 163, 164
top toolbar options, board
board menu 15
filtering 13, 14
members and roles 15
sharing 12, 13
starring 11
visibility 11, 12
trash icon 177
Trello 3, 4, 107
account, creating 7
boards 9
cards 27
desktop app 5
features 5
lists 23, 24
mobile app 5
non-work-related use cases 6, 7
uses 5
using, via web 5
work-related use cases 6
workspaces 8

Trello card
    actions 41, 42
    activity details 39
    activity details, adding 40
    comments 39
    comments, adding 40
    dates, creating 34
    descriptions, editing 31
    descriptions, using 31
    labels. creating 32-34
    members, adding 37
    name 31
    watching 38
Trello-made Power-Ups 226
Trello Premium account 73
Trello template 87, 88
    copying 89-91
    creating 102-104
    information, viewing 88, 89
Trello, using for Kanban and Agile workflow management 91, 92
    board structure 92, 93
    cards, representing tasks 93
triggers 108
    accessing 109, 110
    advanced mode 110

U

Unito 265, 266
    flow, creating 266
    flow, testing 272
    URL 266
    using 265
Unito, flow
    connecting, tools 266-268
    direction, selecting 268
    information, specifying 270, 271
    launching 271
    syncs, selecting 269

V

Voting
    on card 223
Voting Power-Up 117, 221, 222
    adding 222, 223
    list, sorting by votes 225

W

watching 38
Workspace views 83
    calendar views 84, 85
    Table view 85

Packtpub.com

Subscribe to our online digital library for full access to over 7,000 books and videos, as well as industry leading tools to help you plan your personal development and advance your career. For more information, please visit our website.

Why subscribe?

- Spend less time learning and more time coding with practical eBooks and Videos from over 4,000 industry professionals
- Improve your learning with Skill Plans built especially for you
- Get a free eBook or video every month
- Fully searchable for easy access to vital information
- Copy and paste, print, and bookmark content

Did you know that Packt offers eBook versions of every book published, with PDF and ePub files available? You can upgrade to the eBook version at `packt.com` and as a print book customer, you are entitled to a discount on the eBook copy. Get in touch with us at `customercare@packtpub.com` for more details.

At `www.packt.com`, you can also read a collection of free technical articles, sign up for a range of free newsletters, and receive exclusive discounts and offers on Packt books and eBooks.

Other Books You May Enjoy

If you enjoyed this book, you may be interested in these other books by Packt:

Automate Everyday Tasks in Jira

Gareth Cantrell

ISBN: 978-1-80056-286-8

- Understand the basic concepts of automation such as triggers, conditions, and actions
- Find out how to use if–then scenarios and conditions to automate your processes with practical examples
- Use smart values to achieve complex and more powerful automation
- Implement use cases in a practical way, including automation with Slack, Microsoft Teams, GitHub, and Bitbucket
- Discover best practices for writing and maintaining automation rules
- Explore techniques for debugging rules and solving common issues

Enhancing Productivity with Notion

Danny Hatcher

ISBN: 978-1-80323-208-9

- Understand how to set up and build on any device
- Navigate, share and alter the appearance of your workspace
- Import and export data to and from Notion
- Understand how to use all the database views, filters, sorts, and properties
- Create task, wiki, and project management systems
- Connect Notion to third-party applications with the API

Packt is searching for authors like you

If you're interested in becoming an author for Packt, please visit `authors.packtpub.com` and apply today. We have worked with thousands of developers and tech professionals, just like you, to help them share their insight with the global tech community. You can make a general application, apply for a specific hot topic that we are recruiting an author for, or submit your own idea.

Share Your Thoughts

Now you've finished *Supercharging Productivity with Trello*, we'd love to hear your thoughts! Scan the QR code below to go straight to the Amazon review page for this book and share your feedback or leave a review on the site that you purchased it from.

`https://packt.link/r/1801813876`

Your review is important to us and the tech community and will help us make sure we're delivering excellent quality content.

Download a free PDF copy of this book

Thanks for purchasing this book!

Do you like to read on the go but are unable to carry your print books everywhere? Is your eBook purchase not compatible with the device of your choice?

Don't worry, now with every Packt book you get a DRM-free PDF version of that book at no cost.

Read anywhere, any place, on any device. Search, copy, and paste code from your favorite technical books directly into your application.

The perks don't stop there, you can get exclusive access to discounts, newsletters, and great free content in your inbox daily

Follow these simple steps to get the benefits:

1. Scan the QR code or visit the link below

   https://packt.link/free-ebook/9781801813877

2. Submit your proof of purchase
3. That's it! We'll send your free PDF and other benefits to your email directly

Milton Keynes UK
Ingram Content Group UK Ltd.
UKHW031833140923
428706UK00007BA/46